REGIONALISM AND MULTILATERALISM

This book discusses the impact of cultural diversities and identities on regional and interregional cooperation, as well as on multilateralism.

Employing a comparative approach to organizations such as ASEAN, MERCOSUR, SAARC, and the African and European Unions, this volume seeks to understand their distinctive features and patterns of interaction. It also explores the diffusion of multidimensional interregional relations, including but not limited to the field of trade. Scholars from several disciplines and four continents offer insights concerning the consequences of both multiple modernities and the rise of authoritarian populism for regionalism, interregionalism, and multilateralism. The Covid-19 pandemic confirmed the decline of hegemonic multilateralism. Among alternative possible scenarios for global governance, the "new multilateralism" receives special attention.

This book will be of key interest to European/EU studies, economics, history, cultural studies, international relations, international political economy, security studies, and international law.

Thomas Meyer is Professor Emeritus of Political Science at the Technical University of Dortmund, Germany, and Editor-in-Chief of the monthly political magazine *Neue Gesellschaft/Frankfurter Hefte*.

José Luís de Sales Marques is President of the Institute of European Studies of Macau (IEEM).

Mario Telò is the Jean Monnet Chair of International Relations at the Université Libre de Bruxelles and Rome's LUISS, and a member of the Royal Academy of Sciences, Brussels.

Globalisation, Europe, Multilateralism Series

Series Editor:
Mario TELÒ,
Université Libre de Bruxelles, Belgium, and LUISS-Guido Carli, Rome, Italy.
Series Manager:
Frederik PONJAERT,
Université Libre de Bruxelles, Belgium.

With the institutional support of the Institut d'études européennes-Université Libre de Bruxelles

The series offers an interdisciplinary platform for original peer-reviewed publications on the institutions, norms and practices associated with Globalisation, Multilateralism and the European Union. Each published volume delves into a given dynamic shaping either the global-regional nexus or the role of the EU therein. It offers original insights into: globalisation and its associated governance challenges; the changing forms of multilateral cooperation and the role of transnational networks; the impact of new global powers and the corollary multipolar order; the lessons born from comparative regionalism and inter-regional partnerships; as well as the distinctive instruments the EU mobilises in its foreign policies and external relations.

International Editorial Board

Amitav ACHARYA, American University, Washington

Shaun BRESLIN, University of Warwick

Ramona COMAN, Université Libre de Bruxelles

Marise CREMONA, EUI, Florence

Louise FAWCETT, University of Oxford

Andrew GAMBLE, University of Cambridge

Robert O. KEOHANE, Princeton University

Nicolas LEVRAT, Université de Genève

Christian LEQUESNE, IEP-Paris

Leonardo MORLINO, LUISS-Guido Carli, Rome

Tamio NAKAMURA, Waseda University, Tokyo

Yaqing QIN, CFAU, Beijing

Ummu SALMA BAVA, JNU, New Dehli

Vivien SCHMIDT, Boston University

Leonard SEABROOKE, Copenhagen Business School

Karen E. SMITH, LSE, London

Anne WEYEMBERGH, Université libre de Bruxelles

Michael ZÜRN, WZB, Berlin

Regionalism and Multilateralism
Politics, Economics, Culture
Edited by Thomas Meyer, José Luís de Sales Marques, and Mario Telò

"As the world debates the future shape of international order, this volume, bringing together some of the best academic scholars on regionalism, offers a feast of ideas about how different actors and forces might reshape modernity, and redefine the theory and practice of multilateralism."

– Amitav Acharya, *American University, Washington, DC*

"This innovative edited volume is not only collecting the best worldwide specialists of regional cooperation and interregional relations, but it also provides us with inspiring inputs beyond the epistemic community of scholars, policy makers and citizens who are interested and committed to the construction of a new post-hegemonic, multilayered and more legitimate multilateralism."

– Maria João Rodrigues, *President of the Foundation European Progressive Studies, Brussels*

"This is a wonderful and inspiring book on the concepts, perceptions and realities of regionalisms in our globalized world. It contrasts competitive and cooperative regionalism and outlines a vision of cooperative multipolarity."

– Eun-Jeung Lee, *Freie Universität Berlin*

REGIONALISM AND MULTILATERALISM

Politics, Economics, Culture

*Edited by Thomas Meyer,
José Luís de Sales Marques
and Mario Telò*

This Publication is supported by Macau Foundation

First published 2019
by Routledge
2 Park Square, Milton Park, Abingdon, Oxon OX14 4RN

and by Routledge
52 Vanderbilt Avenue, New York, NY 10017

Routledge is an imprint of the Taylor & Francis Group, an informa business

© 2019 selection and editorial matter, Thomas Meyer, José Luís de Sales Marques, and Mario Telò; individual chapters, the contributors

The right of Thomas Meyer, José Luís de Sales Marques, and Mario Telò to be identified as the authors of the editorial material, and of the authors for their individual chapters, has been asserted in accordance with sections 77 and 78 of the Copyright, Designs and Patents Act 1988.

All rights reserved. No part of this book may be reprinted or reproduced or utilised in any form or by any electronic, mechanical, or other means, now known or hereafter invented, including photocopying and recording, or in any information storage or retrieval system, without permission in writing from the publishers.

Trademark notice: Product or corporate names may be trademarks or registered trademarks, and are used only for identification and explanation without intent to infringe.

British Library Cataloguing in Publication Data
A catalogue record for this book is available from the British Library

Library of Congress Cataloging in Publication Data
A catalog record has been requested for this book

ISBN: 978-0-367-89667-6 (hbk)
ISBN: 978-0-367-89665-2 (pbk)
ISBN: 978-1-003-02040-0 (ebk)

Typeset in Bembo
by Wearset Ltd, Boldon, Tyne and Wear

CONTENTS

List of illustrations — ix
Notes on contributors — x
Foreword — xvi
Acknowledgments — xix
List of abbreviations — xxi

Introduction — 1
Thomas Meyer and Mario Telò

PART I
Multiple modernities and regional/ interregional multilateralism — 15

1 Constrained diversity: modernities, regionalism, and polyvalent globalism in world politics — 17
Peter J. Katzenstein

2 Multiple modernities and regional multilateralism: a political–cultural point of view — 36
Thomas Meyer

3 Transnational governance and multiple multilateralisms — 48
Yaqing Qin

Contents

4 Regional diversity, interregional/transregional
dialogues, and the new multilateralism   66
Mario Telò

PART II
**History and drivers of regional
cooperation: trade, identity, security**   **93**

5 The future of regionalism: competing varieties
of regional cooperation   95
Andrew Gamble

6 The evolution of competitive Latin–American
regionalism   108
Louise Fawcett

PART III
**Case studies: competing regionalisms or
pluralistic and post-hegemonic multilateralism?**   **127**

7 Russia and Eurasian regionalism: how does it
fit into comparative regionalism research?   129
Alexander Libman

8 Chinese multilateralism in Central and
Southeast Asia: a relational perspective   143
Jianwei Wang and Weiqing Song

9 South Asia between nationalism and regionalism   166
Ummu Salma Bava

10 Multilateralizing regionalism in East Asia   178
Moonsung Kang

11 The Asia–Europe Meeting (ASEM): multilateral
interregionalism beyond trade relations   188
Evi Fitriani

12 Is the world ready for cooperative multipolarity?   202
Antonio de Aguilar Patriota

Index   217

ILLUSTRATIONS

Figure

3.1 Multilateralism: common features and different anchoring practices — 51

Tables

6.1 Latin American regionalisms, 2019 — 119
10.1 Multilateral trade negotiations — 179
10.2 WTO dispute cases with the US as a respondent during the Trump administration (as of March, 2019) — 181
10.3 New regional trade agreements since the Trump administration took office — 182

CONTRIBUTORS

Ummu Salma Bava holds the Jean Monnet Chair and Chairs the Centre for European Studies at Jawaharlal Nehru University. With 30 years of teaching and research experience, Professor Bava is one of the leading Indian experts on the EU, German and Indian foreign and security policy, regional integration, emerging powers, norms and global governance, and peace and conflict resolution. The author of numerous publications, she also has been a visiting professor at the Universities of Würzburg in Leipzig and the ULB in Brussels. In addition, in 2012 she was awarded the prestigious Order of Merit (Bundesverdienstkreuz) by the President of the Federal Republic of Germany. Professor Bava is a board member on the Berlin-based Research Advisory Council, Stiftung Wissenschaft und Politik, and sits on the Academic Advisory Board at the German Institute of Global and Area Studies in Hamburg.

Louise Fawcett is Professor of International Relations and the Wilfrid Knapp Fellow and Lecturer in Politics, St Catherine's College, University of Oxford (1995-present). She is currently Head of Oxford's Department of Politics and International Relations. Previously she served as Senior Tutor and Vice Master at St Catherine's College. Her research focuses on comparative regionalism and the international relations of developing countries, notably the Middle East. Major publications include: *Iran and the Cold War* (Cambridge University Press, 2009); *Regionalism in World Politics*, co-edited by Andrew Hurrell (Oxford University Press, 1995; Japanese edition, 1998); *The Third World Beyond the Cold War* ed. with Yezid Sayigh (Oxford University Press, 2000); *The International Relations of the Middle East* (Oxford University Press, 2005, 2009, 2013, and 2016); *Regionalism and Governance in the Americas* (co-edited by Monica Serrano, Palgrave, 2005); *Interregionalism and the European Union* (co-edited by Mario Telò and Frederik Ponjaert, Ashgate 2015). Professor Fawcett currently is working on a fifth revised edition of *The International Relations of the Middle East* as well as a single-authored book on international relations over the past century. She serves as a member of the editorial board of the UK journal, *International Affairs*.

Evi Fitriani is a Senior Lecturer in the International Relations Department, Faculty of Social and Political Sciences, Universitas Indonesia (Dept. HI FISIP UI), which she also chaired from 2012 to 2016. Currently, she is the Head of Miriam Budiardjo Resource Center of FISIP UI. She is co-founder of the University's Masters Program in European Studies as well the ASEAN Study Center of FISIP UI. In addition, she is the Indonesian Country Coordinator for the Network of East Asian Think-Tanks, a second track platform of the ASEAN Plus Three. Professor Fitriani completed her doctorate at the Australian National University in 2011. Trained in international relations in a variety of countries—Indonesia, the UK, the USA, Japan, Sweden, the Netherlands, and Hungary—she has won more than 13 international awards. The latter include the British Chevening Awards, a Fulbright Scholarship, Australian Development Scholarships, JICA and SIDA Grants, EU Fellowships, and—as a member of an Asia–Europe consortium—a Jean Monnet Network Grant. Over the last 20 years, she has been involved in numerous international collaborative research projects. Professor Fitriani's research interests center around Indonesian foreign policy, ASEAN, Asian regionalism, Indonesia–Australia relations, and Asia–Europe relations. Her publications include studies of Southeast Asia and the Asia–Europe Meeting, the interests of states, and the longevity of institutions. She is the author of eight book chapters in volumes written with international peer groups including *Asian Countries' Strategies towards the European Union in an Inter-regionalist Context* (National Taiwan University Press, 2015); *Europe in Emerging Asia* (Rowman & Littlefield International, 2015); *The Yudhoyono Presidency: Indonesia's decade of stability and stagnation* (ISEAS Singapore, 2015); and *Inter-regionalism and the European Union: Competing Perspectives on Regional Cooperation* (Ashgate, 2015) as well as *Muddy Boots and Smart Suits: Researching Asia-Pacific Affairs* (ISEAS Singapore, 2017). She also contributed to policy recommendation to the ASEM Summit, Asia–Europe Connectivity Vision 2025: Challenges and Opportunities (ERIA, 2016). Her latest articles appear in the *Journal of Contemporary Southeast Asia* on "The Trump Presidency and Indonesia" (2017) and in the *Pacific Review* on "Indonesian Perceptions of the Rise of China: Dare you, dare you not" (2018).

Andrew Gamble is Professor of Politics at the University of Sheffield and Emeritus Professor of Politics at the University of Cambridge. He is a Fellow of the British Academy and the Academy of Social Sciences and a professorial Fellow at the Sheffield Political Economy Research Institute (SPERI). His most recent books are *Crisis without End? The unravelling of western prosperity* (Red Globe Press, 2014) and *Can the Welfare State Survive?* (Polity Press, 2016). Professor Gamble, who served as a joint editor of the journals *Political Quarterly* and *New Political Economy* for over a decade, has published widely on political economy, British politics, and political theory. In 2005 he received the Isaiah Berlin Prize from the UK Political Studies Association for his lifetime contributions to that field.

Moonsung Kang received his BA in Economics from Korea University and his PhD in Economics from the University of Wisconsin at Madison. In 2006, he joined the faculty of the Division of International Studies at Korea University, and now serves as its Associate Dean. Previously, he worked at the Korean Institute for International Economic Policy, a government-funded research institution, as Research Fellow. Professor Kang has participated in multilateral and regional trade negotiations and advised the Korean government on international trade policy. His research interests include theoretical analyses on strategic trade policy and international trade rules and institutions, encompassing the multilateral trading system and regionalism. Professor Kang's recent articles include "Korea's Growth-Driven Trade Policies: Inclusive or exclusive?," "Northeast Asian Economic Cooperation in the Gradual Unification Process and Planning for Economic Integration of North and South Korea," "Protection of Intellectual Property Rights and Subsidy Policy for Foreign Direct Investment," "Industry-Specific Effects of Antidumping Activities: Evidence from the U.S., the EU, and China," "Asia's Strategic Participation in the Group of 20 for Global Economic Governance Reform: From the perspective of international trade," "Strategic Investment Policy: Role of knowledge spillovers," "Regional Production Networks, Service Offshoring, and Productivity in East Asia," "Understanding Agreements on TRIPS and Subsidies in Tandem." His book, *The Great Recession and Import Protection: The Role of Temporary Trade Barriers*, was published by CEPR and the World Bank.

Peter J. Katzenstein is the Walter S. Carpenter, Jr. Professor of International Studies at Cornell University, where he has taught since 1973. His research and teaching interests lie at the intersection of the fields of international relations and comparative politics. His current project is focused on worldviews in international politics. Professor Katzenstein's recent books include *Protean Power: Exploring the Uncertain and Unexpected in World Politics* (Cambridge University Press, 2018), co-edited by Lucia Seybert; *Anglo-America and Its Discontents: Civilizational Identities beyond West and East* (Routledge, 2012); *Sinicization and the Rise of China: Civilizational Processes beyond East and West* (Routledge, 2012); and *Civilizations in World Politics: Plural and Pluralist Perspectives* (Routledge, 2010). He is the author, co-author, editor and co-editor of over 40 books, edited volumes, or monographs and over 100 articles or book chapters. Professor Katzenstein served as President of the American Political Science Association from 2008–09. He holds six honorary degrees and has won numerous awards for his teaching and scholarship.

Alexander Libman is Professor of Social Sciences and Eastern European Studies at the Ludwig Maximilians University of Munich. Previously, he worked at the German Institute for International and Security Affairs SWP as an associate in the Eastern Europe and Eurasia Division and at the Frankfurt School of Finance & Management as an assistant professor of International Political Economy. Professor Libman holds a PhD from the University of Mannheim. His main research interests include Russian politics (especially its sub-national dimension) and regional organizations in post-Soviet Eurasia. His work was awarded the Knut Wicksell Prize from the European Public Choice Society; the Gordon Tullock Prize from the Public Choice Society; and the Ovsievich Memorial Prize from the Russian Academy of Sciences and the Leontieff Center. His most important publications include "Re-Evaluating Regional Organizations: Beyond the Smokescreen of Official Mandates" (2017, with Evgeny Vinokurov); "Causes and Consequences of Democratization: The Regions of Russia" (2015, with Anastassia Obydenkova); *Autocratic and Democratic External Influences in the Post-Soviet Eurasia* (2015, co-edited by Anastassia Obydenkova); "Holding-Together Regionalism: Twenty Years of Post-Soviet Integration" (2012, with Evgeny Vinokurov); and "Eurasian Integration: Challenges of Transcontinental Regionalism" (2012, with Evgeny Vinokurov). His articles have appeared in *World Politics*, *Comparative Political Studies*, *Political Studies*, *Review of International Organizations*, *Review of International Political Economy*, and *Post-Soviet Affairs*.

José Luís de Sales Marques has been President of the Board of Directors of the Institute of European Studies, Macau (IEEM) since January of 2002. From 1993–2001, he served as the Mayor of Macau. His research, teaching, and writing focus on Asia–Europe relations, EU–China dialogue, regional integration, and urban studies.

Thomas Meyer is Emeritus Professor Doctor of Political Science at the Technical University of Dortmund and Editor-in-Chief of the monthly political magazine, *Neue Gesellschaft/Frankfurter Hefte*. He has held visiting professor and guest lecturer positions at numerous universities, particularly in East and Southeast Asia, including Todai University, Tokyo; Beida University, Beijing; and the Indian Institute of Management, Bangalore. He directed projects for the well-respected German Research Foundation on such topics as political communication in the media (1995–2001) and the theory and practice of social democracy (2002–06). From 2000–07 he served as Academic Advisor to the European Commission for the Social Sciences and Humanities, and from 2004–08 he was a member of the GARNET Network of Excellence, funded by the European Commission. Professor Meyer's research focuses on comparative social democracy, European studies, mass media and politics, religious and political fundamentalism, and the cultural foundations of politics. Among his many books are *The Theory of Social Democracy* (Polity, 2007), *Identity Mania* (Zed, 2001), and *Media Democracy* (Polity, 2002).

Antonio de Aguilar Patriota was appointed as Brazil's Ambassador to Italy, Malta, and San Marino in August of 2016. Prior to serving in that capacity, he had been Brazil's Permanent Representative to the United Nations (2013–16), Foreign Minister (2011–13), Deputy Foreign Minister (2009–10), and Ambassador to the United States (2007–09). During his period as Ambassador to the UN, he was Chair of the 60th and 61st sessions of the Commission on the Status of Women and of the Peacebuilding Commission of the UN (2013–14). During his diplomatic career, he was posted to Geneva (1983–87 and 1999–2003), New York (1994–99), Beijing (1987–88), and Caracas (1988–90). Born in Rio de Janeiro in 1954, Ambassador Patriota graduated from Brazil's Diplomatic Academy in 1979, having studied philosophy at the University of Geneva. He was awarded an Honorary Doctorate in Public Service by Chatham University in 2008. Among his publications are "The UN Security Council after the Gulf War" (1998) and two volumes of "Speeches, Articles, and Interviews" during his period as foreign minister. His chapter in this volume is reprinted from the journal *CEBRI* (Brazilian Center for International Relations). Ambassador Patriota is a member of the Team of External Advisors of the 72nd United Nations General Assembly, and has been appointed to the "Leaders for Peace" initiative under the chairmanship of former French Prime Minister Raffarin.

Yaqing Qin is Professor of International Studies at China Foreign Affairs University (CFAU), Executive Vice-President of China National Association for International Studies (CNAIS), and Associate Member of the Royal Academy of Belgium and Global Fellow at the Peace Research Institute, Oslo. Previously, he served on the Resource Group for the UN High-Level Panel for Threats, Challenges, and Change (2003–04), organized by the then-UN Secretary General, Kofi Annan, and worked as Special Assistant to the Chinese Eminent Person, China–ASEAN Eminent Persons Group (2005). Professor Qin has served on numerous national and international editorial boards, including *Global Governance, East-West Policy Studies Series*, and *The Chinese Journal of International Politics*. His academic interests include international relations theory, global governance, and regionalism. He has written for numerous journals, including *International Studies Review, The Chinese Journal of International Politics* and *International Relations of the Asia-Pacific*. His most recent publication is *A Relational Theory of World Politics* (Cambridge University Press, 2018).

Weiqing Song is an Associate Professor of political science and coordinator of the MA Program in European Studies, with the Department of Government and Public Administration, Faculty of Social Sciences at the University of Macau. He holds a PhD in political science from the University of Siena, Italy. His research focuses on Chinese foreign policy, particularly in its neighborhood and with respect to global governance, and on European politics, with an emphasis on the European Union and European foreign policy. Professor Song is the author or editor of several books on Chinese foreign policy and Sino-European relations, including *China's Approach to Central Asia: the Shanghai Cooperation Organization* (Routledge, 2016) and *China, the European Union and*

International Politics of Global Governance (Palgrave Macmillan, 2015). In addition, his articles have appeared in various international peer-reviewed academic journals and edited volumes.

Mario Telò is the Jean Monnet Chair of International Relations at the Université Libre de Bruxelles, where he is the coordinator of the Global Europe Multilateralism (GEM) international doctoral program and the past president of the Institute for European Studies. He also teaches at the LUISS University and School of Government in Rome, and has been a visiting professor at numerous universities worldwide. Professor Telò has served as a consultant to the European Council, European Parliament, and European Commission. He is the author of 32 books and over 100 articles, published in seven languages. His recent works include *Europe: A civilian power?* (2006); *European Union and the New Regionalism* (2014); *International Relations: A European perspective* (2016); and *Regionalism in Hard Times* (2016). Professor Telò participates vigorously in public debates concerning international relations and the future of the European Union.

Jianwei Wang is Professor in the Department of Government and Public Administration at the University of Macau. He holds a PhD in Political Science from the University of Michigan and a BA and MA in International Politics from Fudan University (Shanghai). Previously, he was Distinguished Professor of Political Science at the University of Wisconsin-Stevens Point. He also has served as a research fellow and visiting scholar at George Washington University's Sigur Center for Asian Studies, the Atlantic Council of the United States, the East–West Center (Hawaii), and the United Nations Institute for Disarmament Research in Geneva. His teaching and research focus on East Asian politics and security, Chinese and American politics and foreign policy, Sino-American and Sino-Japanese relations, and UN peacekeeping operations. He has published extensively in these areas.

FOREWORD

The Institute of European Studies of Macau (IEEM) has organized a series of conferences on the topic of "multiple modernities and multilateral convergence" inspired by the pioneering work of sociologist Shmuel Eisenstadt and, more generally, has supported multidisciplinary research on multilateral governance. We think that this agenda is of the utmost importance not only for illuminating the dynamics and challenges of international cooperation today but also for laying the foundations of a genuine, sustainable multilateralism, one that takes into account the diversity of background cultures.

The high quality of the academic dialogue generated during the 2016 inaugural session encouraged us to continue promoting a series of annual conferences on the theme of multiple modernities, leading to the decision in 2019 to establish a permanent forum on the subject.

Following the usual anonymous referee process, Routledge Press, and notably the GEM Series (Globalisation, Europe, Multilateralism), offered to publish two books featuring the best papers presented at the first pair of annual meetings: *Multiple Modernities and Good Governance*, edited by Thomas Meyer and José Luís de Sales Marques, and *Cultures, Nationalism and Populism: New challenges to multilateralism*, edited by Thomas Meyer, José Luís de Sales Marques, and Mario Telò.

The 2017 conference focused on a different set of political challenges: populism, authoritarianism, and nationalism, and the threat they pose to existing national and international orders. It too featured essays prepared by scholars from around the globe, with perspectives drawn from empirical experiences in their own or neighboring states.

This new volume contains a selection of revised papers presented and discussed during the third conference of the series, held at the IEEM in November of 2018, which focused more narrowly on the future of regional, interregional, and multilateral cooperation in an age of resurgent nationalism and identity politics. In a context where the legacy of hegemonic multilateralism is dwindling because of deficits in both legitimacy and efficiency, the challenge is to deepen the dialectic between the diversity of modernity and modernization processes and the institutionalized, multilayered forms of multilateral cooperation.

We initiated the Macau seminars not only because the world was changing fast, but because we wanted to understand (and help to influence) the direction that change would take. We were especially keen to assess the political consequences that the idea of multiple modernities might have, given how it raised questions about established notions of modernization, good governance, the good society, and the nature of people's individual and collective rights in a global pluralist context.

Why did we focus this book on regionalism and interregionalism? With the US-led liberal order in decline, it seems urgent to examine continuities and discontinuities in the global governance of a diverse planet. We live in a transitional era, the outcome of which is hard to predict. Recent events in the US, Asia, Latin America, and Europe have had a destabilizing impact on world politics, while stopping short of sparking a new Cold War. Far-right and ultra-conservative forces have fared well in several recent national elections, although they clearly were held in check by the EU parliamentary election of May 2019. The Association of Southeast Asian Nations (ASEAN) and the EU continue to prove that resilient, dynamic, and open regional cooperation is still possible. That is why the theoretical agenda surrounding multiple modernities needs to focus on two interrelated questions: first, to what extent (if at all) do multidimensional regional entities canalize feelings of cultural identity; and second, how do such entities interact with one another as they try to establish interregional ties?

Even when they are under pressure from power politics and threatened with disintegration, multipurpose, bottom-up forms of regional cooperation have evolved on every continent as a third level between nation-states and global institutions. Nevertheless, we also can observe the emergence of competitive forms of authoritarian, top-down regionalism, for example those that have been sponsored by Vladimir Putin in the territory of the former Soviet Union, notably the Eurasian Economic Association. In various ways all of the book's contributors ask whether regional cooperation might be able to reverse or slow nationalist disintegration and power politics and whether it can revive multilateralism in new forms. Comparative empirical research is needed to address those questions. This volume contributes to that project by presenting the findings of some outstanding specialists, including experts in regionalist studies, which by now has become an established multidisciplinary field.

The second focus of this anthology is on interregional relations. Regions create their own unique forms of international relations, and those arrangements are relevant for our research agenda for three main reasons. First, to the extent that regions express cultural backgrounds and civilizations, interregional dialogues play a relevant role in damping down Huntington-style "clashes of civilizations." Second, the regional dimension is an intermediate cultural and normative level between nationalism and globalism, combining local particularism with abstract cosmopolitanism. Third, the shared aim of our authors is to move beyond an arrogant Euro- or Western-centric universalism while counteracting the drift toward cultural relativism. This last goal may be attained only by means of dialogues in which each participant seeks to understand the deep cultural background behind the values and principles of the others.

Global governance, multilateral cooperation, and interregional dialogue are in a precarious position today. In the context of contradictory signs such as global economic growth coupled with turbulent political disorder, the world is drifting toward greater instability and mutual suspicion. Thus, this volume represents a contribution both to a multidisciplinary research agenda and to the pluralist and collective efforts to explore joint solutions to global challenges. The latter would include, among many others, efforts to halt climate change, promote sustainable development, and ensure international peace and security.

José Luís de Sales Marques
President, Institute of European Studies of Macau

ACKNOWLEDGMENTS

Neither this anthology nor the third annual Conference on Multiple Modernities held in November of 2018 and sponsored by the Institute of European Studies of Macau (IEEM) would have been possible without the generous backing of the Macau Foundation, the leading funding mechanism for culture, science, and education of the Macau Special Administrative Region government.

The conference was jointly chaired by the President of IEEM, José Sales Marques; Thomas Meyer, visiting Professor at IEEM and former Chair of the Department of Political Science at the Technical University of Dortmund; and Mario Telò, visiting Professor at IEEM, professor of International Relations and emeritus President of the "Institut d Études Européennes" of the Université Libre de Bruxelles, and Member of the Royal Academy of Sciences and Arts of Belgium. Prof Qin Yaqing, emeritus President at China Foreign Affairs University (CFAU), also offered much-appreciated support to the conference.

The editors are grateful to the GEM program, the academic network coordinated by Professor Telò on behalf of the Institute of European Studies at the Université Libre de Bruxelles, funded by Horizon 2020 under the auspices of the EU Commission Research Directorate General. The latter also provided support for the work of several of the contributors to this volume and for the book itself.

The Brazilian journal *CEBRI* (*Centro Brasileiro de Relações Internacionais*) graciously granted permission to reprint material contained in the chapter by Antonio de Aguilar Patriota, which originally appeared under the title, "Is the World Ready for Cooperative Multipolarity?" in its October, 2018 issue.

We also are indebted to a long list of individuals and institutions whose contributions made this book possible, particularly to Beatrice Lam for her invaluable assistance throughout the entire process. We thank the students and academicians of IEEM, the University of Macau, who attended the annual Multiple Modernities conference and whose questions and comments enriched our discussions. We would also like to thank the anonymous referees and staff at Routledge who helped us to complete the final manuscript.

A special word of appreciation goes to Professors Lew and Sandy Hinchman of the United States, who assisted the editors and the authors in preparing this anthology for publication.

LIST OF ABBREVIATIONS

ACP	African, Caribbean, and Pacific Group of States
ACFTA	ASEAN–China Free Trade Agreement
ADB	Asian Development Bank
AFTA	Asian Free Trade Association
AIIB	Asian Infrastructure and Investment Bank
ALBA	Bolivarian Alliance for the Peoples of Our America
APEC	Asia–Pacific Economic Cooperation
APT	ASEAN Plus Three
ARF	ASEAN Regional Forum
ASEAN	Association of Southeast Asian Nations
ASEF	Asia–Europe Foundation
ASEM	Asia–Europe Meeting
AU	African Union
BIT	Bilateral Investment Treaty
Brexit	British exit from the EU
BRI	Belt and Road Initiative (China)
BRICS	Brazil, Russia, India, China, South Africa
CASCF	China and the Pacific Island Countries and the China-Arab States Cooperation Forum
CELAC	Community of Latin American and Caribbean States
CENTO	Central Treaty Organization
CETA	Comprehensive Economic and Trade Agreement (EU and Canada)
CFAU	China Foreign Affairs University
CIS	Commonwealth of Independent States
COC	Code of Conduct
COP	Conference of Parties

CCP	Chinese Communist Party
CPTPP	Comprehensive and Progressive Transpacific Partnership
CSTO	Collective Security Treaty Organization
CU	Customs Union
DDA	Doha Development Agenda
DOC	Declaration on the Conduct of the Parties in the South China Sea
EAEU	Eurasian Economic Union
ECJ	European Court of Justice
ECLA	Economic Commission for Latin America and the Caribbean
ECOWAS	Economic Community of West African States
ECSC	European Coal and Steel Community
EDC	European Defense Community
EEC	European Economic Community
EFTA	European Free Trade Association
EPA	Economic Partnership Agreement
EU	European Union
FDI	Foreign direct investment
FTA	Free Trade Agreement
FTAA	Free Trade Area of the Americas
GATT	General Agreement on Tariffs and Trade
GDP	Gross Domestic Product
GEM	Globalization, Europe and Multilateralism
ICC	International Criminal Court
IFI	International financial institutions
ILO	International Labor Organization
IMF	International Monetary Fund
IR	International relations
LAFTA	Latin American Free Trade Association
MC	Ministerial Conference
MENA	Middle East, North Africa, Afghanistan, Pakistan (Greater Middle East)
MERCOSUR	Mercado Común del Sur (Southern Common Market)
MNC	Multinational corporation
NAFTA	North American Free Trade Agreement
NAM	Non-aligned Movement
NATO	North Atlantic Treaty Organization
NGO	Non-governmental organization
OAS	Organization of American States
OPENAL	Tlatelolco Treaty
OSCE	Organization for Security and Cooperation in Europe
PA	Pacific Alliance
PRC	People's Republic of China
PROSUR	Forum for the Progress and Development of South America

RCEP	Regional Cooperation Economic Partnership
RTA	Regional Trade Agreement
SAARC	South Asian Association for Regional Cooperation
SACU	South African Customs Union
SADC	South African Development Community
SCO	Shanghai Cooperation Organization
SEATO	Southeast Asia Treaty Organization
SNA	Social Network Analysis
TAC	Treaty of Amity and Cooperation
TAFTA	Transatlantic Free Trade Association
TEU	Treaty of the EU
TFEU	Treaty on the Functioning of the EU
TPP	Transpacific Partnership
TTIP	Transatlantic Trade and Investment Partnership
UDHR	Universal Declaration of Human Rights
UNASUR	Union of South American Nations
USMCA	United States–Mexico–Canada Agreement
USRB	Union State
USSR	Union of Soviet Socialist Republics (Soviet Union)
USTR	United States Trade Representative
WTO	World Trade Organization

INTRODUCTION

Thomas Meyer and Mario Telò

This book presents an analysis of recent global trends in international relations, with special emphasis on the connections between cultural pluralism; political regionalism and interregionalism. New actors and varieties of cultural politics have challenged not only the Western model of modernization (along with its philosophical justifications) but also Western-derived forms of democracy. Among the emergent actors that have offered wide-ranging alternatives to the culture of modernity as represented by the West, three deserve special attention. First, there are various forms of political authoritarianism (seen, for example, in Russia, Turkey, and China) that claim to defend national or regional traditions against the logic of homogenization. Next, there are several variants of religious and political fundamentalism that pursue the politics of identity (e.g., in Iran, Saudi Arabia, and India) and advocate some sort of theocracy. Third, and most recently, neo-populist movements have gained ground even in electoral democracies like the United States, United Kingdom, Hungary, Poland, and Italy. By appealing to nationalist, ethnic, or religious identities as a way to mobilize support at the polls, those movements implicitly have attacked the model of Western modernity as such. All three of these tendencies affect the functioning and development of regional cooperation as well, since each invokes a strongly nationalistic and protectionist anti-multilateralism. During the ongoing upheaval in the global system of international relations, the cultural factor—that is, different worldviews and identities, and the use that political actors make of them—plays a crucial yet highly ambivalent or even contradictory role in politics, ideological debate, and intellectual discourse.

Culture and civilization exist in the modern world only in the plural. Although the great civilizations of the world all have come under the influence of the West, each has tried to develop its own set of generative principles. Of course, those principles differ from one another, yet all are understood to be the antithesis of the previously dominant source of legitimacy: traditional authority rooted in history. The dominant cultures today are not simply imitating or appropriating "Western modernity"; rather, each is interacting with it in the context of its own modernizing or anti-modern traditions. In referring to the "dominant culture" of a society, we mean the totality of the concepts, values, norms, habits, practices, and religious and secular convictions that shape and give meaning to human actions within it (whether wittingly or unwittingly). The meaning-bestowing power of culture touches nearly every sphere of a given society, including its politics, economy, art, and private life. The prevailing culture serves as the exclusive source against which all claims to legitimacy raised by institutions and actions, whether in domestic or international politics, must be measured. In short, culture molds the identities of actors and provides motivations for their actions.

No culture is an immutable, homogeneous entity; rather, all cultures are contested, dynamic spaces of discourse in which the interpretation of tradition unfolds under the impact of various social, political, and economic interests as well as of transnational interdependence. Cultures are constantly being constructed and reconstructed, but always under the influence of tradition. Yet, they are dynamic social facts of *longue durée* and cannot be fabricated arbitrarily under the direction of power. Thus, only by understanding and respecting the cultural dimension of every society and every actor can we establish solid foundations for fruitful cooperation and peaceful multilateralism in today's international environment. Moreover, if we understand culture broadly enough, as background knowledge, we recognize that it also nurtures social theory and enables theoretical innovation to flourish. The proper understanding of the concept of culture and its implications thus serves as the starting point for the dialogue that we hope this book will inspire.

On the one hand, we can observe that since roughly the end of World War II, and especially after the end of the Cold War's bipolarity, nations with close geographic and historical ties, nurtured by feelings of common belonging that flow upward from the grassroots, have aspired to construct a shared cultural identity alongside the more prosaic trade relations that they have maintained and developed. Their experiences are addressed by a large academic literature on "regionalism." On the other hand, both the determination to defy universalistic norms and values in the name of cultural regionalism/nationalism and the trend toward aggressive religious fundamentalism—the sort that attacks the very foundations of human civilization—have grown increasingly aggressive and conspicuous. Various economically successful authoritarian models of development in the Eurasian macro-continent recently have emerged as serious rivals to Western modernity. The European model has been called into question almost everywhere, including some countries that were considered to be centers of Western modernity until quite recently.

This book distinguishes carefully between authoritarian populism and "multiple modernities" (the plurality of paths toward modernity). Nevertheless, it tries to add to our understanding of both phenomena and their respective impacts on regionalism, interregionalism, and multilateralism. To cite an example, the European Union (EU), one of the most highly developed systems of new regionalism in the world, understands itself as a culturally pluralist democratic polity and as a proactive agent working for peaceful cooperation, conflict resolution, and economic development in the world as a whole. Cultural diversity, whether in Europe or elsewhere, can be an asset that supports a society's creativity and wealth-generation as well as its productivity and cultural richness. And, as the EU demonstrates, it also can be a force promoting political regionalization and interregional cooperation abroad. Since the 1990s, new forms of regional cooperation have been consolidated on every continent, albeit in diverse and distinctive ways, and have led to the development of multidimensional and multilayered interregional relations.

The following chapters suggest at least one broad generalization: that regionalism is changing and, in some cases, losing some of the impetus it once had. Emergent political or socio-economic conflicts—especially in times of crisis—have begun to chip away at multilateral regimes while giving a boost to exclusivist cultural politics as purveyed by identity entrepreneurs from various cultural, political, and religious communities. Thus, for the EU, with its increasing cultural pluralism, the impending challenge will be to strike a proper balance between the expectation that there should be one common civic culture for all and the claims raised by the multitude of cultural and nationalist identity groups for recognition and protection of their unique attributes. Within this unpredictable global context, in which the US and some emergent powers are exacerbating economic and political tensions, every neo-regional organization confronts three main problems: how to respond to the competition from authoritarian and hierarchical regionalism; how to combine the deepening of internal ties with influence-broadening and external cooperation; and how to support the development of a new multilayered multilateralism.

The contributions to the present volume consider many of the diverse forms and functions of regionalism across distinctive cultural contexts and their consequences for the politics of regional and interregional political cooperation. Employing a comparative approach, the book seeks to expose and understand the specific patterns of interaction between the cultural factor and social, economic, and political developments in determining the success or failure of efforts toward political regionalization. Moreover, it investigates the convergences and divergences between multiple modernities and transnational and interregional ties.

We have frequently alluded to the Western model of modernization. Needless to say, whole libraries could be devoted to analyzing its many facets, but here we wish to focus mostly on how a paradigm of international relations that was developed in seventeenth-century Europe allowed for the emergence of the secular state and the pursuit of political power in ways that were less destructive and more amenable to rational solutions than the system that preceded it.

The 1648 Peace of Westphalia, which ended (more or less) the Thirty Years War, gave rise to a certain idea of how international relations should be understood and practiced, one that today often is described as "realism" or, as many of the scholars writing for this volume would put it, as "power politics." The Westphalian system, with its rules for power, wealth, and territory undeterred by moral or religious scruples, endured for at least 150 years (indeed, according to some scholars, it persisted until World War I). But things began to change in the latter half of the eighteenth century, when some European philosophers began to question the logic of that Westphalian order. Immanuel Kant proposed an entirely new international system that would, he argued, ensure "Perpetual Peace." In Kant's view, only a republican form of government could guarantee such an outcome, for its rulers would have to seek the approval of the people in order to wage wars, and the latter would be unlikely to assent, fearing that they might end up as cannon fodder. Extending that logic, Kant believed that republics—today we would say "democracies"—would be disinclined to fight each other. Moreover, aside from championing republicanism at the national level, Kant advocated the establishment of transnational networks at the level of civil society, thereby moving beyond the traditional understanding of international relations as an activity conducted exclusively between states.

About the same time that Kant wrote his essay on perpetual peace, Adam Smith launched a revolution in political economy that rested on two insights. First, free markets generate greater prosperity or "wealth" than do monopolies and closed commercial empires. The point of political economy should not be to accumulate gold and silver in the state treasury or even to make sure that exports exceeded imports. The "invisible hand" of the market will make everyone better off in the long run. Trade and manufacturing are not a zero-sum game; hence, the more open the trading system, the more likely it is that all parties will benefit from economic growth. Smith's conclusion was reinforced by David Ricardo, whose "law of comparative advantage" claimed to prove that countries, and not just individuals, can specialize in producing certain commodities and then exchange them for items produced more efficiently elsewhere. Foreshadowing these antiprotectionist sentiments, Kant himself had underscored the need to institute a fair legal framework for free trade, one that would restrain, if not entirely eliminate, colonial economic hierarchies and similar inequities.

This complex set of ideas, which we today would call "liberalism," laid the foundations for a new approach to international relations, one that however would not really bear fruit until the mid-twentieth century. The European powers continued to expand their empires whenever and wherever they could, then sealed them off against trade with their rivals and prepared for the likelihood of armed conflict. The result was the debacle of World War I, which proved to many thoughtful people that the power-politics system inherited from Westphalia was bankrupt, and that the intellectual impulses stemming respectively from Kant and the British political economists ought to be given a chance. This entailed a stab at multilateralism, a term that needs to be defined carefully. Yaqing Qin, one of the scholars contributing to this volume, defines it as "a process of communicating, consulting, and coordinating among several actors, who should be more or less on an equal footing." The latter criterion means that states, like citizens in a republic, should have an equal voice even when they differ drastically in their wealth and power. Politically, after World War I, multilateralism in this sense found expression in the League of Nations. Economically, multilateralism was taken to mean that everyone would benefit if the principle of comparative advantage were respected. Unfortunately, empires controlled by European powers, especially Britain, Belgium, Portugal, and France, continued to operate by mercantilist principles to some extent, not allowing their colonies to trade freely and making them dependent instead on goods manufactured in the mother country. In short, although multilateralism appealed in theory, few if any states were ready to practice it even after the carnage of the Great War.

Only after World War II, the brutality and devastation of which far exceeded that of its predecessor, did the leaders of many countries begin to take multilateralism seriously. They did so in two different ways, both of which are at central to the subject of this anthology.

First, world leaders revived the global multilateralism behind the League in the form of a United Nations (UN), especially that body's General Assembly, which grants each country one vote, regardless of its size and power. Thus, for example, the Maldives and Haiti there are on par with China and the United States. Second, the UN still embodied the older great power politics in the form of its Security Council, which enables any one of its five permanent members to exercise a veto. Global multilateralism took other forms as well. Inspired by liberal doctrines and by the constructive hegemonic design associated with Franklin D. Roosevelt, world leaders meeting in 1944 at Bretton Woods in New Hampshire established a gold standard based on the US dollar; founded the International Monetary Fund (IMF) to stabilize exchange rates, prevent global recessions, and bail out floundering economies; and created the World Bank to finance growth-oriented projects in the developing world. Three years later, efforts to reduce barriers to international economic exchange culminated in the General Agreement on Tariffs and Trade, which in 1995 was reconstituted in a more robust form as the World Trade Organization (WTO). Today, although the institutions associated with Bretton Woods have been targeted by numerous critics, almost no one would prefer to abolish them. They give evidence that multilateralism finally has been accepted by most countries and their citizens as a legitimate form of international relations, alongside the older Westphalian model.

In addition to the UN and the Bretton Woods system, many nations attempted to pursue a second kind of multilateralism, this time in the form of regionalism. While Cold War tensions and/or great power politics might limit the effectiveness of global-level multilateralism, regional-scale organizations have the potential to enjoy greater success, especially when—to one degree or another—they consisted of "republics" in Kant's sense. The European Common Market (instituted in 1957), which eventually evolved into the European Union (1992), proved to be the most durable and successful of such efforts, inspiring other experiments in regional multilateralism.

It is at this point that we arrive at the intersection between multiple modernities and multilateralism/regionalism that animates this volume. Regional associations seem to thrive best when the participants have cultural traditions in common. For example, most of the EU's member nations share a heritage of Christianity, political democracy, commitment to human rights, related languages, and—perhaps most importantly—the experiences of the two world wars, which demonstrated that the Westphalian system of exclusive sovereignty and balance of power politics could lead to catastrophe. Convergent background cultures also may help to explain the success of other regional groupings, such as Assocation of Southeast Asian Nations (ASEAN), the Southern Common Market (MERCOSUR), and the African Union.

From these considerations, three fundamental questions follow. First, do different civilizational backgrounds foster different types of regional cooperation? Second, how and to what extent does regionalism pose a challenge to multilateralism? Are regional associations irreconcilable expressions of what Samuel Huntington called "civilizations," pitted irretrievably against one another and simply carrying on power politics at a higher level? Or is regionalism the launching pad for genuinely global cooperation and multilateralism that can arc across civilizational barriers and bring together countries that are all striving to be modern in different ways? Third and finally, can interregional cooperation and cultural dialogue counter the fragmentation of global governance?

According to some scholars, the interplay between regionalism and democratization may provide a key to addressing these questions. As discussed above, Kant had argued that republics, rather than autocracies, are best positioned to reach and maintain a durable peace and find multilateral solutions to common problems. Some regional associations, especially the EU, consist almost entirely of regimes that derive their legitimacy from democratic procedures and respect for fundamental rights. Others, such as the Eurasian Economic Union (founded by Vladimir Putin) and the Shanghai Cooperation Organization, bring together a mix of regime types, most of which are authoritarian to some degree. Yet the latter often proclaim their commitment to multilateralism and back it up, at least at times, with a willingness to cooperate with global multilateral organizations such as the WTO and its multilateral trade policy. Meanwhile, supposed "republics" such as the United States and Brazil recently have thumbed their noses at international agreements and norms, apparently regressing to Westphalian-style power politics and a fixation upon national sovereignty. Can authoritarian and democratic regimes find common ground that cuts across civilizational lines, so that the world does not end up with a Huntingtonian clash of civilizations? Does the domestic politics of a country still matter when it comes to addressing global problems such as trade, climate change, and terrorism? These are just a few of the issues that our contributors address in the pages of this volume.

In the leadoff essay of Part I, Peter Katzenstein points out that the multiple modernities approach pioneered by Israeli sociologist Shmuel Eisenstadt traces the different versions of modernity seen today back to the Axial Age (the eighth through the third centuries BCE), when many of the world's major religious and ethical traditions began to take shape. As Katzenstein puts it, "[t]he legacies of different world religions thus create multiple modernities." The formative power and durability of those traditions is impressive; in fact, there is no reason to believe that the process of modernization ever will homogenize all regions and cultures, since "forces of convergence are always balanced against forces of divergence." But, against Huntington, Katzenstein emphasizes that the space for divergence is not limitless. For example, regionalism is not shaped merely by culture or geography, but also by political and economic realities. That is why Italy, a Mediterranean country, joined the North Atlantic Treaty Organization and why Greece and Turkey, historical enemies from different civilizations, followed suit. These examples illustrate Katzenstein's insight that regional groupings (and for that matter states) operate within a spectrum of "constrained diversity." Moreover, the political order in any region also exhibits "variants of modernity," a less ambitious claim about the diverse ways in which modern societies have responded to common challenges posed by the "one general model of modernity." In short, Katzenstein's approach to regionalism, constrained diversity, "helps discover spaces for new political possibilities that Huntington's language of clash conceals."

Like Katzenstein, Meyer (in Chapter 2) questions Huntington's assumption that civilizations—or the regional associations that flow from them—are monolithic, closed, mutually suspicious, and always on the verge of clashing. In Meyer's view, the multiple modernities approach offers a far more empirically accurate and normatively defensible way to conceptualize cultural/political differences. He argues that cultures are always internally contested, always engaged in a tug-of-war between traditionalist, modernist–liberal, and fundamentalist elements, each seeking to appropriate and assign its own specific meanings to cultural traditions. There is no inherent reason that different civilizations or regional associations cannot cooperate, unless the fundamentalist strain in a given culture becomes utterly dominant. All forms of fundamentalism "lack both the proper cultural foundations for consistent multilateralism and the willingness to cooperate with other political cultures/civilizations on an equal footing." Still, those observations leave the question open: Can republics (today's democracies) cooperate with non-democracies that nevertheless share a commitment to certain crucial principles of modernization and multilateralism, such as the rule of law and good governance? Meyer suggests that such multilateral cooperation is indeed possible, since it would be wrong "to infer from Kant's notion of republicanism the superiority of American or European-style institutional patterns."

Yaqing Qin begins Chapter 3 by posing a question that is seldom asked: "What sustains multilateralism?" To address it, he argues, we must realize that multilateralism takes at least three different forms: hegemonic, institutional, and relational. In the first, one great power, the hegemon, imposes an order on the rest of the world, as the United States did after World War II. Aside from spearheading multilateral institutions like the UN and the IMF, the US encouraged the development of regionalism in various parts of the world, most notably Europe, in the service of containing the Soviet empire. What maintains this form of multilateralism, for Qin, is simply power. Although hegemonic power may be necessary, at least at times, it is in tension with multilateralism, which rests on the principle that member countries should be "on an equal footing." Institutional multilateralism is best illustrated by the European Union. That association, lacking a hegemon, has developed an elaborate set of rules, norms, and treaties to coordinate policies and economic relations among its 27 member states. As it has evolved, the EU has gradually transformed itself from an intergovernmental organization into what Qin calls a "supranationality," since the member states have transferred some of their sovereignty to higher-level bodies like the European Commission, Parliament, and Court of Justice, as well as to the Council, when it operates on the basis of a qualified majority voting procedure. Finally, relational multilateralism, exemplified by ASEAN, is less about rules, laws, and institutions than it is about consensus-seeking to maintain good relations among member states. At the theoretical level, Qin has transposed Confucian ideas about the centrality of social relationships to the realm of international relations.

Mario Telò picks up the thread of Qin's reasoning and takes it in a different direction. He contends that the regional multilateral cooperation developed over the past 70 years is on shaky ground, beset on the one hand by populist nationalism and old-fashioned power politics and challenged on the other hand to upgrade toward political integration. While he recognizes that trade has been an important motivator for the formation of many regional and global multilateral bodies, such as the EU and WTO, he remarks that "regional and interregional arrangements may be driven by factors other than trade interests." These factors include "cultural identities and feelings of common belonging." Multipurpose interregional and multilateral relations combined with trade could generate a sophisticated regulatory framework capable of combatting a wide range of domestic and international problems, including "anarchy, nationalism, competition, ethnocentrism, protectionism, and fragmentation." In this light, he analyzes emerging challenges to the EU's multiple interregional ties with every continent. For Telò, interregional relations have a potentially enormous role to play in defusing trade wars, political conflicts, and even Huntington's so-called clash of civilizations. The EU is now explicitly threatened by the Trump administration in the US, which favors Brexit and other expressions of nationalism; by Russia, which is proactively undermining the solidarity of the EU; and, implicitly, even by China, which de facto divides the EU through its 17+1 policy. Like Meyer, Telò sees merit in Kant's essay on perpetual peace as a guidepost for reflections on the future of multilateralism in a world of multiple modernities. In particular, he endorses combining the agenda of the EU strategic autonomy with enhanced transnational ties at the level of civil societies (what Kant called "cosmopolitanism") as the fundamental condition for peaceful cooperation in the post-Westphalian world.

The authors contributing to Part II of this volume seek to lay bare the historical roots of regional multilateral cooperation in specific settings. In Chapter 5, Andrew Gamble focuses especially on the rise and decline of multilateralism in the twentieth and twenty-first centuries. To elucidate that historical trajectory, he distinguishes between open and closed regionalism. In the former, regional associations are regarded as "stepping stones" to more encompassing forms of cooperation, first at the interregional and ultimately at the global level. Closed regionalism, by contrast, features a hegemon that attempts to seal off its sphere of influence from trade and cooperation with the outside world. Imperial Japan's project of establishing an East Asian Co-Prosperity Sphere (1935–45), and the Soviet-dominated Eastern Europe (COMECON) prior to 1991, provide examples. Gamble argues that the heyday of open regionalism—which began just after World War II, reached its zenith in the 1990s, and crumbled in the wake of the Great Recession of 2008—is passing into history. Its demise is due to the upsurge of populist nationalism in many countries and the actions of the Trump administration to terminate or disparage so many of the treaties and alliances that once underpinned the American system of hegemonic multilateralism, in favor of bilateral relations in which the US can impose its will on weaker countries under the banner with of "America First." Like Telò, Gamble focuses on the development of the so-called "new regionalism" in the EU, which he fears could become just "a multilateral island in a sea of competing nationalisms." Aside from the EU, Gamble recognizes other forms of regionalism, such as the "minimalist" variety; the illiberal variety exemplified by the Russian-led Eurasian Economic Union (EAEU, discussed below); and the enigmatic variety now pushed by China in parallel with its interregional Belt and Road Initiative (BRI). But none of the latter seems likely to restore anything like the globally oriented multilateralism that once seemed to be on history's agenda.

Complementing Gamble's analysis, Louise Fawcett in Chapter 6 elaborates the "historical institutionalist approach" to the development of regionalism in Latin America. Although the continent often is regarded as being outside the global mainstream, regionalism in South America has a long tradition. Its history extends to the early nineteenth century, when newly independent countries sought to preserve their political and economic independence first from the European great powers and later from the United States as it became a hegemon in the Western hemisphere. A choice that confronted Latin American leaders from the beginning was whether to "cohere around a pan-American or hemispheric ideal of regionalism" or embrace "Southern alternatives" to US primacy. As the advantages of regional organization became apparent by the mid- to late-twentieth century,

South American countries sometimes opted for deeper and more defensive regional schemes such as the Community of Andean States and MERCOSUR, in competition with broader US-led associations like the Free Trade Area of the Americas. Ratification of the Asunción Treaty (1991) in the context of domestic democratization and the "new regionalism" wave signaled a commitment by South American states to apply the lessons of the EU to their own affairs. Organizations such as MERCOSUR aimed to stimulate economic growth and development through a common market. Nowadays, according to Fawcett, MERCOSUR—once greeted with enthusiasm—faces a crisis due to its inability thus far to overcome the conflicts of economic interest among its member states. These difficulties threaten to favor the alternative Pacific Alliance, an organization oriented merely to the FTAA model. But the recent arrangement of a complex, multidimensional trade deal between the EU and MERCOSUR suggests that interregional agreements still remain a live option.

Part III includes several case studies on experiments in regionalism and interregionalism. We may read these contributions as efforts to test the general hypotheses about multilateralism and regionalism found in earlier chapters.

The essay by Alexander Libman on Eurasian regionalism (Chapter 7), in the form of the Eurasian Economic Union, suggests a sobering question: Are regional associations, to one extent or another, stepping stones toward a more robust version of global multilateralism? Or, as perhaps in the case of the Eurasian Economic Union (EAEU), are we dealing merely with a "façade of multilateralism and economic cooperation [that] hides a power hierarchy?" What is most striking about the evolution of Eurasian regional cooperation—and especially the EAEU, its most advanced organization—is the enormous influence that the EU has had as a template for establishing customs unions out of independent countries with a common cultural and political history. But, as Libman emphasizes, the EAEU cannot truly emulate the EU, because most of its member states are authoritarian regimes, whereas the EU contains only democracies, at least in principle. Putin's Russia, seeking to enhance its status in global power politics, regards the EAEU as a counterweight to the EU, one that is designed to promote autocracy rather than democracy (e.g., by certifying fraudulent elections results as free and fair). In brief, Eurasian regionalism appears to be a throwback to what Libman calls the "authoritarian regionalism" that prevailed after World War I, and thus hardly inspires hope that regionalism of this sort can move us any closer to reformed global multilateralism.

In Chapter 8, Jianwei Wang and Weiqing Song—drawing on Qin's theory of "relational regionalism"—offer an innovative analysis of China's multilateral relations with two regions: Central Asia (mainly via the Shanghai Cooperation Organization) and Southeast Asia, with its principal regional body, ASEAN, along with its concentric circles of ASEAN plus 1, plus 3 and plus 6. Relational theory (a.k.a. social network analysis) is based on the premises that "all human actors are shaped by and become social beings via relational interactions" and therefore "cannot be understood atomistically." This generalization supposedly holds true not only for individuals, but equally for states. The relational approach, as the authors point out, clearly reflects the influence of Confucian thought, although one might add that it also has Western comparisons, especially in the philosophy of Hegel. In Central Asia, Chinese diplomacy has sought common ground on which these mostly Muslim states could cooperate with Beijing, and they have found it primarily in the struggle against terrorism and in infrastructure projects such as the BRI. By contrast, the authors note that China and the ASEAN countries could build on "shared historical experiences and cultural values," especially the Southeast Asian countries' tradition of consensus-building. But according to Wang and Song, we should be aware that China and ASEAN have shaped each other's identities and goals in a process of mutual multilateral accommodation. China's turn toward multilateralism actually began with its discovery that diplomacy with the ASEAN countries worked better on a multilateral than on a bilateral basis. The results of that diplomacy have been impressive in the field of trade, but much less so in the area of security cooperation, mostly because ASEAN opposes China's position on its "rights" in the South China Sea (although even here China's hard line has softened a bit). The larger point is that ASEAN–China ties have been a "two-way street" in which China's goals, views, and norms have evolved along with those of the ASEAN ten.

While China's forays into multilateralism and regionalism have been somewhat encouraging, the same cannot be said for the states of South Asia, as Ummu Salma Bava shows in Chapter 9. To be sure, those countries—including India and Pakistan—have founded a regional body (South Asian Association for Regional Cooperation, SAARC) that promotes cooperation among them, but it has accomplished little. The stumbling-block to mutually beneficial arrangements has been the mistrust that exists between India and Pakistan as well as between those states and others, including Bangladesh and Sri Lanka. As Bava explains, the end of colonialism in South Asia and the emergence of new states raised urgent questions of national identity. Relatively quickly, identity became linked to religion in some places (especially Pakistan and Bangladesh) and to territory and boundaries in many others, with the result that "boundaries and sovereignty became defining aspects of identity in each of the countries." Harking back to our earlier discussion of the origins of modern-day international relations theory, Bava notes that "the Westphalian idea of the state, which links sovereignty to territory, had acquired prominence in that region." Of course, the Westphalian idea of sovereignty never has ceased to be a cornerstone of international relations everywhere, but in Europe and to a lesser extent in Southeast Asia and elsewhere, it has been sharply modified by the perceived advantages, shared norms, and legal agreements associated with regional multilateralism. Not so where India, Pakistan, Bangladesh, and other such countries are concerned. Indeed, recurrent international conflicts in South Asia challenge the hypothesis of a dynamic interplay between regionalism and multilateralism.

Dating back to the era of Smith and Ricardo, global free trade has been touted as a win–win arrangement for all countries that engage in it. As we have seen, that conviction did not stop colonial nations like Britain and France from protecting their imperial markets, nor did it prevent countries from seeking to protect domestic markets during the Great Depression. Supposedly, the surge of US-led multilateralism after World War II gave proof that most countries finally had grasped the advantages of free trade after the catastrophic nationalism and protectionism of past decades. The best prospects for global multilateralism seemed to be precisely the ones involving trade. But, as Moonsung Kang argues in Chapter 10, the consensus over the virtues of free trade is fraying badly nowadays. The United States, once the most powerful advocate of lower tariffs, has withdrawn from or bad-mouthed global multilateral global and regional trade agreements from the WTO to the Trans-Pacific Partnership (TPP) and Transatlantic Trade and Investment Partnership (TTIP). As a result, other countries have sought to escape a relapse into mere transactionalist bilateralism by negotiating a series of agreements that, in effect, supplant the regional and global multilateralism practiced under the pro-free-trade auspices of the US as hegemon. Kang recommends the regionalist and interregionalist strategy for East Asia and notes with satisfaction that "East Asia is the place where regionalism is growing fastest." But, he observes, regional trade agreements are not enough. If we are to rebuild some semblance of the old global multilateral trading system that the US presently is disrupting, then trade agreements should be "multilateralized" at the global level as well, since the present webwork of regional agreements is "too complex and redundant." In Kang's approach, regionalism is thus, in trade-specific context, part of a process of reconstructing a multilateral world and preserving mutually beneficial exchange from American truculence and bullying.

Like Kang, Evi Fitriani in Chapter 11 wishes to preserve and expand multilateralism, arguing that this goal can be accomplished by means that go "beyond trade relations." She reposes great hopes in interregional cooperation on many fronts. These are best exemplified by the Asia–Europe Meeting (ASEM), a "multidimensional form of interregionalism" established in 1996. Fitriani is well aware that the EU and its Asian counterpart, ASEAN, were originally founded to serve the national interests of their member states in a rather Westphalian spirit. But she insists that this is not the end of the story. Instead, she asks whether "Asian and European regional entities, originally the expressions of the power and interests of regional states … [can] amicably deploy their power to safeguard multilateralism and support global governance?" In other words, Fitriani wonders whether ASEM could be the prototype for a bottom-up reconstruction of the multilateral global order that now seems to be disintegrating. Although Fitriani concedes that "trade was the main justification for the creation of ASEM," she argues that it has evolved beyond its original, narrow mandate to embrace a range of other objectives, running the gamut from education, employment, and social issues to green growth, intellectual property rights, and more. In fact, the "social, cultural, and educational pillar" of ASEM has flourished, as has the "economic pillar." The trouble is that the "political pillar" has not, because the issues there are too delicate and too intertwined with questions of national sovereignty and power. Nevertheless, Fitriani counsels patience, noting that trust-building and institutional development are slow processes and that ASEM has made great strides during the nearly 25 years of its existence. In sum, she rejects critics who dismiss it as a talk-shop that never accomplishes anything worthwhile. On the contrary, she avers that "ASEM can lay a solid foundation upon which to build a cooperative world order."

Among the contributors to this volume, Antonio de Aguilar Patriota, a highly-regarded Brazilian diplomat and former UN Representative, sounds the most optimistic note on the future prospects of global cooperation, remarking that an opportunity for "posthegemonic multilateralism may be at hand." Of course, his hopes have been tempered by the turn of American foreign policy back toward unilateralism, a trend our other authors also have deplored. But he emphasizes in Chapter 12 that the current world order is far more "multilayered" than it ever has been, including not only rising powers such as the BRICS (Brazil, Russia, India, China, and South Africa), but also a variety of non-state actors. He cites the UN's 2030 Agenda on Sustainable Development as an example of what can be accomplished when all of these actors work together to reach consensus. More broadly, Patriota thinks that problems such as terrorism, Ebola, and climate change simply cannot be resolved without broad multilateral cooperation. In this respect, the multilateralism of today ("a unifying element") differs greatly from that of the Concert of Europe, to cite an older case, which was designed to preserve a balance of power on the European continent and thus serve the interests of the major nation-states of that era. To overcome challenges of this kind we need "enlightened leadership and effective diplomacy," especially a willingness on the part of the great powers to accommodate developing countries in allocating UN positions and, above all, broadening the Security Council's membership, ground rules, and mandate. In this respect, Patriota's approach to multilateralism differs to some extent from that of most of our authors. He does not envision a process in which global multilateralism will gradually re-emerge from regionalism; instead, he argues that we can move directly toward the goal of global multilateralism without going through the detour of regional associations. We live in a densely interconnected world in which we already have functioning global multilateral institutions such as the UN and the Bretton Woods system. We need to resist unilateral, go-it-alone impulses and place our trust in those institutions.

The survey of multilateralism and regionalism presented in this volume thus admits several conclusions. Most of our authors equate the Kantian ideal of a "federation of republics" with post-hegemonic multilateralism: that is, a global order built on mutual respect and equality. That ideal holds the promise of gradually moving the world past the Westphalian system of state sovereignty and power politics. But making a transition to a new multilateralism will not prove easy to achieve. The lure of national sovereignty and exclusive cultural identities remains powerful, and although the EU and ASEAN, especially, appear to be resilient and dynamic, some competitive regional arrangements seem to be little more than smokescreens for the pursuit of national self-interest. And although multilateralism is still alive and well via regional and trade agreements, that is a thin reed upon which to build a more robustly cooperative world order. Most contributors to this volume would probably agree that the best thing that could happen to the project of global or even regional multilateralism would be the re-commitment of the United States to supporting and participating in cross-national institutions and regimes.

However, in contrast to the past hegemonic era, reviving the willingness of the US to abide by the rules and norms that underlie what remains of the postwar multilateral system will not suffice. Efforts to build a new multilateralism also will require new actors and new drivers, as well as broad-based tendencies to promote peaceful cooperation, democratization, and the pooling of sovereignty at the regional and interregional levels. That project, in turn, must be rooted in respectful dialogue among diverse cultural identities and multiple forms of modernity.

PART I
Multiple modernities and regional/interregional multilateralism

1

CONSTRAINED DIVERSITY

Modernities, regionalism, and polyvalent globalism in world politics

Peter J. Katzenstein

Apposite for this chapter, Jacob Viner (1991: 227) writes that "most abstract terms ending in 'ism' inevitably accumulate about them a haze of uncertainty and imprecision."[1] The chapter focuses on civilizational and regional politics. It maneuvers between two sets of claims articulated after the end of the Cold War. Francis Fukuyama's (2006) end-of-history thesis interpreted the victory of liberalism over communism and fascism as the end of different programs for modernity and the beginning of stultifying sameness. Samuel Huntington's (1996) clash of civilization thesis viewed the same victory as setting the stage for bitter civilizational clashes across deep fault lines. The first views the world in terms of convergence toward harmonious cooperation, while the second views it in terms of divergence into fundamentally irreconcilable differences. Polyvalent globalism, I argue, describes a situation of constrained diversities that characterizes contemporary world politics more accurately than either of these perspectives. A recognition of constrained diversities makes it easier to resist Fukuyama's urge of imputing to history a teleology and helps discover spaces for new political possibilities that Huntington's language of clash conceals.

Multiple modernities and variants of modernity

How do we characterize and account for the mixture of difference and sameness in contemporary world politics? Explanations that feature "multiple modernities" or highlight variations on the theme of modernity offer related though different answers. Looking at historical developments dating back to the sixth century CE, the theory of multiple modernities stresses the never-ending potential for constrained diversities in the nature of constitutive institutions, including political orders, collective identities, and the character of public spheres. Informed primarily by the history of the last two centuries, variants-of-modernity theories emphasize instead the pervasiveness of constrained diversities. They focus typically on regulatory institutional and organizational arrangements, including the strength and autonomy of state agencies, societal groups, and social movements.

Multiple modernities[2]

Joined by many other scholars, Shmuel Eisenstadt (1982, 1996, 1999a, 1999b, 2000a, 2000b, 2000c, 2003) developed the concept of multiple modernities and applied it to many different settings.[3] The key distinction lies between two types of civilizations. Axial Age civilizations emerged together with the major world religions around the sixth century BCE (Arnason *et al.* 2005; Bellah 2011; Bellah & Joas 2012),[4] a formative period of religious innovation. The delayed impact of different religious traditions embodied in distinctive civilizational frameworks has had powerful effects down to the present. Continuous reconstruction of religious traditions creates struggles and innovations in political orders, collective identities, and public spheres. Proto-fundamentalism is an inescapable byproduct of those struggles. In this view, Jacobin impulses are not evanescent phenomena. The civilization of modernity (Eisenstadt 2001), by way of contrast, is a product of the very recent past, starting with the scientific and technological revolution brought about by the European Enlightenment and marked by an unprecedented openness to novelty and uncertainty. The two types of civilizations interact and reconfigure each other in unending dynamic relations of mutual reconstitution. Together they have helped bring about the emergence of one global civilization containing multiple modernities.

Eisenstadt took the concept of the Axial Age from Karl Jaspers (1953; see also Levine 1995, 2004). It denotes a formative period in world history when a number of powerful cultural developments in China, India, Iran, Palestine, and Greece occurred independently from one another. Humankind moved at that pivotal moment in world history from an instinctual disposition to a self-reflexive striving for human agency, transcendence, self-determination and, eventually, future-oriented progress (Eisenstadt 2000b: 3–5; Meyer 2018a: 5–7; Meyer 2018b: 17–20). For Jaspers and Eisenstadt, the sixth century BCE is an axis that divides history, a transformative break brought about by the appearance of the world's great religions and the onset of humankind's spiritualization.

Eisenstadt's core argument holds that the impact of different Axial Age religions and civilizations is eventually transmitted to one global civilization containing multiple modernities. Following Max Weber, Eisenstadt argues that the different religious cores and cultural programs of Axial Age civilizations are historically grounded, continually reconstructed traditions. The religious cores of civilizations thus continue to have a strong impact on the unending restructuring of their respective states. Eisenstadt dissents from Weber's Eurocentrism by insisting that, in all civilizations, this reconstruction is shaped by specific antinomies:

transcendental vs. mundane, universalistic vs. particularistic, totalistic vs. pluralistic, orthodox vs. heterodox. These antinomies motivate political struggles that affect political institutions, social and economic structures, and collective identities. It is noteworthy that all Axial Age civilizations have generated proto-fundamentalist movements. In the West, Jacobinism became an oppositional movement in European civilization that exploded in the twentieth century under the banners of communism and fascism. Modern fundamentalism in non-Western civilizations combines the impact of Western Jacobinism with indigenous fundamentalist movements. Jacobin impulses in modernity thus are not passing phenomena in the history of civilizations. Instead, they are its permanent features. Fundamentalism is an engine of change in all civilizations and a key aspect of the civilization of modernity. In general, Western patterns of modernity are not the only authentic ones; they merely precede other versions and thus often act as cognitive reference points (Eisenstadt 2000b: 2–3).

Early modernities (from the sixteenth to the eighteenth century) provide a transitional phase between Axial Age civilizations and full modernity that exemplify and deepen the theme of multiple modernities (Eisenstadt & Schluchter 1998). Language offers a good illustration of this period of transition. The turn to vernacular languages occurred in both Europe and India. In Europe, but not in India, it was accompanied by the emergence of more clearly defined territorial boundaries. In India, but not in Europe, vernacular languages complemented rather than replaced the sacred languages of Sanskrit and Pali (Pollock 2006: 259–80). In China and Japan, classical languages and political orders survived those turbulent centuries. While China experienced a major break in the age of axial religion, Japan, as the only state coterminous with a civilization, did not. Yet in both states a public sphere evolved in early modernity, although one that was not tied, as in Europe, to civil society. Instead, China's public sphere became the world of the academies and the literati, which was closely linked to the official sphere (Woodside 2006). In Tokugawa Japan, people and territory were united (*kokka*). But even in that holistic conception, politically relevant distinctions emerged between the official and the non-official and between the social and the non-social. As in China, the realm of the private was denigrated and widely regarded as undercutting the pursuit of the common good. By contrast, in Islamic law, Sufi orders constituted a dynamic public sphere that operated quite independently from the political or official realm. Charting such a multiplicity of early modernities undercuts the charge of Eurocentrism in Eisenstadt's civilizational analysis (Pasha 2007: 65, 70). Europe is, as Eisenstadt and Schluchter argue, an analytical ideal type, not a normative reference point (Eisenstadt & Schluchter 1998: 6–7, 15).

The first civilization of modernity was Western European. Based on the Enlightenment and crystallized politically in the American and French revolutions, it developed in the specific context of European Christianity. Its cultural core was a bundle of cognitive and moral imperatives insisting on more individual autonomy, fewer traditional constraints, and increased control over nature. The first modernity was constructed and reconstructed in the specific context of Judeo/Greek/Christian cultural universalism and in the political pluralism of its various center-periphery relations and political protest movements. Subsequently, Western European modernity spread to Central and Eastern Europe, North and South America, and other non-European civilizations. For Eisenstadt (2001), the civilization of modernity is defined not by being taken for granted, but by becoming a zone of contestation, an object of uninterrupted conflict engaging both pre- and post-modern protest movements (Kocka 2001). The civilization of modernity embodies a multiplicity of cultural programs and institutions that derive from the interaction between West European modernity and the various civilizations of the Axial Age.

In contrast to theories of variants of modernity, for theories of multiple modernities, modern societies are therefore not converging on a path involving capitalist industrialism, political democracy, modern welfare regimes, and pluralizing secularisms. Instead, the different religious traditions serve as cultural sources for the enactment of different programs of modernity. For example, West European modernity was transformed in the United States under the specific circumstances of a settler and immigrant society. In America fundamentalist religious movements remain relevant for the multiple traditions and various dimensions of political identities, political institutions, and collective identities of the American state (Roniger & Waisman 2002; Kurth 2010). A second example is provided by Japan's reconstruction of modernity. Japan's is the only civilization that did not experience a rupture during the Axial Age. It is based on specific patterns of emulation and selection that evolved a distinctive set of sociopolitical structures and collective identities. Since the Meiji revolution the country's deeply anchored syncretism of religious belief systems has been highly eclectic in the values that it has adopted and flexible in the interpretation of the dramatic shifts in political context that it has confronted (Eisenstadt 1996; Leheny 2010).

As sources of cultural innovation, the legacies of different world religions thus create multiple modernities. In the evolution of the socio-economic, political/legal and technical/scientific dimensions of the civilization of modernity, forces of convergence are always balanced against forces of divergence. Modernity is inescapably multiple and undergoing a constant process of reinvention in which all traditional elements that rebel against it have a modern, Jacobin character. In sum, although the aspirations of the world's important civilizational states may be totalistic, they are pluralistic in their cumulative impact on multiple civilizational modernities (Sternberg 2001: 80–81; Arjomand & Tiryakian 2004: 3).

Variants of modernity

Between the thirteenth and nineteenth centuries, modernity acquired various conventional, interrelated markers: culturally, the Renaissance; scientifically, the

Enlightenment; politically, the French and American revolutions; and economically, the rise of industrial capitalism. Variants-of-modernity theory regards these ruptures as fundamental and transformative. In its strong version, modernization theory holds that over time these ruptures will diminish greatly or eliminate the differences among all polities. Gaining in prominence in the 1950s, the strong version's central claim holds that modernization is a homogenizing process that ultimately leads to a convergence in practices, policies and institutions. Daniel Lerner (1958) and Walt Rostow (1960), for example, acknowledged different rates of social change, but were confident that Western-style modernity would eventually prevail the world over (Huntington 1971). In this view, Europe is the maker of universal history, modernization is basically the same as Westernization, and all states and societies eventually will adopt the model of North America and Western Europe (Bhambra 2007: 2–5).

Rather than insisting on a monolithic form of modernity, weak versions of the variants-of-modernity approach recognize different outcomes confined by one general model of modernity (Schmidt 2006). German, Japanese, and Russian history in the nineteenth and twentieth centuries gave ample evidence that authoritarian modernization offered viable avenues for polities opposed to the Western model, even though these alternatives ultimately led to disaster (Snyder 2018). In our own day, the rise of China is a poignant reminder of the viability of authoritarian, illiberal modernization. Technical and bureaucratic rationality without political competition can produce stable growth. What remains an open question is how long authoritarian, illiberal modernization can succeed. Years or decades? A few decades or many decades? A century or several centuries? Advocates of multiple modernities tend to count in terms of centuries, while their variants-of-modernity counterparts count in terms of decades. Unavoidably, this discrepancy leads to different conclusions about present conditions and future trends.

Variants-of-modernity approaches also stress the interconnectedness of modernity in relations of dependence and interdependence. Modernity is not Eurocentric but global. "Methodological cosmopolitanism" begins with the observation that variants of modernity are profoundly interdependent. The era of the "world risk society" requires a rethinking of the concept of modernity. All societies are now marked by interpenetrations that run so deep that no society can withstand them. All translate aspects of the second, cosmopolitan modernity into their domestic structures and repertoires of practice (Beck & Grande 2007, 2010).

A third version of the variants-of-modernity approach focuses on capitalism as a driving force of modernity. Although capitalism existed before modernity, modern capitalism is more dynamic and encompassing than its forebear—hence the designation of capitalism in the singular rather than plural. The varieties of capitalism literature acknowledges capitalism's different institutional and organizational forms: specifically, liberal and coordinated (Hall & Soskice 2001). It focuses primarily on regulatory norms and practices. This distinction is informed only by American and European models. Japan since the 1960s, the Newly Industrializing

States since the 1970s, and China since the 1990s require us to go beyond the West in understanding the dynamics of contemporary capitalism.[5] Differences in the varieties of capitalism are family resemblances in one system of global capitalism rather than different types of capitalisms. Varieties of capitalism illustrate constrained diversity. They take "existing differences seriously without giving them too much weight" (Schmidt 2006).

Variants-of-modernity arguments are readily extended to other spheres that also show evidence of constrained diversity. Social policy regimes, for example, have shown constrained diversity among similar institutional and organizational forms (Esping-Andersen 1990). And so have public opinions as measured by public opinion surveys, and theorized by the world polity model (Inglehart 1995; Meyer et al. 1997). In these approaches economic and cultural modernization go hand in hand. Without insisting on it, like other variants-of-modernity approaches, they leave open the possibility of a delayed modernization in some community-oriented political cultures that, in due time, still may converge with the more individualistic mores that characterize some parts of the West (Schmidt 2006).

In short, theories of multiple modernities stress long-term historical development and focus on the effects of religious and cultural patterns of evolution on constitutive institutions. Variants-of-modernity theory focuses primarily on historical developments of the last two centuries, and on the effects of economic and social factors on regulatory institutions. The two theories are complementary. Together they offer a compelling explanation of the constrained diversity that characterizes world politics.

Regionalisms and regionalization[6]

As is true of many other "isms" that project the image of unity and coherence, regionalism and regionalization have conceptually fluid and porous boundaries. They blend easily into the global, international, and national domains. Conceived as both structure and process, regionalism and regionalization co-evolve in different ways in different parts of the world. That difference, however, is constrained by the global, international, and national contexts in which regionalism and regionalization unfold. A world of regions and regionalization is a world of constrained diversity.

"Any interpretation of world history in the twentieth century ought to begin with a decisive emphasis on regionalism in global politics" (Bright & Geyer 1987). Regional acronyms such as EU, ASEAN, ECOWAS, NAFTA, SADC, and MERCOSUR are legion. All national governments engage with regional organizations. And so do many business and civil society actors. Distinctive regional orders are important in shaping national politics, policies, and practices. All regional orders are indissolubly linked to both the larger international and global systems and the various national and sub-national systems of which they are a part, and which they help to constitute.

Regional orders evolve along peculiar historical trajectories. In the 1930s, Nazi Germany and Imperial Japan pursued autarchic policies, practiced trade wars as precursors to World War II, and attempted to build autarchic regional blocs: a German-led European New Order and a Japan-led East-Asian Co-Prosperity Sphere. While the bloc and trade war language remains a staple of today's punditry, that language fails to capture accurately the open and porous character of contemporary regions, which persists even in the era of aggressive, unilateral American tariff policy initiated by President Trump. These traits give politics a wide sway in the constitution of regions. When Italy, a Mediterranean country, joined the North Atlantic Treaty Organization in 1949, it defied the laws of geography while obeying the laws of politics. So did, a few years later, Greece and Turkey, thus pacifying their deep-seated enmity through joint membership in an anti-Communist alliance.

Because of the strong impact of internationalization and globalization on contemporary world politics, regions cannot be closed or self-contained. Internationalization describes the increasing cross-border exchanges of goods, services, capital, peoples, and ideas, while globalization expresses the compression of time and space. Like the internet and the worldwide web, the two processes are deeply intertwined. Their joint impact on regionalism and regionalization processes constrains regional diversity.

With the possible exception of Central America, where US influence has been massive, since 1945 the distinctive role of the US has been to play a significant but not dominant part in all world regions. Superpower status thus is modulated by regional dynamics. American-led regional alliances such as NATO, SEATO and CENTO were permissible forms of organization under Article 51 of the UN Charter that guaranteed states the right to collective self-defense. While these alliances served America's anti-Communist grand strategy in the 1950s, many other regional alliances (such as the OAS, OAU, the Arab League, and the Gulf Cooperation Council) served broader, regional purposes. So did regional free trade areas and customs unions, first in Europe, Latin America and East Africa, and later Southeast Asia, South Asia, North America, and the Caribbean. Some of these institutions are now under stress as President Trump seeks to force a renegotiation of their basic terms. But many prove to be resilient as they face an unpredictable US foreign policy.

Regionalization processes take different forms, emanate often from large regional states, and are not necessarily spatially confined. Americanization, Europeanization, Sinicization, Japanization, and Indianization are prominent examples, and so is Islamicization, which lacks a clear regional focus. Regionalization is an open-ended process of emulating and adapting to distinctive patterns of production and consumption of material and symbolic objects as well as distinctive patterns of social and political behavior. In this view, globalization and internationalization are the sum total of intersecting, intermingling, and circulating regionalization processes. This is a far cry from the linear diffusion processes, conceptualized by theories of globalization that look to "the West" as the center of dynamic change in world politics.

Regionalism has a general historical lineage. No particular part of the world has originated or owns regional politics. It is therefore a mistake to compare "success" in one region with "failure" in another. Such a view invites the unwarranted assumption that one region's experience is setting the standards by which another's can or should be measured. We are better off acknowledging instead that regionalization processes vary across many dimensions and in and across different world regions. Comparative analysis, for example, can help identify elements of Asian and European distinctiveness. It highlights, specifically, the inclusive character of an Asian market and network-style integration in contrast to the European emphasis on formal and legalistic integration that tend toward exclusion. Multiple modernities and variants of modernity are thus reflected in, and refracted by, the emergence and persistence of different regional orders and regionalization processes (Katzenstein 1997, 2005; Katzenstein & Shiraishi 1997).

East Asia's economic rise has transformed world politics. First Japan, then Southeast Asia, then China and the economy of "Greater China," and now Vietnam and other Asian states have brought about a significant shift of the global political economy's center of gravity. Most analysts agree that the relative economic size of the United States and the European economies will continue to shrink. However, as Japan's economic history of the last half century illustrates, it is in the nature of all catch-up growth that it must come to an end. Asian societies confront daunting demographic, environmental and political challenges that will have unknowable effects on future economic growth rates and productivity changes. The rate of relative economic decline of the United States and Europe thus remains uncertain.

The growth of intra-Asian economic exchange has occurred in regional markets that were exceptionally open to the global economy. The consumption-driven American growth model was of enormous importance for Asia's export-led growth strategy and its accumulation of trillions of dollars of US assets. Enormous current account deficits in the American balance of payments made Asian holders of those assets subject to a long-term "devaluation" tax imposed by America's easy monetary and lax fiscal policies. Although hardly welcome, this tax was not sufficiently high to dissuade Asian states and producers from changing their basic strategy.

Asian regionalism is defined foremost in market terms. These markets express institutional and political relationships that deeply implicate both business and government in their operations. Following the growth of direct foreign investment, multinational corporations now control, to an unprecedented degree, the trade and investment flows of all major economies. The production chains forged by multinational corporations (MNCs) make for dynamic and intricate market relations. Asian states have assisted this development through the establishment of myriad special production zones and investment corridors. Market transactions do not resemble either economic textbook descriptions of arms-length transactions among anonymous players or the mercantilist search for trade surpluses that is driving US trade policy under Trump.

Compared to market networks, Asia's formal regional institutions are designed to be less extensive and well developed. The reason is historical. East Asian states had fought hard to regain sovereignty from Europe's imperialist powers and were not eager to relinquish the sovereignty gains they had made after 1945. In the 1960s a number of Japanese political initiatives in regional institution-building were met with a mixture of indifference and opposition. Political suspicion of Japanese motives and Japan's economic dynamism and size were the main reason. In the 1970s, however, a number of economic, non-governmental organizations had greater success. They diluted Japanese influence and typically featured a broader Asian–Pacific membership. So did ASEAN, arguably East Asia's most important political consultative body. Summarizing the findings of their edited volume, Frankel and Kahler (1993: 4) distinguish between the "soft" regionalism of Asia and the "hard" regionalism of Europe, which is based on politically discriminatory arrangements.

In contrast to Europe's experimentation with multilateralism, US foreign policy after 1945 operated along bilateral lines in Asia (Katzenstein 1996, 2005; Hemmer & Katzenstein 2002). This fact has made it much more difficult for Asian states to develop broad, interlocking and institutionalized political arrangements of the kind that have characterized the European type of regionalism. Furthermore, the distinctive character of Asian state institutions has militated against a type of regionalism typical of Europe: sanctioned by public international law and legitimating formal international institutions that create sharp boundaries between members and non-members. In short, Asian regionalism and regionalization characterize and operate in a world of constrained diversity.[7]

As is true of Asia, Europe's regionalism is a variegated, multidimensional, and complex set of political phenomena that cannot be reduced to a simple formula. The EU as its most prominent institution has its roots in a cataclysmic war that ravaged Europe both physically and psychologically. Out of the rubble emerged the political purpose of "never again." Ascendant after 1945, Christian Democracy had three political leaders—Schumann, De Gasperi, and Adenauer—who committed themselves to the task of mapping a road to European integration. The European Coal and Steel Community (ECSC) was designed both to place Germany's military–industrial complex under international control and to form a region-wide cartel. Similarly, the European Defense Community (EDC) and Euratom were intended to put Germany's military and future nuclear industry under international control. This daring plan was upended by the French Assembly when, in 1954, it refused to ratify the EDC. Rather than internationalizing all areas of "high politics," with the 1957 founding of the European Economic Community (EEC) the fallback option became the "low politics" of economic integration. Its aim was three-fold: to tame German power; to guarantee a peaceful resolution of all conflicts; and to assure social stability through economic growth and prosperous welfare states. By providing a security umbrella, the US became a vital silent partner in this endeavor.

The original customs union (EEC) had six members: France, Italy, Germany, and the Benelux countries. It excluded Britain, which founded a rival free trade area (EFTA) in 1959. The UK twice was thwarted by De Gaulle when it sought to join the EEC in the 1960s. It finally succeeded in 1972, in the first round of EEC enlargement, after *Le Général* had retired from politics. The next 40-plus years never reconciled a significant part of the British Conservative Party and public to Britain's EU membership. The 2015 Brexit vote extended rather than ended a foundational disagreement in British politics. On the continent, six additional enlargement rounds followed after 1972, leading to an EU that now has 28 member states and encompasses virtually all of Southern, Central, Eastern, and Southeastern sections of the continent. Throughout the enlargement process, Britain's preference for a larger and shallower Europe and France's for a smaller and deeper one were brokered by Germany, which both mediated between Britain and France and acceded to and pushed for a bigger and deeper Europe. Thus, Germany sought to avoid serious conflicts with either Britain or France. Although they were successful for many decades, Germany's preferences for both larger and deeper integration have displayed weaknesses that are becoming more evident by the day as the European project faces grave challenges on multiple fronts.

Legal unification was equally important. In what can only be described as a legal coup d'etat by a handful of judges, two decisions of the European Court of Justice (ECJ) established in the mid-1960s the primacy of European over national law. How and why European leaders, and in particular De Gaulle, the champion of European nation-states, could have overlooked such a far-reaching change remains one of the great unsolved mysteries of twentieth-century European history. In any case, European law has direct, binding effects on both states and individuals. By contrast, no mystery surrounds the series of treaties that gradually strengthened and expanded Europe's legal foundations: the 1965–67 unification treaty of the institutions created in the 1950s; the 1985–95 Schengen Agreement eliminating intra-European border controls; the 1986–87 Single European Act that revised the Treaty of Rome and sought to complete the creation of Europe's internal market; the 1992–93 Treaty of Maastricht that created the European Union and introduced the euro; the 1997–99 Treaty of Amsterdam that increased the power of the European Parliament and strengthened Europe's common security and foreign policy; the 2001–03 Treaty of Nice that streamlined institutions to cope with the EU's Eastern enlargement; and the 2007–09 Treaty of Lisbon that achieved the full legal unification of the European Union. The ECJ has done its utmost to "constitutionalize" these treaties.

The outcome of these various regionalization processes has been the creation of a regional order in the form of a multilevel polity, embodying multilateral practices that accept the condition of associated rather than full sovereignties. The EU is a system of political incrementalism and veto-politics that is informed by the German principle of taming power rather than the American one of separating it. Those, especially in larger states, wishing decisive action are often disappointed; those, especially in smaller states, cherishing go-slow policies are often satisfied. As a novel governance system operating at the regional level, the EU affects, is affected by, and helps shape its national members, global markets, and the international state system. More than a deregulated market and less than a supra-state, the EU fuses rather than concentrates power. It is an institutionalized polity that expresses variable and contested norms and interests and thus embodies constrained diversity.

Polymorphic globalism[8]

Polymorphic globalism tries to capture the mixture of difference and sameness in world politics resulting from both the layering of constitutive institutions (such as the nature of the political order, collective identities, and the character of the public sphere) that the multiple modernities perspective highlights and the regulatory institutional and organizational arrangements (such as the strength and autonomy of state agencies and societal groups and movements) that remain the focus of variants-of-modernity theory. Furthermore, it also seeks to capture the porousness between regionalism and regionalization and global, international, and national structures and processes. Polymorphic globalism talks of the modern world in the singular: globalism. And it acknowledges difference and divergence in the layering of constitutive and regulatory institutions: polymorphism. Adapting the terminology of Murakami (1996) and Mann (1993: 44–91), similarities and differences create never-ending political currents of peaceful negotiations, conflictual bargaining, and violent war.

Two intersecting political currents, in particular, command our attention. The first pits a secular against a religious politics. With the desacralization of Christianity and the rise of science and technology, the content of the emerging global polity has become both secular and religious. In recent decades, the historical foundations of the global polity and the renewed vibrancy of several of the world's major religions have made religious movements once again an integral part of world politics. Religion and science offer different worldviews and world orders.

Phillips (2011) has inquired into the constitution, operation, and eventual decay of two such orders: Latin Christendom before the mid-seventeenth century, and the Sinocentric world order in the nineteenth. Latin Christendom and its decaying canon law were undermined by the confessional splintering that accompanied the Protestant Reformation. Sectarian violence increased at the very time that technological innovations increased the cost, scale, and destructiveness of warfare. After the Habsburgs had failed to shore up a unified Christendom along imperial lines, Europe's princes began enforcing confessional conformity in their own realms. Religious heresy came to be equated with political treachery, and a century of warfare ensued. At its end, the Westphalian system of sovereign states began to separate an international, secular order from private, religious ones.

Nineteenth-century China experienced a similar split between a religious and a secular politics. The Sinocentric world order, however, confronted not only internal but also external shocks. Dynastic decline was accelerated by millenarian peasant rebellions and an incipient military revolution that destroyed the East Asian order and plunged China and much of the region into a century of upheaval. Emboldened by a revolution in naval warfare, imperialist Western powers opened China by force to satisfy their commercial and cultural interests. The Taiping rebellion was a puritanical millennial movement that incorporated evangelical Christianity into Chinese folk religion and created a ferocious insurgency. Although it was ultimately defeated, this rebellion hollowed out China's centralized state, thus opening the path toward the system's ultimate demise, Japanese occupation, and—after a bloody civil war—the Communist seizure of power.

Is today's international order likely to go the way of medieval Latin Christendom and the Sinocentric world in the nineteenth century? The intermingling of secular and religious elements in contemporary world politics is not just a matter of the different types of actors—state versus non-state, secular versus religious—vying for primacy. It is also a matter of the principles that constitute contemporary world politics. Do secular or religious elements provide the core organizing principles (Mendelsohn 2012)? Although the Westphalian system is structured along secular lines, the weakening of scores of states in recent decades has given more political space to religious actors. In seeking to substitute religious for secular principles in the organization of world politics, a small number of these actors pose a radical challenge to secular authorities. The wave of jihadist politics is one such effort. It seeks not to advance its preferred outcomes within the existing Westphalian order, but to create a new one. The secular state system is organized around multiple sovereign centers of authority that respect territorial borders, subscribe to the sanctity of law and the legitimacy of international organizations, and deny that there exists one single truth governing world politics. A religious world order might not respect territorial borders, and it would recognize only one center of authority, deny the sanctity of law and the legitimacy of international organizations, and insist on the existence of only one source of divine Truth. Calling for such an order poses a systemic and total, not national and partial, threat. Today there is no state seeking to affect such a dramatic change, and only a few non-state actors, among them Al Qaeda- and ISIS-led jihadist movements.

Polymorphic globalism exists also at a second and less familiar intersection. Rather than dividing secularism from religion, Yasusuke Murakami (1996) underlines the similarities in the transcendental tendencies of historical religions *and* modern science. Both science and religion are based on transcendental thought. Religious politics holds to an unquestioned belief in the divine, whereas secular politics has an unshaken belief in the attainability of ultimate truth. In their contrasting revolutionary aspirations and impact, both are in tension with the conservative historiological and hermeneutic tendencies of East Asian civilizations. The former is possessed by the belief in various forms of religious redemption or secular progress. The latter remains firmly grounded in the world of the profane, which lends itself to limitless reinterpretations of and existence in multiple realities.

In developing his argument, Murakami follows Weber in his sociological treatment of historical religions. Distinctive of Christianity, and the Western civilizations based on it, is a transcendental orientation. Divided into a high-level, intellectual and a lowbrow, popular form, Eastern religions and civilizations lack this transcendental orientation. For Murakami, a decline in international liberalism and a rise in polymorphic globalism would not end history. It would merely end a historical era dominated by Western states: specifically, the Anglo-American symbiosis of two great empires, British and American, that has shaped world politics during the last 300 years. History will continue, sustained by the dialectical relations between these two types of reflexive practices: transcendental, scientific/religious on the one hand and hermeneutic, historical/practical on the other.

For Murakami the religions that are part of the Judeo–Christian–Islamic tradition have an absolute character, promise salvation in the afterlife, and are prone to violence. In their highbrow, intellectual, and lowbrow, popular forms, Eastern religions instead are defined by syncretism, a promise of salvation in earthly life, and a tendency toward peaceful coexistence. According to Murakami, the prospect for cultural commensurability in a polymorphic world depends on a partial move away from universal justice-based standards and a transcendental style of thought in a world dominated by Western states, to accommodate contextual, rules-based standards and a hermeneutic style of thought in a world inhabited also by East Asian and (we might add) a number of other states operating in a variety of civilizational and regional complexes.

The analysis of polymorphic globalism is enriched further by the institutional analysis that John Meyer (1989) has provided. Meyer argues that the culture of Latin Christendom has shaped the organizational form as much as the substance of a secular world polity. Christianity brought together local mobilization of individual effort and general, universalistic long-distance relationships. It offered an institutional model of collective life that accorded political prominence to states as ideologically validated units, thus avoiding global segmentation and disintegration. For many centuries, the Church owned much of the world's productive land and provided the ideology that both defined the content of the political practices of princes and justified the management of the Church's vast worldly affairs. Christianity offered a general frame for Western civilization that brought together elites and mass publics as well as central and peripheral organizations of the global polity. In doing so, it helped create and sustain the political and economic vitality and imperialist thrust of the West.

Karl Deutsch (1944) has provided a complementary, materialist account of why the civilization of Latin Christendom was able to unite, and why subsequently it was fated to split apart. He argues that the spiritual, linguistic, and cultural unity of medieval Christendom—its common Latin language, the shared legal and spiritual authority of the Pope, the common political leadership provided by the Holy Roman Emperors, and the collective enterprise of the crusades—was a transitory historical stage that eventually was destroyed by the very forces that gave rise to it. In this view, scarcity in goods, services, and skilled personnel was the economic foundation of the international civilization of Latin Christendom. Scarcity permitted the growth of a thin web of supranational trading communities sharing a common language, customs, spirit, laws, traditions, and family connections. In this web, specialized nodes of productive skill-sets diffused over long distances—provided, for example, by Irish monks, German knights, Lombard traders, French master builders, and Flemish peasants knowledgeable in advanced agricultural techniques. While at the local level the linguistic fractionalization of an immobile peasantry persisted, the thin web of supranationalism created the conditions for a superficial internationalization of three major civilizations—Western and Byzantine Christianity and Islam—knit together by commerce, politics, and intellectual life. As the rate of national mobilization began to outpace the rate of international assimilation, increasing contacts between village, manor, and town eventually gave rise to the conditions that led to the demise of Latin Christendom.

Polymorphic globalism expresses not a common standard but a loose sense of shared values entailing often-contradictory notions of diversity in a common humanity. This loose sense centers on the material and psychological well-being of all humans. The rights and well-being of all "humans" are no longer the prerogative or product of any specific civilization or political structure. Instead, science and technology, which serve these ends, are de-territorialized processes that have taken on a life of their own and provide the script for all civilizations and regions. Polymorphic globalism does not specify the political route toward implementation. It does offer a script, often not adhered to, that now provides the basis for political authority and legitimacy everywhere. All polities claim to serve the well-being of individuals, and all individuals are acknowledged to have inherent rights. The existence of these processes exemplifies the constrained diversity that inheres in every civilization and region. And it also undercuts both the imperialism of imposing single standards and the relativism of accepting all political practices.

Conclusion

Multiple modernities, variants of modernity, regionalisms, and regionalization processes reflect a condition of constrained diversity and the grafting of a cosmology of science and technology onto the world's main religions. Interacting religious and scientific legacies are sources of diversity, innovation, and political change. Their antinomies reflect the post-sixteenth century "flight from ambiguity" in language and thought and the value placed on univocal representations of social reality. Additionally, based on the assumption that knowledge is or can be common, they aim at developing general theories that travel (Levine 1985). But they also reflect the experiential ambiguities of practical life that require multivocality and a toleration of ambivalence reflecting local conditions that are captured by the tacit dimension of knowledge and find their expression in different worldviews.[9] In the form of Reason or God, transcendental forces undercut binary notions such as Western vs. non-Western. This constrained diversity pushes everywhere "the painful process of de-parochialization," leaving contested spaces for special epistemologies (Santos 2008, 2016; Godrej 2011; Jenco 2015: 4).

Constrained diversity allows for, but does not guarantee, both a rebuilding of balanced interconnections that can reconstitute the identities and practices of all actors and a global circulation of practices and learning effects that are not derivative of any one part of the world. Being different and making a difference through interconnections and learning effects remain possible but not necessary under conditions of constrained diversity (Bhambra 2007; Duara 2015). Shaped by material and institutional conditions, constrained diversity coalesces around states that are more similar in form than in substance (El Amine 2016; Katzenstein 2019). Global politics is not an iron cage. Constrained diversity leaves space for variably construed worldviews about peoples as self-actualizing subjects; history as a human-made construction; improvement in human well-being as an ideology; and the pursuit of justice through responsive governance as an established right (Comaroff & Comaroff 2012).

Constrained diversity in world politics is a constant. What differs is the institutional order that it takes. The mixing of different ethnic and religious groups attracts talent. Such institutional orders operate primarily as constitutional structures (as meta-values defining units of political authority and the character of rightful political action) and fundamental institutions (as basic institutionalized practices that facilitate coexistence and cooperation among different centers of political authority), rarely as issue-specific regimes (as commonly discussed in international relations; Reus-Smit 2017). The nineteenth-century "standard of civilization" tied to the institution of empire and the primordial conceptions of ethnicity tied to the nation-state provide good examples. The resulting hierarchies subordinated "uncivilized" peoples in Africa, Asia, and the Pacific and "minority peoples" in Europe. After the Holocaust sovereignty was tied to civic not ethnic nationalism. And after decolonization had run its course in the 1960s, empire was eliminated as a unit of rightful rule and civic nationalism was deepened by the norms of multiculturalism and human rights.

Today, modernities and regionalisms offer the main vehicles for articulating agreements and disagreements, for example, about the meaning and relevance of political and economic human rights (Beitz 2009). Furthermore, they reveal the existence of repertoires of shared practices reflected in both cognitive-common and experiential–tacit dimensions of knowledge (Taylor 1984). Constrained diversity is not the West writ large, and its ecumenical processes are not the same as Westernization. It constitutes and makes legitimate some units of political authority more than others. Further, it is always open to change in response to past grievances, new claimants, and shifting constellations of power. It provides the durable foundation for world politics in the twenty-first century.

Notes

1. I would like to express here my profound gratitude to Routledge Press for its graciousness in permitting me to open this essay with a quotation from Jacob Viner, who died in 1970.
2. This section draws on Peter Katzenstein (2010: 15–17).
3. Eisenstadt's scholarship on this topic is a partial revision of his own writings on modernization dating back to the 1950s and 1960s, and a forceful dissent from the main claim of contemporary globalization theory. My summary of Eisenstadt's encompassing thought and voluminous writings is indebted to the discussions in Arnason (2003), Spohn (2001), and Mandalios (2003).
4. Nelson (1973) locates a different kind of "axial shift" in the twelfth and thirteenth centuries, which witnessed an intermingling between Western Christianity, Islam, Byzantine Christianity, Jews, Mongols, China, and Africa. Nelson's dating is important theoretically because it highlights the decisive role of inter- and trans-civilizational encounters in Afro-Eurasia, a first instance of what today we call globalization (Arnason 2003).
5. Schmidt (2002) has proposed a three-fold distinction between market, managed and state capitalism, recalling Katzenstein's (1978) three-fold distinction in his analysis of comparative capitalism. Boyer (2005) operates with a four-fold distinction.
6. For some of the arguments developed in this section see Katzenstein (2005). For reasons of length, I am neglecting the topic of interregionalism. Söderbaum (2016) discusses it, together with quasi-interregionalism and transregionalism, at considerable length, calling it a "conceptually and theoretically underdeveloped" subject (174–93).
7. It is too early to judge whether President Trump will succeed in breaking European political and global trade institutions. The purposes informing the policies of his administration are clear. But the pushback in Europe and Asia as well as in American domestic politics is formidable.
8. This section draws on Katzenstein (2012: 237–42).
9. The inherently and inescapably contestable core constructs of the social sciences—power, capital, status, value—create multivocality and ambiguity. They reflect the social world and constitute all efforts to explicate it.

References

Arjomand, S. & E. Tiryakian, 2004. "Introduction." *Rethinking Civilizational Analysis*. Thousand Oaks, CA: Sage, pp. 1–13

Arnason, J. 2003. *Civilizations in Dispute: Historical questions and theoretical traditions*. Leiden, The Netherlands: Brill

Arnason, J., S. Eisenstadt, & B. Wittrock (eds.), 2005. *Axial Civilizations and World History*. Leiden, The Netherlands: Brill

Beck, U. & E. Grande, 2007. *Cosmopolitan Europe*. Cambridge, UK: Polity

Beck, U. & E. Grande, 2010. "Varieties of Second Modernity: The cosmopolitan turn in social and political theory and research." *British Journal of Sociology* 61(3): 409–43

Beitz, C. 2009. *The Idea of Human Rights*. New York: Oxford University Press

Bellah, R. 2011. *Religion in Human Evolution: From the Paleolithic to the Axial Age*. Cambridge, MA: Belknap Press of Harvard University Press

Bellah, R. & H. Joas (eds.), 2012. *The Axial Age and Its Consequences*. Cambridge, MA: Belknap Press of Harvard University Press

Bhambra, G. 2007. *Rethinking Modernity: Postcolonialism and the sociological imagination*. New York: Palgrave

Boyer, R. 2005. "How and Why Capitalisms Differ." *Economy and Society* 34(4): 509–57

Bright, C. & M. Geyer, 1987. "For a Unified History of the World in the Twentieth Century." *Radical History Review* 39: 69–91

Comaroff, J. & J.L. Comaroff, 2012. *Theory from the South: Or how Euro-America is evolving toward Africa*. Boulder, CO: Paradigm Publishers

Deutsch, K. 1944. "Medieval Unity and the Economic Conditions for an International Civilization." *Canadian Journal of Economics and Political Science* 10(1): 18–35

Duara, P. 2015. *The Crisis of Global Modernity: Asian traditions and sustainable future*. New York: Cambridge University Press

Eisenstadt, S. 1982. "The Axial Age: The emergence of transcendental visions and the rise of clerics." *European Journal of Sociology* 23(2): 294–314

Eisenstadt, S. 1996. *Japanese Civilization: A comparative view*. Chicago, IL: University of Chicago Press

Eisenstadt, S. 1999a. *Fundamentalism, Sectarianism, and Revolution: The Jacobin dimension of modernity*. Cambridge, UK: Cambridge University Press

Eisenstadt, S. 1999b. *Paradoxes of Democracy: Fragility, continuity, and change*. Baltimore, MD: Johns Hopkins University Press

Eisenstadt, S. 2000a. "The Civilizational Dimension in Sociological Analysis." *Thesis Eleven* 62(1): 1–21

Eisenstadt, S. 2000b. "Multiple Modernities." *Dædalus: Journal of the American Academy of Arts and Sciences* 129(1): 1–29

Eisenstadt, S. 2000c. "The Reconstruction of Religious Arenas in the Framework of 'Multiple Modernities.'" *Millennium* 29(3): 591–612

Eisenstadt, S. 2001. "The Civilizational Dimension of Modernity: Modernity as a distinct civilization." *International Sociology* 16(3): 320–40

Eisenstadt, S. 2003. *Comparative Civilizations and Multiple Modernities*. Leiden, The Netherlands: Brill

Eisenstadt, S. & W. Schluchter, 1998. "Introduction: Paths to Early Modernities: A comparative view." *Dædalus* 127(3): 1–18

El Amine, L. 2016. "Beyond East and West: Reorienting political theory through the prism of modernity." *Perspectives on Politics* 14(1): 102–20

Esping-Andersen, G. 1990. *The Three Worlds of Welfare Capitalism*. Cambridge, UK: Polity

Frankel, J. & M. Kahler, 1993. "Introduction." *Regionalism and Rivalry: Japan and the United States in Pacific Asia*. Chicago, IL: University of Chicago Press, pp. 1–18

Fukuyama, F. 2006. *The End of History and the Last Man*. 2nd ed. New York: Free Press

Godrej, F. 2011. *Cosmopolitan Political Thought: Method, practice, discipline*. New York: Oxford University Press

Hall, P. & D. Soskice (eds.), 2001. *Varieties of Capitalism: The institutional foundations of comparative advantage*. New York: Oxford University Press

Hemmer, C. & P. Katzenstein, 2002. "Why Is There No NATO in Asia? Collective identity, regionalism, and the origins of multilateralism." *International Organization* 56(3): 575–607

Huntington, S. 1971. "The Change to Change: Modernization, development and politics." *Comparative Politics* 3(3): 283–322

Huntington, S. 1996. *The Clash of Civilizations and the Remaking of World Order*. New York: Simon & Schuster
Inglehart, R. 1995. "Changing Values, Economic Development and Political Change." *International Social Science Journal* 145: 379–403
Jaspers, K. 1953. *The Origin and the Goal of History*. London: Routledge & Kegan
Jenco, L. 2015. *Changing Referents: Learning across space and time in China and the West*. New York: Oxford University Press
Katzenstein, P. 1978. "Conclusion: Domestic structures and strategies of foreign economic policy." In P. Katzenstein (ed.), *Between Power and Plenty: Foreign economic policies of advanced industrial states*. Madison, WI: University of Wisconsin Press, pp. 295–336
Katzenstein, P. 1996. "Regionalism in Comparative Perspective." *Cooperation and Conflict* 31(2): 123–59
Katzenstein, P. (ed.), 1997. *Tamed Power: Germany in Europe*. Ithaca, NY: Cornell University Press
Katzenstein, P. 2005. *A World of Regions: Asia and Europe in the American Imperium*. Ithaca, NY: Cornell University Press
Katzenstein, P. 2010. "A World of Plural and Pluralist Civilizations: Multiple actors, traditions, and practices." In P. Katzenstein (ed.), *Civilizations in World Politics: Plural and pluralist perspectives*. New York: Routledge, pp. 1–40
Katzenstein, P. 2012. "Many Wests and Polymorphic Globalism." In P. Katzenstein (ed.), *Anglo-America and Its Discontents: Civilizational identities beyond West and East*. New York: Routledge, pp. 207–47
Katzenstein, P. 2019. "Fractures and Resilience of Liberal International Orders." Unpublished manuscript
Katzenstein, P. & T. Shiraishi (eds.), 1997. *Network Power: Japan and Asia*. Ithaca, NY: Cornell University Press
Kocka, J. 2001. "Multiple Modernities and Negotiated Universals." Paper presented at the conference on Multiple Modernities. Social Science Research Center (WZB), Berlin
Kurth, J. 2010. "The United States as a Civilizational Leader." In P. Katzenstein (ed.), *Civilizations in World Politics: Plural and pluralist perspectives*. New York: Routledge, pp. 41–66
Leheny, D. 2010. "The Samurai Ride to Huntington's Rescue: Japan ponders its global and regional roles." In P. Katzenstein (ed.), *Civilizations in World Politics: Plural and pluralist perspectives*. New York: Routledge, pp. 114–36
Lerner, D. 1958. *The Passing of Traditional Society: Modernizing the Middle East*. Glencoe, IL: Free Press
Levine, D. 1985. *The Flight from Ambiguity: Essays on social and cultural history*. Chicago: University of Chicago Press
Levine, D. 1995. *Visions of the Sociological Tradition*. Chicago: University of Chicago Press
Levine, D. 2004. "Note on the Concept of an Axial Turning in Human History." In S. Arjomand & E. Tiryakian (eds.), *Rethinking Civilizational Analysis*. Thousand Oaks, CA: Sage, pp. 67–70
Mandalios, J. 2003. "Civilizational Complexes and Processes: Elias, Nelson and Eisenstadt." In G. Delanty & E. Isin (eds.), *Handbook of Historical Sociology*. Thousand Oaks, CA: Sage, pp. 65–79
Mann, M. 1993. *The Sources of Social Power: The rise of classes and nation-states, 1760–1914*. Cambridge, UK: Cambridge University Press
Mendelsohn, B. 2012. "God vs. Westphalia: Radical Islamist movements and the battle for organizing the world." *Review of International Studies* 38: 589–613

Meyer, J. 1989. "Conceptions of Christendom: Notes on the Distinctiveness of the West." In M. Kohn (ed.), *Cross-National Research in Sociology*. Newbury Park, CA: Sage, pp. 395–413

Meyer, J., J. Boli, G. Thomas, & E. Ramirez, 1997. "World Society and the Nation State." *American Journal of Sociology* 103: 144–81

Meyer, T. 2018a. "Introduction." In T. Meyer and J. de Sales Marques (eds.), *Multiple Modernities and Good Governance*. New York: Routledge, pp. 1–11

Meyer, T. 2018b. "Multiple Modernities and Good Governance." In T. Meyer & J. de Sales Marques (eds.), *Multiple Modernities and Good Governance*. New York: Routledge, pp. 15–28

Murakami, Y. 1996. *An Anti-Classical Political-Economic Analysis*. Stanford, CA: Stanford University Press

Nelson, B. 1973. "Civilizational Complexes and Intercivilizational Encounters." *Sociological Analysis* 34(2): 79–105

Pasha, M. 2007. "Civilizations, Postorientalism, and Islam." In M. Hall & P. Jackson (eds.), *Civilizational Identity: The production and reproduction of "civilizations" in international relations*. New York: Palgrave, pp. 61–79

Phillips, A. 2011. *War, Religion and Empire: The transformation of international orders*. New York: Cambridge University Press

Pollock, S. 2006. *The Language of the Gods in the World of Men: Sanskrit, culture, and power in premodern India*. Berkeley, CA: University of California Press

Reus-Smit, C. 2017. "Cultural Diversity and International Order." *International Organization* 71(4): 851–85

Roniger, L. & C. Waisman (eds.), 2002. *Globality and Multiple Modernities: Comparative North American and Latin American perspectives*. Brighton, UK: Sussex Academic Press

Rostow, W. 1960. *The Stages of Economic Growth: A non-communist manifesto*. Cambridge, UK: Cambridge University Press

Santos, B. de Sousa (ed.), 2008. *Another Knowledge is Possible: Beyond Northern epistemologies*. Vol. 3 of *Reinventing Social Emancipation*. London: Verso

Santos, B. de Sousa (ed.), 2016. *Epistemologies of the South: Justice against epistemicide*. London: Routledge

Schmidt, V. 2002. *The Futures of European Capitalism*. Oxford, UK: Oxford University Press

Schmidt, V.H. 2006. "Multiple Modernities or Varieties of Modernity?" *Current Sociology* 54(1): 77–97

Snyder, J. 2018. "Alternative Modernities on the Road to Nowhere." In T. Meyer & J. de Sales Marques (eds.), *Multiple Modernities and Good Governance*. New York: Routledge, pp. 45–59

Söderbaum, F. 2016. *Rethinking Regionalism*. New York: Palgrave

Spohn, W. 2001. "Eisenstadt on Civilizations and Multiple Modernity." *European Journal of Social Theory* 4(4): 499–508

Sternberg, Y. 2001. "Modernity, Civilization, and Globalization." In E. Ben-Rafael & Y. Sternberg (eds.), *Identity, Culture, and Globalization*. Leiden, The Netherlands: Brill, pp. 75–92

Taylor, C. 1984. "Philosophy and Its History." In R. Rorty, J. Schneewind, & Q. Skinner (eds.), *Philosophy in History: Essays on the historiography of philosophy*. New York: Cambridge University Press, pp. 17–30

Viner, J. 1991. "The Economist in History." In D. Irwin (ed.), *Jacob Viner: Essays on the intellectual history of economics*. Princeton, NJ: Princeton University Press, pp. 226–47

Woodside, A. 2006. *Lost Modernities: China, Vietnam, Korea, and the hazards of world history*. Cambridge, MA: Harvard University Press

2
MULTIPLE MODERNITIES AND REGIONAL MULTILATERALISM

A political–cultural point of view

Thomas Meyer

Kant's "Perpetual Peace" and beyond

When Immanuel Kant first conceived his famous, ironically-titled essay on "Perpetual Peace" (1795/1983), the notion of political regionalism had not yet been invented by political philosophers, much less put into effect. By now that slim pamphlet has become paradigmatic for discussion of the normative foundations of global multilateralism. When the League of Nations was founded after World War I, it served as a blueprint for the League's vision, and it has remained an inspiring reference for reflections about the foundations of a just international system ever since. Does the essay still offer guidance for understanding regions and civilizations? Kant drew on Enlightenment philosophy to sketch the outlines of what he took to be a just (based on equality), prudent, and stable multilateral world order. Even though its intellectual roots lie so far in the past, it would seem that, at least in their substance and normative content, his ideas are insightful and constantly inspiring for all levels and variants of international multilateralism. They provide a solid middle ground in the contemporary debate that is characterized by the antipodal and extreme positions of Samuel Huntington (1996) and Francis Fukuyama (1992), both of which have proven to be too simplistic to help us grasp the current political–cultural reality in the world. The question is, are the world's geo-cultural regions quasi-natural, homogenous cultural blocs? Alternatively, are they malleable and dynamic entities on an ineluctable historical path toward convergence on the European model? Or could they be something else entirely?

Let us start with Kant. In his first definitive article for the creation of a cosmopolitan federation of free nations, he postulates that "the civil constitution of every state should be republican" (Beck 1963: 93). Only when that condition is met will all states enjoy a secure and durable peace on the basis of equal rights for each and every citizen. According to Kant, the republican constitution is the only just one and, due to the public character of its decision-making, the only political order capable of generating trust. All citizens are (potentially) involved in decision-making; moreover, such decisions are easy to understand because they have been reached in a process that is transparent both internally and externally, and they are thus both predictable and reasonable. In republican constitutions, the freedom of all (as human beings) is combined with the subjection of all under the laws (as *passive* citizens) and with the equality of the *active* citizens who created the law. In this manner, Kant defines the core of legitimate political authority as understood by Western modernity. In the fifth preliminary article in this same essay, Kant insists that "No state shall by force interfere with the constitution or government of another state" (Beck 1963: 89). This condition calls to mind one of the crucial components of the Westphalian international order. By stating these conditions, Kant raises the question of whether a stable multilateral order is possible at all as long as there are countries that are not "republics" in his sense. From the perspective of the multiple modernities approach, it is interesting to clarify the meaning of Kant's criteria of republicanism for divergent cultures and for the institutionalization of political order. Can these criteria function as conditions or goals for a desirable regional and/or global multilateralism? Kant elucidates the principles of individual liberty, equal treatment, and political equality, all at the core of republicanism, in the following way: the freedom of the individual person and political equality enjoin people to obey only those laws "to which [they] could have given consent." Legal equality means that "all are subject in the same way to the prevailing laws" (Beck 1963: 93).

Kant cites two related arguments in support of his philosophical assumption that only a federation of republics can establish a cooperative and peaceable world order built to last: Only such an order will be just, and only a *just* order can be *stable* in the long run and thus *amenable to peace*. In the vein of Enlightenment optimism, Kant here presupposes that a just order is transparent and stable simply because it is understood as fully legitimate and therefore meets with the unconditional support of all its citizens. His thesis that only a worldwide union of republics in this sense could guarantee permanent peaceful cooperation on an equal footing is ambivalent. as it allows for both a descriptive and a normative reading.

From Kant's arguments we can infer three interesting questions for multiple modernities and multilateralism.

- Kant's principles of republicanism are intended to be universal; are they also meaningful in a transcultural context?
- Is Kant's republicanism a useful idea for the creation of sustainable multilateralism (regional and global) in the world of multiple modernities?
- Is Kant's "federation of free states" a fruitful paradigm for regional and/or global multilateralism?

Republicanism and multiple modernities

The question arises whether Kant's principles of republicanism are compatible with Shmuel Eisenstadt's definition of the common core of the several variants of modernization. Answering it also would shed light on the subsequent question of whether there can be a common understanding about basic criteria of good governance among the different modernities and (regarding our key issue) also for the basic norms of mulitlateralism. Eisenstadt's common core consists of *reflexivity* or *subjectivism*: i.e., the reducibility of all collective projects to the reflecting subjects who authorize them, which implies equality and good government. Certainly, the spokespersons of most countries from almost any civilization would agree that equality and good governance should be considered as both conditions and objectives of their voluntary cooperation. Yet, the question remains unanswered: How much normative content can they jointly derive from such broad formulas?

Like Kant's criterion for the federation of republics, Eisenstadt's core content of multiple modernities can be read in both descriptive and normative ways. Understood in the first sense, it is completely unproblematic. If new candidates for modernization enter the global scene, we could simply enlarge the definition of the common core. But the scenario changes if we regard that core as a normative criterion enabling us to distinguish those variants of modernization that are to be considered as legitimate members of the family—the *ecumene of types of modernization* as conceived by Peter Katzenstein (2009)—from the rest, such as fundamentalism and totalitarianism. The latter two variants of counter-modernization can be labeled modern only in the sense that they are merely contemporaneous with modernized socieites or their "shadows," inherently in contradiction with and antagonistic to the former. In that case "modernization" would be reduced to the name of a historical epoch.

We should be more explicit about this normative dimension, since it is often suppressed or omitted in the respective debates. Either explicitly or implicitly, the discussion about multiple modernities always concerns equal legitimacy and its limits. This is the main idea that underlies Jürgen Kocka's argument that none of the competing versions of modernity is entitled to decide for the others what the concrete content of this common core shall be; instead, he says, the core content should emerge from a dialogue among all the candidates (Kocka 2018). That controversy might not be settled definitively until the competing versions, exercising their equal right to a voice, reach a consensus—if indeed they ever do.

Presumably, representatives of (e.g.) several distinct Chinese, Islamic (perhaps Indonesian), Indian, Brazilian, or other claimants upon modernization could make sense out of both Eisenstadt's core and Kant's definition of republicanism by reformulating them in their own conceptual terms and adjusting them to fit a different set of institutional practices. At bottom, what is at stake here is the fact that, under modern conditions, political legitimacy can only emerge from the reflection of the associated subjects concerning the kind of order under which they would like to live together and the awareness that they cannot just assume that order but instead must create it themselves.

To be sure, those conclusions imply that the external conditions must be met that would enable them to construct such a legitimate order in the first place. This is the point where the disputed issues in intercultural political discourse come to the fore.

In this context it needs to be mentioned that in another work Kant appears in part to have left equal rights to political participation as a kind of virtual reality limbo (Kant 1795/1983). This is true in the sense that, according to him, all citizens must be able reasonably to imagine that they in fact (if given the opportunity) would have consented to the laws that have been passed, because the latter are objectively rational (in the well-considered interest of everyone), having been approved after public consultation. But even in a republican commonwealth there is a distinction to be drawn, in principle, between passive citizens who are equal only with respect to the laws that have been enacted and active citizens (those who are educated and own property), who—in addition—have equal opportunities to participate in the framing and approval of the laws. This comes very close to the legitimizing argument of some contemporary authoritarian regimes that are probably "output inclusive" even without much "input inclusion."

It would be a mistake straightaway to infer from Kant's notion of republicanism the superiority of American or European-style institutional patterns. Nevertheless, the normative essence of republicanism, like that of Eisenstadt's core, can serve as a stimulating starting point for the intercultural modernization dialogue—which could have a trust-building effect for multilateral politics at all levels.

The logic and dynamics of modernization

Even the constructivist approach to interpreting the multiple modernities conceptual scheme takes into account Eisenstadt's claim that there are two limits upon permanent construction and reconstruction in processes of modernization. Constructivists seeking to apply that approach to an exegesis of multiple modernities would have to recognize that they do not have unrestricted leeway for interpretations. The process of modernization itself imposes limits on the construction and reconstruction of its content. The cultural context sets the first limit, while reflexive subjectivity—i.e., the need for an intersubjective justification—establishes the second.

From these reservations there emerges a conception of modernization as an unavoidably tri-polar process. It is always a dynamic interchange among many social actors with different power resources; it always takes place via the reconstruction of a traditional substratum; and everywhere it follows similar principles of modernization in appropriating the tradition to be interpreted. The constraints that flow from internal differentiation and global networking help to shape these principles, which constitute a "logic of modernization."

Due to the progress of modern construction and reconstruction, the "primordial" elements that have come down to us from the Axial Age enter into a reciprocal relationship with the imperatives of the logic of modernization originating in the global context. In every case, those elements are available to us only in the form of interpretations, and in this sense they may be constructed but not arbitrarily chosen. From this process there emerges a dynamic of modernization, the contemporary manifestations of which exhibit a different look in every culture and at every point in time, as the German sociologist Richard Münch points out (Münch 1984).

The principles of the logic of modernization identified by Münch can be linked not only to Kant's republicanism but also to Eisenstadt's core elements of multiple modernities: individualism, equality, secularism, rationalism, and universalism. Depending on the cultural context and on how far those processes have advanced, those core elements may generate different effects, resulting in divergent dynamics of modernization (cf. Katzenstein 2009).

The mistaken claim that one has gained direct access to a "primordial substance" is the definitive feature of political fundamentalism. By contrast, Samuel Huntington's clash of civilizations theory, which identifies the logic of modernization with "Western culture," presupposes an essentialist *or* naturalistic concept of culture unsupported either by history or by current empirical observation. In principle, both theories conflict with the political–cultural foundations of international multilateralism.

Social actors and interpretations

The dynamic of modernization does not follow its own inherent logic "automatically" by the very power of its ideas (as Hegel would have it); instead it takes place in and through political struggles between competing actors with diverging interests. Within limits, the outcome and durability of these processes are open-ended. As Max Weber emphasized, it matters a great deal which political classes in any given epoch gain supremacy over the interpretation of tradition in a culture (e.g., merchants, intellectuals, the clergy, civil servants, etc.). Here, economic and social relations, interests, and control over the means of education and communication play a vital role. "Freely invented" constructions of a dominant political culture based exclusively on the interests of power elites in maintaining their own rule may prevail for a time due to repressive measures. But generally speaking such interpretations are in a state of permanent and dysfunctional conflict with society, as was the case, for instance, with the political culture of Marxism–Leninism in Eastern Europe (cf. Almond & Verba 1963).

In most countries and regions, one often finds competing claims to social, cultural, and political hegemony existing alongside one another, among which several might potentially occupy that role for a long stretch of time (a pattern that is presently evident in the United States and Europe). Sometimes—depending on the impact of crisis or wars—they alternate for short periods in assuming the hegemonic role.

Levels of cultural identity and political cooperation

To gain a fuller understanding of the differences among the various roads to modernization and their internal consistency, it is instructive to take a glance at the different social levels of cultural identity. There are four main social levels of cultural identity that ought to be distinguished carefully:

- metaphysical or religious notions of salvation largely focused on the individual;
- collective cultures of everyday life or lifestyles;
- social or civic cultures that influence interactions in society; and
- political culture (legitimation, the ways in which the roles played by the political self or by political institutions and style are understood).

As modernization advances, the links among these levels tend to loosen. Each level may develop a high degree of relative autonomy. However, there are always many-faceted reciprocal relations between the social and political cultures. Individuals or milieus may thus share a cultural identity at one of the levels (e.g., metaphysics) while belonging to other cultural collectives on the remaining levels (e.g., everyday life, politics). This process produces what Pierre Bourdieu has described as milieu segmentation, a phenomenon characteristic of modern societies (Bourdieu 2010). Today the basic units of cultural identity tend to be more and more the socio-cultural settings and not the nation or the region—in particular when it comes to the political culture.

Political culture is crucial for the political level in every dimension: the political self, polity, politics, and policy. This generalization holds true for international relations as well, particularly the willingness of states to cooperate with one another on an equal footing (multilateralism). Authoritarian political cultures marked by national populism and fundamentalism, whether religious or secular, are especially ill-suited to construct the foundations of a sustainable multilateralism committed to the principle of equality. But they are rarely stable in the long run and can be toppled quickly from their positions of hegemony should wars or other crises supervene. That is especially true when a democratic framework is already in place.

Issues such as which institutions of the state (polity), which policies, and what version of power politics will count as "culturally embedded" and thus as legitimate and worthy of social support get decided at the level of political culture. Institutional systems and political cultures are in a process of permanent interaction, but if the match between them is not exact, or if it deteriorates over time due to a lack of good governance, the institutions tend to be overthrown, as evidenced by the Eastern European revolution of 1989.

Here we need to bear in mind that culture in all its dimensions is inevitably always both discourse and practice, explicit and tacit knowledge. A particular political culture is nothing but that specific part of the general culture of a political entity (nation/milieu) that relates directly to the political realm in all its dimensions. Thus, the "foundational practice" of a political community in the form of tacit or implicit political knowledge is regularly a core part of the respective political culture (Qin 2020). Yet, it remains beyond discussion only so long as it functions seamlessly and does not rise to the level of explicit, conscious awareness and thus is not called into question. As soon as it loses this taken-for-granted character, whether in a pragmatic manner (via alternative practices, disruptive action, deviation, etc.) or discursively (doubt, negation, alternative values or norms, growth of alternative milieus), the hidden norms and facts, the tacit knowledge and routine habits are pulled into the limelight and reveal their normative status.

It is obvious that much of political life both domestically and internationally is based on cultural habits (tacit knowledge) in the above-mentioned sense. In ordinary practice, as long as cooperation between the involved actors works smoothly, it does not require discursive cultural justification by reference to the larger cultural context or an explicit cognitive consensus. This is what regularly happens in the interaction among people of very diverse cultural backgrounds at all levels of life and what sometimes even happens between people of diverse cultural backgrounds at the level of international politics. Only when interaction is disrupted, and a spontaneous adoption of the relevant habits does not occur, will justification of the underlying principles potentially be required.

We know from empirical research on political culture that the foundational political practice of people with different cultural backgrounds in modernizing societies may converge, while people who share a cultural tradition may still live in different worlds of tacit practical knowledge concerning their political behavior.

Regions, cultures, and identities

All of the contemporary cultural units in all regions of today's world, whether defined as religio-cultural or ethno-cultural, are marked by a very high degree of internal differentiation. At the macrocosmic level (above the level of the sociocultural settings) these differentiations may be called mutually contradictory "styles of civilization": i.e., patterns of giving actual meaning to what the cultural tradition in question has to say to the challenges of the present age (civilization in the sense of Norbert Elias 2000). Research on fundamentalism has shown convincingly that, in today's world, every single culture presents itself as a dialectical and dynamic social discourse-system in which three principal styles of civilization try to bring the tradition up to date and struggle for hegemony in a variety of ways (Marty & Appleby 1994, 1995).

Traditionalism adapts grudgingly and defensively to modern culture and social development, accepting from the latter only what it must. It defends the values of tradition, inequality (including that of the genders), hierarchy, and authority.

Modernism/liberalism interprets tradition more or less consistently in the light of the predominance of the values of individualism, pluralism, activism, and rationalism. It allows for major differences in the interpretation of the culture in question, and thus eventually becomes the main driver of the process of modernization.

Fundamentalism is a reaction against the various economic, social, and cultural deprivations and crises that arise in the process of modernization. It is a modern form of opposition against modernity, since it makes use of some of the most cutting-edge modern products such as weaponry, organization, and mass communication but does so precisely in order to fight against the basic values of modernism—particularly against legitimate difference, openness, relativity, pluralism, democracy, gender equality, and individual rights. It is omnipresent and takes different forms in all cultures.

Fundamentalism is the most conspicuous among the styles of civilization in certain contemporary cultures, most notably Islam. In attempting to retrieve past stages in the development of its respective mother-culture, it dogmatizes one particular historical pattern of its interpretation as the absolutely unshakeable foundation of cultural identity and political legitimacy. Doubts expressed about the dogma are not tolerated—at least not when voiced by anyone who wants to be recognized as a true member of the cultural community in question. Varying models of a closed society and polity are evaluated against the allegedly absolute certainties of cultural identity. All forms of fundamentalism tend, with differing degrees of comprehensiveness and consistency, toward theocracy of some kind. Internal cultural differences are considered to be altogether destructive, alien to the true nature of the given cultural heritage, and as bearing poisonous seeds of modernism within them.

However, current research confirms unequivocally that no religion or culture (including Islam) is inescapably fundamentalist by its very nature. Nowhere can fundamentalism rightfully claim to be the unchallenged expression of the cultural identity of a community. Every culture—including e.g., Buddhism, Hinduism, Judaism, Islam, Christianity, and Confucianism—today presents itself in this dialectical shape, and that includes above all the West. The relative political and social scope and influence of each of the three competing styles of civilization within each culture are constantly changing, albeit at different rates. The pattern of such changes depends very much upon the historical situation, the socio-economic constellation, the acceptance and performance of the political class that succeeds in establishing itself as the key interpreter of the tradition, and the modes and pace of change in a given society as induced by globalized communication and economic relations.

Thus, it is not cultural identity itself that determines the social and political role of the different cultures; rather, social and political forces exercise a crucial measure of control over its mainstream interpretation in a given historical, social, and economic context. All cultures in the modern world provide vast scope for internal differentiation and modernization. The clashing styles of civilization obviously have more in common with their counterparts in other cultures than with their rivals within their own culture of origin. In short, culturally-based coalitions for political action can extend to transnational and transcultural levels. Their capacity to do so is particularly well illustrated by the multilateral networks of the institutions of civil society.

With respect to the *initial question* about regions, a realistic answer needs to stress that all the different styles are present in each geo-cultural region. Everywhere, dialectical strife *among those cultural styles* is happening, but always influenced by the general situation that prevails, the level of development that has been attained, and the nature of the host culture (or civilization). In some countries the modern style of civilization prevails (Europe, North America); in others, the traditionalist style dominates (China, parts of East Asia); in still others the fundamentalist style sets the tone (Iran, Saudi Arabia). Some regions display a mixture of styles over long periods of time (e.g., Europe in the first half of the twentieth century, South Asia, Southeast Asia). Some are currently in an open stage of transition with different versions of fundamentalism (religious or ethnic) gaining ground.

Change in political culture

We may conclude that political stability and predictability in international relations in the post-Kantian era of multiple modernities are now—contrary to what Kant had thought—less a function of the convergence or overlap of the political regimes and constitutions of all the involved states. Instead, stability, trust, and predictability seem to be influenced more by whether or not the respective governments are solidly embedded in the culture of their own society, whether they have adopted a justifiable and socially well-supported scheme of good governance, and whether their political culture accommodates a reliable pattern of cooperation and mutual understanding. During transitional periods, the latter point also may hold true of the more inclusive varieties of authoritarianism, so long as their policy outputs demonstrably serve the interests of the entire society, even when their participatory structures (inputs) are weakly developed.

A polity is likely to be stable internally as long as there is an adequate match between its political culture and political system and a shared understanding of what good governance has been achieved. There is a striking similarity between the styles of civilization and the types of political culture as analyzed in Almond and Verba's still classic study, *The Civic Culture* (1963). Close correspondences exist among

- fundamentalism and parochialist political culture (identity fixed/closed);
- traditionalism and subject political culture; and
- modernity and participatory political culture.

The stability and legitimacy of a polity persist either when there is a good fit between the prevailing political culture and the dominant set of institutions, or when both develop together without disruption of the balance (though sometimes institutions may move a step or two ahead of political culture, as they did in Germany after World War II).

Transcultural milieu research encompassing Europe, Asia, and the Americas (Sinus-Institut 2017) and comprehensive transcultural studies on fundamentalism (Marty & Appleby 1994, 1995) have demonstrated that all contemporary societies worldwide display a similar pattern of cultural segmentation with respect to both the milieu-pattern and the styles of civilization that embrace and influence neighboring milieus. There is no cultural homogeneity within nations and still less within regions. Instead, the special shape of the milieus and styles and (in particular) their relative size differ from country to country. That fact suggests that they have highly different weights in their respective societies and in the political sphere within a given period of time. Pivots, caesuras, and backsliding concerning both the political constitution and the dominant political culture everywhere remain possible and often happen. This is especially the case when the majority political culture is challenged by relevant oppositional groups or counter-cultures with an effective communications infrastructure and organizational network.

As far as I can tell, these observations are valid for all regions and cultures, including Europe, both historically and currently. The most conspicuous contemporary examples are furnished by the European Union, with the Visegràd countries as its problem cases, and the US, where the pendulum has swung toward a new Trump-style, nationalistically tinged version of unilateralism. In many instances, political and cultural transformations such as these barely touch the deeper cultural layers of metaphysical group identities and the lifeways associated with them. By the same token, those deeper layers do not determine how such changes in political culture will play out. What often happens in such constellations is the sharpening and deepening of the conflicts between rival milieus of political culture up to the point of cultural civil war.

Given favorable conditions, democratic political cultures with strong affinities for multilateralism can emerge from any cultural tradition as evidenced by their presence in every region of the world. Cultural (or civilizational) pluralism is not an obstacle to the development of regional or global multiculturalism. Societies and political elites so disposed can promote policies in that direction without betraying their own cultural traditions (Qin 2020).

"Perpetual peace" revisited

The implications for regional and global multilateralism are as follows.

1 Assuming the validity of the multiple modernities approach, an ecumenical culture of international cooperation among the various forms of modernity

is crucial for developing a sustainable brand of multilateralism that does not insist on the pre-eminence of a certain kind of political system and/or its adoption by other countries. Instead, it will build upon the recognition of and cooperation with different versions of modernization. All the different modernities need to be understood as complex, dynamic, and highly differentiated social spaces. This fact holds true for nations and even more so for regions. What matters most for multilateral cooperation is whether or not a coalition of socio-cultural settings that shares a political culture of understanding and cooperation attains a dominant position.

2   Fundamentalist and other culturally monopolistic regimes that believe in their own superiority always present a special problem for multilateralism, both regionally and globally. They lack both the proper cultural foundations for consistent multilateralism and the willingness to cooperate with other political cultures/civilizations on an equal footing.

3   The core content of the Kantian imperative to seek "perpetual peace" through sufficient correspondence between the legitimizing foundations of the cooperating countries must be achieved. Yet, it has to be uncoupled from its linkage to Western European and American institutions, and related instead to accommodating political cultures and the politics of good governance. Kant's idea of a federation of free states can then be reinterpreted along these lines as a very idealistic type of multilateralism among other meaningful types—regionally and globally.

References

Almond, G. & S. Verba, 1963. *The Civic Culture: Political attitudes and democracy in five nations.* Princeton, NJ: Princeton University Press

Beck, L. (ed.), 1963. *Kant on History.* New York & Indianapolis, IN: Bobbs-Merrill

Bourdieu, P. 2010. *Distinction: A social critique of the judgment of taste.* London & New York: Routledge

Elias, N. 2000. *The Civilizing Process: Sociogenetic and psychogenetic investigations.* Oxford, UK: Oxford University Press

Fukuyama, F. 1992. *The End of History and the Last Man.* New York: Free Press

Huntington, S. 1996. *The Clash of Civilizations and the Remaking of World Order.* New York: Simon & Schuster

Kant, I. 1795/1983. "Zum Ewigen Frieden." In W. Weischedel (ed.), *Immanuel Kant: Werke in zehn Bänden,* vol. 9. Darmstadt, Germany: Wissenschaftliche Buchgesellschaft

Katzenstein, P. (ed.), 2009. *Civilizations in World Politics.* New York: Routledge

Kocka, J. 2018. "Plural Modernity and Negotiated Universals." In T. Meyer & J. de Sales Marques (eds.), *Multiple Modernities and Good Governance.* London & New York: Routledge, pp. 161–67

Marty, M. & R.S. Appleby, 1994. *Fundamentalisms Observed.* Chicago, IL: University of Chicago Press

Marty, M. & R.S. Appleby, 1995. *Fundamentalisms Comprehended.* Chicago, IL: University of Chicago Press

Münch, R. 1984. *Die Struktur der Moderne*. Frankfurt/Main: Suhrkamp Taschenbuch
Qin, Y. 2020. "Populism, Globalization and Future World Order." In T. Meyer, J. de Sales Marques, & M. Telò (eds.), *Cultures, Nationalism, and Populism*. London & New York: Routledge, pp. 149–63
Sinus-Institut, 2017. Heidelberg. Available at www.sinus-institut-de

3
TRANSNATIONAL GOVERNANCE AND MULTIPLE MULTILATERALISMS

Yaqing Qin

The end of the Cold War witnessed the disappearance of the two major political blocs of East and West and the removal of conventional barriers between countries. As a result, the world is becoming increasingly connected and globalized, entering what some have called an "era of transnational threats" (Jones *et al.* 2009). Transnational problems, such as global economic development, environmental deterioration, and terrorism, have emerged from time to time, constituting major threats to international society and human security. Since none of these problems can be solved by a single country, no matter how powerful it happens to be, transnational governance, or governance beyond national borders, has become a crucial issue in world politics.

Due to the anarchical nature of the international system, governance of the transnational commons differs from governance in a domestic setting. It is generally and correctly believed that transnational governance relies on multilateralism. This chapter therefore focuses on one question: What sustains multilateralism? To provide an answer, we need to realize from the very beginning that there has been more than one model of multilateralism. Although the various forms of multilateralism have much in common—their goals and principles, for example—they differ obviously in terms of practice. In the history of world politics since the end of World War II, we can identify, *inter alia*, three multilateral approaches to transnational governance at the global and the regional levels: namely, hegemonic multilateralism, institutional multilateralism, and relational multilateralism, represented respectively by US unipolarity at the global level and by the European Union and Association of Southeast Asian Nations (ASEAN) at the regional level. Although these three multilateral approaches share certain features, we also observe practical divergences, mainly by virtue of different underlying realities and cultural backgrounds. This chapter compares the three models, arguing that the elements that sustain each of them are not the same. In fact, there are multiple pathways to governance beyond national borders, a situation that will continue to prevail. Therefore, a conscious blending of the positive elements of each model may help to generate more effective and legitimate transnational governance in today's multiplex world.

Multilateralism as practice

Transnational governance involves the management of the transnational commons through joint efforts, under the condition that there is no single authority comparable to a government in charge of domestic affairs. "Governance without government," in the words of Rosenau and Czempiel, reflects an essential feature of governance in a transnational society (Rosenau & Czempiel 1992). Although some thinkers have argued forcefully that there is no clear demarcation line between domestic and international societies (Milner 1993), the existence of a single governing entity characterizes domestic politics in today's world, whereas sovereignty, a principle established by the Westphalian agreements, continues to be a strong norm and common practice in international politics.

Due to the special requirements of transnational governance, multilateralism has become the most accepted principle (Ruggie 1993). It is the natural and perhaps the only right choice that international society can make, for on the one hand there is no one authoritative political unit in the world, and on the other hand there are many transnational problems to be solved. However, when we talk about multilateralism, we tend to think of it in the singular form, believing that it is the "practice of coordinating national policies in groups of three or more states" (Keohane 1990: 731). This definition identifies the minimum requirement for multilateralism: that there should be at least three states that come together to coordinate their national policy or their relations. Ruggie has correctly pointed out that this definition is merely nominal, lacking a substantive or qualitative element, i.e., "principles." He therefore defines multilateralism as "coordinating relations among three or more states in accordance with certain principles" (Ruggie 1993: 8), holding that multilateralism is a modifier of institutions or the multilateral form of international institutional arrangements (Ruggie 1993: 6). Furthermore, multilateralism is described as characterized by three principles: non-discrimination, indivisibility, and diffuse reciprocity. In a transnational era, however, we need to add one more element, "for the purpose of transnational governance," to clarify the objective of multilateralism as the principle and chief mechanism to manage the global and/or regional commons and to deal with transnational threats. Thus, drawing on the previous arguments, I understand multilateralism to be "the *practice* of coordinating national policies in groups of three or more international actors in accordance with certain principles for the purpose of transnational governance."

This definition has general application, wherever multilateralism is adopted. However, no matter how it is defined, multilateralism usually is taken as an institutional design and a principled enterprise, thus neglecting one of its most significant features: i.e., multilateralism as practice. We place special emphasis on "practice," a term used rather casually by Keohane, and argue that multilateralism is practice in the first place.[1] We therefore need to realize that since it is practice, it is performed in various ways across geographical and geo-cultural spheres. Even if there are significant commonalities of multilateralism, individual instances of multilateralism inevitably will vary in style. For example, when we think about a crucial element of multilateralism, we may ask what sustains multilateralism or multilateral institutions so that they stand and work for governance across national borders? This is a question about how multilateralism works, or the nature of the working mechanism of multilateralism and multilateral cooperation that multilateralism always implies (Caporaso 1993: 51–90). More simply, we are talking about multilateralism more as a practice in its everyday performance rather than as a general principle or an institutional design.

In line with this practice approach (Pouliot 2008; Adler & Pouliot 2011), I hold that human activity in general depends greatly on practice, and that multilateralism is a case in point, being performed according to the practical or background knowledge of the actors involved. Since background knowledge will diverge in different geo-cultural settings, multilateralism may well be practiced in multiple ways even though it has the same form (three or more states coming together), the same substance (coordinating national policies in accordance with certain principles), the same principles (non-discrimination, indivisibility and diffuse reciprocity), and the same objectives (for transnational governance). In other words, if we understand multilateralism as practice, then its performance differs, just as actors perform in different styles even if have the same script and stage (Ringma 2012).

Multilateralism assumes various styles. Here I would like to use the concept of "anchoring practice" for a comparative study. By "anchoring practice," I simply mean *the practice that makes other practices possible*. Sending and Neumann (2011) elaborate on this concept as follows:

> Employing Ann Swidler's concept of "anchoring practices," we focus on what Adler and Pouliot refer to as "subordination"—how some practices are dominant and organize others. For Swidler, practices are anchoring by virtue of enacting constitutive rules and principles. We broaden this conceptualization by also considering how—as the editors highlight—practices can be anchoring also in other ways—for example, by making other practices possible.
>
> (Sending & Neumann 2011: 234)

An anchoring practice is therefore foundational. It usually comes from the long historical tradition of a community and becomes central to its culture. Members of the community take it for granted and follow it almost out of habit (Hopf 2010). Drawing on Searle, the nonintentional and pre-intentional are what enable intentional states of functioning (Searle 1995: 129). Simply stated, we are talking about ways in which members of a given community tend to do things. As such, an anchoring practice provides a foundation for other practices and an infrastructure for the behavior of the community's members. To realize the same objective of transnational governance, for example, different communities of practice have unique approaches. One of the reasons for that uniqueness is that their anchoring practices differ.

The anchoring practice is also the pervasive practice. Since it is embedded in the background and internalized over ages, it is the most persistent and penetrating practice that binds a community together. Not only has such a practice endured over the ages, but it also has implicit impacts on almost every aspect of communal life, pervading practices in various areas and across various issues. In this respect, an anchoring practice is very much like the "invisible hand" analogy in economics, shaping people's thinking and orienting their behavior. For example, we can discern it during the whole process of practicing multilateralism, including its physical architecture, its organizational structure, and its decision-making style.

In sum, the anchoring practice is thus what sustains a community of practice, underpins the thinking and doing of its members, and makes its collective life possible. It is a long-lasting practice based on background knowledge and performed almost as though it were habitual. I do not place particular emphasis on "subordination," which distinguishes between dominant and secondary practices. But I do stress the anchoring role of a certain practice without which other practices would not be possible. In the particular situation of multilateralism, the anchoring practice is what underpins multilateral arrangements in practice and makes them work. Nowadays, we may see different styles of multilateralism in different regions, and scholars generally maintain that European multilateralism differs from the Asian, African, or Latin American forms. Therefore, it is useful to take a comparative perspective in the study of multilateral institutions (Acharya & Johnston 2007).

I argue that existing forms of multilateralism, while sharing important common features, differ in actual performance by virtue of their discordant anchoring

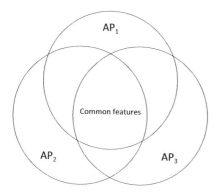

FIGURE 3.1 Multilateralism: common features and different anchoring practices (AP).

practices (see Figure 3.1). Using this concept of anchoring practice enables us to set up an analytical frame for a comparative study of multilateralism as it has developed over the last few decades.

Multilateralism in practice

Since the end of World War II, the three most common manifestations of multilateralism have been the hegemonic, the institutional, and the relational forms. It is true, as discussed above, that each approach contains features found in other approaches, so they are not mutually exclusive. They do share certain common properties: Specifically, there must be three or more than three countries trying to coordinate their policies or positions to achieve cooperation according to some generally agreed principles, such as indivisibility and diffuse reciprocity. But when we turn to the issue of how to make multilateralism function well and realize its objectives successfully, we find that diverse practices have been adopted. In what follows, I will examine each in some detail so that we can gain a better understanding of multilateralism in a multiplex world.

Hegemonic multilateralism: *Pax Americana*. The term hegemonic multilateralism refers to multilateralism sustained and maintained by the predominant power of the hegemon in the international system. Its anchoring practice is power-directed. Other practices are made possible by maintenance of the hegemonic power; in other words, hegemonic power is the linchpin of the system as a whole, determining how it operates. Here, in the final analysis, power rules.

One might argue that the concepts of hegemony and multilateralism are contradictory, with the latter by definition negating the former. It is true that multilateralism, more often than not, constitutes a daunting challenge to hegemony. In history, hegemons usually did not take multilateralism seriously. Although they might have entertained some multilateral arrangements, they tended to stop at the threshold of a genuinely institutionalized multilateralism. Be that as it may, hegemonic multilateralism does exist in practice. As Ruggie argues, all hegemonies are not alike, and American hegemony is an exception. Thus, he describes the post-World War II international order as an America-led multilateralism. As he puts it, "For American postwar planners, multilateralism in its generic sense served as a foundational architectural principle on the basis of which to reconstruct the postwar world" (Ruggie 1993: 25). What he terms "*American* hegemony" rather than "American *hegemony*" (Ruggie 1993: 31, italics in original) can be properly interpreted as American-led multilateralism or hegemonic multilateralism.

For the purpose of this study, it is important to ask what sustains this type of multilateralism. The answer is obvious: The system's sustaining force is the overwhelming power of the hegemon. Take the post-World War multilateral arrangements in the economic field, where it is most obvious, as an example. Behind all the important architectures, the International Monetary Fund (IMF), General Agreement on Trades and Tariffs (GATT), the World Bank, and the status of the US dollar, American power underpinned their establishment and existence. Without the inexorable rise of globalism (Ambrose 1985) and the US commitment of its power to the construction of the postwar global order, it would have been impossible to develop these multilateral institutions. Since the cost of building such architectures is extremely high, hegemonic power evidently was required. Thus, many social scientists, especially hegemonic stability theorists, argue that hegemony is the necessary condition at least for the formation of multilateral international regimes (Krasner 1983; Keohane 1984).

It is not only the formation or creation of multilateral institutions that needs hegemonic power, but also the sustainability of multilateralism. Charles Kindleberger traces the roots of the Great Depression to the absence of global leadership caused by the inability of the Great Britain and the unwillingness of the United States to assume such a role at that historic juncture. He therefore calls for a stabilizer—*one* stabilizer, as he has emphasized—to underpin a sustainable world economic order (Kindleberger 1973: 305). Interestingly enough, Kindleberger's study was published when the United States as the hegemon began to show signs of decline and perhaps was no longer able to play the role that hegemonic stability theorists expected it to play. It was because the theory of hegemonic multilateralism was so widely accepted that the possible decline of the hegemon led to so much anxiety about the world order in general and multilateral institutions in particular. Numerous studies subsequently came out to discuss the "post-hegemonic" world order, and many observers believed that multilateral arrangements would wither away with the decline of American power.

Thus, hegemonic power is crucial for establishing and sustaining international multilateral architectures. Keohane, though arguing that international institutions can stand on their own because nations need them for cooperation in an anarchical international setting, also believes that hegemonic power is crucially important at least for the formation of international institutions (Keohane 1984). In the 1970s and 1980s, people began to fear that the decline of American material capabilities would bring about a vacuum in leadership in the world and that as a result, postwar multilateral institutions would collapse (Gilpin 1981; Krasner 1983). A commonly voiced proposal both during that period and thereafter was to increase American power so that the international order and the multilateral institutions would remain safe and sound. After all, a liberal international order needed multilateralism, which in turn presumed the existence of a hegemon.

To a large extent, multilateralism in the West during the Cold War years was practiced and operated under the American power. That helps explain why worries spread when US capabilities were on the decline, especially when President Nixon in 1971 announced the delinking of the US dollar from the gold standard. It is undeniable that the United States played a crucial role in making this multilateral system work and was both able and willing to perform as that role required. This phenomenon became even more conspicuous when the end of the Cold War witnessed the collapse of the Soviet Union and, by default, left the United

States as the world's only superpower. That development led to greater confidence in the ability of the United States to establish a liberal, constitutional order on a global scale (Fukuyama 1992; Ikenberry 2001), one based on multilateral institutions under the leadership of the United States, which was both the most powerful and the most willing and committed. The American globalist belief joined hands with American power: hence, we got hegemonic multilateralism.

As globalization has spread and transnational threats increasingly challenge international society, the appeal of hegemonic multilateralism has grown. To deal with transnational threats in an increasingly globalized world, hegemonic multilateralism is needed even more than before to ensure a stable international order. As Jones, Pascual, and Stedman argue,

> Building this order depends on four prerequisites: effective international leadership by the United States; institutionalized cooperation between the United States and the major and rising powers; negotiated understandings of the applicability of responsible sovereignty to different issues; and effective institutions that provide legitimacy, mobilize resources, and coordinate multiple actors toward common goals.
>
> *(Jones et al. 2009: 15)*

The assumption was that after the fall of the Soviet Union, the United States as the victor in the Cold War should use its overwhelming power to construct and lead an international order operating through multilateralism. American power, a crucial factor for multilateralism, should serve the common good while advancing its own values. The 30-years-long post-Cold War order largely witnessed such a development at the global level, often referred to by American scholars as "a liberal international order" (Keohane 2012). What was not foreseen was the phenomenon of "hegemonic defection: the possibility that the hegemon that played such an important role in establishing and maintaining multilateral arrangements would begin to abandon them. Peter Cowhey has argued that the nature of the American domestic polity decides the credibility of its reliable commitment to multilateralism, especially to its "American version" (Cowhey 1993: 164). However, with Donald Trump in the White House, the United States has adopted a "policy of withdrawal," abandoning multilateral institutions if it believes they cannot serve US national interests in the here and now. If people worried about American capabilities in the 1980s, now the concern is more about US willingness and commitment to sustain multilateral projects, together with its relative decline in power.

Institutional multilateralism: European integration. Unlike hegemonic multilateralism, institutional multilateralism is sustained by international or supranational institutions. Reliance on and maintenance of those institutions constitutes its anchoring practice. For institutional multilateralism, rules rule.

Europe has taken a distinctive path to regional governance. I term this form of multilateralism "institutional" mainly because it works more through institutional structures and the rules and the norms thereof than through the backing of a hegemonic power. In other words, it is regional institutionalization that most distinctively characterizes European multilateralism. The replacement of "power rules" by "rules rule" has become a hallmark of the European multilateralism. To a large extent, the history of the European Union is a history of building institutions and institutionalizing regional rules and norms (Checkel 2005).

The practice of institutional multilateralism is evidenced during the entire course of the EU's development. Its first and most distinctive phase was characterized by using legal procedures and especially multilateral treaties to forge institutions. The very beginning of the European Union witnessed the establishment of three major institutions: the European Coal and Steel Community (ECSC) in 1952 by the Paris Treaty and the European Economic Community and the European Atomic Energy Community in 1957 by the Treaty of Rome. If the Paris Treaty was the result of negotiations mainly between Germany and France, the ECSC was created as a multilateral institution with Italy, Belgium, the Netherlands and Luxembourg joining France and Germany as members. The historically significant Treaty of Rome demonstrated the vital role of legal mechanisms in binding the countries of Western Europe closer together. Acting jointly, the three communities provided the foundation for regional cooperation during the Cold War years. Thus, from the very beginning, multilateral arrangements in Europe followed a legalistic-institutional approach. The rule of law was not only a principle and the code of conduct, but also a long-time practice in the history of European civilization.

After World War II, Western Europe lacked a regional hegemon, but it was protected by the United States in security affairs and aided by the Marshall Plan in economic development. Although Germany became increasingly important, especially after its reunification at the end of the Cold War, and now boasts the largest economy in the EU, European multilateralists always have cautioned against a preponderant German influence in EU affairs, let alone a German hegemon. Europe began its experiment in regional multilateralism with the support of the United States, which believed that even though European multilateralism would restrain its freedom of action to some degree, it would serve American interests in the long run (Katzenstein 2005). However, this nascent multilateralism followed the European legalistic tradition and took more of an institutional approach than one might have predicted. European multilateralism, therefore, was more European than American in both scope and character.

Subsequent developments have demonstrated this feature of European multilateralism in even more conspicuous ways. Structurally, the European Union has relied heavily on treaties to establish its architectural framework, ranging from the Council of the European Union, the European Commission, the European Council, the European Parliament, and the Court of Justice to the Court of Auditors, the Central Bank, and the Investment Bank. Together, these institutions constitute all the necessary formal elements of a nation-state, representing the administrative, legislative, and judicial branches. Moreover, the European Council, consisting of heads of states or governments, provides political leadership, while the Council of the European Union, composed of relevant ministers from EU member states, is the union's important decision-making body, owing to the fact that there are different national interests and concerns to be addressed and coordinated. Because its member states pool their sovereignty, and to the extent that its ambition is to establish a "United States of Europe," the EU legitimately might be termed a "supranationality" rather than merely an intergovernmental organization (Haas 1958).

Moreover, decision-making procedures in the European Union largely follow the legalistic practice of modern institutions: i.e., by voting that usually follows the principle of majority rule. This trend became more apparent beginning in 1987, when the Single European Act was signed. It was a most significant event along the path of European multilateralism, considering the decades of stagnation in the 1960s and 1970s. Since then, and especially since the end of the Cold War, the European Union has developed rapidly, taking the lead in multilateral institution-building and transnational/supranational governance at the regional level. It is noteworthy that one of the most important and meaningful reforms ushered in by the Single European Act was change in the decision-making procedures. While previously the EU was unable to act unless all member states were in agreement, the Single Europe Act adopted the practice of qualified majority voting. As expressed by the European Commission, "the now fully accepted possibility of adopting a decision by a qualified majority forces the delegations to display flexibility throughout the debate, thus making decision making easier" (cited in Keohane & Hoffmann 1991: 7).[2]

These features mean that European multilateralism is institutional in nature. The multilateral treaties that propelled its development both established physical institutions and set rules and norms for member states to follow. To a significant extent, the European Union with its rule-based governance is a typical example of the institution-building process. Though France and Germany are the two single largest members of the Union, they cannot perform like hegemons and in most cases do not have the final say in decision-making. The union has established numerous rules and principles through treaties and treaty-like agreements, which are highly binding on its members. If member states disagree over a particular policy proposal, they can vote on what course of action to take. Once that decision is made, all members, including those who had been in opposition, are expected to implement it. In fact, for that reason the European Commission is often called the "Guardian of the Treaties" (Pease 2000: 27).

The sort of institutional multilateralism that is exemplified by European practice is the most relevant approach to transnational governance. As noted above, it is supranational, transferring certain aspects of national sovereignty to a higher institution that governs with the power delegated to it by the member states. Its organizational architecture resembles that of a nation-state, encompassing a legislature, an executive and administrative system, and the judicial functions. In addition, there are some important institutions that respect the principle and reality of sovereignty and represent the national interests of the member states. The EU's institutional architecture is mainly composed of principles and rules that every member state is expected to abide by. It is commonly acknowledged that the European Union displays the highest degree of institutionalization among all regional schemes of cooperation and integration in today's world. As such, it constitutes a great practical achievement.

Institutional multilateralism, however, has inherent weaknesses. Before a region becomes a single, unified state, it necessarily faces the problem of coordinating national and supranational interests and preferences. Contradictions exist between sovereignty and supranationality, some of which are difficult to resolve through mechanisms of coordination. That reality is clearly reflected in the evolution of the EU's internal architectural arrangements and the decision rules that they impose. As noted, when disagreements arise among individual states, they typically are resolved by means of a vote, the result of which is binding on all members. Though the initial Luxemburg Compromise required unanimity, the Single Europe Act revolutionized this compromise by establishing the rule of a qualified majority. The fact that the outcome must be respected by all members requires greater relinquishment of state sovereignty. Moreover, the principle of "enhanced cooperation" has enabled eight Council members to make a decision. Thus, on the one hand the EU is moving toward an even higher level of institutionalization and facilitating multilateral governance; but on the other hand, institutional multilateralism is still multilateral in nature and the member states continue to retain much of their autonomy. Problems surrounding the refugee crisis, the maintenance of a single currency, and admission to or exit from the union illustrate the difficulty in mediating between sovereignty and supranationality. The Brexit, to some extent, can be seen as the culmination of this contradiction. If rules are too rigid, solidarity breaks down.

Relational multilateralism: ASEAN regionalism. Relational institutionalism has as its anchoring practice reliance upon and maintenance of positive and cooperative relations among members of the multilateral process. Undoubtedly, this kind of multilateralism needs power and institutions. However, relations tend to be given a higher priority than either power or institutions. We are talking about a form of multilateralism in which relations rule.

The Association of Southeast Asian Nations (ASEAN) offers an important example of transnational governance. Kofi Annan, the former Secretary-General of the United Nations, once praised ASEAN as follows:

> Since the latter half of the 20th century, regional organisations have emerged in many of the world's regions. Much focus has been devoted to the success story of the European Union, yet another regional organisation deserves our recognition: ASEAN. It is hard to overstate ASEAN's contributions to peace, prosperity and transnational cooperation across

South East Asia. Its positive impact is felt by millions of people in what has traditionally been one of the more complex and divided regions.

(Cited in Mahbubani & Sng 2017)

ASEAN regionalism is said to be a miracle thanks mainly to its elasticity and eclecticism. I term it a form of "relational multilateralism" because it pays extraordinary attention to governing and maintaining positive relationships among its constituent nations (Qin 2018: 318–56)—what one might call the "hanging together" of its member states (Khong & Nesadurai 2007: 32). This does not mean that ASEAN cares little about institution-building or prefers not to have any rules governing its internal operations. But what it does suggest is that maintenance of good relations among members is of the utmost importance, sometimes even at the cost of institution-building and rule-following.

ASEAN, as an organization aiming at regional cooperation, has maintained basic peace and stability among its members since its initiation in 1967, when the ASEAN Declaration was signed by five nations (Indonesia, Thailand, Singapore, the Philippines and Malaysia) in Bangkok. Now it includes all the states in Southeast Asia and covers an area of almost 5 million square kilometers with a population of more than 500 million, of whom 240 million are Muslim, 130 million Christian, 140 million Buddhist, and 7 million Hindu. The members of ASEAN are highly diversified, with different religious beliefs, regime types, social systems, cultural traditions, and levels of economic development. Compared with the European Union, it is more inclusive, especially concerning political, economic and social systems, implying that in principle, friendly relations are possible among all peoples. Having stayed together for a long time, they succeeded in completing the ASEAN Community by the end of 2015. Moreover, ASEAN took the lead in establishing Asia–Pacific Economic Cooperation (APEC) in 1989; the ASEAN Free Trade Area (AFTA) in 1992; the ASEAN Regional Forum (ARF) in 1994; and the ASEAN Plus Three (APT) in 1997. By and large, it has managed to play a central role in regional affairs even when major powers such as China, India, Japan, Russia, and the United States have become involved.

There is little doubt that the impressive achievements of ASEAN have been facilitated by many factors. But, as suggested above, the organization has not based its integration on homogeneity, nor has it worked for homogeneity, which in truth is not possible in its part of the world (or perhaps any part of the world). Rather, it has grounded regional coordination and integration on management of the complex relations among diversified actors, both within and without. Although lacking centripetal political institutions similar to those of the European Union, it rests on huge spiderweb-like relational circles that are concentric and multilayered. The inner core is ASEAN, which occupies the driver's seat, while the second layer encompasses the Plus 3 dialogue partners, including China, Japan and South Korea, together with whom ASEAN established the 10+3 regional cooperative process. The third circle was formed by ASEAN's expansion to include

India, Australia and New Zealand, with the United States and Russia joining in later; and the fourth and final circle is the world at large. The organization can be analogized to a ripple,[3] geographically, politically, and socially.

As observed above, ASEAN does not have governing institutions on the model of the European Union. Its main institutionalized mechanisms include the summit, the Coordinating Council, the three ASEAN Community Councils, meetings of various ministers, and the Secretariat. The ASEAN Chairmanship rotates annually in an alphabetical order and the country that controls the chair also heads the ASEAN summit and all other meetings. A permanent secretariat based in Jakarta manages the daily routines of the association. By 2015, when the ASEAN Community was declared completed, it was composed of the Political-Security Community, the Economic Community, and the Socio-Cultural Community. Since that time, three councils have been established, and the secretariat accordingly has set up three major departments dealing respectively with political security, economic matters, and socio-cultural affairs. There are no bodies that perform legislative and judicial functions. ASEAN prefers to use the word "process" rather than "structure" to describe its activities. And although the evolution of ASEAN has been marked by declarations and statements, very few treaties have been signed,[4] especially when compared with the European Union.

There are, however, numerous informal consultations at all levels, including among governments and non-governmental institutions. Common within the organization are frequent visits with counterparts and friends designed to enhance mutual relations in an informal way. Kishore Mahbubani, a diplomat-scholar from Singapore, has suggested that peace in Southeast Asia is inseparable from playing golf, in that many thorny issues have been solved "after a happy round of golf that generated friendship and camaraderie." Wong Kan Seng, the former Foreign Minister of Singapore, readily agreed with that assessment, remarking that golfing together reduces tension and promotes friendship. Accordingly, the two men organized ASEAN golf matches on the weekend when delegates were attending the annual UN Assembly. In Wong's view, the outing "was a show of unity. Ministers' wives would come and shake people's hands—that was not seen in other regional organizations. There were memorable but simple gifts as well. Orchids would be given at the end of the reception. A lot of people would turn up, including the UN secretary-general" (Mahbubani & Sng 2017: 50–1). Such informality seems quite often more relevant than formal institutions in the practice of ASEAN multilateralism.

Furthermore, decision-making styles in ASEAN differ obviously from those that prevail in institutional multilateralisms. Voting, the most effective way to make a decision and widely adopted in most organizations, is a procedure that ASEAN member states prefer not to use. It is unanimity that rules, but this unanimity also diverges from the unanimity characteristic of institutional multilateralism. Usually, before a decision is made, there have been long and seemingly endless informal discussions and consultations among members. All the questions and concerns raised in these conversations are taken into consideration. When a proposal is actually submitted for adoption at the decision-making meeting, long and even tedious deliberations are again a common practice. The objective is to reach a complete consensus that every participant not only accepts but also feels comfortable with. Serious concessions are made, and rewording here and there is done; the deletion and addition of words, sentences, and paragraphs is common here. Sometimes, for lack of agreement among participants, the effort at decision-making grinds to a halt. Only after everyone feels comfortable can the process continue (Qin & Wei 2008). Formal voting is avoided within ASEAN for fear that it might result in one faction imposing its will upon recalcitrant others.

Unique to ASEAN, this "comfort level" norm reflects a desire for complete consensus. The aim is not merely that all those involved in framing a policy will find the outcome tolerable on some level. Instead, focusing on making sure that everyone is comfortable is a way to express unconditional respect for people who hold positions with which one might not agree. The management of these complex relations has always been a strategic priority and a cherished practice within ASEAN. Norms and rules are more often designed to manage relations among individual actors than to regulate their behavior. Although this is done sometimes at the cost of effectiveness and efficiency, it should be seen not as a sacrifice of principle but rather as a way to preserve cooperative relations. The operative belief is that cooperation cannot be achieved if relations are broken. Therefore, maintaining good relationships among the participants and avoiding the breakdown of cooperative processes appear to be more important than achieving immediate and tangible results. In sum, the management of relations is as an important element of the ASEAN way. It may not be as effective as the majoritarian voting rule prevalent in the European Union, but it is also less likely to derail the process of regional integration. Following a time-honored practice, then, ASEAN member states focus on maintaining good interstate relations rather than on achieving immediate results; on finding common ground rather than debating their differences; and on attending to everyone's comfort level rather than imposing a majority decision. As an organization composed of highly diverse nations, it thereby remains more resilient, and the cooperative agreements it manages to achieve are all the more durable.

Relational multilateralism, like other types, has its characteristic deficiencies. The most obvious is the lack of effectiveness due mainly to the softness of its internal institutionalization. On the one hand, lengthy discussions show full respect for member states and their concerns; on the other hand, the deliberative process becomes extremely time-consuming. The comfort-level norm leads to slowness in making and implementing decisions. For this reason, the ASEAN way has been criticized as a "talking shop" and described as a "spaghetti bowl" (Wei 2010). The three ASEAN communities continue to have weak and soft institutions if measured by the EU standards.

Multilateralism in prospect

Multilateralism, as we have seen, varies in practice. In hegemonic multilateralism, overwhelming power provides the foundation for multilateral architecture and sustains its functioning. Power-directed practice constitutes the life of the multilateral arrangements and makes other practices possible. In institutional multilateralism, institutional rules maintain the coordination and cooperation of various international actors and orient them toward cooperation. Rule-based norms anchor other practices. In relational multilateralism, the maintenance of friendly or at least workable relationships is the most important consideration, sometimes even at the cost of shelving issues and failing to arrive at decisions. The practice of maintaining friendly relations is thus "anchoring" in the sense that it makes other practices possible.

Of course, the three approaches are not mutually exclusive. Hegemonic multilateralism and relational multilateralism also need institutions and rules, just as institutional multilateralism needs power and relationships, too. American hegemonic multilateralism established important institutions, such as the IMF, the World Bank, and the GATT (now the World Trade Organization or WTO), but these institutions were rooted firmly in American power, and when disputes arise, its interests tend to prevail. European multilateralism focuses on institution-building, using primarily rules to facilitate cooperation. At the same time, however, power and friendship also remain important. ASEAN multilateralism almost always stresses institution-building. But compared with the EU, the institutions it has established are softer and much more flexible; its level of institutionalization is relatively low; and its emphasis on friendship is far greater than is the case with the other two forms of multilateralism. Comparatively speaking, ASEAN's relation-oriented practice, more often than not, trumps its rule-based practice. Thus, it is meaningful to argue that power, institutionalization and relationality constitute the most distinctive feature and the anchoring practice respectively of each form of multilateralism.

Transnational governance relies on multilateralism. Although in today's world multilateralism faces serious challenges, it will continue to be the most important practice in a world that is more than ever interconnected and inseparable. Multilateralism has been the most reasonable and appropriate form of transnational governance in human affairs. However, as this chapter has emphasized, multilateralism is far from a unitary phenomenon. Several types of multilateralism have coexisted in the past few decades, and while they may not vary in principles and objectives, they do differ in practice in regard to their sustaining mechanisms. The coexistence of these models of multilateralism reveals the importance of comparative study, which can improve our understanding of the relationship between multilateralism and transnational governance and, in the best case, may encourage the different systems to learn from one another.

Of the three forms, hegemonic multilateralism is perhaps the most effective. Possessing overwhelming material power, the hegemon finds it relatively easy to set objectives, make rules, and enforce implementation. Hegemony, however, is inherently contradictory to multilateralism, for the former requires a single leader to sustain the system and make it work, while the latter, by definition, is a process of communicating, consulting, and coordinating among several actors, who should be more or less on an equal footing. Moreover, hegemonic multilateralism relies heavily on the willingness and capability of the hegemon. In the 1970s and 1980s, although the willingness of the US to sustain the international order it had established in the wake of World War II was not in doubt, its material capacity to do so raised concern. Today, by contrast, President Trump's policies and strategies have led observers to question both the capabilities and the willingness of the US to continue to lead. Rising populism, narrow-minded nationalism, anti-globalization movements, and strong-man regimes in many parts of the world conspire to worsen the situation. Given that multilateralism hinges primarily on the power of a single hegemon and is sustained largely on power-led practice, the world faces huge risks. Any form of hegemonic multilateralism will not constitute a solid foundation for transnational governance in the future.

Institutional multilateralism, with its focus on rules and institutions, will continue to be the most relevant form. To be sure, the European Union, as its foremost exemplar, faces great challenges today, including Brexit, refugees, populism, and right-wing governments and policies. Previously, the European Union succeeded in overcoming other formidable obstacles that—especially in the 1970s and 1980s—had led many people to question its future prospects. By confronting such problems proactively, the EU turned the situation around. The end result was to speed up its progress toward pooling national sovereignties and achieving a higher level of supranational integration. This precedent gives us reason to hope that despite the EU's present difficulties, institutional multilateralism will continue to be a vital force in world politics. All things considered, rules-based multilateralism appears much more enduring and reliable than its power-based counterpart. The danger is that institutional multilateralism may become a victim of its very success, relying so heavily on rules that it grows rigid. If institutional determinism dominates, the whole organizational architecture may suffer due to lack of resilience and sensitivity to the human element as manifested in personal relationships and a quest for concordance (Qin 2011).

Thus far, relational multilateralism has been quite ably practiced in ASEAN. Its most obvious strength lies in its elasticity and pliability. Undeniably, the difficulty is tremendous when nations that differ in almost every important aspect have managed to forge close ties with one another and to cohere for five decades, eventually culminating in the completion of the ASEAN community. ASEAN has neither a high level of institutionalization nor the fully developed bodies that would be required for a polity. Its decisions generally have taken the form of declarations without strict and well-defined binding force, and its institutional arrangements are soft and flexible. The anchoring practice of and for institutionalization found in the European Union is obviously missing or at least not emphatically stressed in ASEAN, while the practice of maintaining and strengthening concordant relations seems to have been something that each member state does with every other in its daily interactions. As a result, ASEAN is highly resilient. It has not developed quickly, and sometimes it seems to be less effective than the other two multilateral systems under discussion, but it has moved forward steadily and would be difficult to undermine. In brief, resilience has become one of its most distinctive features while inadequate effectiveness is said to be the most obvious weakness.

In the future, multilateralism will continue to take multiple forms. Hegemonic multilateralism will be the least likely to succeed and multiple forms of multilateralism the most likely. Since multilateralism is practice, it is closely related to local conditions, cultures and circumstances that, together, foster a variety of anchoring practices. As we have seen, a legalistic environment contributes a great deal to European multilateralism, while a relational background nurtures ASEAN multilateralism. It is desirable that the two learn from each other, especially in an effort to compensate for their respective weaknesses. A multilateralism that is rules-based and relation-attuned, for example, might better combine effectiveness and resilience. But we should not expect to see an ASEAN community of practice that would look identical to a European community of practice. Using one set of standards to evaluate all types of multilateralism tends to enforce and enhance homogeneity, which in today's multiplex world is even more unattainable than it was in the past (Acharya 2018: 29–30). It is therefore important to encourage comparative studies of various types of multilateralism, not for the formation of a uniform model, but for mutual learning, inspiration and enlightenment.

Notes

1. Keohane uses "practice" largely in its general sense, while I place more emphasis on the term from the perspective of the international practice approach. See Schatzki *et al.* 2001; Adler & Pouliot 2011.
2. It is true that in the EU important decisions still need unanimity and EU foreign policy decisions, for example, usually require it. But it differs from the unanimity of the ASEAN, because—in the latter—more than adequate informal discussions and consultations are carried out before the decision is made. Since for ASEAN voting is never a choice, its unanimity is unanimity without voting, while the unanimity in the EU is one with voting.
3. The ripple analogy was made by the late Chinese sociologist Fei Xiaotong to describe social relations of the Chinese society. One's relational circles are like ripples made by a stone thrown into the quiet lake, one after another. See Fei 2012.
4. A significant exception is the Treaty of Amity and Cooperation in Southeast Asia, signed in Indonesia in 1976.

References

Acharya, A. 2018. *Constructing Global Order: Agency and change in world politics*. Cambridge, UK: Cambridge University Press

Acharya, A. & A. Johnston, 2007. "Comparing Regional Institutions: An introduction." In A. Acharya and A. Johnston (eds.), *Crafting Cooperation: Regional international institutions in comparative perspectives.* Cambridge, UK: Cambridge University Press, pp. 1–31

Adler, E. & V. Pouliot, 2011. *International Practices.* Cambridge, UK: Cambridge University Press

Ambrose, S. 1985. *Rise to Globalism: American foreign policy since 1938.* 4th ed. New York: Penguin Books

Caporaso, J. 1993. "International Relations Theory and Multilateralism: The search for foundations." In J. Ruggie (ed.) *Multilateralism Matters: The theory and praxis of an institutional form.* New York: Columbia University Press, pp. 51–90

Checkel, J. 2005. "International Institutions and Socialization in Europe: Introduction and framework." *International Organization* 59(4): 801–26

Cowhey, P. 1993. "Elect Locally—Order Globally: Domestic politics and multilateral cooperation." In J. Ruggie (ed.) *Multilateralism Matters: The theory and praxis of an institutional form.* New York: Columbia University Press, pp. 157–200

Fei, X. 2012. *From the Soil: The foundation of the Chinese society.* Beijing: Foreign Languages Press

Fukuyama, F. 1992. *The End of History and the Last Man.* New York: Free Press

Gilpin, R. 1981. *War and Change in World Politics.* Cambridge, UK: Cambridge University Press

Haas, E. 1958. *The Uniting of Europe: The political, economic and social forces, 1950–1957.* Stanford, CA: Stanford University Press

Hopf, T. 2010. "The Logic of Habit in International Relations." *European Journal of International Relations* 16(4): 539–61

Ikenberry, G.J. 2001. *After Victory: Institutions, strategic restraint, and the rebuilding of order after major wars.* Princeton, NJ: Princeton University Press

Jones, B., C. Pascual, & S. Stedman, 2009. *Power and Responsibility: Building international order in an era of transnational threats.* Washington, DC: The Brookings Institution Press

Katzenstein, P. (ed.), 2005. *A World of Regions: Asia and Europe in the American Imperium.* Ithaca, NY & London: Cornell University Press

Keohane, R. 1984. *After Hegemony: Cooperation and discord in world political economy.* Princeton, NJ: Princeton University Press

Keohane, R. 1990. "Multilateralism: An Agenda for Research." *International Journal* 45(1): 731–64

Keohane, R. 2012. "Twenty Years of Institutional Liberalism." *International Relations* 26(2): 125–38

Keohane, R. & S. Hoffmann (eds.), 1991. *The New European Community: Decision-making and institutional change.* Boulder, CO: Westview

Khong, Y. & H. Nesadurai, 2007. "Hanging Together, Institutional Design, and Cooperation in Southeast Asia: AFTA and the ARF." In A. Acharya & A. Johnston (eds.), *Crafting Cooperation: Regional International institutions in comparative perspectives.* Cambridge, UK: Cambridge University Press, pp. 32–82

Kindleberger, C. 1973. *The World in Depression, 1929–1939.* Berkeley, CA: University of California Press

Krasner, S. (ed.) 1983. *International Regimes.* Ithaca, NY: Cornell University Press

Jones, B., C. Pascual, & S, Stedman, 2009. *Power and Responsibility: Building international order in an era of transnational threats.* Washington, DC: The Brookings Institution Press

Mahbubani, K. & J. Sng, 2017. *The ASEAN Miracle: A catalyst for peace.* Singapore: Ridge Books

Milner, H. 1993. "The Assumption of Anarchy in International Relations Theory." In D. Baldwin (ed.), *Neorealism and Neoliberalism: The contemporary debate.* New York: Columbia University Press

Pease, K. 2000. *International Organizations: Perspectives on governance in the twenty-first century.* Upper Saddle River, NJ: Prentice-Hall

Pouliot, V. 2008. "The Logic of Practicality: A theory of practice of security communities." *International Organization* 62(2): 257–88

Qin, Y. 2008. *A Relational Theory of World Politics.* Cambridge, UK: Cambridge University Press

Qin, Y. 2011. "Rule, Rules, and Relations: Toward a synthetic approach to governance." *The Chinese Journal of International Politics* 4: 117–45

Qin, Y. & L, Wei, 2008. "Structure, Process, and the Socialization of Power: East Asian community building and the rise of China." In R. Ross & Z. Feng (eds.), *China's Ascent: Power, security, and the future of international relations.* Ithaca, NY & London: Cornell University Press, pp. 115–40

Ringma, E. 2012. "Performing International Systems: Two East-Asian alternatives to the Westphalian order." *International Organization* 66(1): 1–25

Rosenau, J. & E-O. Czempiel (eds.), 1992. *Governance without Government: Order and change in world politics.* Cambridge, UK: Cambridge University Press

Ruggie, J. (ed.), 1993. *Multilateralism Matters: The theory and praxis of an institutional form.* New York: Columbia University Press

Searle, J. 1995. *The Construction of Social Reality.* New York: Free Press

Sending, O. & I. Neumann, 2011. "Banking on Power: How some practices in an international organization anchor others." In E. Adler & V. Pouliot (eds.), *International Practices.* Cambridge, UK: Cambridge University Press, pp. 231–54

Schatzki, T., K. Cetina, & and E. von Savigny (eds.), 2001. *The Practice Turn in Contemporary Theory.* London & New York: Routledge

Wei, L., 2010. *Guifan, Wangluohua yu Diquzhuyi (Norms, Networking and Regionalism).* Shanghai: Shanghai People's Publishing House

4
REGIONAL DIVERSITY, INTERREGIONAL/TRANSREGIONAL DIALOGUES, AND THE NEW MULTILATERALISM

Mario Telò

Introduction

How might multilateral cooperation survive in a multipolar world characterized by both increasing cultural diversity within regions and assertive power politics? Having been enriched by the theoretical debates sparked by the multiple modernities approach, we should be talking about multilateralisms as a plural noun. However, this does not mean submitting to cultural relativism and fragmentation; rather it suggests that we should be looking for unprecedented terms of multilateral convergence. Are regional and interregional arrangements part of the problem or perhaps part of the solution in paving the way to new forms of multilateral convergence? That is the focus of this chapter.

In Chapter 3 of this volume, Qin asks how regionalisms might dovetail with multilateralisms now that the era of hegemonic multilateralism is over. To this important question we should add some subsidiary issues. In a context of power shifts and enhanced multipolar confrontation, are we witnessing a crisis, an ambiguous evolution, or a dramatic reappraisal of some regional cooperation projects as milestones along more competitive and instrumental paths? To what extent are "polymorphic globalism" (as conceptualized by Katzenstein in Chapter 1) and diverse "socio-cultural milieus" (Meyer, Chapter 2) instrumental to regional/global power politics? And, how might regional cooperation among neighbors and interregional dialogues or trade arrangements between geographically distant partners contribute to a new post-hegemonic multilateralism?

The interlinked phenomena of regionalism and interregionalism are both essential aspects of the current debate about the evolution of multilateral cooperation in a context of cultural diversity. While regionalism is about relations among neighboring countries belonging to the same continent, interregionalism bridges different continents. Students of comparative politics will find it instructive to follow the lead of Gamble (Chapter 5) and Fawcett (Chapter 6) in exploring the achievements and failures of alternative regional models. Do similar cultures foster a shared identity?

Interregionalism concerns intercontinental relationships among diverse models and cultures of modernity. Should we regard the contours emerging in the post-hegemonic era as a shift toward an intercultural clash between irreconcilable regions (Huntington 1996) or as the potential start of a new multidimensional dialogue between diverse partners (Acharya 2014; Qin 2018)? Earlier anthologies based on papers delivered at the Macau conferences on multiple modernities (Meyer & de Sales Marques 2018; Meyer et al. 2019) uncovered a host of challenges, such as populist nationalism, that could seriously undermine both regional and multilateral forms of cooperation. However, the traditional global order is contested both inside and outside the states. How should our comparative studies interplay with a new multilateralist research agenda?

Convergences and divergences in national debates about the coming world order

One major, and highly controversial, line of inquiry sheds light on the evolving global power framework. Beyond the well-publicized divergent viewpoints articulated by Fukuyama (1992) and Huntington (1996) in the aftermath of the Cold War, various theses have been developed about the end of the global American hegemonic order (Keohane 2015; Acharya 2014; Kupchan 2012). Haass (2008) has argued that the world is moving toward a fragmented, non-polar system as US power recedes. By contrast, Ikenberry and Deudney (2018) remain convinced that global institutions are robust and resilient enough to cope with the new historic challenges. Nevertheless, they add, the world still needs a more inclusive, flexible kind of American hegemony. Surprisingly, the pessimistic front has enrolled Allison (2017), who forecasts the possible, though not inevitable, shift from trade wars to military rivalry between the two main powers, the declining United States and the emerging China. An unstable neo-bipolar scenario for the next decade ("Thucydides' trap") will confirm the conviction that international politics will never change, and competitive power politics will prevail. Similar arguments have surfaced in China and elsewhere (see for example Yan 2019).

Turning to the EU, the dilemmas of continental Europe are expressions of the conflictual coexistence of two logics. On the one hand, we have the EU's institutional paradigm of reconciliation among erstwhile enemies, designed to put an end to "security dilemmas." On the other we are witnessing the neo-nationalist trend, correctly analyzed by Qin in this volume (Chapter 3) as animated by "populist realism." Even though they performed poorly in the 2019 European Parliament elections and has been chastened by the new EU leadership, nationalistic and populist far-right parties remain a long-term challenge. For example, in

France *La Déclaration de Paris* (Bénéton et al. 2018) has revived reactionary or nationalist associations that were once deemed outmoded. Consider the lineup of those who advocate neo-nationalist paradigms: Alain de Benoist (2019) and, within a different cultural context, Michel Onfray (2017), on the one hand, and Alain Finkielkraut (2016) and Regis Debray (2019), on the other. All contest the previously dominant paradigm of post-sovereignism championed by scholars like Badie (1999), Bourdieu (1999), and Hassner (1991).

In Italy the comeback of the old "geopolitics" has been accompanied by the revival of national fascist thought, while extreme right-wing populists are inpired by Ezra Pound and Alexander Dugin. The Europeanist perspective articulated, among others, by Norberto Bobbio (1999), Altierro Spinelli (cf. Glencross & Trechsel 2010), and Umberto Eco (2012) has been put on the defensive, even though it is by no means marginalized.

Even in Germany, Habermas's post-national idea of a European public sphere, based on the reconciliation of previous enemies and the construction of supranational democratic governance, has been challenged increasingly, not only by the legacy of the sovereignst tradition championed by Carl Schmitt, but also by various neo-nationalist approaches, including the "social welfare nationalism" of Fritz Scharpf (2015) and Wolfgang Streeck (2013).

It is worthwhile to draw some analogies between the current pluralist debate in China about the coming world disorder/order and alternative scenarios and the three main alternative paradigms within the international relations (IR) debate currently going on in that country. On the one side, the most creative advocate of "moral neo-realist" thought, Yan Xuetong, forecasts a resurgent bipolar structure for the international system. Even though it will not necessarily provoke a war, the coming "new bipolarism" (Yan 2019) is driven by the economic, trade, and security competition and increasing military tension between two alternative models of modernization: those of the US and China. The Trumpist "undemocratic leadership" and transactionalist form of trade associated with it also could be juxtaposed to the emphasis on diversity in "China's model" and "Sinicization" as a power model (see Chapter 1 in this volume).

On the other side, two post-realist approaches have emerged clearly in China. First, the idea of "all under heaven" (Zhao 2016) represents a Confucian vision of the global Sinocentric harmony, where international politics could be transformed into "friendly relations." That would mean something similar to the European concept of "diffuse" as opposed to "specific" reciprocity (Telò 2014, 2017). Second and more important, there is an emerging alternative paradigm that combines divergences and convergences, as embodied in Qin's interpretation of traditional Chinese thought (Chapter 3 of this volume). That approach builds bridges to the contemporary global debate in international relations theory. Qin is attempting to develop a new post-hegemonic, pluralist, and participatory form of multilateralism that would include openness to various regional models and interregional partnerships as well as forging ties of cooperation.

On a de facto basis, these national debates converge, drawing two alternative scenarios for the future. The world is headed either toward hard power politics, based on a multipolar or bipolar confrontation, or toward a heterogeneous system that features new forms of multilateral cooperation. Logically, only the latter paradigm is potentially respecful of the "constraining diversities" that characterize our current situation (see Chapters 1 and 2 of this volume). And only the latter offers other global actors—such as the EU, India, the African Union, ASEAN, and MERCOSUR—a relevant role in regional, interregional, and global governance.

Conceptualizing and comparing interregionalist partnerships as a test for intercultural dialogue

Interregional relations are understudied even though they are crucial in modifying the debate about the global order and the development of regional entities (Rüland 2006). The first conceptual debate about the role of interregional relations started in the 1990s, under the auspices of the "Rio process" between the EU and Latin America. The Asia–Europe Meeting (ASEM), which celebrated its 12th summit in Ulaanbaatar on October 18, 2018, was launched in Bangkok in 1996. Many scholars also would include the former African, Caribbean, and Pacific Group of States (ACP), started in 1973 via the Yaoundé Convention, in the same conceptual framework because the EU's partners in that organization were located in other parts of the world: namely, Africa, Oceania, and Central America. Multiple conceptual controversies emerged in the academic world around the turn of the new century. At that time, it became clear that the US had developed its own interregional relationships, based on Fred Bergsten's theory of "emerging markets" (Bergsten 1994). These included ties with Latin America (the Free Trade Area of the Americas (FTAA), formed in 1994, which failed in 2005); with Asia and the Pacific (Asia–Pacific Economic Cooperation (APEC), formed in 1994); and with Europe (the new Transatlantic Agenda of the 1990s). For its part, the EU—in the context of its new ambitions as global actor—negotiated almost a dozen parallel strategic partnerships (with China in 2003, India in 2004, Brazil in 2007, and seven more later on) and several trade arrangements with individual countries. These initiatives raised some important theoretical issues: e.g., whether in a de facto sense such strategic partnerships (as well as some Economic Partnership Agreements (EPA) with single African countries) were opposed to region-to-region partnerships, and/or to bloc-to-bloc relations (Santander 2016).

However, the majority of the epistemic community shares a flexible and comprehensive concept of interregional relations which could be summarized as follows: "multidimensional relations between one region, on the one hand, and a region or a large state on the other, belonging to two or three different continents." By this definition, the EU–China partnership, Belt and Road Initiative (BRI), Transatlantic Trade and Investment Partnership (TTIP), and Transpacific Partnership (TPP) all would count as interregional relations. To characterize this second type of interregional relations with greater precision, the concept of "hybrid interregionalism" has been proposed and now is shared by several scholars (Fawcett et al. 2015; Rüland 2015; Soederbaum et al. 2016).

The main point to be brought out here is that a regional organization may play a decisive role as at least one of the partners within a scheme of interregional cooperation. In this respect, we are witnessing a multiplication of interregional relations, such as those launched by ASEAN, MERCOSUR, and the African Union.[1]

By this encompassing definition it is possible to assert that interregionalism is a structural feature of an increasingly multilayered system of global governance in which the global multilateral set is no longer the sole framework for institutionalized cooperation. As a significant development of the UN Charter of 1945, the balance between the regional/interregional level of governance and the global level is shifting in favor of the former. Both Boutros Boutros-Ghali and Kofi Annan recognized, on behalf of the UN, the increasing relevance of the sub-global (notably the regional) dimension of governance in helping to prevent or manage conflicts and establish economic cooperation. The fact that two UN Secretaries-General saw the value of regionalism itself has had an impact, helping to sustain regional organizations and foster regional identities.

But there is another, less positive take on this trend. Globalist economic liberals, reflecting on the place of such ties within the system of global governance (Bhagwati 1992), likely might see regionalism and interregionalism as a symptom of the fragmentation of the global framework. However, undoubtedly, regional cooperation eventually encourages interregional ties, trade partnerships, and sometimes even cultural dialogues. Thus, the normative criticisms that were leveled by Bhagwati against regional and interregional trade arrangements are outdated, but his remarks suggest a different and stimulating observation. Regional and interregional arrangements may be driven by factors other than trade interests. As scholars of the new regionalism assert, the explosion of these phenomena can be analyzed comparatively as a trend toward a "world of regions" (Katzenstein 2005), a *longue durée* and structural process of multilayered transformation of global governance (Fawcett & Hurrell 1995; Gamble & Paine 1996; Hettne et al. 2001; Hettne 2008; Telò 2001/2006/2014, 2016; Risse & Börzel 2016). Normative condemnations in the name of economic neo-liberalism seem inappropriate for a multidisciplinary research agenda. Regions develop their own identities and interregional relations, including by trade arrangements. Such regional relationships are no longer a matter of mere rational choice alone; instead, they reflect political decisions, as well as shared values, standards, and ways of life.

All in all, the development of multipurpose regionalism and interregionalism also can be seen as the only way possible to revive and reform global multilateralism, by enhancing not only its efficiency but also its legitimacy. In this way, the new regionalism goes beyond the limits of the famous debate between Bhagwati and Summers in the early 1990s, which was limited to trade dimensions (see Morin et al. 2015; De Block & Lebullinger 2018).

In terms of its theoretical implications, interregionalism is a form of multidimensional cooperation that may include cultural identities and feelings of common belonging, which together may help to ward off, or at least to limit, anarchy, nationalism, competition, ethnocentrism, protectionism, and fragmentation. Interregionalism belongs to the realm of new complex institutional sets and frameworks, operating within a highly contested scheme of global governance. In these ways, it transcends the old realist thought, even if the latter appears to have made a comeback, being revived by the nationalist challenge posed by "populist realism" (Qin 2018) in many countries.

Diachronic dimensions of EU interregionalism from the 1990s to the present

A second relevant debate within the international epistemic community has concerned the evolution of interregional relations in the aftermath of the Cold War. During the first decade, which Gamble (2014) has termed the era of "liberal peace," the Clinton/Bergsten approach to regional cooperation was essentially economic and instrumental, focusing on free trade areas in the three directions mentioned above. As Qin points out in Chapter 3 of this volume, that approach revived a hegemonic style: hegemonic in the sense meant by Keohane (1984/2004). The Clinton/Bergsten approach also would contain the hegemonic decline of the United States, which began in 1971. Nevertheless, it was consistent with the so-called "Washington Consensus" and Western neo-liberal culture. In the three cases—APEC, FTAA, and New Transatlantic Agenda—it sparked bitter conflicts with deeper regional organizations such as MERCOSUR in Latin America, ASEAN in the Asia–Pacific zone, and the EU in the transatlantic area. These three examples of regional cooperation encompassed political and cultural dimensions as well, which were incompatible with the US's neo-hegemonic and rational-choice approach to international relations.

The effort by George W. Bush to subordinate interregional agendas to security concerns after 2001—the era of "liberal war," according to Gamble (2014)—sharpened the resistance of the various partners. As a result, the interregional projects of the US largely went nowhere. This debacle confirmed the deadlock of the attempts by Clinton and by G.H.W. Bush to revive the declining hegemonic, US-led multilateralism by relying on interregional arrangements, whether focused on free trade or security. Such interregional setbacks were paralleled by the shortcomings of the WTO–DDR from Seattle (2000) to Cancún (2003) and the failure of the "liberal wars" in Iraq and Afghanistan. During the same period, the Southeast Asian economic crisis provoked a regionalist reaction against the IMF and the Washington Consensus as well as the deepening of the ASEAN integration process. The latter began expanding into monetary, political, and cultural fields. For example, the "Chang Mai Initiative" for a regional fund that began in 2000 was supported by ASEAN, China, Japan, and South Korea.

Academics at this time, at least in the field of international relations, still focused on comparing the competing US-led and EU-led interregional endeavors. Two main differences between the approaches of the EU and USA, as underlined by prominent scholars like Hettne (2007), stood out. First, while the EU's interregional relations were multipurpose (economic, cultural, environmental, social, and political), US-led arrangements were either only free trade-oriented or security-oriented (e.g., in the realm of anti-terrorism). EU interregionalism included three baskets: socio/cultural and environmental cooperation, economic cooperation, and political dialogue. That approach could be considered an example of the politicization of interregional partnerships in defense of multilateralism. The condemnation of the United States' preventive war in Iraq by the EU–Community of Latin American and Caribbean States (CELAC) interregional meeting of 2003 in Guadalajara suggests what such politicization might accomplish.

A second difference in this regard is that interregional relations started by the EU typically supported multidimensional regional integration abroad, whereas US-led efforts were at cross-purposes with deeper regional integration. The EU approach made it possible to engage in various form of regionalist "diffusion" (Risse & Börzel 2016), while avoiding excessive emulation and mimesis and downplaying the early arrogant normative emphasis on the "EU model" and "normative power" (Manners 2002).

The emergence of competing interregionalism: convergences, failures, and power relations

Since 2010, the international scholarly debate has changed dramatically due to the economic and financial crisis, the rapid emergence of China, and the rise of the BRICS. An issue raised years ago by Hettne (2007) has gained saliency in the present political context: do interregional relations facilitate the cohesion of regional partners or are they more likely to divide and disintegrate the partner organization as a bloc? Bloc-to-bloc negotiations (e.g., EU/ASEAN, EU/African Union (AU) and EU/MERCOSUR) are an identity marker in which each partner has a direct mirror interest in mutually supporting the other's current and future integration. The EU's policy on cooperation with ASEAN for disaster relief and security issues provides a positive example (cf. Globalization, Europe, Multilateralism (GEM) research, notably that by Tercovich 2019). In what follows, we will try to assess whether interregional factors spur integration or division around the world. As will become apparent, the role of the leading partner—whether that be the US, Russia, China, or the EU—is often decisive in determining the answer.

Under the Trump administration, the US has been abandoning the enhanced global role sought by President Obama through mega-interregional trade arrangements. The turning point was Trump's decision to delegitimize the global multilateral network (WTO and its panels) and to dismantle the final attempt to revive

US interregional hegemony though the TPP and TTIP. The only alternative to those efforts that Trump accepts—aside from national protectionism and trade wars—is to undertake hierarchical revisions of previous regional and interregional arrangements that allegedly will favor US interests, if only in symbolic terms. Regional arrangements in the wake of NAFTA illustrate this tendency. NAFTA was transformed into the US–Mexico–Canada Agreement (USMCA) in order to put the US first even in the acronym while deleting the acronym Free Trade Agreement (FTA). We may define this sort of regionalism as a form of hierarchical transactionalism, the opposite of true multilateral regionalism. In the event that Trump should propose the same for the US with Japan, the UK, China, or the EU relations, heightened tensions will occur. The partner matters, as well as its politics and/or vision of the best possible combination of bilateralism, interregionalism, and multilateralism.

In this context it is notable that both the US under Trump and Russia under Putin explicitly seek the dismemberment of the EU. Putin is funding far-right, anti-EU nationalist parties in order to weaken and divide the Union. For his part, Trump famously proposed Brexit to EU member states as a model and described NATO as "obsolete," throwing the organization into a crisis that may presage its decline. These policies imperil transatlantic interregionalism, much as the US withdrawal from the Trans-Pacific Partnership Agreement vitiated prospects for enhanced trans-pacific cooperation.

Particularly relevant for the future of pan-European, East/West interregional relations is the way that Putin's policies toward Georgia and Ukraine have transformed the potentially complementary EU and Eurasian constructs into strategically competing projects (cf. Chapter 7 of this volume). Under this new regime, defections from the Eurasian Community in favor of pro-EU arrangements may be either punished by military invasion, as has occurred in Eastern Ukraine, Abkhazia, and South Ossetia, or subjected to blackmail by the withholding of energy supplies, as happened to Armenia. To be sure, Russia's conduct was motivated by what it perceived to be the threat in its own backyard posed by NATO's eastward expansion after 1991. Still, that conduct, which led to the EU's unanimous sanctions against Russia, indicate the dangerous collapse of the peaceful pan-European interregional architecture established after 1990–91, as embodied in the Council of Europe, Organization for Security and Cooperation in Europe (OSCE), Russia–NATO Council, and strategic partnership between the EU and Russia.

Authoritarian regimes like Putin's Russia sometimes work to foster regional and interregional cooperation. Typically, they do so for geopolitical defensive advantages, or when they think that such moves will promote autocracy and/or a "hard" version of multipolarity. However, as far as Putin's vision and practice of regional cooperation is concerned, the absence of democracy, bottom-up drivers, and civil society actors all are factors limiting regional cooperation. Furthermore, one must consider the internal mechanisms enabling or constraining relations between autocrats. In this context, security is the main engine of regime-building. Because of its internal rules and procedures, this top-down, hierarchical version of regionalism cannot be multilateral. Notwithstanding these limits, it is very interesting that today large states, including Russia, want to coordinate policies at the regional level, thus moving, to some extent, beyond the old imperial concept of spheres of influence that prevailed in the nineteenth century. Interregional relations may matter by shaping the future of regional entities characterized by alternative values and identities. So, on the one hand, the EU potentially could influence potential members of the Eurasian community, such as Moldova, Ukraine, and the Caucasus. On the other hand, China's regional policy in Central Asia, notably the Shanghai Cooperation Organization (with its "Chinese characteristics"), may be critical in the future evolution of the Eurasian Economic Union (EAEU).

As far as the EU is concerned, the quasi-continental enlargement policy, reflected in that body's growth from 12 to 28 member states plus 5 applicants, is widely regarded as a success story. By contrast, the EU's attempt to establish interregional relationships with the "arc of crisis" countries, from Ukraine and Belarus to Libya and the Arab nations—exemplified in the "Barcelona process" and the European neighborhood policy—largely can be judged a quasi-failure, at least so far, and a challenge awaiting future resolution. Cultural cleavages do affect this failure, not only on the Southern flank (cf. the poor record of the EU's multiple attempts at a cultural dialogue with Islam), but also on the Eastern flank, as shown by the oscillating relationship with Moldova, the Caucasus states, and Belarus, and the deadlock in educational and cultural cooperation with Russia. The latter shows up in the frozen bilateral strategic partnerships between the EU and Russia in both the Council of Europe (regarding the crucial dimension of human rights protection) and OSCE (regarding the monitoring of democratic transitions).

Comparative studies offer evidence of the authoritarian evolution of top-down regional cooperation organizations elsewhere, notably in the cases of the Gulf Cooperation Council. The latter has been described as an instrument of Saudi Arabia's hierarchical rule, exemplified in its campaign against Qatar, which has been accused of complicity with Iran. Another case of such authoritarian evolution is Bolivarian Alliance for the Americas (ALBA), a political instrument of the declining Venezuela. Authoritarian regionalism is an alternative model, distinct from soft/relational and deep/institutionalized regionalism (see Chapters 3, 5, and 6 of this volume) based on bottom-up legitimacy and multilateral rules. The latter would include the EU, ASEAN, MERCOSUR, and Southern African Development Community (SADC), no matter what the main driving factors (security, trade, or institutions) behind them may have been.

China's interregional relations in the Xi era and the "post-peaceful rising period" that was openly proclaimed by the 19th CCP Congress are instructive. The Belt and Road Initiative (BRI) exemplifies a unilateral interregional global project of staggering magnitude. Are China's interregional policies in Asia, Africa, Europe, and Latin America evolving toward a multilateral or hierarchical pattern, and are they uniting or dividing the various regional/continental partners? In regard to China's relations to Europe, we are witnessing a paradox. For many decades the consensus among international observers was that China strongly supported the unity of the EU as well as further integration, with the purpose of counterbalancing the power of the US and the USSR/Russia. Despite recent visits to Brussels by Xi Jinping, it has become apparent that we must temper that insight. The attempt to reach out to Europe, manifested most recently in Xi Jinping's 2018 and 2019 visits to Brussels, has deep roots in Chinese history, extending not only back to Deng Xiaoping but even to Mao Zedong's vision of a multipolar world and a politically united Europe's balancing role both in trans-Atlantic and pan-European relations. Moreover, Xi's support for the EU runs parallel to China's controversial political and financial support for the African Union. China has offered to build the AU's headquarters in Addis Ababa and promised to upgrade Chinese investments within the AU. On the other hand, as part of its BRI, China is now institutionalizing its relationships with 17 European countries, including several EU members. Thus, in a de facto sense, China is dividing the EU, much to the chagrin of those in charge of the European Union's institutions.

The shift in China's European policy is part of a broader sea change. In the Xi Jinping era, China has increased its assertiveness as a global actor. It is in the process of developing its own practices, characteristics, and ideas of global multilateralism and regionalism, both in its own neighborhood and in interregional relations with Africa and Europe (via the BRI) as well as Latin America. The China–Africa partnership has developed enormously since 2010, and these interregional economic ties are supported by political objectives.[2] Most analyses of China's offensive diplomacy in Africa have focused on Beijing's thirst for economic benefits in regard to energy and raw materials. That is why its behavior often is dubbed "energy diplomacy" or "economic diplomacy," implying that China, like Japan in the 1980s, seeks to become a "geo-economic power." But if one looks at the history of the PRC's foreign policy, one realizes that Beijing has seldom pursued its diplomacy based on purely economic considerations. Chinese interregionalism in Africa should be viewed through a political lens, in light of geo-strategic calculations, political and security ties with African countries, peacekeeping and anti-piracy efforts, and support for African regionalism. China's diplomatic expansion in Africa, while partially driven by its need for economic growth, cannot be fully understood without taking into consideration the strategic impulses accompanying its accelerating emergence as a global power. Africa's interregional partnership is one of China's diplomatic "new frontiers," as exemplified by new Chinese leader Xi Jinping's maiden foreign trip to Africa in 2013. However, the huge FDI plan for Africa has been interpreted by some international commentators as an excellent opportunity, but also as posing a risk of division and geopolitical domination.

In short, recent events are obliging neutral observers to address the question of the nature of China's interregionalism by typing in a question mark. The deepening of relations between China, on the one hand, and 17 European countries (plus bilateral arrangements made with Portugal and Italy in 2019), on the other, is weakening the institutional role of the EU as the main coordinator of Europe's external cooperation, trade, and partnerships. They are also de facto strengthening Euro-skeptical sovereignist governments such as those of Orbán in Hungary, Kaczyński in Poland, and Salvini in Italy. In the context of the economic decline of Southern EU member states after the 2009–17 financial crisis, it is also worthy of mention that China's decision to prioritize individual relations with single EU countries, notably with the weak ones like Greece, provokes worries regarding its political designs.

The Belt and Road Initiative presents an interregional opportunity of historic importance for all, including Africa, Asia, Latin America, and the EU. Presented by Xi Jinping as the "project of the century," it is one of the pillars of the "Third Chinese Revolution" (after those spearheaded by Mao and Deng: cf. Economy 2018), beyond the period of the so-called "peaceful rise." It will be a crucial test for China's interregionalism and multilateralism.

The US opposes the BRI as a major rival to its own global influence and a risky bargain for weak states. Does the launch of the BRI presage a neo-hegemonic shift? If its implementation openly serves the geopolitical interests of a single great power, thereby promoting a one-sided understanding of globalization, it will provoke resistance, criticism, and containment. Comparisons with the American Marshall Plan of 1947–57 may be useful. The Marshall Plan's inspiration was innovative and enlightened Keynesianism. John Maynard Keynes believed that the shortcomings of the Versailles conference in 1919 stemmed from (among other things) a flawed understanding of international economic relations that he had tried and failed to correct. He ended up "winning" at the Bretton Woods conference in 1944, basing the new postwar economic order on multilateral agreements. However, largely due to Stalin's opposition, the Marshall Plan by 1947 had become de facto an instrument of the Cold War and the containment policy suggested by George Kennan. In combination, the Marshall Plan and the policy of containment became the twin linchpins of US hegemony (Keohane 1984/2004; Ruggie 1993; Patrick 2009). That hegemony involved providing international public goods, promoting the European Organization for Economic Cooperation as a new multilateral institution, and applying the logic of power politics to the bipolar confrontation between the US and the USSR. Especially in the wake of Stalin's 1948 refusal to allow the participation of Czechoslovakia and Yugoslavia in the Marshall Plan, it became effectively impossible for US aid recipients to reject demands to join NATO.

We are not (not yet) in an era of bipolar confrontation, and there is no "Thucydides trap" between China and the West lurking around the corner (Allison 2017). But what still remains inspiring in this troubled time for a true hegemonic project is that the multilateral approach taken by the US after World War II managed to expand during and beyond the Cold War, thanks to both its links to global economic growth and the attractiveness of the "American way of life" as a form of soft power. Assuming that China is not seeking to use the BRI to pursue international hegemony as a single superpower, it will need to expand the nature of its international public goods provision, offer its autonomous partners opportunities for economic growth, enhance its soft power dimension, and foster shared interregional leadership within a revived multilateral network, in order to limit the impact of negative feedback and foil policies of containment by the US and other actors. The quality of its partnership with the EU[3] and possible convergences both at the global and interregional levels are crucial. These are the key variables that may influence this potentially virtuous interregional scenario. Here, a triangular partnership among China, the EU, and Africa would be a relevant test.

The most daunting challenge facing a pluralist, multiple-style multilateralism is how to combine trade with other interregional issues, thereby linking external relations to internal policies. Traditionally, trade was a matter of technocratic, de-politicized global or interregional relations. However, this is changing dramatically, as a comparison of Chinese and EU approaches to foreign policy makes clear. Whereas the accent in China is on "multilateralism with Chinese characteristics" (19th CCP Congress 2017), the EU strives to embody its own values in the making of foreign policy. In other words, the EU's cultural traditions extend even to its trade policy, which is a linkage that multiple modernities theory would lead us to expect. Of course, future post-hegemonic multilateralism will have to be based on pluralist convergence among very diverse approaches, political styles, background cultures, and divergent ways of making policy. That is why neglect of the multiple modernities principle has slowed progress in expanding multilateral trading relations. No country wants to buy another's values in addition to its commercial products.

According to the Treaty of Lisbon provisions, which went into effect in 2009, the EU attempted to create a comprehensive approach to foreign policy and a kind of single pillar of external relations. Legally framed by the Treaty of the EU (TEU) and the Treaty on the Functioning of the EU (TFEU), that approach obliges policymakers to promote human rights and sustainable development, among other general aims. EU Trade Commissioner Cecelia Malmström's 2015 paper, entitled "Trade for All," emphasized that "economic growth goes hand in hand with social justice, respect for human rights, high labor and environmental standards, and health and safety protection" (2015: 10). Finally, the "EU Global Strategy" approved in 2016, following a proposal by the High Representative for Foreign Policy Federica Mogherini, commits the EU to "harmoniz[ing] trade arrangements not only with development goals but also with sustainable development, environmental protection, health, safety, human rights protection and foreign policy strategy."

This approach is counterbalanced by a strong emphasis on regional and interregional partnerships, in which the EU does not have to provide lessons to the partners. The previous Eurocentric and arrogant perspective of "normative power

Europe" (Manners 2002) is largely over, and not only because it provoked negative feedback on every continent, as Acharya (2014) and other scholars have underlined.

What can be said about the impact of this controversial evolution? Between 2010 and 2018, the EU negotiated and signed a series of relevant "second generation trade arrangements" with interregional partners like South Korea, Vietnam, Japan, Canada (De Block & Lebullinger 2018). Similar arrangements are under negotiation with MERCOSUR, Australia, and New Zealand. These complex and multipurpose interregional partnerships are politically relevant, notably in the Asia–Pacific region, because they address the huge vacuum created by the inward-looking and protectionist policy of Donald Trump. Although investments were located in the sphere of EU competence by the Lisbon Treaty, this competence was fine-tuned by the European Court of Justice in 2019, providing not only the EP but also the national parliaments with ratification power. For that reason, the difficulties involving several ongoing negotiations, including the Bilateral Investment Treaty (BIT) with China, are understandable. Is China likely to agree to seek some relevant improvements in respect for the rule of law in general and labor law in particular? Transparency and fairness in business are the conditions for attracting foreign investments, increasing trade, building financial and economic partnerships. Consequently, they are among the goals of President Xi Jinping, as announced at the party congress of 2018. However, many problems exist that touch on the domestic impact of multilateral standards. For example, divergences in the notions of the rule of law and human rights have not yet been successfully addressed by the EU–China "human rights dialogue" (Ding et al. 2018). In addition, the question of labor rights is affecting the BIT agenda.

Could the EU simply forget about complying with its demanding treaty and strategy provisions? Doing so would not be easy, first because of the Lisbon Treaty provision that has altered the process through which trade policy acquires legitimacy. The treaty calls for enhanced democratic accountability and transparency by bestowing an oversight role on the EU Parliament. Moreover, that body has the final word on ratification and, consequently, carries on a constant dialogue with very persistent NGOs. The Lisbon Treaty thus has changed the parameters and now requires closer cooperation among the Commission, the Council, and the Parliament. In effect, it integrates the Parliament into the established decision-making system. Furthermore, after the declaration by the Commission that some trade and investment arrangements such as Comprehensive Economic and Trade Agreement (CETA) are "mixed treaties" that require the signatures of and ratification by both the EU and the member states, some of the latter have accepted and even supported the bottom-up politicization of EU trade policy. They have chosen to submit treaties to national and even sub-national (in the case of Belgium) majority decision-making. According to many observers, that procedure may undermine the credibility of the EU in international and interregional negotiations.

Is this more rigorous process on the part of the EU a sign of unilateral arrogance that will make beneficial trade deals harder to negotiate and less effective once they are? Or should the new system be considered a constructive factor, fostering higher standards in commercial arrangements, as it did in several instances, notably in the cases of Canada, Mexico, MERCOSUR, Japan, and Asia–Pacific? It is too early to answer this question.

Interregionalism and new multilateralism: five issues

One highly encouraging implication of this book is that it displays multiple convergences on a new multilateralist agenda. The contribution of Professor Qin Yaqing to this dialogue (Chapter 3) should be particularly welcomed, as well as those by other non-European authors (Chapters 8, 9, 10, 11, and 12). However, there is a problem of common language and cultural dialogue that has to be addressed. We need to be precise about the evolving nature of multilateralism in a context in which regionalism and interregionalism are expanding. What are the implications of regional identities and interregional cultural and trade dialogues for the theory and practice of the "new multilateralism"?

Classic references in the literature clearly articulate the two central ideas animating the postwar scheme of multilateral cooperation: "reciprocity" and the "general principle of conduct" (Ruggie 1993; Telò 2014). The issue that arises is whether those pillars suffice to sustain multilateralism in the twenty-first century. What can be said about efforts to deepen the features of the "new multilateralism" and about the role of regional organizations and interregional relations and dialogues within it?

Recent scholarship has opened up new avenues of research. Multilateral cooperation may decline because it is too inefficient and its legitimacy is too contingent. But it is also threatened by external factors such as the possible defection of its main stakeholder, the previously hegemonic US, which weakens the system of multilayered governance. All of these drawbacks may mean that it will be impossible to cope with the emergence of power politics, fragmentation, and spheres of influence without upgrading the idea and practice of multilateral cooperation. A new multilateralism is on the agenda of relevant actors, from UN Secretary General António Guterres, to the EU High Representative for Foreign Affairs, as well as many states and regional entities, and the epistemic community on every continent (Acharya 2014; Telò 2014; Qin 2018). Convergences and divergences are inevitable within what Katzenstein (Chapter 1, in this volume) calls "polyvalent globalism." However, as Katzenstein goes on to argue, although "constrained diversity" may be a "constant" in international relations, it assumes a variety of institutional forms.

Because the quality of multilateralism is a function of the institutional order, the main issues on the agenda of a new multilateralism are of an institutional nature. The changing institutional framework is the independent variable shaping the possible movement of multiple and diverse modernities toward enhanced policy-convergence. Here, several key issues are at stake.

First: The new multilateralism can only be *post-hegemonic* (cf. Chapter 3 in this volume). This means not only that the US will be unable to stop its decline, but that neither the EU nor China is, or can be, a candidate to replace it. However, a post-hegemonic vacuum is dangerous for peace. Only a collective and cooperative leadership within stronger common institutions may ensure sustainable and fairer multilateral governance. Moving from the G7 to the G20 was a step in the right direction during the worst years of crisis (2008–10), even if recently the G20 has lost some of its relevance. Moreover, the US under Trump is disengaging from traditional liberal multilateralism (Ikenberry & Deudney 2018). Does the end of US hegemony signal the end of the best aspects of the liberal idea of a rules-based, transparent, and fair system of global governance beyond the state? This legacy has its roots in the Kantian institutional and legal pacifism. Could the Kantian idea be translated into the languages of modern regional and national cultures in India, China, and elsewhere? The new multilateralism is neither an arrogant nor a unanimous European demand. Europe is currently divided between (on the one hand) an elevated Habermasian, revised/regulated, post-American brand of liberalism and (on the other hand), illiberal tendencies driven by populist nationalist and protectionist parties. These nationalist strands of European politics are profoundly rooted in Europe's tragic history and political thought, from Carl Schmitt to Giovanni Gentile (Gamble 2020).

Second: The new multilateralism should enhance the relevance of fair, well-balanced *communicative action*, in two ways: via interregional partnerships and by containing asymmetries and recasting dynamics beyond all illusions about the EU as a single "normative power." Every power is a normative power. Norms are the consequences of various knowledge-backgrounds (Qin 2018) and of various cognitive priors (Acharya 2017). Multilateralism is essentially the antithesis of merely hierarchical international power relations. However, in a post-hegemonic context, the concept of "partnership" stands out, as emphasized by Qin's contribution to this volume as well as in the large literature on "post-revisionist" interregional relations (Fawcett & Telò 2015). Scholars in this camp are engaged in the quest for a third way between Western-centrism and fragmented relativism (cf. Meyer & Sales Marques 2018). The main global actors need to usher in a third, multidimensional cultural era of interregional relations between equals, beyond universalism and relativism. In the case of the EU, that means going beyond both the Eurocentric period and the Euroskeptical one.[4] The same of course holds true for the interregional relations launched by the EU, the US, India, Brazil, South Africa, ASEAN, and China.

Third: The new multilateralism must be more *multilayered* than the version that prevailed in past decades: it should include the role of regional organizations and of interregional relations as crucial frames integrating partners within their respective continents as well as between the continents. It must move beyond Cordell Hull's 1948 vision of the UN, with its primary focus on the global level, as institutionalized in both the UN and the Bretton Woods agreement (1944) creating the World Bank, International Monetary Fund, and, in 1947, the General Agreement on Tariffs and Trade, and its commitment to global rules-based trade and financial multilateral cooperation. Former UN Secretaries General Boutros Boutros-Ghali and Kofi Annan as well as several regional leaders from each continent argued that an authentic renewal would require a multilevel and regionalist reform of international organizations beyond the West-centric globalist model that proved successful in the aftermath of World War II. To cope with the challenges of nationalism and protectionism, multilateral forms of governance operating beyond the state must try to generate enhanced efficiency and legitimacy by building a set of regional and interregional pillars supporting connectivity, transnational ties, and regulation beyond the state.

Fourth: Multilateralism is becoming more "*institutionalized*," according to a broader understanding of that expression, as it evolves from informal fora, networks, and arrangements into intergovernmental consultative bodies and even true organizations. This inevitably means that multilateral cooperation becomes more intrusive and (whether *de facto* or *de jure*) more binding. In this new context, novel forms of interaction inside and outside the state pose major political and cultural challenges, including for multidimensional interregional relations, as we can ascertain through comparative analysis of Europe and East Asia and especially of the EU and China.

EU–Asia interregional relations have entered a critical phase. In light of Trump's new tariff policy and the uncertain future of NATO after the Brussels summit held in mid-July of 2018, the EU is sealing important deals with Japan, China and other relevant partners. These new agreements would complement the existing economic relations between the EU and other key Asian regional actors. The recent adoption of the EU–Japan Economic Partnership Agreement (EPA) has set the stage for a more dynamic multipurpose partnership. At the same time, the 20th EU–China summit also focused on strengthening economic ties and overcoming the difficulties of the BIT. The Xi-Junker Joint Declaration of April 9 expressed the hope that BIT negotiations could be wrapped up in 2020.

In this context, the ASEM summit of October 18–19, 2018 has been crucial to strengthening further multipurpose EU–Asia ties.[5] How has the Europe–Asia Meeting developed so far as a soft interregional multilateral framework, and what can be achieved in coming years? And how does ASEM dovetail with domestic policy in the EU, China, and other powers such as India, Japan, and Indonesia?

The impact of such interregional cooperation on domestic politics and policies has increased in weight and complexity, as the examples of the EU and East Asia show, notably in the case of China. The inward-looking and protectionist trade policy and aggressive trade wars pursued by the United States have stimulated the EU to become a more proactive participant in reshaping global and interregional trade rules. However, it has evolved domestically in the aftermath of the Lisbon Treaty. On one hand, it now has bestowed a veto power over trade deals upon the European Parliament and included trade within a single comprehensive approach to external relations, all to be based on EU values. On the other hand, the intrusion of national and sub-national majoritarian politics as well as the pressure exerted by NGOs for transparency and value-consistency indicates a potential contradiction between external effectiveness and internal legitimacy. Why? Because the standard-setting established by the Treaty and the "Trade for All" strategy (2015) is a one-way street due to internal legitimacy and transparency requirements. That is, trade deals no longer can be signed by the EU unless they meet exacting internal requirements and legitimacy constraints.

FTA negotiations with India are deadlocked and will not be resumed as long as India sticks to its exceedingly low standards on environmental and social protection (making problems for the Regional Comprehensive Economic Partnership (RCEP) as well). Furthermore, the EU has a legal obligation to withdraw from negotiations for free trade when potential trading partners are found to violate EU values systematically, especially values involving sustainable development and human rights. This matters because values-based negotiations might rule out trade deals with certain countries, e.g., with Myanmar (in light of its persecution of Rohingyas) and Cambodia (where the government limits opposition rights), Yet, oddly enough, those values did not stop the EU from signing and ratifying a treaty with Vietnam and starting negotiations with ASEAN as a regional bloc that includes Thailand, Myanmar, and Cambodia. At the same time, the EU Commission has launched in 2019 a legal attack on South Korea for not implementing the bilateral clause of a trade arrangement that commits it to ratify International Labor Organization (ILO) conventions.

This comprehensive approach may have an impact on the outcome of complex negotiations with China on the Bilateral Investment Treaty, in the event that the partner refuses to sign ILO conventions on labor rights. Of course the EU should exercise prudence and flexibility. If it truly followed a rigid "normative power" approach (Manners 2002), the EU could bargain only with Norway, Switzerland, and a few other countries in today's world. That is why we need an intercultural dialogue on fundamental values. A serious intercultural dialogue at the level of civil societies would be extremely useful, especially if combined with trade and diplomatic negotiations. EU Trade Commissioner Cecilia Malmström said that "negotiations are more complex and difficult, but the current positive record in East Asia and South America says that they are possible."[6] Meanwhile, other trading actors like Canada likewise have upgraded their standards-requirements for trade negotiations.

For its part, China is drifting toward a serious dilemma. On the one hand, it has to defend the multilateral trade system from which it has benefitted so much since 2001. That would mean that it must implement consistent measures to respect the rule of law in domestic affairs and make its commitment to multilateral and interregional cooperation both sustainable and credible. On the other hand, the implications of multilateral cooperation in regard to respect for the rule of law may have troubling domestic consequences, such as pressure for internal reform, including adherence to labor standards such as the right of free association, the right to strike, and limited standards-setting. Yet all this would have to happen with no talk of human rights protections, since those are not yet included in the government's program as proclaimed by the Chinese Communist Party's (CCP) innovative but rather "leftist" Congress of 2017.

The EU is not the only agent addressing the challenging question of how to institutionalize an enhanced and more "pluralist" form of government (whether softer or deeper) "beyond the state," both in trade and human rights realm. Other international actors such as the UN and WTO, individual states, transnational social movements, and regional organizations like ASEAN also are highlighting the need to strengthen the role of the international courts and to implement Kofi Annan's "responsibility to protect." Of course, that broad concept of responsibility may need revision after some controversial performances and in light of the proposal aired by the previous Brazilian government that the international community should assume "responsibility while protecting."

Fifth: Many scholars claim that the new multilateralism cannot avoid empowering a larger and deeper scheme of *citizens' participation* (cf. Chapter 3 in this volume). That would mean greater input legitimacy bestowed by an enhanced role for civil society associations, actors, and networks. Such enhancement would have to begin during the negotiation process itself, i.e., before the multilateral arrangements were even made. Moreover, civil society groups would need to monitor the multilateral arrangements themselves and, relying on decentralized oversight and follow-up, try to ensure consistent implementation. All such modes of governance would naturally require full transparency and accountability. However, we are witnessing two conflicting tendencies in the current world: on the one side, enhanced nationalist and protectionist opposition to multilateralism, and, on the other, a variety of constructive cultural, economic, and political dialogues.

In almost every Western country, including (among many others) the US, the UK, Italy, Hungary, and Poland, plenty of evidence suggests that democratic participation and direct democracy (e.g., via social networks and referenda) are manipulated as powerful instruments of national populism: channels of irrational, inward-looking feelings and of nationalist and protectionist "mobilizations of fear," whether against "others," against Europe, against migration, and in general against international cooperation, especially with China (see Chapter 5 of this volume). Of course, populist parties have not had the same degree of electoral success in all the countries mentioned above, but the trend is clear. In short, populism is a form of extreme nationalism, opposed to multilateral cooperation.

And yet it must be emphasized that multilateral and interregional institutions still matter, including interregional regimes and arrangements, as channels of information, communication, and cultural dialogue. Not only do they foster spillover effects and allow the reduction of transaction costs; they also encourage mutual cultural knowledge and people-to-people contacts that are fundamental for the future of interregional ties to expand beyond the Westphalian diplomatic legacy.

Several initiatives have been proposed that would move us in that direction, for example on the occasion of the 12th ASEM summit, held in 2018 (for background, see Chapter 11). For weeks in advance, that summit was preceded and followed by meetings of civil society networks.[7] Similar trends are emerging in the EU-Latin American interregional partnership. The EU–Islamic intercultural dialogue in Istanbul and the EU's multiple interparliamentary dialogues with Mediterranean, Latin American, and Indian partners are headed in the same direction, even if their records are mixed and less impressive so far (cf. Jancic 2019).

This rich ongoing process of intercultural interaction is directly relevant to our theoretical discussion of multiple modernities and global governance. Is it a mere rhetorical exercise, subordinate to legitimacy imperatives, or is it a step in the right direction to cope with new domestic challenges and interregional cultural differences?

Conclusions

Interregional multipurpose dialogues are significant in many fields, including trade, economics, and politics. However, they cannot progress without a substantial upgrading, and without seriously addressing the respective background cultures and their profound differences. To cite just one case in which the background culture has an enormous impact on politics, we should consider China. There, the benefits of the Confucian legacy are not merely rhetorical; they are one of the country's strong points. Despite their disagreements, eminent Chinese scholars do agree on this, including Qin (2007), Yan (2011) and Zhao (2016), all of whom have argued eloquently for the continuing relevance of Confucianism in China (April 2018 conference at China Foreign Affairs University (CFAU) University, Beijing). Turning to the European Union, we would encounter broad agreement that, at least on the continent and excluding the UK, the Enlightenment tradition still matters a great deal. The Kant–EU connection proposed by Thomas Meyer (Chapter 2 in this volume) is essential even if, of course, not unique. Christian, liberal, and social democratic thought constitute some of the indispensable building blocks of the shared European background culture that supports peaceful, cooperative governance beyond the state and between the states (Telò 2018). However, for Europe, Kant matters in particular, since his was the first rational theory offering strong arguments on the linkage between the internal and external polities and legal orders, i.e., those inside and outside the state.

To answer this crucial question, we need to update and upgrade the theory behind our discussion of multilateralism as the institutional frame for "perpetual peace." The chapter by Thomas Meyer in this volume is crucial for identifying the tension between the two Kantian concepts of "republicanism" (participation in domestic policy, jus *publicum*) and "federation" (international law, equality of states) as a dialectical framework that might enable a synthesis of divergence and convergence. That, incidentally, is an issue also ably addressed by the Qin and Katzenstein chapters in this volume. However, my thesis is that republicanism and federation only can be synthesized only on the basis of deepening *transnational ties/networks* at the citizen and civil society levels as well as by a new form of reciprocity known as "*diffuse reciprocity.*" The Kantian concept of a "right to visit" can be updated as a philosophical anticipation of today's transnationalism. In fact, over the past 50 years it has been adapted to contemporary international relations theory by many scholars, especially Keohane and Nye (2014).

As a first step we should establish that republicanism for Kant means not merely the opposite of monarchy but also the antithesis of any tyrannical system, i.e., a constitutional polity. His concept of "federation" looks like a third way between federation in the usual sense and confederation, while the "freedom" of each participating country is not constrained. However, in my opinion these two definitive articles of the "Perpetual Peace" essay risk playing contradictory and even incompatible roles if they are unable to overcome the limits of the Westphalian paradigm. For example, those two elements are seen as contradictory in the original thought of Sun Yat-Sen, who opposes internal freedom and external freedom. Sun claims that borderless internal freedom (human rights, etc.) risks undermining and destroying the nation and weakening its external freedom against imperial and colonial powers. In their chapters in this volume, Bava and Fitriani demonstrate that precisely this post-colonial legacy explains the emphasis on sovereignty and non-interference in the post-colonial countries. Much the same point was made in the Bandung Declaration of 1955, in which leading figures of the day, including Sukarno, Nehru, and Chinese foreign minister Zhou Enlai, participated. However, more than 60 years later we are witnessing the failure of regionalism, whenever the sovereignty principle is pushed to extreme limits. At the same time, we must welcome the achievements that have been made in the construction of new kinds of multilateralism at the regional level, although they remain timid and soft forms of governance beyond the state, as exemplified by ASEAN. We also know that the WTO panel system implies a form of law that supersedes that of its member states. That certainly provides a good example of governance beyond the state, much to the dismay of the current US administration which is boycotting the panel system. Finally, in 2005 Kofi Annan inaugurated a new debate, arguing that it was impossible for the international community to remain indifferent to massacres occurring on a vast scale.

That is why we need to look for new, creative, pluralist theories of governance beyond the state, and identify the sources of thought and action that might implement such governance in the polymorphic international life of the twenty-first century.

In this context, as Europeans we must begin with Kant, of course with the intention of going beyond Kant, jointly with some of the non-European cultures.

How does the Kantian tradition of constitutionalism help bridge the gap between internal constitutionalism and international cooperation? The essay on "Perpetual Peace" should be read in the context of all Kant's writings during the 1790s including the *Groundwork for the Metaphysic of Morals* and the *Critique of Practical Reason*. This method (as practiced by Bobbio 1999) leads to the conclusion that the single most innovative of Kant's concepts—the one bridging the gap between republicanism and "cosmopolitanism"—is cosmopolitanism itself, the main precondition for perpetual peace. But let it be noted that none of this amounts to a utopian call for a centralized world government, as found in current cosmopolitan *vulgata* represented by Held (1995) and his school, an approach that risks a move toward what Kant would condemn as a "universal monarchy." It means an emphasis on the driving role of social connectivity among societies and individuals beyond the realist interstate paradigm and an institutional construction above and beyond mere free trade liberalism of the kind advocated by Montesquieu, Smith, and Ricardo. It therefore includes principles such as the free movement of people (not only of merchants but also of ordinary citizens who have a right to visit other countries, which must welcome them) as well as trade regulations intended to avoid hierarchies and colonialism.

Consequently, not only republican states but also multiple transnational networks, people-to-people relations, and intercultural dialogue increasingly are becoming the driving forces behind peace-building. In other words, they are fostering the difficult combination of republicanism and federation. That combination would enable us, step by step and with Kantian prudence, to move beyond the traditional Westphalian paradigm toward an interregional/transnational institutionalized regime of peace.

Is this European "background knowledge" compatible with intercultural dialogue and "relational multilateralism" (cf. Chapters 1 and 3 of this volume)? Beyond traditional universalism we will need differentiated universalism as a bottom-up means to overcome the risk of relativism (Marramao *et al*. 2015). As I see it, these should be topics for our research program. In any case, it is a matter of fact that the transnational dimension of the world polity plays a crucial role in sustaining interregionalism in several ways, notably by making it more efficient, more legitimate, and more able to frame balanced dialogue among cultures. Thinkers such as Habermas (2001), Bourdieu (1999), and Bobbio (1999), among others, have made it clear that this cathartic feature of European political culture marked a radical turning point against centuries of tragic conflicts and wars provoked by extreme nationalism during the first decades of the twentieth century, the most violent period in European history. In the very moment at which movements have arisen that revive the pre-1945 specter, it is important to underline this feature of the European political culture, one that is the very soul of European reconciliation and is open to intercultural dialogue.

The alternative would be the nightmare of a cultural and civilizational regression toward extreme nationalism, perhaps a kind of Huntingtonian clash between irreconcilable regions (Huntington 1996). Peaceful transnationalism based on internal reconciliation is not the only tendency emerging from European societies in 2018, even if it has lasted for 70 years as a critical factor in promoting peace though socio-economic integration and governance beyond the state. As a consequence of the financial crisis that began in 2007–08, nationalism has returned in the form of populism, protectionism, and intolerance. It poses a threat to both domestic democracy and multilateral cooperation. What is new is that the populist rhetoric deploys democracy as a rhetorical weapon against three targets: openness, European integration, and interregional relations with other continents, notably with East Asia and China.

Let us conclude by returning to Kant and considering what he means by "cosmopolitanism." He did not intend it to replace feelings of national belonging and patriotism by a vague global citizenship. On the contrary, civic republicanism includes patriotism as a background for international cooperation and enduring peace. But this delicate balancing of patriotic sentiment and cosmopolitanism will be realistic only on the assumption that international relations not only are paralleled but also legitimized by a variety of transnational ties combining civil society networks and building bridges between domestic "republicanism" and what Kant defines as interstate "federalism." The latter differs profoundly from the inward-looking perspectives of Fichte and Rousseau, later replicated by Sun Yat-sen in China. On every continent, splendid examples of a combination between civic republicanism and institutionalized cooperation among states and cultures have emerged. Pan-Africanists such as Henry Sylvester Williams, Kwame Nkrumah, Julius Nyerere, and Kofi Annan (Yusuf 2014) and Pan-Americanists like Simón Bolívar have much to add concerning the synthesis between patriotism, freedom, and regional cooperation. This innovative way forward might lead to a confidence-building process, a trust-building dialogue, while gradually allowing governance beyond the state to be transformed from an instrumental into a binding process. This gradual revision of the traditional Westphalian paradigm is already underway and should be inspired more and more by Mahatma Gandhi's advice: "Relationships are based on four principles: respect, understanding, acceptance, and appreciation."

Notes

1. According to the EU trade commissioner the EU negotiations with individual countries are a stepping stone toward bloc-to-bloc negotiations, which are the objective of the EU trade policy (interview in Brussels, October 16, 2018).
2. China poured more than $86 billion in commercial loans into African governments and state-owned entities between 2000 and 2014, an average of about $6 billion a year. In 2015, at the sixth Forum on China–Africa Cooperation (FOCAC), President Xi Jinping pledged $60 billion in commercial loans to the region, which would increase lending to at least $20 billion per year.
3. "China Watch" (2018) focused on certain priorities in the EU's relationship with China; the parenthetical annotations are mine. (1) *Engagement* (which requires trust);

(2) *reciprocity*, including FDI, trade, and political reciprocity; (3) *security screening* (which is indispensable where China's FDI in strategic sectors of Europe is at stake); (4) *multilateralism* (which requires shared values to move forward); (5) *demands to the rule of law and to defend technological competitiveness*. In this context I would emphasize the interplay between China's foreign policies and its internal fragilities, including a huge public debt, delayed reforms, and the risk of economic crisis.

4. Fawcett, Telò, and Ponjaert (2015) identify three epochs of EU interregionalism and define the features of a post-revisionist approach to interregional relations:

    A   EC/EU interregionalism started with the ACP program in 1957 and the Yaoundé and Lomé conventions as a consequence of the de-colonization process. However, after 1989–91 and the end of the bipolar world, the EU interregional relations became a distinctive feature of external relations at the global level. Hettne (2007) and Rühland (2015) highlight both the differences and the competition between the EU-centered and the US-centered interregional partnerships: on the one hand, the US initiative toward "the emerging markets" (APEC, FTAA, the new Transatlantic Agenda) and, on the other, the EU initiative of the Rio process, the Cotonou convention and ASEM. The EU did feel then like a normative power (Manners 2002) exporting its model of regional integration.

    B   There were some radical revisions at the end of the liberal peace period of the 1990s. The beginning of the new century saw a second period of rejection, linked to both internal EU problems, and the emergence of the BRICS. Both factors strengthened the partners' resistance against the importation of the EU model and spurred the search for new forms of regional and interregional relations. Rejection of EU normative power, alternative cognitive priors (Acharya 2009) and other factors explain this Euro skeptical trend in Southeast Asia, Latin America, and elsewhere.

    C   The current period is best understood as "post-revisionist," because for some years now the EU has been looking for a more modest and balanced approach to interregional relations. With few exceptions, the BRICS revealed their economic strengths and weaknesses as alternative models, while the post-crisis EU appeared to many observers as a still-relevant economic, commercial, and framing power, able to cope with the worst economic crisis of the postwar era and to revive interregional relations. Interregional relations appear most likely to respect the idea of "multiple modernities" (Meyer & Sales Marques 2018), which represents a third way between Western arrogance and relativism.

5. As noted above, the 12th ASEM summit took place in Ulaanbaatar on October 18, 2018 (the first one having been held in Bangkok in 1996) with 51 states participating, including 30 from Europe and 21 from Asia. Regional organizations from both sides also attended. Discussions focused on one controversial topic: "Europe and Asia: global partners for global challenges." Leaders did seek to strengthen dialogue and cooperation between the two continents on a wide range of areas, including trade and investment, connectivity, sustainable development and climate, and security challenges such as terrorism, non-proliferation, cyber-security, and irregular migration. The ASEM summit was followed by the EU–Korea summit and the region-to-region EU–ASEAN leaders' meeting, convened on October 19. Not surprisingly, Europe is trying to diversify its economic and trade portfolio in light of Donald Trump's threats to impose tariffs on European goods and services.

6. Interview in Brussels Press house on October 16, 2018.

7. ASEM provides an excellent case study. European and Asian representatives of civil society-based, transnational networks discussed how to reinforce the interregional and multilateral system. The ASEM parliamentary meeting was hosted by the EP on September 28–29 of 2018 (see the Final Declaration of the Asia–Europe Parliamentary Partnership meeting). The ASEM young leaders' summit focused on ethical leadership.

Asian and European students, as well as young professionals, discussed leadership development over 5 days, from October 15–19, 2018. The Asia–Europe economic forum, focusing on monetary and housing policy, global climate change, international trade, and Asia–Europe connectivity, was hosted by the think tank Bruegel in Brussels on October 17–18. The ASEM business forum, sponsored by *Business Europe* on October 18, 2018, discussed how to strengthen trade and investment relations between the two continents. The ASEM cultural festival took place in Brussels from October 18–30, displaying the creativity and cultural diversity of Asia and Europe through dance, film, music, theater, digital art, and the visual arts.

References

Acharya, A. 2009. *Whose Ideas Matter? Agency and power in Asian regionalism*. Ithaca, NY & London: Cornell University Press

Acharya, A. 2014. *The End of American World Order*. London: Polity

Acharya, A. 2017. *Global Governance in a Multiplex World*. Fiesole, Italy: IUE papers

Allison, G. 2017. *Destined for War*. Melbourne: Scribe

Badie, B. 1999. *Un Monde sans Souveraineté*. Paris: Fayard

Bénéton, P., R. Brague, & C. Delsol, 2018. *La Déclaration de Paris: Une Europe en laquelle nous pouvions croire. Le manifeste!* Paris: Cerf

Bergsten, F. 1994. "APEC and the World Economy." In R. Garnaut & P. Drysdale (eds.), *Asia Pacific Regionalism*. Sydney: Harper, pp. 218–25

Bhagwati, J. 1992. "Regionalism versus Multilateralism." *The World Economy* 15(5): 535–55

Bobbio, N. 1999. "Etat et Democratie Internationale." In M. Telò (ed.), *Démocratie et relations internationals*. Bruxelles: Complexe, pp. 143–58

Bourdieu, P. 1999. "Pour un Movement Social Européen." *Le Monde Diplomatique*, pp. 1–16

"China Watch," 2018. Rhodium Group. Translated into Italian in *Aspenia*, no. 82. Milan, Italy, pp. 13–32

De Benoist, A. 2019. *Contre le libéralisms*. Monaco: Le Rochee

De Block, C. & J. Lebullinger, 2018. *Génération TAFTA/CETA: Les nouveau partenariats de la mondialisation*. Montreal: Université de Montréal, 2018

Debray, R. 2019. *L'Europe Phantôme*. Paris: Gallimard

Ding C., X. Zhang, & M. Telò (eds.), 2018. *Deepening EU-China Partnership. Bridging ideational and institutional differences*. Abingdon, UK: Routledge

Eco, U. 2012. "It's Culture, Not War, that Cements European Identity." *The Guardian*, January 26

Economy, E. 2018. *The Third Revolution; Xi Jinping and the new Chinese state*. Oxford, UK: Oxford University Press

Fawcett, L. & A. Hurrell, 1995. *Regionalism and World Politics*. Cambridge, UK: Cambridge University Press

Fawcett, L., M. Telò, & F. Ponjaert (eds.), 2015. *Interregionalism and the EU*. London: Routledge

Finkielkraut, A. 2016. "Nul n'est Prêt à Mourir pour l'Europe." *Le Point*, June 30

Fitriani, E. 2014. *South East Asians and ASEM*. Singapore: ISEAS

Fukuyama, F. 1992. *The End of History and the Last Man*. New York: Free Press

Gamble, A. 2014. "Regional Blocs, World Order, and New Medievalism." In M. Telò (ed.), *EU and New Regionalism*. Burlington, VT: Ashgate, pp. 21–36

Gamble, A. 2020. "The Crisis of the Western Liberal Order and the Rise of New Populism." In T. Meyer, M. Telò, & J. de Sales Marques (eds.), *Cultures, Nationalism, and Populism: New Challenges to Multilateralism*. Abingdon, UK, & New York: Routledge, pp. 133–46

Gamble, A. & A. Payne (eds.), 1996. *Regionalism and World Order.* London: Red Globe
Glencross, A. & A. Trechsel (eds.), 2010. *EU Federalism and Constitutionalism: The legacy of Spinelli.* London: Lexington
Haass, R. 2008. "The Age of Non-polarity: What will follow the US dominance." *Foreign Affairs* 87(3). Available at www.foreignaffairs.com/articles/world/2017-02-13/internet-whole-and-free
Habermas, J. 2001. "A Constitution for Europe?" *New Left Review* 11: 1–15
Hassner, P. 1991. "L'Europe et le Spectre des Nationalismes." *Esprit*, October issue, pp. 5–20
Held, D. 1995. *Democracy and Global Order.* Cambridge, UK: Polity
Hettne, B. 2003. "The New Regionalism Revisited." In F. Söderbaum and T. Shaw (eds.), *Theories of New Regionalism. A Palgrave Reader.* Basingstoke, UK: Palgrave Macmillan, pp. 22–24
Hettne, B. 2007. "Interregionalism and World Order: The diverging EU and US models." In M. Telò (ed.), *EU and New Regionalism.* Burlington, VT: Ashgate, pp. 75–105
Hettne, B., 2008. "Regionalism and World Order." In M. Farrell, B. Hettne, & L. Van Langenhore (eds.), *Global Politics of Regionalism.* London: Pluto Press, pp. 269–86
Hettne, B., A, Inotai, & O. Sunkel (eds.), 2001. *Comparative Regionalism.* London: Palgrave
Hull, C. 1948. *The Memoirs of Cordell Hull.* 2 vols. New York: Macmillan
Huntington, S. 1996. *The Clash of Civilizations and the Remaking of World Order.* New York: Simon & Schuster
Ikenberry, J. & D. Deudney, 2018. "Liberal World: The resilient order." *Foreign Affairs* 94(4): 1–15
Jancic, D. 2019. "The Role of the EP in EU-China Relations." Collège of Bruge Conference, Brussels
Katzenstein, P. 2005. *A World of Regions.* Ithaca, NY: Cornell University Press
Keohane, R. 1984/2004. *After Hegemony.* Princeton, NJ: Princeton University Press
Keohane, R. 2015. "Contested Multilateralism." In J. Morin, T. Novotna, F. Ponjaert, & M. Telò (eds.), *The Politics of Transatlantic Trade Negotiations.* Burlington, VT: Routledge, pp. 17–27
Keohane, R. & J. Nye (eds.), 2014. *Transnational Relations and World Politics.* Cambridge, MA: Harvard University Press
Kupchan, C. 2012. *No One's World.* Oxford, UK: Oxford University Press
Malmström, C. 2015. "Trade for All." Brussels: Report of EU Commission, pp. 10–20
Manners, I. 2002. "Normative Power Europe: A contradiction in terms?" *Journal of Common Market Studies* 40(2): 235–58
Marramao, G., P. Baler, S. Franchi, A. Lantz, M. Jay, M. Marchesmi, A. Moreiras, P. Palou, C. Rodrigues, T. Vilaros, & H. White, 2015. "On Giacomo Marramao's 'The Passage West.'" *Politica Commun,* special issue 8. Ann Arbor, MI: University of Michigan Press
Meyer, T. & J. de Sales Marques (eds.), 2018. *Multiple Modernities and Good Governance.* London & New York: Routledge
Meyer, T., J. de Sales Marques, and M. Telò (eds.), 2019. *Cultures, Nationalism and Populism: New Challenges for Multilaterlism.* London & New York: Routledge
Morin, J., T. Novotna, F. Ponjaert, & M. Telò (eds.), 2015. *The Politics of Transatlantic Trade Negotiations.* Burlington, VT: Routledge
Onfray, M. 2017. *Décadence: Vie et mort du judéo-christianisme.* Paris: Flammarion
Patrick, S. 2009. *The Best Laid Plans.* Lanham, MD: Rowman & Littlefield
Qin, Y. 2007. "Why is There No Chinese International Relations Theory?" *International Relations of the Asia-Pacific* 7(3): 40–62
Qin, Y. 2018. *A Relational Theory of World Politics.* Cambridge, UK: Cambridge University Press

Risse, T. & T Börzel (eds.), 2016. *The Oxford Handbook of Comparative Regionalism.* Oxford, UK: Oxford University Press

Rüland, J. 2006. "Interregionalism: An unfinished agenda." In H. Hänggi, R. Roloff, & J. Rüland (eds.), *Interregionalism and International Relations.* London: Routledge, pp. 295–313

Rüland, J. 2015. "The Unintended Consequences of Interregional Democracy Promotion: Normative and conceptual misunderstanding in EU-ASEAN relations." In M. Telò & L. Fawcett (eds.), *Interregionalism and the European Union.* Abington, UK: Routledge, pp. 267–83

Ruggie, J. (ed.), 1993. *Multilateralism Matters.* New York: Columbia University Press

Santander, S. 2016. *Concurrences Régionales dans un Monde Multipolaire Emergent.* Bruxelles: Peter Lang AG

Scharpf, F. 2015. "After the Crash: A perspective on multilevel European democracy." *European Law Journal* 21(3): 384–405

Soederbaum, F., F. Baert, & T. Scaramagli (eds.), 2016. *Intersecting Interregionalism.* Doedrecht, The Netherlands: Springer

Streeck, W. 2013. *Buying Time: The delayed crisis of democratic capitalism."* London & New York: Verso

Telò, M. (ed.) 2001/2007/2014. *European Union and New Regionalism.* Burlington, VT: Ashgate

Telò, M. (ed.), 2014. *Globalization, Multilateralism, Europe: Towards a better global governance.* Burlington, VT: Ashgate

Telò, M. 2016. *Regionalism in Hard Times: Competitive and post-liberal trends in Europe, Asia, Africa, and the Americas,* Abingdon, UK: Routledge

Telò, M. 2017. "The Emerging Conflict between Democratic Legitimacy and the EU's Common Commercial Policy Risks for the EU as a Civilian Power and for the Multilateral order." *Annals of the Fondazione Einaudi,* January 12: Turin

Telò, M. 2018. "L'EU Face à la Multiplication des Interconnections Commerçiales Inter-régionales et à Leurs Implications Politiques." In C. De Block (ed.), *Generation TAFTA: Les nouveaux partenariats de la mondialisations.* Rennes, France: Presses Universitaires de Rennes, pp. 37–55

Tercovich, G. 2019. *The EU Interregional Influence in Comparison: The case of institutionalization of ASEAN disaster management.* PhD dissertation. GEM program, Université Libre de Bruxelles & Warwick University

Yan, X. 2011. *Ancient Chinese Thought, Modern Chinese Power.* Princeton, NJ: Princeton University Press

Yan, X. 2019. *Leadership and the Rise of Great Powers.* Princeton, NJ: Princeton University Press

Yusuf, A. 2014. *Pan-Africanism and International Law.* The Hague: Academy

Zhao, T. 2016. *A Possible World of All Under Heaven System: The world order in the past and for the future.* Beijing: CITIC Press Group

PART II
History and drivers of regional cooperation
Trade, identity, security

5

THE FUTURE OF REGIONALISM

Competing varieties of regional cooperation

Andrew Gamble

The world faces at least two major existential challenges this century: the continuing threat of nuclear war and the newer looming threat of irreversible climate change (Cerutti 2007). Until recently, there has been widespread agreement that if human societies are to have any chance of meeting these challenges, they must build on and extend the fragile forms of multilateral cooperation among states that have been achieved in the last 70 years. One form that multilateral cooperation has taken in recent decades, particularly since 1991, is regionalism. A variety of regionalist projects emerged in different parts of the world, with varying levels of integration and ambition. They tended to be examples of open regionalism in the sense that they were mostly outward-looking instead of inward-looking and were therefore compatible with, rather than antagonistic to, globalism. Many of those who theorized the new regionalism saw these regionalists projects as stepping stones to forms of cooperation at the global level (Fawcett & Hurrell 1995; Gamble & Payne 1995; Hettne & Soderbaum 2000; Hettne et al. 2001; Telò 2014). The existence of distinct regionalisms in different parts of the world encouraged the development of interregionalism: dialogue between representatives of the different regionalisms about how to learn from each other's experience and how to coordinate their policies.

In more optimistic times, open forms of regionalism and the promotion of interregionalism appeared to foreshadow a new kind of world order, one that moved beyond the need for a single state to play the role of hegemon to guarantee international cooperation within a framework of rules (Kindleberger 1987; Gilpin 2001) and also beyond the idea that only one form of modernity and modernization was either possible or desirable. Western-centric notions of modernity increasingly have been challenged, both intellectually and politically. The rapid development of China and India since the end of the Cold War irreversibly transformed the future character of the world system. Modernity and development no longer remain the virtual monopoly of a small club of Western nations. Just as there are many globalizations, so too are there are multiple modernities (Eisenstadt 2003; Meyer 2018). Although some common economic and technological features are shared by all forms of modernity, these increasingly are accompanied by cultural divergences in regard to social and political organization.

This fact has led to what Peter Katzenstein, in Chapter 1 of this volume, has called "constrained diversity." The economic and technological transformations of the world associated with capitalism created complex networks of economic interdependence that have increased over time and have constrained the choices of all human societies. But while the economic and social intercourse of the world population has increased, political authority has remained fragmented into separate and often rival jurisdictions, each claiming sovereignty over a territory and a people. The dynamic between these two forces creates cycles of cooperation and conflict that have played out in every era (Wallerstein 1974). Modernity has always been characterized by unevenness; periods of smooth progression and relative peace, harmony, and prosperity have given way to periods of economic and political turmoil and frequently wars, during which many of the gains of earlier times have been sacrificed.

On the whole, harmonious relations characterized the period after 1991. It was a time when globalization reached its full extent, when the balance of the world economy fundamentally shifted, and when the Western project of modernity and modernization temporarily seemed to be triumphant, ostensibly ushering in a period of liberal peace in which all nations would cooperate within the framework of a new world order regulated and policed by the United States. Regionalist projects emerged, expanding and forging links to take advantage of opportunities created by the breakdown of the bipolar superpower rivalry. However, this relatively benign period did not last. New local and regional wars, as well as the willingness of the US and its allies to pursue wars of liberal intervention to reshape parts of the world deemed resistant to the new order, changed the political atmosphere. Still, regionalism and interregionalism continued to grow. But a much more significant change took place in 2008 with the financial crash and subsequent recession, which was followed by a very slow recovery, and the increasing resort to austerity to push the consequences of the financial collapse onto households and public services (Gamble 2014; Streeck 2014).

In the years since the crash, even the most successful and longest established regionalist projects have looked vulnerable because they have no longer been able to count on the stable institutional framework of a world order guaranteed by the United States. That framework has come under pressure from two directions. The first of these has been the inability and unwillingness of the major players, including the US, to agree to new rules and structures for global governance that would reflect a world of multiple modernities and the much more equal balance of economic and financial capacity among the great powers. The second is the insurgency within Western societies themselves against globalism, multiculturalism, the rule of law, and the principles of a liberal order. The new cultural divides within the West threaten the project of a liberal world order from within (Müller 2016; Mudde & Kaltwasser 2017; Zielonka 2018).

These developments have posed serious challenges to emergent regionalism. Some regionalist projects are in danger of either foundering or becoming defensive and protectionist. Open regionalism once seemed part of the solution to a transition to a new kind of world order, one that acknowledged multiple modernities and the need to find a common core through dialogue to make possible international cooperation in global governance. Although that possibility continues to exist, the rise of populist nationalism at the very least has complicated it. There is a risk that regionalism turns inward and becomes increasingly closed.

In this chapter, I first review the different historical phases in the development of regionalism, noting how closely tied open regionalism has been to a globalist project and the provision of public goods by a hegemonic power. I then consider the prospects for regionalism in a world without a hegemon and with a culturally divided and fragmenting West.

Regionalism in the 1930s

Regionalism has passed through several phases since 1900. Before 1914 there were examples of regional cooperation and many regional identities, but little that would be described today as political projects seeking to promote regional cooperation or regional integration among a number of states. Instead, the world was dominated by Western colonial empires and rivalry between the great powers. The modernization unleashed by industrialization in Europe and the consequent competition for trade, resources, and population saw the emergence of a Eurocentric world order presided over by Great Britain as the dominant industrial, commercial, financial, and naval power. Britain played a key role in establishing rules and norms for international trade and finance. While the country's unilateral free trade policy did not apply to its own empire, which was a protected sphere for British manufacturers and involved the destruction of much local industry, it did help to establish a greatly expanded sphere of trade and commerce. The opportunities that Britain gave other developed countries to sell food and raw materials into its domestic market created an international commercial society: an informal empire that was not territorially based and therefore was not under Britain's direct control. The advantages conferred upon Britain included the acceptance of sterling as the international currency and the demand for the financial and commercial services organized from London. Thus, without it having been in any way the conscious design of British policy, the basis for a rudimentary multilateral world order was created. Only a small number of countries ever became full participants, and some of them, notably Germany and the United States, broke the rules by protecting their industries with very high tariffs to allow them to develop free from British competition. Britain itself had no way of enforcing its rules or making others abide by them. Though it was proud of its empire of free trade, it grew even prouder of its territorial empire, which shared with the other European empires the belief in the superiority of European civilization. Very few non-Western states avoided penetration and subjugation by the Western powers. Japan remained the main exception, achieving its independent status by ruthlessly suppressing many aspects of its traditional culture and embracing European models of modernization (Moore 1967).

Britain enjoyed naval but not overall military superiority over the other great powers, and Germany's challenge to its hegemony brought about the collapse of this original liberal world order in the carnage of World War I (Kennedy 1983). Attempts to restore that order during the 1920s failed and, following the 1929 financial crash and the 1931 collapse of the gold standard, the world fragmented into rival currency, trading, and military blocs. Several of these blocs were regional in nature, formed around regional hegemons like the United States, Germany, the USSR, and Japan. France and Britain maintained global empires, and Britain in particular had never been a regional power, except in relation to the UK itself. The blocs were highly protectionist and jealous of one another, and sought to expand by taking over territory of their rivals. This led inexorably to a war on an even greater scale than in 1914–18. Germany's principal aim during World War II was to destroy the USSR and subjugate its population, while Japan aimed to seize the Eastern territories of European Empires and create a co-prosperity sphere controlled from Tokyo.

Regionalism during the Cold War

In 1945 the Axis powers were defeated, and the closed regional blocs they had tried to construct fell apart. Although the United States was the undisputed victor, another major regional bloc, the USSR, was greatly strengthened by the war and its victory over Germany, and proceeded to make Eastern and Central Europe its own co-prosperity sphere. The European colonial empires never recovered from the defeats and humiliations they had suffered at the hands of the Axis. Decolonization proceeded apace, and within three decades of the end of World War II formal empires had almost entirely disappeared. A novel mosaic of regions and independent states emerged, key elements of the new multilateral and multicultural world, signaling the possibility of multiple modernities rather than just a single variety.

This new political condition took time to emerge. After 1945 the liberal international order was reconstructed under US leadership. The US was firmly against the continuation of regional blocs and generally hostile toward the colonial empires, which it regarded as forms of closed regionalism. Accordingly, it encouraged the dissolution of the colonial empires and inaugurated an era characterized by freer movement of goods, capital, and people. American hegemony proved a much more comprehensive and intrusive form of domination than the British ever had exercised (O'Brien 2003). But it was still very much a Western phenomenon, committed to a Western version of modernity and the concomitant belief that Western civilization was inherently superior to all others, albeit without some of the overt racist discourses of the European empires.

The United States was not encumbered by a formal empire, and after its involvement in World War II no longer thought of itself primarily as a regional power. Its global hegemony did not extend to the Soviet Union, which organized itself like a pre-war regional hegemon, dominating a closed regional bloc, sealing off its territory and population from the rest of the world, and engaging in military and ideological rivalry with the US. One of the strengths of the United States in this contest was precisely that it was not a closed regional bloc. Its hegemony rested on the public goods it provided through sustaining a liberal world order in which all non-Communist states were free to participate, and on the network of security alliances it used to project its power around the globe (Ikenberry 2011).

Within the Western liberal order, the US encouraged regionalist projects as a way of building cooperation between its allies in different parts of the world. It participated directly in security regionalist organizations such as the North Atlantic Treaty Organization (NATO) and the Southeast Asia Treaty Organization (SEATO), but not in organizations that were primarily economic, like the European Economic Community that eventually developed into the EU. In American eyes, the difference between these kinds of regionalist projects and the closed regional blocs of the past was that the former fit within the US globalist project; rather, they were compatible with it and did not pose a fundamental challenge. The politicians and political parties that led them were firmly committed to political and military alliances with the United States and accepted the constraints and disciplines of joining in the trade and commercial and investment opportunities offered by the liberal world order. The United States became keen to foster regional cooperation and the formation of regional identities between states, especially when they had been bitter enemies in the recent past, like Germany and France. Such countries became an important part of building a unified "West" under American leadership. The US supported moves to add more members to the European Economic Community (EEC); in particular, it was a strong advocate of Britain's membership, and remained so consistently over four decades. But its support always assumed that these projects would be compatible with the global policy that the US wished to pursue. They would not threaten or obstruct it, but rather would be complementary and supportive.

Regionalism after the Cold War

With the collapse of the USSR in 1991, a third phase of regionalism opened, which became known as the new regionalism. A new international order was proclaimed: the return of "One World" and "the end of history" (Fukuyama 1989). One World evoked memories of the political and economic situation that prevailed before 1914, only this time it meant an environment in which there were no significant challenges to the rules-based Western liberal paradigm presided over by the United States. Some even predicted the rise of a borderless world in which nation-states—aside from the US itself—would wither away (Ohmae 1999). The reunification of the world economy, the opening up of previously closed areas to trade and investment, and most significantly the emergence of new rising powers like China, India, and Brazil began to transform the distribution of power and influence in the global economy. It also made possible the emergence and extension of many regionalist initiatives—some long established like the EU, but others much newer like the Association of Southeast Asian Nations (ASEAN) and the Southern Common Market (MERCOSUR).

In 1991, the world appeared for a brief time to be unipolar, with only one superpower, the United States, which was dominant across the board. But this pattern quickly began to change as the balance in the world economy was transformed and the relative decline in the US position became more and more apparent. For the first time in the modern era, the possibility arose of an international order that was not Western- or Eurocentric, but that might include all the world's major states in its governance and might recognize that there was not just one way to be modern but many. Increasingly, the prospect of a world order for the future was seen to depend on whether a form of governance and cooperation could be devised that was able to cope with multiple modernities and a multipolar rather than unipolar environment.

The regionalist projects that developed in the 1990s were not at all like those of the 1930s. Committed to open regionalism, they were regarded as building blocks for multilateral interregionalism as well as multilateral global institutions. They were seen not as rivaling US power but as complementing it, working within the rules-based order and its institutions that the US had done so much to create and sustain. But tensions began to develop as the regionalist projects took advantage of the more relaxed security atmosphere of the 1990s. American resentment of what it perceived as free-riding by some of its former allies, and disagreements over regulations for important sectors such as agricultural production, ensued. Regionalism was seen as a way to give regional economies greater independence, resisting economic pressures from the United States where necessary. It suggested a return to the greater diversity of the 1950s, the era of so-called "embedded liberalism" (Ruggie 1998). But embedded liberalism had been tolerated and even promoted by the United States at a time when its greatest priority was to weld the Western nations into a cohesive alliance against the Soviet Union. Much of that tolerance for diversity had disappeared in the reconstruction of the world order along neo-liberal lines during the 1970s and 1980s. Its re-emergence in the 1990s was not altogether welcome to the United States, and long before Donald Trump was elected president, strong currents of political opinion in the United States began to urge that the country was bearing too many burdens and should pursue a policy of "America First" (Rapkin 2005).

The new regional groupings were not states and thus lacked the capacity or the will to challenge the position of the US. But their growing importance in international politics led the US to launch its own bid for interregional partnerships, particularly with Asian countries, but also in its own hemisphere, with NAFTA. By the end of the Obama presidency the United States was pursuing ambitious interregional agreements through the Transpacific Partnership (TPP) and the Transatlantic Trade and Investment Partnership (TTIP). These were seen both as ways of restarting growth after the 2008 financial crash and of restoring US power and leadership in two crucial regions of the world economy.

Regionalism after the crash

The triumphalism that followed the end of the Cold War in 1991 was short-lived. Challenges quickly emerged, which showed the limits of US power in the new world order. The US became embroiled in costly and relatively unsuccessful wars, while the advance of globalization meant that the balance of power in the world economy began to shift away from the West. The 2008 crash and the subsequent recession and painfully slow recovery further weakened American leadership, because the United States lacked the capacity to restore its old dominance and at the same time lacked the political will to make the compromises necessary to facilitate the transition to a world order that was appropriate to the times. If it were to reflect the new geopolitical and political economy realities, such an order would have to be based on sharing responsibility for the governance of the international system with established regional blocs like the EU as well as with rising powers, particularly China and India. Some moves were made in this direction. The G-20 (Group of Twenty) received a higher status, and the newly established Financial Stability Board gave authority to central banks to devise a framework of financial regulation designed to prevent another financial crash (Mackintosh 2017). But little more proved possible, and other initiatives stalled. A decade after the crash there were no signs that the G20 was about to become the forum where deals could be brokered and decisions made to improve the rules of the world order and foster cooperative, multilateral solutions to existing problems.

Even the limited progress that had been made before 2016 was quickly reversed with the election of Donald Trump in November of 2016. The advent of the Trump administration signaled a new phase in the evolution of the world order and the role of the United States within it. President Trump was hostile to globalization and free trade, which he blamed for US decline, and was also a critic of many of the postwar institutions and alliances by means of which the US had secured its power and influence. Through his words and actions both during the presidential campaign and since taking office, he showed a strong preference for bilateral arrangements with other states (Laderman & Simms 2017). During his first 2 years in office he withdrew from numerous treaty obligations and regularly disparaged multilateral institutions. He encouraged populist nationalist forces seeking to break up the EU and defined China as the major strategic competitor of the United States, launching a trade war in a bid to contain China and blunt its rise. By the end of 2018, Trump's policies had begun to unsettle global markets because of the mutual dependence of China and the United States in terms of markets, production chains, and the management of debt. At one level, Trump's policies represented a return to nativist, protectionist, isolationist strands in US political culture (Mead 2002), but on another level they were an astute recognition of the long-term decline of the US and what needed to be done to reverse that trend or at least limit the damage. Accordingly, Trump sought to break up multilateral institutions and reframe US relationships with other countries in bilateral terms so that the US once again might dominate the global scene.

This "America First" policy of the Trump administration is an attempt to restore US power, which has been seriously eroded over the last two decades. But the methods chosen to accomplish that goal involve destroying or undermining many of the institutions which successive US administrations forged since 1945 to create an encompassing rules-based order. These include many of the regionalist projects that often were directly supported and promoted by the US. In this respect, among others, the Trump administration displays a strong contrast to its predecessors. It is instinctively opposed to regionalist projects like the EU, which it sees as undermining American power, and it would prefer to deal with EU states on an individual basis, rather than as a unified bloc. This explains why Trump welcomed the British vote to leave the EU, and why he supports populist nationalists in other parts of Europe. If the US is successful in encouraging national populist challengers to multinational institutions, the EU and other regional trade associations could disintegrate. The Trump team seeks a much more hierarchical structure of international relations, one in which the US deals with other states as their clear superior. By contrast, successful regionalist projects establish the conditions for multilateralism and mutual respect in international relations.

Since his election Trump has enjoyed disrupting the rules-based international order, undermining traditional allies, and forging close bilateral ties with autocratic rulers and authoritarian regimes. Although the increasingly fragmented world economy, the threats to prosperity and democracy, and the rising tensions did not originate with Trump, his administration has significantly added to them. After initial amazement that a United States president could be behaving in such a destructive way, US allies have shown increasing resistance. Regionalist projects in particular have been defended because suddenly their value appears in a new light: as a bulwark against a hegemon that is behaving capriciously and only in its own self-interest. More and more, the US is perceived by most of the international community as no longer interested in providing the public goods on which the world had come to rely. The difficult question for other states to answer is whether this is a temporary phenomenon that will cease with Donald Trump's presidency or whether it marks a permanent shift in US policy.

The challenge of populist nationalism

Regionalism is threatened by a United States no longer interested in sustaining the rules-based multilateral framework that had made open regionalism possible. It is also threatened by the surge in populist nationalism mobilized against established elites and governments, a phenomenon that has been growing in intensity since the 2008 financial crash and the austerity measures instituted in its wake. What is novel is that the two biggest successes of this illiberal insurgency so far have occurred in the two states that once were the most committed to the creation and sustaining of a liberal world order: the United States as the global hegemon and Great Britain as the former hegemon. There is no likelihood of a return to the regionalist blocs of the 1930s or the Cold War era. Globalization and internationalization have made the world too interdependent for that. But in this new aggressive climate, the jealousy of trade and investment that had been a key driver of state competition since the beginnings of modern commercial society is set to intensify (Hont 2010).

That sobering fact has conflicting implications for the future of regionalism. In many areas of the world where regionalist institutions are not firmly rooted, we can discern a tendency for states to fall back on emphasizing their national sovereignty and abandon regional cooperation, except in very basic forms. This seems to be the pattern in Latin America, the Middle East, Africa, and South Asia alike. But in some areas of the world, regionalist institutions may strengthen in order to increase their competitive edge against other actors, particularly against some of the most powerful states. The EU, if it withstands the populist nationalist surge and finds a way to deal with its most pressing internal problems such as migration and the euro, could still emerge stronger from the present period, a multilateral island in a sea of competing nationalisms, although many analysts are pessimistic about its chances of success (Kearns 2018). In Eurasia, the Eurasian Economic Union (EAEU) increasingly sees itself as a rival to the EU rather than as a partner. This kind of regionalism is no longer part of a move toward wider multilateral cooperation but instead a vehicle for strategic competition with rival blocs. China offers a third model. It is pushing ahead rapidly with its own regional partnership, the Belt and Road Initiative, which underlines both its growing power and reach and its ability to pursue policies independently of the US, forging relations with other states and regions.

The rise of China, the weakening of Eurocentrism, and the apparent eagerness of the US to disengage from its former hegemonic role all make this period significantly different from anything that has preceded it. While there is a superficial comparison with the Cold War between the US and the USSR, that rivalry was primarily military and territorial in nature. Except for a brief period, the USSR never looked like a credible challenger to the economic superiority of the United States. China, by contrast, is a strategic competitor in a different way. Its challenge is primarily economic rather than military, although military rivalry is growing.

Like the USSR in the 1950s, it offers an alternative model to the US, a pole of attraction that is already winning influence both within China's own region and beyond. What that also provides is space for other regionalist initiatives and projects, with or without explicit Chinese sponsorship. We are seeing an increasing variety of regionalist cooperation as a result. Chinese soft power is much less developed than that of the United States, but this may start to change unless Trump's policies are reversed.

The problem for all forms of regional cooperation is that if an overarching framework of multilateral institutions that are supported by all or most of the leading powers no longer exists, regionalisms either tend to turn inward and become defensive or they become defunct. This is particularly true now that trade wars once again are used as instruments of state policy and lauded as easy to win. Open regionalisms have thrived most when there is a globalist project to which they can relate. A return to the fragmentation of political authority into territorial sovereign jurisdictions will produce an order of a sort, but at the cost of further hindering the development of multilateral cooperation to deal with global challenges. In a world of multiple modernities, regionalism at its best can promote such cooperation, both by providing models for how similar states within a region can cooperate and also by making possible forms of interregional dialogue.

Varieties of regionalism

The brief moment after 1991, when it seemed that the dream of One World might be in reach after all the bitter divisions and conflicts of the twentieth century, was always illusory. The globe is too fragmented and diverse for any simple unity imposed by one power on the rest ever to be viable for long. But few expected that within two decades of the end of the Cold War, the international system once again would be moving away from cooperation by electing leaders and adopting policies to undermine the achievements of multilateralism, which had been so painfully won. These changes have been depicted as an insurgency of the people forgotten by globalization, the left-behind middle-income citizens who had lost faith in their elites and felt threatened culturally and economically by the pace of change and the influx of immigrants. But although this is a factor in the rise of populist nationalism, it overlooks how from the start this has been a contest between elites. Many of the leaders of the populist nationalists see themselves as part of a transnational anti-globalist movement. They are bitter enemies of what they call the globalist elite, but that is only because they are aiming to replace the existing elite with their own.

The new political climate of fragmentation and division is affecting all types of political regimes, including regionalist ones. Just as there are different worlds of welfare, varieties of capitalism, and multiple modernities, so now more than in the past we can see different forms of regionalism.

The first of these is minimalist, or lowest common denominator, regionalism. Minimalist regionalism puts renewed emphasis on state sovereignty, and remains hostile to any further pooling of sovereignty or wider cooperation. Here the regionalist projects are scaled back and regional cooperation is in retreat. The fate of NAFTA is an illustration. It has been renamed US–Mexico–Canada Agreement (USMCA) to reflect Donald Trump's insistence on America First, although Justin Trudeau, still committed to salvage what he can of multilateral cooperation, refers to it as the new North American Free Trade Agreement.

A second form of regionalism is illiberal and authoritarian. Illiberal regionalism is both defensive and protectionist. It favors policies that harden borders and place obstacles in the way of trade and investment. Closed rather than open, such regionalism promotes rivalry rather than cooperation. The aim is to enhance the strength of the regional association in order to deploy it as a weapon against other states and other regional associations. The EAEU provides a salient example. After its founding in 1994, there were strong hopes that it might become complementary to the EU and form part of an interregional dialogue, but in the last decade relations have become increasingly confrontational as the EAEU has become an arm of Russian foreign policy.

A third form of regionalism is being developed around China, in a series of regional partnerships linked together by the Belt and Road Initiative. China is now once again the dominant economic and political force in its region, and what is not yet clear is whether the regionalism that the Chinese state fosters will be genuinely multilateral and consensual or whether it will be used to project Chinese power. China has an opportunity to build a different kind of regionalism from Western varieties, whether minimalist, liberal, or illiberal, and if it succeeds in doing so it may greatly increase its soft power and the attractiveness of its model to other countries of the world. The developing strategic competition between China and the US is likely to damage multilateralism at the global level, but may allow space for a wider variety of regionalist initiatives, both those linked to the two major powers and those independent of them.

The fourth form of regionalism is liberal and multilateralist. Here the EU remains the main example. At one time there seemed a prospect that the EU would be the model for regionalisms around the world, but today there is much less confidence in the possibility or desirability of such an outcome. Liberal regionalism faces many challenges, which (as argued above) are both external and internal. The world's great powers—the United States, Russia, and increasingly China—have an interest in seeing the dissolution or at least the weakening of the EU so that bilateral relations can be developed with individual member states. Breaking the will of the EU member states to act together was also the hope of some of the more enthusiastic proponents of a hard Brexit in the United Kingdom. But these external challenges, as Brexit shows, increase the likelihood that the EU will become more united rather than less so. The internal challenge, however, may prove more difficult to contain. The rise of populist nationalism in many EU countries and the establishment of illiberal democracies in several East European states, notably Hungary, mean that the character of the EU as a liberal regionalism is in peril. Victory by populist nationalists in both national elections and elections to the European Parliament eventually could tip the EU's political balance. If the Council of Ministers were to become dominated by national leaders like Matteo Salvini and Marine Le Pen, and the European Parliament by populist nationalist parties, then the EU (assuming it were able to hold together) would move away from liberal toward illiberal regionalism. For the moment, however, the EU continues to provide the clearest example of liberal regionalism, and as such is a target of attack for anti-globalists and authoritarians everywhere.

Conclusion

Like the liberal world order, regionalism is being remade under the pressures of continuing economic turbulence and political upheavals. If something more hopeful is to emerge from the present travails, the institutional experience and institutional memory of the open regionalisms that emerged over the last 60 years and particularly in the last 30 will be an important resource (Telò 2017). One lesson is that open regionalisms will find it hard to survive if there is no credible globalist project to uphold a type of world order that recognizes the existence of multiple modernities and sustains institutions that promote dialogue and multilateral negotiations. Such a project only makes sense under present circumstances if it is founded on agreement on a common core of principles and rules for governing the world order (Kagan 2018). The current weakening in the ability of any country or group of countries to supply the public goods that the world economy so badly needs and the renewed emphasis on territorial sovereignty alert us to the difficulty of the present task. Multilateral cooperation has become more difficult under present circumstances, but in a world of multiple modernities there is no other recourse if human societies are not to repeat some of the mistakes of the past.

References

Cerutti, F. 2007. *Global Challenges for Leviathan: A political philosophy of nuclear weapons and global warming*. Lanham, MD: Lexington Books

Eisenstadt, S. 2003. *Comparative Civilisations and Multiple Modernities*. Leiden, UK: Brill

Fawcett, L. & A. Hurrell, 1995. *Regionalism in World Politics: Regional organization and international order*. New York: Oxford University Press

Fukuyama, F. 1989. "The End of History?" *The National Interest* 16: 3–18

Gamble, A. 2014. *Crisis without end? The unravelling of western prosperity*. London: Palgrave

Gamble, A. & A. Payne (eds.), 1995. *Regionalism and World Order*. London: Palgrave

Gilpin, R. 2001. *Global Political Economy: Understanding the international economic order*. Princeton, NJ: Princeton University Press

Hettne, B. & F. Soderbaum, 2000. "Theorising the Rise of Regionness." *New Political Economy* 5(3): 457–72

Hettne, B., A. Inotai, & O. Sunkel, 2001. *Comparing Regionalisms: Implications for global development*. New York: Palgrave

Hont, I. 2010. *Jealousy of Trade: International competition and the nation-state in comparative perspective*. Cambridge, MA: Harvard University Press

Ikenberry, J. 2011. *Liberal Leviathan: The origins, crisis and transformation of the American world order*. Princeton, NJ: Princeton University Press

Kagan, R. 2018. *The Jungle Grows Back: America and our imperilled world*. New York: Knopf

Kearns, I. 2018. *Collapse: Europe after the European Union*. London: Biteback

Kennedy, P. 1983. *The Rise and Fall of British Naval Mastery*. London: Macmillan

Kindleberger, C. 1987. *The World in Depression*. London: Penguin

Laderman, C. & B. Simms, 2017. *Donald Trump: The making of a world view*. London: Endeavour Press

Mackintosh, S. 2017. *The Redesign of the Global Financial Architecture: The return of state authority*. London: Routledge

Mead, W.R. 2002. *Special Providence: American foreign policy and how it changed the world*. New York: Routledge

Meyer, T. 2018. "Multiple Modernities and Good Governance." In T. Meyer & J. de Sales Marques (eds.), *Multiple Modernities and Good Governance*. London & New York: Routledge, pp. 15–28

Moore, B. 1967. *The Social Origins of Dictatorship and Democracy*. Boston, MA: Beacon Press

Mudde, C. & C. Kaltwasser. 2017. *Populism: A very short introduction*. New York: Oxford University Press

Müller, J.-W. 2016. *What is Populism?* Philadelphia, PA: University of Pennsylvania Press

O'Brien, P. 2003. "The Myth of Anglophone Succession." *New Left Review* 24: 113–34

Ohmae, K. 1999. *The Borderless World: Power and strategy in the interlinked economy*. New York: Harper Business

Rapkin, D. 2005. "Empire and its Discontents." *New Political Economy* 10(3): 389–412

Ruggie, J. 1998. *Constructing the World Polity: Essays on international institutionalisation*. London: Routledge

Streeck, W. 2014. *Buying Time: The delayed crisis of democratic capitalism*. London: Verso

Telò, M. 2014. *European Union and New Regionalism: Competing regionalism and global governance in a post-hegemonic era*. Farnham, UK: Ashgate

Telò, M. 2017. *Regionalism in Hard Times*. London: Routledge

Wallerstein, I. 1974. *The Modern World System*. New York: Academic Press

Zielonka, J. 2018. *Counter Revolution: Liberal Europe in retreat*. Oxford, UK: Oxford University Press

6

THE EVOLUTION OF COMPETITIVE LATIN–AMERICAN REGIONALISM

Louise Fawcett

Introduction

In 1996, the University of Buenos Aires instituted a 2-year master's degree program in Regional Integration Processes. That program features the study of the problems and opportunities of regional integration with a specifically Latin American and comparative focus. The degree places heavy emphasis on one of the region's then brand-new organization of which Argentina was a founding member, the Mercado Común del Sur or MERCOSUR (www.economicas.uba.ar/posgrado/posgrados/procesos-de-integracion-regional/).

The fact that a leading Latin American university should offer such a course at such a time is unsurprising. After all, that was the age of the "new regionalism," and—in a world of global regionalisms (Farrell *et al.* 2005) and with the refashioned, ostensibly portable European Union (EU) very much at the forefront of the theory and practice of regionalism—the effort to spread the word and study regional processes on one's home continent was both natural and desirable. Latin America in general, and Argentina (as a leading regional state) in particular, were an important part of that development. Buenos Aires is but one of a number of universities around the world that today offer a degree in regional integration targeted specifically to its region. Though Europe led the way in that regard, there are other courses on regional integration in far-flung academic institutions. These include the University of Cape Verde in Africa (www.unicv.edu.cv/en/unicv/3341-mira-eng) and the Institute of European Studies at Macau (IEEM) in Southeast Asia, which was established in 2016 with the explicit aim of serving as a bridge between Europe and the Asia–Pacific region (www.ieem.org.mo/about/index).

The above point is an important one in the context of this chapter, for it focuses attention on one particular type of regionalism at a time when there were multiple options—both competing and complementary—on the table, such as the bold hemispheric project, the Free Trade Area of the Americas (FTAA), and other sub-regionalisms, including ones in the Caribbean, Central America, and the Andean countries. Thus, the privileging of MERCOSUR in the above context opens up many questions about the nature and purposes of Latin American regionalisms, past, present, and future, and their relationships with one another and with wider multilateral processes. These relationships and their implications for regionalism and multilateralism are the subject of this chapter.

Latin American regionalism is, and always was, about much more than MERCOSUR, important though that moment was. Moreover, MERCOSUR itself has experienced significant challenges in recent years, as discussed below. Beyond the excitement of the 1990s, when regionalism in Latin American (and indeed throughout the Americas and the wider world) enjoyed a renaissance, regionalism and the ideas associated with it have a long and distinguished history that can be traced back to the early independence period (Fawcett 2005). Furthermore, the history of regionalism in Latin America both intersects with and complements multilateral processes and the development of international institutions in many different ways, as will be illustrated here. However, despite common features over time, there has not been any singular or linear path toward Latin American regionalism. This observation could also be made about other regionalisms around the world. There have been elements of overall coherence and continuity—reflecting common regional identities and security concerns—but also rupture and discontinuity, revealing a sometimes controversial and competitive pathway, between North and South or between open and closed regionalism. MERCOSUR, as an example of *open* post-Cold War regionalism influenced by EU developments, is but one milestone along this pathway, as it manifests both worldwide trends in new regionalism and regionally specific developments. In what follows, we will track and evaluate that pathway, concentrating on its implications for regionalism in the Americas and trends in global regionalism. The findings, while derived from Latin American experience, may also apply to other regions, particularly those of the so-called developing world. In that respect the chapter shares some of the concern of the "Global International Relations (IR)" project: namely, to decenter the study of international relations and to take seriously the contributions of the Global South. In the words of Acharya (2016a: 4), it encourages us to "embrace greater diversity, especially by recognizing the places, roles and contributions of 'non-Western' peoples and societies."

This chapter suggests that we take seriously the processes of regionalism in Latin America. It adopts an historical, institutional approach toward Latin American regionalism, arguing that much can be learned about current patterns and practices by looking back at the processes leading to institutional start-up and change over time (Pierson 2004). In a similar vein, a recent study of regional geographies states that we need to "go back to move forward": Just as history and tradition are important to the study of regions and territories, they are important to the study of regionalism (Passi *et al.* 2018: 2).

The story of Latin American regionalism is complex, not only because of the powerful shadow of the North, which has been a constant conditioning factor and one against which most Latin American regionalisms have been measured, but also because of the very diversity of Latin America itself. Initially, given the recent experience of European colonialism, it was European intervention in the Americas that remained the major concern for new states. Early Latin American thinking about regionalism saw the United States as a useful counterweight to and natural republican ally against a still dominant Europe, and the Monroe Doctrine was understood in this light. However, as European power waned and US hegemony became more established, the perception of threat and opportunity shifted and balancing against (as well as bandwagoning with) the US became the priority. So, from a very early stage, the US and its hegemonic position in the Americas has been involved, both positively and negatively, in supporting and influencing regional activity and development. Though bilateral trade and other links continued, EU countries would collectively re-enter the frame through the promotion of regionalism in the Americas and the export of European practices. Over the *longue durée* both Europe and the US have had substantial input into Latin American regionalism, but this is no simple story of hegemonic regionalism.

Another linked and complicating issue is that of "Latin America" itself. It is certainly not the case that the continent's politics reflect either a monolithic culture or the sense of having a shared space. While there are many commonalities provided by history, geography, language, and culture, Latin American states are divided among themselves and divided over time, not least over the position that should be adopted toward the North. Some states have tended to cohere around a pan-American or hemispheric ideal of regionalism, while others have resisted that trend and promoted Southern alternatives, and still others have combined hemispheric and sub-regional approaches to maximize their room for maneuver. For geo-strategic reasons, Central American and Caribbean countries have been particularly subject to US influences, to some extent forming their own sub-regions, but South American states have also adopted distinctive positions, as reviewed below. Not least, Brazil—one of the region's most important powers today, with its distinctive colonial history and culture—did not consider itself as part of "Latin" America until around the mid-twentieth century, and even thereafter often followed a distinctive path (Bethell 2010). These divides, like the impact of US influence on the region, have not been constant but have evolved over time. To give one example, events since the start of the twenty-first century have seen renewed "counter-hegemonic" moves in institutions like the Bolivarian Alliance for the Americas (ALBA), the Union of South American Nations (UNASUR), the Community of Latin American States (CELAC), and the Pacific Alliance (PA). But there also has been convergence between certain Latin American states and the US as they have jointly tried to negotiate an FTAA and the Trans-Pacific Partnership (TPP), from which the US withdrew in 2017. Nonetheless, despite all these caveats about distinctiveness and diversity over time and place, the argument advanced here is that a discernible common line of Latin American regionalism has existed, but has been subject to both internal and external pressures leading at times to fragmentation and competition between and within the Americas (Riggirozzi & Deciancio 2018).

Looking back: a history of Latin American regionalism

As indicated above, Latin America is an unusual, even unique case in the global history of regionalism because of its early independence from Spain (and later Portugal, in the case of Brazil), its evolving relationship with an increasingly powerful North, and a rich, if neglected, history of involvement in international institutions and organizations from the Hague Conferences to the United Nations and Bretton Woods institutions and beyond. Latin America, therefore, was both an important part of the history of regionalism, and of "the urge to internationalism" (Mazower 2012: 116–17; Telò, 2014).

An early template for regionalism was established in the post-independence period, when the newly emerging states and their leaders imagined a union of *South* American states free from external influence. Simón Bolívar's attempt to organize a regional congress in Panama in 1826—a first for the Americas—is one prominent and well-known example, but there were to be many more (Cleven 1928: 225). In the mid-nineteenth century, one post-independence publicist, the author of the most important contemporary treatise on international law, inquired:

> Who could doubt the enormous interest of our young republics in strengthening their friendship, their mutual commercial interests and in offering each other all possible forms of support to promote their security and well-being? Between the American republics there is an alliance formed by nature.
>
> *(Cited in Fawcett 2012: 694)*

This early vision was an important marker in the emerging and competitive world of American regionalisms. South Americans were staking out a position for themselves in the international order and seeking to embed that position in international law by demanding equal treatment for weaker states, a position particularly relevant to those emerging from colonialism. Significantly, this early vision did not initially include the US. Indeed, despite the early enthusiasm for the revolutions in its "sister republics" (Fitz 2016), the US Congress deliberated long and hard over an invitation to send a representative to the Panama Congress (Cleven 1928). However, as the century progressed, South Americans increasingly coalesced around a "hemispheric" idea of regionalism (Scarfi & Tillman 2016); they emphasized the ties that bound the two continents, believing this would afford them greater protection against a still-interventionist Europe. The Congress at Lima in 1864–65 was the last purely South American affair, with delegates debating whether or not they should open the door to "all representatives of the New World," including the US (Frazer 1949: 325). In this instance, pan-American voices prevailed, although the underlying distinction and tension between the two positions remained. It continues to be pertinent today, as regional governance in the Americas is contested among competing and overlapping visions of hemispheric and sub-regional entities (Riggirozzi & Tussie 2012).

The move to hemispheric regionalism was facilitated through the work of then-US Secretary of State James Blaine, and resulted in the Inter-American Conference in Washington in 1889, the first of a series of (mostly) 5-yearly conferences between 1889 and 1945, extending, with a few interruptions, through the two world wars. The establishment of the International Union of American Republics (later the Pan-American Union) followed in 1890. This development, reflecting shared commercial and security interests, was not, as is sometimes imagined, a purely North American project, but counted on significant South American input. From the start prominent South American leaders, diplomats, and lawyers lobbied US representatives to gain their support for an interpretation of a pan-American doctrine that, while necessarily aligned with the North, also recognized and accommodated the distinctive interests of the South. Inspired by figures like Alejandro Alvarez and his colleagues at the American Institute of International Law, pan-Americanism therefore represented a fusion of different continental ideas and emerging practices concerning regional order and international law (Scarfi 2017). Latin American leaders and legal scholars were also jostling for position, seeking to influence agendas with the aim of increasing their influence in a highly competitive system (Petersen & Schulz 2018). Important debates during this period concerned the arbitration of disputes, the principle of non-intervention, and (more generally) the equal treatment of all states in international law. Such issues had been addressed earlier by publicists like Andrés Bello and Carlos Calvo, but it was Argentine foreign minister Luis Drago who—in a doctrine bearing his name—effectively argued the case for prohibiting the use of armed force by one country for the purposes of debt collection in another.

If pan-Americanism rather than Latin Americanism became the central leitmotif for regionalism from the late nineteenth century onwards, and indeed right through the interwar period and beyond, it did not always provide the desired formulas for autonomous development and security. Nor was it uncontroversial. Pan-Americanism may have offered some such benefits, but it also offered a cover for US unilateralism, including interventions against regional states, which drew critical fire. Critics included prominent literary figures like José Enrique Rodó and Ruben Dario (Fawcett 2005: 33). As Rodó (1988: 90) presciently warned in 1900, "Let us refuse to see an exemplary civilization where there exists only a clumsy, though huge, working model." Pan-Americanism, however, was not the only outlet for Latin American participation on the international stage; new arenas for multilateral action also opened up, revealing the complex evolving environment in which states operated in the early twentieth century. Because of their nearly 100 years of independence and sheer weight of numbers, Latin American states played an early and prominent part in the evolving parallel multilateral order. While only one Latin American state, Mexico, responded to an invitation to participate in the First Hague Conference in 1899, by the time of the Second Conference in 1907, there were 19 attendees, which presented an opportunity for lobbying on behalf of the so-called Drago Doctrine, described above, that recently had been adopted by the Pan-American Conference. On this occasion, the presence of a large delegation gave the Latin Americans increased visibility, creating a wider international space for refining their diplomatic skills and enhancing their status and influence (Schulz 2017).

Armed with such advantages, Latin American states once again formed a significant element in the League of Nations. By 1920, 17 of the then 20 Latin American republics were members (Wehrli 2015: 2). This further involvement in multilateralism could be seen as another marker of their equality and status. However, the absence of the United States also meant that as a potential venue to balance or lobby the US, the League would prove disappointing. Further, the League Covenant included an explicit mention of the Monroe Doctrine—a constant reminder of US power. Yet, while accounts of Latin American involvement in the League reveal frustration at the limits of that organization from the perspective of smaller and weaker states, whether in respect to US imperialism (in the Dominican Republic and Haiti, for example) or Mexico's failed "defense" of Ethiopia following the Italian invasion (Herrera León 2015), this is arguably too narrow a view. On one level, some disputes were brought to the League's attention and ultimately resolved, notably the Chaco War and the conflict between Peru and Colombia over Leticia. On another, the League's wider architecture, particularly in respect of social, economic, and intellectual issues, offered not only participation but also valuable access to global networks. For example, the International Labor Organization saw significant Latin American input, with delegates pressing the case for a separate Latin American ILO conference (Ferreras 2015: 86–87). Such participation, alongside their earlier involvement in both regional and multilateral institutions, permitted the Latin American states to develop contacts and expertise, which led to further and deeper involvement in the subsequent crafting of the Inter-American, Bretton Woods, and United Nations systems, as discussed below. To some extent, therefore, the limitations of the pan-American system could be mitigated by these parallel multilateral initiatives. And, in the 1930s, US President Franklin Roosevelt sought to reset US–Latin American relations, taking a softer political line in the so-called Good Neighbor Policy. At the 1938 Lima Conference, new support was voiced for a "united hemisphere against external threats" by Brazil's Foreign Minister, Oswaldo Aranha, a strong adherent of the pan-American approach. World War II and its immediate aftermath were marked by displays of hemispheric solidarity, though some states (notably Argentina, which stayed neutral throughout) remained outliers.

Regionalism after 1945

It would be naïve to present any simple picture of the empowerment of Latin America in the early twentieth century, whether in respect to regionalism or multilateralism. Relations with the United States fluctuated widely and would continue to do so. Further, there were serious and recurring divisions and conflicts between states, as in the cases noted above. Nonetheless, both pan-Americanism and multilateralism, as practiced in the interwar period, offered an important space for Latin American engagement, even when the terms of engagement were heavily skewed. As such there were significant and enduring, if interrupted, Latin American initiative and involvement in regionalism and multilateralism prior to World War II. These eventually would provide the basis for later developments.

Against such a backdrop, it was unsurprising that in foundational United Nations debates, as well as those relating to the formation of international financial institutions, the so-called Bretton Woods System, and the development of the inter-American system, enjoyed significant Latin American input. Scholars have recorded the role of Latin American states at Dumbarton Oaks and San Francisco in contributing to Charter provisions, notably in regard to the roles of regional agencies (Claude 1964: 5–6; Smith 1966: 140). Twenty-odd Latin American states were among the 51 founding members of the UN, thereby enjoying a relative numerical (if not hard power) advantage, though this would change quite quickly as the processes of decolonization continued and member states multiplied. Helleiner (2014) has shown, for example, how pre-war Latin American initiatives around the proposed development of an Inter-American Bank were influential in the subsequent crafting of the Bretton Woods institutions, notably the International Bank for Reconstruction and Development and the International Monetary Fund, particularly in strengthening their focus on economic development. The Inter-American Development Bank itself, founded in 1959, was also another important all-American initiative with significant Latin American input, and one that served many Latin American states well, providing them with financial and technical support for multiple development projects. With all member countries as major shareholders, Latin American states have seen this institution as "their" bank (Tussie 1995: 2).

Another hitherto neglected instance of activism that bridged the multilateral– regional divide was the contribution of Latin American legal scholars to an emerging human rights regime. The longstanding commitment of Latin American states to the equal rights of states on issues such as sovereignty and non-intervention already has been noted. However, this commitment was linked to a wider concern regarding the extension of international law principles to human rights (Lutz & Sikkink 2000: 639; Sikkink 2014). The Latin American role here has unsettled the commonly held assumption about the emergence of a human rights regime as a purely Northern project culminating in the Universal Declaration of Human Rights (UDHR). In ratifying a similar American Declaration of the Rights and

Duties of Man eight months before passage of the UDHR, Latin American states thereby contributed to "the first broad enumeration of rights."[1] One could argue that this commitment was the product of a century of Latin American efforts to achieve equality between states and peoples in the still highly unequal international system. This story of activism would continue when Latin American, specifically Argentine, lawyers influenced the design of new international legislation at the International Criminal Court (ICC) to bring to trial former leaders and politicians accused of human rights abuses (Sikkink 2011).

The Inter-American Human Rights System was an integral part of the new institutional landscape of the Americas that evolved from the pan-American system after World War II (Pope Atkins 1997: 4–5; Engstrom 2016). The Pan-American Union was formally replaced by the Organization of American States (OAS), which continued to serve as the permanent secretariat for the pan-American conferences. Other significant innovations were the Rio Treaty of 1947 and the Inter-American Development Bank, established in 1959. While there was considerable enthusiasm among many Latin Americans over the new postwar institutional frameworks and their part in them, older hemispheric tensions re-emerged as the Cold War progressed. When US efforts to prevent its revolution failed, Cuba was expelled from the OAS and thus began a long period of isolation from the inter-American system that continued until the death of Fidel Castro. United States intervention in the Dominican Republic in 1965 was designed precisely to prevent that state following the Cuban path.

If such issues divided Latin American countries, there were other options for them to exercise autonomy outside the inter-American system. Their role in the UN and the Bretton Woods system has been noted. In particular, the UN General Assembly (whose first President was a Colombian) saw an increasingly lively defense of the rights of newly independent states, which generated tensions with major powers. The Economic Commission for Latin America and the Caribbean (ECLA), in turn, became a major source of economic policy for Latin American countries and the wider developing world. Inspired by the dependency school, associated with the Argentine economist Raúl Prebisch, policies of import-substitution industrialization (ISI) were advocated to protect the infant industries of weaker developing countries. ECLA provides an instance of how one of the UN's regional commissions carried real weight in influencing continental, even global development and thinking. The fact that the early *dependentista* literature originated with Latin American scholars from this period is noteworthy, as it links back to earlier distinctive ideas about autonomy and development and forward to later ideas about Latin American roles in the post-Cold War order.

Another Latin American security initiative of this period was the Tlatelolco Treaty (OPANAL), named after the Mexican city where it was signed in 1967, which prohibited the use, testing, or production of nuclear weapons throughout the region. First discussed at an OAS conference in 1958, further negotiations over the proposal followed the Cuban Missile Crisis, where a Cold War standoff took place between the US and the USSR regarding the stationing of Soviet missiles on Cuban territory. Initially a free-standing treaty, OPANAL represented an important collective regional commitment in respect of the creation and preservation of a nuclear free zone. It also became a model for other regions in establishing similar zones of their own.

The (sub-)regional level also provided opportunities for action. Latin American states were early participants in the "first wave" of regionalism, involving not only groupings like the OAS but a wider range of sub-regional bodies. Influenced by the example of European institutions, on the one hand, and the protectionist prescriptions of ECLA, on the other, Latin America was home to multiple proposals to foster regional trade through the construction of customs unions like the Central American (1961) and Caribbean (1973) Common Markets and the Andean Pact (1969), as well as free trade areas like the Latin American Free Trade Association (LAFTA) (1960). The early record of such initiatives was mixed, given the underdeveloped nature of the regional economy, but they provided some alternative platforms for collective Latin American engagement in the global economy and bases upon which to build in the future. Nearly all these groups survived and were rejuvenated in the second regional wave, to be discussed below.

By the 1980s, the prevailing economic orthodoxy shifted again, and ISI was gradually abandoned. Debt crises and a changing regional and global environment saw Latin America enter a sustained period of economic restructuring that followed neo-liberal guidelines derived from the so-called Washington Consensus. Once more, Latin America became closely entwined with US policy and the accompanying prescriptions of international financial institutions. Although these changes preceded the end of the Cold War, the latter, by also discrediting the Soviet economic and political models, helped further to accelerate the effects of economic and political liberalization in Latin America and beyond.

The post-Cold War environment duly witnessed a "second wave" of regionalism, dubbed *new* regionalism for its revised content, ambition, and vision in an era of globalization (Fawcett & Hurrell 1995; Sodebaum & Shaw 2003). Here again, Latin America was closely associated with this wave, though it took different and competitive forms (Fawcett & Serrano 2005). On the one hand, the new post-Maastricht European Union presented a further set of options to would-be regionalizers, including a much more sophisticated set of interregional policies. On the other hand, the US—realizing the benefits of a regional trade approach within a wider multilateral strategy—advanced an ambitious hemispheric trade project: the FTAA, first mooted at the Summit of the Americas in 1994. After more than half a decade of negotiations, the latter failed to materialize, though the NAFTA Treaty of 1994 secured an important free trade agreement among Canada, Mexico, and the US. In an environment of trade liberalization and "open regionalism," Latin America saw the renewal and reform of existing organizations alongside the creation of new bodies and agreements, most notably MERCOSUR.

Borrowing from the European experience of integration and institution-building, and benefitting from the rapprochement between Argentina and Brazil and ongoing democratizing processes in the Southern Cone, MERCOSUR was hailed as an exemplary model, a flagship for the new regional era. Founded in 1991, within 5 years the grouping had recorded a 10 percent trade increase inside the bloc. Given Argentina's leadership role, it is unsurprising that it features prominently in the course at the University of Buenos Aires that was mentioned at the start of this chapter. However, the coexistence of the FTAA project with MERCOSUR and other revived regional projects in Central and South America and the Caribbean also was indicative of the competing visions and enduring tensions between sub-regional and hemispheric regional patterns. While MERCOSUR reflected longstanding ideas about greater South American autonomy in the international arena, providing an alternative and balance to the all-embracing US free trade area, the new, more assertive regional stance of Latin America was reflected in its wider global roles. The World Trade Organization, established in 1995, saw significant Latin American input, particularly in the Doha Development Round.

At first, the liberal regional wave attracted considerable attention from scholars and policy makers alike, but old tensions soon resurfaced. While regionalists applauded its progress and novelty, especially in addressing emerging issue areas and reaching beyond the state, multilateralists worried about the possibility of competing regional blocs. But the reality was, and still is, one of coexistence in a complex and multilevel international order in which the local, regional, and international layers were combined. Initially promising developments, both in MERCOSUR and also in reformed institutions like the Andean Community (formerly the Andean Pact), incorporated a number of EU-type innovations. However, neither regional integration properly understood—as an exercise in sovereignty transfer to supranational institutions—nor any wider FTAA emerged. Scholars would later comment that Latin American regionalism had never been a "liberal" or simple integration project, but much more a pragmatic and rational response to regional economic and security opportunities (Gomes de Mera 2005; Nolte 2016). It was also highly political and dependent on the common interests of incumbent regimes (Malamud & Giardini 2012).

Given the factors enumerated above, it was perhaps unsurprising that by the early twenty-first century, only a decade or so after the start of Latin America's new regional wave, a revised *post*-liberal consensus emerged to challenge previous prescriptions and models, resulting in the establishment of four new organizations in less than 10 years. Reflecting new regional power dynamics and advocating a "Latin America first" approach, it highlighted longstanding tensions within the Americas, some already evident during the Cold War period or indeed even earlier (Fawcett 2005: 37), and introduced new debates about the ownership, direction, and identity of Latin American regionalism.

Spearheaded by a new generation of Latin American regimes, some of these new regionalisms cast themselves as deliberately Southern and anti-Western, implying a return to more indigenous or continental roots. The Venezuelan-led ALBA, standing for Bolivarian Alliance for the People of Our Americas,[2] which was founded in 2004; the Brazil-led UNASUR, founded in 2008; the all-encompassing CELAC, founded in 2010; and the Pacific Alliance (PA), founded in 2011, all issued—though in different ways—firmer statements regarding the need for greater autonomy in regional affairs. While the PA recognized the growing influence of China in South America, the pendulum had swung once more away from the US and EU to the promotion of alternatives and represented, if not a distinct break, at least an alternative to the features of the inter-American system.

Some commentators duly heralded a new era of post-liberal or post-hegemonic regionalism (Riggirozzi & Tussie 2012). This development, in turn, appeared to send a clear message that the twenty-first century multilateral order would look rather different than some had imagined it, with a much stronger *Southern* dimension. Identity politics was writ large in such new regionalisms, endorsing the work of constructivist scholars in supplanting purely material explanations for regionalism and highlighting the new roles and viewpoints of emerging countries in the Global South. Therefore, it accorded with, or possibly went beyond, what might be called a post-revisionist view of regionalism representing both a synthesis and extension of the old and new (Telò *et al.* 2015). Other scholars were more cautious, noting that there was little novel in the idea of post-hegemonic regionalism, since this had been practiced, albeit in sporadic fashion, since the very inception of the modern Latin American state system (Petersen & Schulz 2018). To some extent, all regionalisms were part of this ongoing tension between hegemony and counter-hegemony, and states had regular recourse to alternative regional and multilateral forums. Still others worried that the very multiplicity of competing and overlapping regionalisms in Latin America was a sign not of progress but of confusion and disorder. The fear expressed here was that Latin American regionalism had "peaked" or "gone too far" (Malamud & Gardini 2012; Riggirozzi & Deciancio 2018: 479), revealing nothing but a muddle, or an alphabet soup of acronyms. "Cumbritis," a term adopted from the Spanish word *cumbre* or summit, referred to the seemingly never-ending series of summits and multiple declaratory statements. In short, rather than bringing forth a new regional order, a new regional anarchy threatened (Heine 2012: 209–10).

All the above reflections have their place. Certainly, by 2015 there were 17 regional bodies excluding NAFTA, as laid out in Table 6.1. And, in support of that claim, one could note contradictory trends since 2015, where there is evidence of further fragmentation, partly due to the ongoing crisis in Venezuela but also to Brazil's economic and political difficulties and the effects of the Trump presidency. Venezuela, having joined MERCOSUR only in 2011, was suspended from that body at the end of 2016; ALBA has lost its original dynamism; and UNASUR has slowly unravelled, losing its core identity and some its members over the handling

TABLE 6.1 Latin American regionalisms, 2019

ACS—Association of Caribbean States
ALADI—Latin American Integration Association
ALBA—Bolivarian Alliance for the Americas
APEC—Asia Pacific Economic Cooperation
CAN—Andean Community
CARICOM—Caribbean Community
CELAC—Community of Latin American and Caribbean States
MERCOSUR—Southern Common Market
OAS—Organization of American States
OECS—Organization of Eastern Caribbean States
OEI—Organization of Ibero-American States
Pacific Alliance
Rio Group
SELA—Latin American and the Caribbean Economic System
SICA—Central American Integration System
UNASUR—Union of South American Nations
PROSUR—Forum for the Progress and Development of South America

Modified from www.as-coa.org/articles/explainer-alphabet-soup-regional-integration-organizations#ACS_explainer

of the Venezuelan crisis. A number of former UNASUR members, including Colombia, Chile, and (most recently) Brazil, have moved to form a new organization, the Forum for the Progress and Development of South America (PROSUR). The election in 2019 of Jair Bolsonaro in Brazil is likely to accentuate a trend toward further fragmentation or reconstruction of regional groups. In respect to US policy, while NAFTA was excluded from the list of 17, it too has been "downgraded" to the US–Mexico–Canada Agreement (USMCA) in 2018 (note here also both the absence of the term "Free Trade Association" from the new bloc's name and the partial construction of a wall along the US–Mexico border).

For some, these steps are merely emblematic of wider trends: an ongoing crisis in global regionalism and multilateralism, generated not only in the US but also in Western countries where economic downturns and migration issues have fed populist movements and ideas that are hostile to integration. Today the notion of a crisis, or at least a critical juncture, in regionalism pervades the literature, whether exemplified by the dilemmas facing the European Union since 2008 after the Greek meltdown and Britain's vote to leave the organization in June of 2016; the US withdrawal from the TPP in January of 2017; or the establishment of the competitor Belt and Road Initiative. To an extent, all regions have been affected by the new nationalist turn in global politics

(Riggirozzi & Deciancio 2018: 479). This is not to speak of MENA (Middle East, North Africa, Afghanistan, and Pakistan) regionalism, which has been seriously weakened since the Iraq War and the events of the Arab Spring. Today, the Latin American continent may be in a state of flux, but not for the first time, nor is it alone in this respect.

In short, in the space of less than 20 years a great deal certainly has changed in the fluid and complex world of Latin American regionalism. Since the early promise of a "new" regionalism delivering on post-Cold War expectations of a liberal economic and political order, there have been subsequent moves away from neo-liberal formulations alongside a continuation of longer-term trends at the continental and sub-regional levels. Yet, almost as soon as the newer anti-hegemonic projects took hold, they in turn faced serious challenges. So, what are we to make of the evidence that supports the chapter title of competitive and even contentious regionalisms? How seriously should we take claims about failure, fragmentation, or crisis?

Such questions have yielded different and often-contradictory answers, all part of the wider discussion with which this volume is concerned. Controversy and competition have been and still remain an ever-present feature of Latin American regionalism. To some extent, though, that surely holds true of every region. Regions and their constituent institutions are social and malleable constructs, subject to different pressures and influences, and their contours and characteristics are not fixed; a region becomes a region because an actor or set of actors decides it should exist for a particular purpose (Van Langenhove 2011: 60). Against this assertion, it might be argued that Latin America is in a unique position, given its history and experience of European colonialism and tensions with its powerful Northern neighbor. But other regions (and sub-regions), including Africa, South and East Asia, and even Europe, also have complex histories, and all have had to conduct regional business with an eye both on a colonial past and on a powerful neighbor. Furthermore, as argued here, the mere fact of having powerful neighbors or fending off hegemonic influences does not necessarily detract from effective regionalism.

In retrospect, if some of the above claims about new trends in Latin American regionalism appear overdone, it is time for taking stock. There is a need to step back from grand statements and rhetorical claims and consider regional processes over the *longue durée*. On the one hand, much of the current terrain of Latin American regionalism reflects enduring trends and developments. Viewed over time, regionalism in the Americas has been less about deep integration, sovereignty pooling, or even pure identity politics and more about the benefits of functional, pragmatic, and sovereignty-hugging cooperation, as visible in the Pacific Alliance, PROSUR, and the now-revamped NAFTA. Regionalism today may appear to be watered down and lacking in dynamism, but that view elides the complexity and vitality of regional processes and their relationships with global processes over time.

Conclusion

This chapter has reviewed Latin American regionalism over the *longue durée* and examined points of contention and competition in respect to different regionalisms, relations with the US, and the wider multilateral system. The intention here has not been to essentialize Latin America nor to paint an unnecessarily rosy or bleak picture of Latin American regionalism, but rather to reflect upon, and offer some analytical pointers about, its multiple experiences in the context of this volume's discussion of regionalism, interregionalism, and multilateralism. Latin American regionalism has an important if hitherto neglected trajectory and contribution in which certain trends, drawing on the region's history, geography, and political environment, can be identified. Acknowledging Latin America's input into the history of international organization—via both regional and multilateral institutions—is important in helping us understand the present conjuncture, and in contributing to a wider discussion about regionalism and the story of the Global South (Deciancio 2016; Fawcett 2020).

A few key points emerge from the analysis. First, there is a rich history of Latin American regionalism that cannot be subsumed under the umbrella of the US or Europe. At times, it has coalesced with hemispheric regionalism or worked closely with European institutions, but it also has frequently diverged and taken separate, sometimes overlapping and sometimes conflicting pathways demonstrating autonomous development. Hegemony, therefore, is an insufficient term to understand Latin American regionalisms. Elements of controversy and competition always have been present.

Second, an appreciation of the present conjuncture requires us to take an historical approach. Inis Claude, in a seminal work on international organization, wrote that the historical approach is important for the obvious reason that the present cannot be understood, nor future prospects adequately assessed, without a grasp of the tendencies and continuities that emerge from the past (Claude 1964: 5). This point is particularly relevant to the Latin American case. If we focus simply on the present, it is clear that we will miss a large part of the story. Latin American regionalism is about much more than the current "crisis," much more than an exercise in measuring integration, following Europe, or contesting US power. A lot of Latin American regionalism concerns recurring, well-established practices and patterns of governance, ways of thinking, and ways of doing, stretching all the way back to the post-independence period. For example, Latin America's contributions to international law and human rights are embedded in its regional history; the inter-American legal architecture will not simply disappear. The complex networks and structures in place for over 150 years will ensure that that remains the case. That is why a *longue durée* approach is helpful. It seems to confirm Braudel's idea that regionalism constitutes the "sum of all its histories" and encompasses all points of view, those of yesterday, today, and tomorrow (Braudel 2009: 182).

A third point is that Latin American/US relations are sometimes competitive and sometimes complementary. They do not operate in a binary fashion. Engagement with regionalism and multilateral processes has been a way of mitigating and managing US hegemony and promoting regional autonomy, but such processes also require constant (re-)negotiation. In them, state strength and sovereignty have always been at a premium. Although relations are evidently asymmetrical (Long 2018), that asymmetry does not prevent meaningful interaction nor does it necessarily reduce Latin America's room for maneuver. At times, the US has shown great indifference to Latin America, treating it as an arena of peripheral concern. The same goes for relations with Europe. Relative neglect by the great powers has caused significant problems for Latin America by rendering interregional cooperation more difficult. However, neglect also creates opportunities. Rather than being subsumed under the European model or wanting to imitate it uncritically, Latin American states, like other developing countries, have cherry-picked European institutional frameworks and practices while seeking to preserve and maintain their own independence. Latin America therefore needs to be considered on its own terms.

A fourth and related point, as demonstrated above, is that as far back as the late nineteenth century, Latin American regionalism always has had a strong multilateral dimension, evident in international conferences, the League of Nations, United Nations, international financial institutions (IFIs), and the BRICS (Brazil, Russia, India, China, South Africa). As argued here, Latin America's deep and enduring presence in the multilateral arena only recently has begun to be appreciated. This deeply intertwined regional/global nexus is an important part of the debate and has allowed Latin Americans some space for maneuver in global governance debates.

Fifth, Latin American regionalism also has had a cultural dimension. It clearly both serves and reflects "identity needs." There is a South or Latin American consciousness and sense of purpose that runs through this story. It isn't a united or even a continuous one. Brazil, for example, was not part of the early South American vision, and even after it emerged as the major regional power its agenda was somewhat distinctive. Still, Brazil has had its pan-Americanists and its regional as well as global or "Southern" agenda, as evidenced in its participation in the BRICS group (Alden & Vieira 2005). Mexico's agenda—or that of Central America—will always be more closely bound to the US, as history shows. Yet despite their divergent interests and goals, Latin American countries also have pursued a broader cultural agenda that has emphasized the linguistic, religious, and intellectual ties among their populations, which at times have given rise to common bonds, similar institutions, and dense networks.

Finally, and reflecting on the above points, it is clear that Latin America can make an important and distinctive contribution to the wider debate about regionalism and multilateralism, a contribution that previously has been neglected. While developments in comparative regionalism have helped to launch this debate, it has been advanced further as part of the so-called post-revisionism and non-Western approaches that this chapter has sought to highlight. Evidently, there are a good many Latin American regionalisms to study and a rich set of experiences to examine: arguably more than elsewhere, simply because Latin America's colonial era lies farther in the past. It therefore has a longer history as the home of independent states carrying on their own foreign policies. Scholars can rightly conclude that Latin American regionalism clearly matters in debates about wider global processes.

This chapter began with a note reflecting the important role that MERCOSUR played in the 1990s as a flagship for the "new" regionalism that characterized that period. To some extent that organization was also a model for the EU-driven policy of interregionalism. It was quite distinct from the pan-American project as expressed in the inter-American system, in allowing Latin America states a proper space in which to advance their political and trade concerns. The European model was also visible in the organization's institutional design. Despite the importance and novelty of MERCOSUR in the context of the 1990s, however, it has been argued here that Latin American regionalism goes far beyond this one body. This is particularly so given the recent MERCOSUR crisis, which has seen declining trade figures, political instability, and the emergence of stark divergences among members, particularly regarding the issue of the political situation in Venezuela. The organization has gone from poster child to what has been termed a "fractious trade bloc" (Felter & Renwick 2018). There has been considerable skepticism about the possibility of recovery, often accompanied by unflattering comparisons between the relative decline of MERCOSUR and the relative strength of the Pacific Alliance, a grouping with a different ethos. With no pretensions to integration or supranationalism, PA is an intergovernmental organization that has been "pragmatic, flexible, goal-oriented and member driven" (Sauvé et al. 2019: x).

To some extent, however, many Latin American regionalisms have shown high degrees of pragmatism and indeed resilience. MERCOSUR has survived previous crises (Gomes de Mera 2005), and there are still grounds for optimism regarding the organization's prospects, even during its current downturn. At the time of this writing, the EU is engaged in negotiating a trade deal with the four founding MERCOSUR states (Argentina, Brazil, Paraguay, and Uruguay) as part of a broader Association Agreement between the two regions. Such efforts, which have a longer history, were hailed as close to conclusion at the end of 2018. While MERCOSUR is a major investor in the EU, it also constitutes an important market for EU goods and services. These robust trade and investment patterns have not been disrupted by the election of Jair Bolsonaro as president of Brazil, despite his aversion to some existing areas of regional cooperation. Hence, both the interregional agenda and the link to the EU continues to be important within the wider regional/multilateral architecture.

Meanwhile, alongside the developments in MERCOSUR or the Pacific Alliance, the wider world of Latin American regionalism, with its long history, remains alive and well, representing a competitive and lively space for regionalism, interregionalism, and engagement with multilateralism. The development of such ties in Latin America forms part of what Amitav Acharya (2016b) has called a "multiplex" architecture "beyond" hegemony. The evidence presented above, drawing upon nearly two centuries of history, exposes the wider picture of Latin American regionalism and positions it in an evolving multilateral order. Subject to fluidity and contestation, Latin American regionalism as policy and project has been dynamic and eclectic, and it has survived in "hard times" (Telò 2016) of crisis, including periods of US neglect, regional rivalries, or populist/nationalist tendencies. In sum, Latin America is embedded within the multilateral system in multiple ways, and will continue to be part of the making and remaking of any global governance architecture.

Notes

1. *American Declaration of the Rights and Duties of Man*, Organization of American States. Available at www.oas.org/en/iachr/mandate/Basics/declaration.asp.
2. The appropriation of the name Bolivar for purposes of this group has obvious significance.

References

Acharya, A. 2016a. "Advancing Global IR." *International Studies Review* 18(1): 4–15

Acharya, A. 2016b. "After Liberal Hegemony: The advent of a multiplex order." *Ethics and International Affairs* 31(3): 271–85

Alden, C. & M. Vieira, 2005. "The New Diplomacy of the South." *Third World Quarterly* 26(7): 1077–95

Bethell, L. 2010. "Brazil and 'Latin America.'" *Journal of Latin American Studies* 42(3): 457–85

Braudel, F. 2009. "History and Social Sciences: The *longue durée.*" Immanuel Wallerstein, trans. *Review [Fernand Braudel Centre]* 32(3): 171–203

Claude, I. 1964. *Swords into Plowshares: The problems and progress of international organization.* 3rd edition. London: London University Press

Cleven, A. 1928. "The First Panama Mission and the Congress of the United States." *Journal of Negro History* 13(3): 225–54

Deciancio, M. 2016. "International Relations from the South." *International Studies Review* 18(1): 106–19

Engstrom, P. 2016. "The Inter-American Human Rights System and US–Latin American Relations." In J. Scarfi & A. Tillman (eds.), *Cooperation and Hegemony in US-Latin American Relations: Revisting the Western Hemisphere idea.* New York: Palgrave

Farrell, M., B. Hettne, & L. Van Langenhove, 2005. *Global Politics of Regionalism: Theory and practice.* London: Pluto Press

Fawcett, L. 2005. "The Origins and Development of the Regional Idea in the Americas." In L. Fawcett & M. Serrano (eds.), *Regionalism and Governance in the Americas: Continental drift.* Basingstoke, UK: Palgrave, pp. 25–51

Fawcett, L. 2012. "Between West and Non-West: Latin American contributions to international thought.'" *International History Review* 34(4): 679–704

Fawcett, L. 2020. "Regionalism." In D. Berg-Schlosser, B. Badie, & L. Morlino (eds.), *Sage Handbook of Political Science*, vol. 3. London: Sage, pp. 1355–71

Fawcett, L. & A. Hurrell, 1995. *Regionalism in World Politics: Regional organization and international order.* Oxford, UK: Oxford University Press

Fawcett, L. & M. Serrano, 2005. *Regionalism and Governance in the Americas: Continental drift.* New York: Palgrave Macmillan

Felter, C. & D. Renwick, 2018. "MERCOSUR, South America's Fractious Trade Bloc." Council on Foreign Relations. Available at www.cfr.org/backgrounder/mercosur-south-americas-fractious-trade-bloc?

Ferreras, N. 2015. "Europe—Geneva—America: The first International Congress of American States Members of the International Labor Organization." In A. McPherson & Y. Wehrli (eds.), *Beyond Geopolitics: New histories of Latin America at the League of Nations.* Albuquerque, NM: University of New Mexico Press, pp. 83–96

Fitz, C. 2016. *Our Sister Republics: The US in an age of American revolutions.* New York: W.W. Norton

Frazer, R. 1949. "The Role of the Lima Congress, 1864–1865, in the Development of Pan-Americanism." *Hispanic American Historical Review* 29(3): 319–48

Gomes de Mera, L. 2005. "Explaining MERCOSUR's Survival: Strategic sources of Argentine-Brazilian convergence." *Journal of Latin America Studies* 37(1): 109–40

Heine, J. 2012. "Regional Integration and Political Cooperation in Latin America." *Latin American Research Review* 47(3): 209–17

Helleiner, E. 2014. "Southern Pioneers of International Development." *Global Governance* 20(3): 375–88

Herrera León, F. 2015. "Mexico and its 'Defense' of Ethiopia at the League of Nations." In A. McPherson & Y. Wehrli (eds.), *Beyond Geopolitics: New histories of Latin America at the League of Nations.* Albuquerque, NM: University of New Mexico Press, pp. 49–62

Long, T. 2018. "The US, Brazil and Latin America: The dynamics of asymmetrical regionalism." *Contemporary Politics* 24(1): 113–29

Lutz, E. & K. Sikkink, 2000. "International Human Rights Law and Practice in Latin America." *International Organization* 54(3): 633–59

Malamud, A. & G. Giardini, 2012. "Has Regionalism Peaked? The Latin American quagmire and its lessons." *International Spectator* 47(1): 116–33

Mazower, M. 2012. *Governing the World: History of an Idea.* London: Penguin

Nolte, D. 2016. "UNASUR: Regional pluralism as a strategic outcome." *Contexto Internacional* 38(2): 545–65

Paasi, A., J. Harrison, & M. Jones, 2018. "New Consolidated Regional Geographies." In A. Paasi, J. Harrison, & M. Jones (eds.), *Handbook on the Geography of Regions and Territories.* Cheltenham, UK: Edward Elgar, pp. 1–20

Petersen, M. & C. Schulz, 2018. "Setting the Regional Agenda: A critique of post-hegemonic regionalism." *Latin American Politics and Society* 60(1): 102–27

Pierson, P. 2004. *Politics in Time.* Princeton, NJ: Princeton University Press

Pope Atkins, G. 1997. *Encyclopedia of the Inter-American System.* Westport, CT: Greenwood Press

Riggirozzi, P. & M. Deciancio, 2018. "Regional Building, Autonomy and Regionalism in South America." In A. Paasi, A., J. Harrison, & M. Jones (eds.), *Handbook on the Geographies of Regions and Territories.* Cheltenham, UK: Edward Elgar, pp. 479–88

Riggirozzi, P. & D. Tussie, 2012. *The Rise of Post-Hegemonic Regionalism in Latin America.* UNU Series on Regionalism, 4. New York & London: Springer

Rodó, J. 1988. *Ariel,* trans. By M. Peden. Austin, TX: University of Texas Press

Sauvé, P., R. Polanco Lazo, & J. Alvarez Zárate (eds.), 2019. *The Pacific Alliance in a World of Preferential Trade Arrangements.* UNU Series on Regionalism, 16. London & New York: Springer

Scarfi, J. 2017. "In the Name of the Americas: The pan-American redefinition of the Monroe Doctrine and the emerging language of American international law in the Western hemisphere." *Diplomatic History* 40(2): 189–218

Scarfi, J. & A. Tillman, 2016. *Cooperation and Hegemony in US-Latin American Relations: Revisting the Western Hemisphere idea.* New York: Palgrave

Schulz, C.A. 2017. "Accidental Activists: Latin American status-seeking at The Hague." *International Studies Quarterly* 61(3): 612–22

Sikkink, K. 2011. *The Justice Cascade.* New York: Norton

Sikkink, K. 2014. "Latin American Countries as Norm Protagonists of the Idea of International Human Rights." *Global Governance* 20(3): 389–404

Smith, G.C. 1966. *The Inter-American System.* Oxford, UK: Oxford University Press

Sodebaum, F. & T. Shaw (eds.), 2003. *Theories of New Regionalism: A Palgrave reader.* New York: Palgrave Macmillan

Telò, M. 2014. *Globalisation, Europe and Multilateralism: Towards a better global governance?* Aldershot, UK: Ashgate

Telò, M. 2016. *Regionalism in Hard Times.* New York: Routledge

Telò, M., L Fawcett, & F. Ponjaert, 2015. *Inter-regionalism and the European Union: A post-revisionist approach.* Farnham, UK: Ashgate

Tussie, D. 1995. *The Inter-American Development Bank.* Boulder, CO: Lynne Reinner

Van Langenhove, L. 2011. *Building Regions: The regionalization of the world order.* Farnham, UK: Ashgate

Wehrli, Y. 2015. "New Histories of Latin America at the League of Nations." In A. McPherson & Y. Wehrli (eds.), *Beyond Geopolitics: New histories of Latin America at the League of Nations.* Albuquerque, NM: University of New Mexico Press, pp. 1–18

PART III
Case studies
Competing regionalisms or pluralistic and post-hegemonic multilateralism?

7
RUSSIA AND EURASIAN REGIONALISM

How does it fit into comparative regionalism research?

Alexander Libman

Introduction

The extent to which the Russian case can be analyzed through the lens of the multiple modernities paradigm has remained a subject of intensive debate in recent decades.[1] The main point of contention is how to interpret the Soviet era. While some view it as a unique pathway to modernity, others emphasize the archaic, premodern—and perhaps even anti-modern—practices of Stalinism. If that take on Stalinism is correct, then it would turn out to be the antithesis of modernity and the continuation of older traditions of rule that dominated Russia for centuries (David-Fox 2006; Maslovskiy 2016). From the 1990s on, a powerful argument has emerged that wants to portray Russia as an example of "fake modernity" (Sztompka 1993; Lewin 2005), meaning that the Communist regime managed to produce artifacts typically associated with modernity (e.g., urbanization or industrialization), but that these artifacts, which are captured in empirical analysis, do not correlate with any change of values and behaviors on the part of the Russian people. To the contrary, Communist "modernization" in fact may have strengthened the illiberal practices in Russian society (Lankina & Libman 2019). At the very least, even if Russian society managed to find its path to a certain version of modernity, the latter has not been matched by the development of the Russian state, which still follows a predominantly archaic approach to governance (Paneyakh 2018).

The debate over Russian modernity also sheds light on the broader issue of Eurasian regionalism, to which this chapter is devoted. From the point of view of some observers (especially in Russian academic circles), regional organizations created by the post-Soviet countries beginning in the early 1990s should be seen as specific regional variants of the same process, one that has been at work across different world regions.[2] Other observers, particularly those versed in the European and American policy discourse on Eurasian regionalism, see it as a qualitatively different phenomenon, associated with the reproduction of the inherently archaic centralist spatial structure of the Russian Empire and of the Soviet Union (Furman 2005). But, from this perspective, Eurasian regionalism is not necessarily unique. On the contrary, it can be considered part of a broader phenomenon of regionalisms in which the façade of multilateralism and economic cooperation hides a power hierarchy and a mechanism of mutual support of authoritarian governments (Obydenkova & Libman 2019). Authoritarian regionalism could therefore be seen as another example of fake modernity, in which there is a wide gap between formal institutions and language on the one hand, and social practices on the other.

The goal of this chapter is to review the development of Eurasian regionalism and to discuss how it can inform the existing research on comparative regionalism, particularly if the latter has to take non-Western models of regionalism into account (Acharya 2016; Söderbaum 2016). I am not claiming that Eurasian regionalism should be seen as typical of a particular class of regionalisms; rather, my objective is to demonstrate that certain processes, which are better observable empirically in the case of the post-Soviet Eurasia, are of interest for understanding the development of regionalism in different parts of the world. In particular, there are three features of Eurasian regionalism that deserve special attention in this context: emulation of the EU by non-democratic actors; the use of regionalism as a tool of regime boosting; and the path that regional organizations may take to become actors in a non-democratic context. In what follows, I will review each of these aspects below.

Eurasian regionalism: a brief description

Before proceeding to a more detailed analysis of Eurasian regionalism, it seems prudent to give a brief overview of what exactly will count as Eurasian regionalism in this chapter. Indeed, the boundaries of Eurasia are particularly blurry, and the very word "Eurasia" has been applied to the region only after the collapse of the Soviet Union. In the recent past, it would have been more common to refer to the region as the "post-Soviet space" or the "new independent states" (cf. Vinokurov & Libman 2012). While all regions are ultimately the outcome of social construction, in the case of Eurasia this process still has a lot farther to go than it does in many other parts of the world. Even in the textbooks and edited volumes on comparative regionalism, the place of Eurasia is never fixed. Post-Soviet regional organizations can end up in the "Europe" chapter, the "Asia" chapter, or even the "interregionalism" chapter.

Today, Eurasian regionalism constitutes a rather loose family of regional organizations, all of which can trace their genealogy to the decisive event that created the "region" and determined the long-term focus of its regional organizations:

the dissolution of the USSR in 1991. The first "Eurasian" organization (which in practice never functioned) was the Economic Community of October, 1991, created by Armenia, Belarus, Kazakhstan, Kyrgyzstan, Russia, Tajikistan, Turkmenistan, and Uzbekistan. It was (or would have been) a very unusual organization, since it included both ex-Soviet republics intent on staying part of a (reformed) USSR, ex-Soviet republics determined to break away from the USSR, and ex-Soviet republics still undecided about which course of action to follow. In December of 1991, the Soviet Union was replaced by the first genuinely international organization: the Commonwealth of Independent States (CIS), which as of today includes 11 post-Soviet countries (it excludes only the Baltic states and Georgia, which left in 2009). Over the subsequent decades, Eurasian countries agreed to establish a number of additional organizations: the first Customs Union (1995, among Russia, Belarus, and Kazakhstan); the Eurasian Economic Community (2000, Russia, Belarus, Kazakhstan, Tajikistan, and Kyrgyzstan); the Single Economic Space (2003, Ukraine, Russia, Belarus, and Kazakhstan); the second Customs Union (2010, Russia, Belarus, and Kazakhstan); the Common Economic Space (2012, the same three countries); the Eurasian Economic Union (2015, Russia, Belarus, Kazakhstan, Armenia, and Kyrgyzstan); the Collective Security Treaty Organization (2002, currently the same five countries); and a sequence of Russia-Belarus regional organizations (from the Commonwealth of Russia and Belarus of 1996 to the Union State of Russia and Belarus of 1999).[3]

The majority of these organizations share three common features. First, they all are characterized by a conspicuous asymmetry of power, with Russia controlling the lion's share of the organizations' economic and military potential. This does not mean that it was Russia that initiated the regionalism processes. On the contrary, in many cases Belarus and Kazakhstan were much more active as initiators. Second, with the exception of the Collective Security Treaty Organization (CSTO) and to some extend the CIS and the Union State (USRB), most Eurasian organizations focus on economic issues and pursue a very similar agenda with several points of emphasis: creating a functioning common market with free movement of goods, labor, and capital, coordinating economic policies, and setting common trade policy. The focus on economic issues can be seen as a legacy of the situation post-Soviet countries faced in the early 1990s, when economic reforms became the most pressing concern for all the newly independent states. But this economic emphasis also reflected Eurasian efforts to emulate the EU experience. Moreover, prior to the establishment of the second Customs Union (CU)—the Common Economic Space and the Eurasian Economic Union (EAEU)—all organizations pushing for Eurasian integration suffered from a huge implementation gap. The ambitious goals of economic integration were not fulfilled by actual policy measures; indeed, over two decades Eurasian countries repeatedly signed agreements with essentially the same content, yet they never complied with any of the obligations they had assumed. The CU and the EAEU differ from all of their predecessors because of the very high level of treaty implementation.

The EAEU, the most advanced regional organization in Eurasia, is a functioning partial customs union with free movement of labor and capital, and a commitment to integrating other policy areas (Vinokurov 2018) as well. This does not mean, however, that Eurasian regionalism prior to the CU remained irrelevant. Rather, it indicates that the real functions of such regionalism could differ from the officially declared goals, and they might be more about regime boosting than economic integration. In fact, these "hidden functions" of Eurasian regionalism will constitute the main topic of the rest of this chapter.

Eurasian regionalism and regionalisms in non-democratic contexts

Emulating the EU

From the very outset, Eurasian regionalism remained a clear-cut example of "downloading the global script" (Jupille *et al.* 2013; Börzel & van Hüllen 2015): designing the regional organization in a way that imitates the European Union (EU) as closely as possible. This is hardly surprising, since the geographic proximity of the Eurasian countries to the EU and the impact the EU had on them during the early years of the transition made Europe an obvious normative benchmark for the schemes of regionalism emerging in the post-Soviet area. However, an inherent contradiction soon came to light. Over time, the majority of the Eurasian countries turned into consolidated autocracies. This is true for all three key countries of the Eurasian regionalist project: Russia under Vladimir Putin (since 2000); Belarus under Aleksandr Lukashenka (since 1994); and Kazakhstan under Nursultan Nazarbayev (who had been in power already in 1990 and stayed there). At the same time, eagerness to imitate the EU project did not diminish. On the contrary, the most recent regional project, the EAEU, clearly follows the EU blueprint. While the scope and the depth of integration in the EAEU of course is much more limited than in the EU, the fundamental design of the EAEU is like that of the EU: i.e., it is based on creating a common institutional framework rather than cultivating informal relations or adapting to the preferences of the hegemon.[4] The EAEU set up a large supranational bureaucracy, the key institution of which, the Eurasian Economic Commission, resembles the EU Commission in many ways. The organization has attempted to follow the same sequence of regional integration steps that the EU did.[5] In short, Eurasia is a region in which autocracies systematically emulate the EU, which—ironically—is one of the principal democratic actors and promoters of democracy in the modern world (Dragneva & Wolzcuk 2015; Vicari 2016).

This contradiction calls for a more careful elaboration of the factors driving the Eurasian states to "download the global script" of the EU. DiMaggio and Powell (1983) point out three possible mechanisms influencing the isomorphic development of institutions: coercion and dependence, socialization, and emulation of models perceived as successful. The extent of the dependence of Eurasian regionalism upon the EU model actually is much less than it is in many other parts of the world. Not only did the EU fail to offer any form of assistance, whether technical or material, to the Eurasian regional organizations, but also very few high-level bureaucrats in Eurasian organizations have ever worked or studied in an EU member country (Furman & Libman 2015).[6] Thus, socialization is unlikely to explain similarities between the EU and the Eurasian regional organizations. So perhaps the best explanation for such parallelism would be the pattern of mimetic isomorphism: the imitation of organizational solutions perceived as successful. Nevertheless, Russian propaganda, at least, is very clear about presenting the EU as an *un*successful case ripped apart by contradictions among its member countries (Neumann 2016). Furthermore, Russian diplomacy pays particularly close attention to bilateral relations with the EU countries rather than prioritizing relations with the EU. In fact, the EAEU was established during a period of escalating tensions between the EU and Russia amid the Ukrainian crisis, a moment when Russia was unlikely to treat the EU as a self-evident blueprint. What is more, one of the factors behind the creation of the CU and the EAEU (although certainly not the only one) was Russia's concern about the European Neighborhood Policy and possible expansion of EU influence in the post-Soviet countries. In other words, besides emulating the EU, Eurasian regionalism also was supposed to constrain the influence of the EU (Stefanova 2018).

How then should we interpret the similarities between the formal design of the EU and the Eurasian regional organizations? Two explanations stand out. The first is the search for the *global status* of the Eurasian organizations. For Russia, Eurasian regionalism is but one aspect of its attempt to reshape the global economic order (Johnson & Köstem 2016). Furthermore, until 2014 it was an important element in Russia's efforts to attain one of the main goals of its foreign policy: gaining recognition as a sovereign and respected equal partner of "the West." As such, Eurasian regionalism ought to resemble the "global blueprint" as closely as possible to in order to ensure that recognition. Recognition can take many forms. For example, since the establishment of the first CU, Russia has insisted on a dialogue between the EU and Eurasian regional organizations. To some extent then, Russia emulates the EU to provide a counterweight to the EU that would be perceived by the latter as legitimate. True, Russia may perceive and/or depict the EU as unsuccessful, but that does not mean it won't emulate the EU in this case. The key objective is not the success of the regional organization as such, but the recognition of the regional organization by "Western" actors in which Russia is interested due to its status anxieties (Furman & Libman 2019).

Yet we should not discount the second plausible explanation for Russia's attempts at replicating the EU model in the Eurasian context (to some extent, at least): the *misperception* of that model by Eurasian elites. Libman (2017), analyzing the discussion of regional integration in post-Soviet Eurasia, indicates that the Russian epistemic community rarely perceives it as a factor *constraining* national sovereignty. On the contrary, regionalism is seen as an *attribute* of great powers, which establish their own regional blocs as tools for influencing the global economic order. The assumption implicitly shared by many Russian observers is that regional organizations are created by powerful actors to strengthen their position in the global competition. This consideration also could induce Russia to support the copying of EU institutions. For example, Russia could perceive the supranationality of the EAEU (giving more power to smaller states) as a sort of redistributive device, encouraging smaller countries to support the Russian foreign policy agenda on strategic issues. The latter, incidentally, are not formally included in the mandate of the EAEU, which has a narrowly economic focus (see Libman & Obydenkova 2018a).

In any case, Eurasian regionalism offers us clear-cut evidence that emulation of the EU, including good political and economic relations with it, does not necessarily go hand in hand with socialization into the norms of the EU or even endorsement of it as a successful model.[7]

Authoritarian regionalism and regime boosting

The authoritarian nature of the Eurasian countries makes it possible to look at Eurasian regionalism from yet another perspective: that of the ability of regional organizations to aid and abet the member countries' shift toward authoritarianism. The scholarly discussion of regional organizations created by democratic associations such as the EU seems to be driven by two somewhat contradictory lines of argument. On the one hand, scholars ask whether the supranational decision-making bodies themselves should be regarded as "democratic," i.e., sufficiently accountable to the population, and how important the risks of a "democratic deficit" happen to be (for a critical discussion of this argument see Moravcsik 2004). On the other hand, others inquire about the extent to which regional organizations can promote democracy at the national level, either through their own conscious efforts or via diffusion of democratic values (e.g., Schimmelfennig & Scholz 2008) or by serving as an anchor to increase the credibility of commitments to democracy (Pevehouse 2005). From this perspective, the decision-making processes of regional organizations comprised primarily of non-democracies are inherently undemocratic; yet they can also potentially strengthen undemocratic regimes by offering them support in the form of both greater legitimacy and economic resources. This is what we mean by the term "regime boosting" (Söderbaum 2004; Libman & Obydenkova 2018b; Kneuer *et al.* 2018). Such support is rarely declared openly and is typically hidden either behind the façade of a purely economic organization or even behind the rhetoric of supporting democracy in the member states, as sometimes happens in Eurasia.

Telò (2017) shows that the hierarchical or authoritarian type of regionalism is not a novel phenomenon. However, authoritarian regionalism is also gaining momentum in the modern world, partly in line with the growing assertiveness of authoritarian powers like China, Russia, Iran, Saudi Arabia, and Venezuela, which play an increasingly important role in global politics.[8] These "authoritarian gravity centers" (Kneuer & Demmelhuber 2016) are not the only reason that authoritarian regionalism is becoming increasingly important. Lesser autocracies also are frequently interested in joining forces within the "authoritarian clubs," where they can support each other. Still, research on the policy implications of authoritarian regionalism is rather limited. Eurasia offers an excellent laboratory for studying whether authoritarian regionalism can have an impact on the autocracy consolidation in the member countries. Eurasia is one part of the world in which undemocratic regional organizations have proliferated. Yet Russia has demonstrated a very strong commitment to multilateralism. That is somewhat paradoxical, given the power asymmetry between it and other member countries, which might have persuaded Russia to prefer a bilateral approach.

Based on the existing research on regional organizations in Eurasia as tools of regime boosting, perhaps the most important conclusion one could draw (Allison 2008; Collins 2009; Obydenkova & Libman 2015; Roberts 2017; Russo 2018; Russo & Stoddard 2018; Yakouchyk 2018) is that regional organizations indeed can contribute to stabilizing and strengthening authoritarian regimes in the member countries, but not all regional organizations created by autocracies do pursue this objective. In some cases, it is possible to identify unambiguously the direct effects of Eurasian regional organizations' support for authoritarian regimes. Thus, since the early 2000s the CIS has systematically engaged in electoral monitoring in its member countries. While the Commonwealth touts its commitment to democracy and human rights, the conclusions it draws from its monitoring missions systematically contradict those of the Organization for Security and Cooperation in Europe (OSCE) and other Western actors and typically whitewash extreme forms of electoral manipulation and fraud (Fawn 2006). For other regional organizations, the effects associated with support for authoritarian regimes are less obvious. Regional organizations contribute to legitimizing authoritarian regimes in Eurasia in several ways. First, they adopt rhetoric approving of the actions of authoritarian leaders. Second, they legitimize the rule of those leaders by calling them supporters of regionalism. That matters because post-Soviet regionalism is very popular in some of the countries of the region, and the existence of the Eurasian organizations allows their authoritarian leaders to present themselves as leading advocates of regional integration. Finally, regional organizations can be used for purposes of redistribution, since they can act as conduits for economic support to flow from Russia to smaller authoritarian countries. The effectiveness of these tools is disputable, but the authoritarian leadership of at least one country (Belarus) has made promoting Eurasian regionalism the cornerstone of its ideology.

However, regional organizations created by non-democracies also can be regime-neutral or they may (surprisingly in the case of Russia) even undermine authoritarian rule and the policies promoting autocracy preferred by their member states. The EAEU is a particularly difficult case to evaluate from the point of view of its potential regime-boosting effects. The organization follows a purely economic agenda and—unlike the CIS or many other Eurasian regional organizations—refrains from establishing any political institutions, whether symbolic or rudimentary. The collective decision-making mechanism in the EAEU has occasionally constrained the Russian Federation in its attempts to exert pressure on other countries of Eurasia. Moreover, the existence of a common internal market makes the implementation of Russian sanctions against democratizing countries in Eurasia more difficult. In the Ukrainian case, since 2014 the existence of the EAEU has reduced Russia's ability to pressure this country rather than increasing it. The economic integration program within the EAEU forces some of the autocracies to implement at least partial economic reforms. Such reforms, in turn, could vitiate to some extent their established mechanisms of authoritarian rule, as has happened in Belarus.

Another important conclusion one can draw from the Eurasian case is that the effect of regional organizations on regime boosting is not necessarily correlated with their actual success in implementing an economic or political integration agenda (Vinokurov & Libman 2017). Even virtually powerless regional organizations can make a difference because they serve as tools to enhance the legitimacy of their member countries. In fact, for smaller autocracies the decision to join weak and ineffective non-democratic regional organizations could be particularly attractive. If an organization has a real policy agenda, it forces its member states to comply with that agenda. But for authoritarian countries, even a limited transfer of sovereignty to the supranational bodies or extensive compliance with the organizations' intergovernmental decisions could be dangerous, because either could be perceived by the national elites and bureaucracies as a sign of regime decay (Libman & Obydenkova 2013). Unlike democracies, in which power-sharing among multiple actors is a part of the normal functioning of the political system, autocracies[9] concentrate all power in the hands of the leadership. Furthermore, the power asymmetry in Eurasia makes smaller countries worry that joining a functioning regional organization might increase their dependence on Russia (Libman & Vinokurov 2018). A defunct regional organization alleviates all these concerns, but still can be useful to the regime for legitimacy purposes.

In short, the Eurasian case shows that it is important to avoid simplifications and generalizations in studying regional organizations created by autocracies. At the same time, it shows that one should not ignore the non-democratic regional organizations as factors favoring the potential consolidation of authoritarian regimes.[10]

Becoming an actor

Acknowledging that regional organizations in Eurasia matter, for instance, for the post-Soviet countries' regime transitions, inevitably leads to yet another question, which unfortunately so far has received very limited attention in the scholarly literature. In the debate over the EU, one of the key questions is the extent to which this regional organization has acquired the status of an actor. That is, to what extent is it able to make and implement independent policy and to emancipate itself from the wishes of the member countries (Jupille & Caporaso 1998)? Without question, other organizations worldwide have a much weaker claim to be actors than does the EU, and it is very likely that regional organizations created by non-democratic states will have more limited claims to the status of actor than democracies. This is the case due to a previously mentioned feature of autocracies: their lesser willingness to accept even limited power-sharing. Does that mean that we should treat authoritarian regionalism merely as a *vehicle* of the foreign policy initiatives of individual countries, whether these are like Russia, the center or gravity of an entire authoritarian system in Eurasia, or simply coalitions of autocrats belonging to the regional organization?

The majority of studies of Eurasian regionalism do seem to share the fundamental assumption that Eurasian regional organizations are simply tools of Russian foreign policy. The studies of the supranational bureaucracy, which in case of the EAEU employs more than 1,000 officials, are very scarce (for a rare exception see Staeger & Bobocea 2018). It appears unlikely that the EAEU bureaucracy ever can really challenge the position of the member states. By contrast, in an authoritarian country, bureaucrats would prefer to err on the side of caution in their attempts to avoid punishment from the political leadership. However, it is possible that the EAEU bureaucrats still attain the status of actors to some degree, not vis-à-vis the political leadership, but vis-à-vis other national bureaucracies. The Eurasian Economic Commission could be competing for the attention of the national leadership with other (national) ministries and agencies, partly attempting to promote its own agenda. This method of rising to the status of actor is much more difficult to recognize and study empirically, yet there have been instances when the EAEU bureaucrats indeed have become vocal in discussing a number of important policy initiatives in the Eurasian countries, about which individual agencies of the national governments were not of one mind.[11] Being an actor in this way makes Eurasian bureaucracy relevant for policy decisions, although perhaps not for the strategic ones, which remain in the hands of the national political leaders. Again, careful study of Eurasia makes it necessary to offer a more nuanced approach to some of the concepts one typically uses in studying regional organizations. But that caution about our conceptual apparatus may also inform research on other non-European regionalisms.

Conclusion

It remains to sum up the main conclusions of this chapter. I started by describing the debate on the historical evolution of Russia in the last century: i.e., whether it can be seen as a country following its own path to modernity or as an example of a state reproducing and strengthening archaic policy and governance practices. Sztompka's (1993) concept of "fake modernity" in the post-Communist world provides an important perspective on this question. Both Communist and post-Communist regimes did manage to achieve certain breakthroughs that, from the point of view of empirical research, resemble what we typically define as proxies for modernization. Yet those pseudo-modern phenomena lead to very different consequences for human behavior. Reviewing the research on regionalism, one similarly could think of the Eurasian regional organizations in the same way. While in form they resemble the processes of regionalism developing in other parts of the world (and, in particular, in the EU), in practice they pursue a very different goal: the preservation of the hierarchically-organized economic space of the Russian Empire and of the Soviet Union. From this point of view, however, it is possible to link Eurasian regionalism to other examples of authoritarian regionalism, which were particularly prolific before and immediately after World War I and seem to be on the rise in the modern world (Telò 2017).

The subsequent analysis presented in this chapter showed that Eurasian regionalism indeed illuminates a number of important phenomena, and those could matter for understanding the emergence and role of regionalism in other regions dominated by authoritarian countries. Thus, the example of Eurasia shows that autocracy can insist on imitating the EU in spite of being heavily and openly critical of the EU model and challenging the growing role of that body in the world. It further shows that autocracies can use regional organizations to support fellow autocracies. At the same time, however, it indicates that not every undemocratic regional organization is a vehicle for the power plays of the leading authoritarian country, nor is it merely a tool of autocracy promotion. Unexpectedly, regional organizations in some cases actually can constrain the power of their authoritarian hegemons. Finally, the Eurasian example also shows some non-traditional paths toward the status of being an actor that could be taken by regional organizations created by non-democracies. Here, however, far more research is needed to investigate these paths empirically.

Thus, Eurasian regionalism is an example of how complex regionalist phenomena can be in a context similar to that of the post-Soviet space. It also suggests how important the hidden effects (different from those declared in the official mandates of the regional organizations) and the unexpected effects may be. As a final remark, it is important to point out that Eurasian regionalism should not be seen only as a process of reproducing and sustaining old economic and social ties inherited from the Soviet Union or, for that matter, even from the Russian imperial past. In addition to these ties (the real focus of this chapter), in the last two decades Eurasia has witnessed a surge of new, market driven interconnections between countries—a vibrant regionalization process which, until 2010, coexisted with rather poor performance of regionalism in regard to economic policymaking. Labor migration from the poorer countries of Eurasia to Russia or Kazakhstan; Russian, Kazakhstani, or Ukrainian foreign direct investments in other Eurasian countries; and the persistence of the common cultural space all offer examples of the bottom-up links among Eurasian societies rather than of the reproduction of hierarchical power structures (Libman & Vinokurov 2012). They, too, must be taken into account when we analyze the Eurasian region.

Notes

1. This chapter is supported by the MOE Project of Key Research Institute of Humanities and Social Sciences in Universities of China (Center for Russian Studies of East China Normal University), Project Number: 16JJDGJW004.
2. See the discussion of the link between regionalism and the multiple modernities framework in the chapter by Katzenstein in this volume.
3. The analysis of this chapter does not cover the Shanghai Cooperation Organization (SCO), since it also includes China and thus differs substantially from other "post-Soviet" regional organizations. However, some of the issues discussed in this chapter—e.g., the role of regionalism as an instrument of regime boosting—in fact do matter for the SCO case as well (Ambrosio 2008; Allison 2018).
4. On the variety of models of multilateralism see Telò (2012) as well as the chapter of Qin in this volume.
5. Thus, it focuses on trade to a larger extent than on other aspects of regionalism, like common infrastructure or migration.
6. This is not surprising: From the very beginning, the EU remained highly skeptical about Eurasian regionalism and until recently designed its policies toward the Eastern neighborhood without taking Eurasian regionalism into account in any way.
7. It is worth noting that the focus on the EU as the normative blueprint diminished in 2016–18. During this period, Russia developed the project of the Greater Eurasian Partnership, which seems to emulate the large transcontinental trade agreements and China's Belt and Road Initiative (Timofeev et al. 2017; Lewis 2018; Li 2018).
8. See also Telò's chapter in this book.
9. At least the personalist autocracies, which dominate the post-Soviet political landscape.
10. An interesting question is whether authoritarian external influences can also matter for established democracies. Research on this topic is virtually non-existent. See Oleinik 2008; Chou et al. 2017.
11. An example is the reform of the import duties for goods purchased on foreign online retail shops, which has been discussed in the EAEU since 2014.

References

Acharya, A. 2016. "Regionalism Beyond EU-centrism." In T. Börzel & T. Risse, T. (eds.). *Oxford Handbook of comparative regionalism*. Oxford, UK: Oxford University Press, pp. 109–30

Allison, R. 2008. "Virtual Regionalism, Regional Structures and Regime Security in Central Asia." *Central Asian Survey* 27(2): 185–202

Allison, R. 2018. "Protective Integration and Security Policy Coordination: Comparing the SCO and CSTO." *The Chinese Journal of International Politics* 11(3): 297–338

Ambrosio, T. 2008. "Catching the 'Shanghai Spirit': How the Shanghai Cooperation Organization promotes authoritarian norms in Central Asia." *Europe-Asia Studies* 60(8): 1321–44

Börzel, T. & V. van Hüllen, 2015. *Governance Transfer by Regional Organizations: Patching together a global script*. Basingstoke, UK: Palgrave MacMillan

Chou, M., C. Pan, & A. Poole, 2017. "The Threat of Autocracy Diffusion in Consolidated Democracies? The case of China, Singapore and Australia." *Contemporary Politics* 23(2): 175–94

Collins, K. 2009. "Economic and Security Regionalism among Patrimonial Authoritarian Regimes: The case of Central Asia." *Europe-Asia Studies* 61(2): 249–81

David-Fox, M. 2006. "Multiple Modernities vs. Neo-traditionalism: On recent debates in Russian and Soviet history." *Jahrbücher für Geschichte Osteuropas* 54(4): 535–55

DiMaggio, P. & W. Powell, 1983. "The Iron Cage Revisited: Collective rationality and institutional isomorphism in organizational fields." *American Sociological Review* 48(2): 147–60

Dragneva, R. & K. Wolczuk, 2015. "European Union Emulation in the Design of Integration." In D. Lane & V. Samokhvalov (eds.), *The Eurasian Project and Europe*. London: Palgrave MacMillan, pp. 135–52

Fawn, R. 2006. "Battle over the Box: International election observation missions, political competition and retrenchment in the post-Soviet space." *International Affairs* 82(6): 1133–53

Furman, D. 2005. "Ot Rossiyskoy Imperii do raspada SNG." http://polit.ru/article/2005/10/05/furman/

Furman, E. & A. Libman, 2015. "Europeanization and the Eurasian Economic Union." In P. Dutkiewicz & R. Sakwa (eds.), *Eurasian Integration—The view from within*. Abingdon, UK: Routledge, 173–92

Furman, E. & A. Libman, 2019. "Imagined Regionalism: Eurasian regional organizations as a Soviet legacy." In A. Moshes (ed.). *What Has Remained of the Soviet Union?* Helsinki: FIIA, pp. 85–101

Johnson, J. & S. Köstem, 2016. "Frustrated Leadership: Russia's economic alternative to the West." *Global Policy* 7(2): 207–16

Jupille, J. & J. Caporaso, 1998. "States, Agency and Rules: The European Union in global environmental politics. In C. Rhodes (ed.), *The European Union in the World Community*. Boulder, CO: Lynne Rienner. Available at: https://papers.ssrb.com/sol3/papers.cfm?abstractid+2242500

Jupille, J., B. Jolliff, & S. Wojcik, 2013. "Regionalism in the World Polity." Mimeo

Kneuer, M. & T. Demmelhuber, 2016. "Gravity Centers of Authoritarian Rule: A conceptual approach." *Democratization* 23(5): 775–96

Kneuer, M., T. Demmelhuber, R. Peresson, & T. Zumbrägel, 2018. "Playing the Regional Card: Why and how authoritarian gravity centres exploit regional organisations." *Third World Quarterly* 40(3): 451–70

Lankina, T. & A. Libman, 2019. "Soviet Legacies of Economic Development, Oligarchic Rule and Electoral Quality in Eastern Europe's Partial Democracies: The case of Ukraine." *Comparative Politics* 52(1): 127–48

Lewin, M. 2005. *The Soviet Century*. London: Verso

Lewis, D. 2018. "Geopolitical Imaginaries in Russian Foreign Policy: The evolution of 'Greater Eurasia.'" *Europe-Asia Studies* 70(10): 1612–37

Li, Y. 2018. "The Greater Eurasian Partnership and the Belt and Road Initiative: Can the two be linked?" *Journal of Eurasian Studies* 9(2): 94–99

Libman, A. 2017. "Russian Power Politics and the Eurasian Economic Union: The real and the imagined." *Rising Powers Quarterly* 1(1): 81–103

Libman, A. & A. Obydenkova, 2013. "Informal Governance and Participation in Non-democratic International Organizations." *Review of International Organizations* 8(2): 221–43

Libman, A. & A. Obydenkova, 2018a. "Regional International Organizations as a Strategy of Autocracy: The Eurasian Economic Union and Russian foreign policy." *International Affairs* 94(5): 1037–58

Libman, A. & A. Obydenkova, 2018b. "Understanding Authoritarian Regionalism." *Journal of Democracy* 29(4): 151–65

Libman, A. & E. Vinokurov, 2012. *Holding-together Regionalism: Twenty years of post-Soviet integration*. Basingstoke, UK: Palgrave MacMillan

Libman, A. & E. Vinokurov, 2018. "Autocracies and Regional Integration: The Eurasian case." *Post-Communist Economies* 30(3): 334–64

Maslovskiy, M. 2016. "The Imperial Dimension of Russian Modernisation: A multiple modernities perspective." *Europe-Asia Studies* 68(1): 20–37

Moravcsik, A. 2004. "Is There a 'Democratic Deficit' in World Politics? A framework for analysis." *Government and Opposition* 39(2): 336–63

Neumann, I. 2016. "Russia's Europe, 1991–2016: Inferiority to superiority." *International Affairs* 92(6): 1381–99

Obydenkova, A., & A. Libman (eds.), 2015. *Autocratic and Democratic External Influences in Post-Soviet Eurasia*. Aldershot, UK: Ashgate

Obydenkova, A. & A. Libman, 2019. *Authoritarian Regionalism in the World of International Organizations*. Oxford, UK: Oxford University Press

Oleinik, A. 2008. "On Negative Convergence: The metaphor of Vodka-Cola reconsidered." *Telos* 145: 31–46

Paneyakh, E. 2018. "Bitva za normu." Available at www.inliberty.ru/article/liberty-paneyakh/

Pevehouse, J. 2005. *Democracy from Above: Regional organizations and democratization*. Cambridge, UK: Cambridge University Press

Roberts, S. 2017. "The Eurasian Economic Union: The geopolitics of authoritarian cooperation." *Eurasian Geography and Economics* 58(4): 418–41

Russo, A. 2018. *Regions in Transition in the Former Soviet Area: Ideas and institutions in the making*. Basingstoke, UK: Palgrave MacMillan

Russo, A. & E. Stoddard, 2018. "Why do Authoritarian Leaders do Regionalism? Ontological security and Eurasian regional cooperation." *International Spectator* 53(3): 20–37

Schimmelfennig, F. & H. Scholtz, 2008. "EU Democracy Promotion in the European Neighbourhood: Political conditionality, economic development and transnational exchange." *European Union Politics* 9(2): 187–215

Söderbaum, F. 2004. "Modes of Regional Governance in Africa: Neoliberalism, sovereignty boosting, and shadow networks." *Global Governance* 10(4): 419–36

Söderbaum, F. 2016. *Rethinking Regionalism*. Basingstoke, UK: Palgrave MacMillan

Staeger, U. & C. Bobocea, 2018. "Bureaucratic Authority and Mimesis: The Eurasian Economic Union's multiple integration logics." *The International Spectator* 53(3): 38–54

Stefanova, B. 2018. *The European Union and Europe's New Regionalism*. Basingstoke, UK: Palgrave MacMillan

Sztompka, P. 1993. "Civilizational Incompetence: The trap of post-communist societies." *Zeitschrift für Soziologie* 22(2): 85–95

Telò, M. (ed.), 2012. *State, Globalization and Multilateralism: The challenges of institutionalizing regionalism*. Heidelberg, Germany: Springer

Telò, M. 2017. *Regionalism in Hard Times: Competitive and post-liberal trends in Europe, Asia, Africa, and the Americas*. Abingdon, UK: Routledge

Timofeev, I., Y. Lissovolik, & L. Filippova, 2017. "Russia's Vision of the Belt and Road Initiative: From the rivalry of the great powers to forging a new cooperation model in Eurasia." *China and World Economy* 25(5): 62–77

Vicari, M. 2016. "The Eurasian Economic Union: Approaching the economic integration in the post-Soviet space by EU-emulated elements." *Revue Interventions Economiques: Papers in Political Economy*, no. 55

Vinokurov, E. 2018. *Introduction to the Eurasian Economic Union*. Basingstoke, UK: Palgrave MacMillan

Vinokurov, E. & A. Libman, 2012. "Eurasia and Eurasian Integration: Beyond the post-Soviet borders." *Eurasian Integration Yearbook*. Almaty, Kazakhstan: Eurasian Development Bank, pp. 80–95

Vinokurov, E., & A. Libman, 2017. *Re-evaluating Regional Organizations: Behind the smokescreen of official mandates*. Basingstoke, UK: Palgrave MacMillan

Yakouchyk, K. 2018. "Governance Transfer by Non-democratic Regional Organizations: The case of the CSTO." In D. Göle & E. Stratenschulte (eds.), *Norm- und Regeltransfer in der europäischen Außenpolitik*. Baden-Baden, Germany: Nomos, pp. 233–56

8
CHINESE MULTILATERALISM IN CENTRAL AND SOUTHEAST ASIA

A relational perspective

Jianwei Wang and Weiqing Song

Introduction

Chinese foreign policy has undergone a remarkable change in recent decades, from being passive and reactive to being proactive and taking the initiative. This tendency has become more salient since Xi Jinping came to power, exemplified by his signature foreign policy initiatives of "One Belt, One Road" (BRI) and the "Community of Common Destiny for Mankind." China's new diplomacy has drawn widespread attention from the international community and students of Chinese foreign policy and given rise to numerous studies and analyses. Most, however, have focused on the geopolitical and utility oriented motivations behind China's diplomatic transformation and their implications for major-power rivalry. Insufficient attention has been paid to the normative and conceptual challenges that China's new diplomacy presents to the traditional Western model and the diplomacy and scholarship associated with it.

One distinctive feature of Xi Jinping's new diplomacy has been China's increasing embrace and even advocacy of multilateralism and regionalism. Just like other major powers, China's practice of multilateralism and regionalism has also carried with it the traditional geopolitical motivations and considerations that enhance its national power and interests, as realists would like to emphasize. However, its practice of regionalism and multilateralism has also featured some "Chinese characteristics," often reflecting China's unique cultural identity and heritage as these pertain to human relations in general and relations among nations in particular. This chapter contends that China's approach to carrying on mainstream Western diplomacy—e.g., via multilateralism and regionalism—cannot be explained adequately by conventional Western theories of international relations. China's rise and its accompanying new diplomacy provide a valuable opportunity to understand more fully the new dynamics of regionalism and multilateralism as practiced by emerging powers such as China. More specifically, this chapter traces the conceptual evolution of China's attitudes and approaches to multilateralism and regionalism as practiced in two of its neighboring regions: Central Asia and Southeast Asia. In so doing, it takes a relational perspective (Emirbayer 1997; Qin 2016).

Multilateralism as a relationship

Multilateralism can be characterized as an integral and important part of the Western liberal international order in the postwar international setting. It underlies international security and financial and economic regimes as exemplified by the United Nations, World Bank, International Monetary Fund (IMF), and General Agreement on Tariffs and Trade (GATT; later the World Trade Organization, or WTO). China, a Communist country isolated from the Western-dominated international system, long has been repelled by and suspicious of Western multilateralism. Its experience of multilateralism with both superpowers during the Cold War period was by no means positive. As late as the late 1990s, some Chinese elites still considered multilateralism to be a taboo that should not be touched by Chinese diplomacy, since it would do more harm than good to China (Wang 2005: 190). Yet, entering the twenty-first century, China has increasingly embraced multilateralism in its diplomacy. Multilateral diplomacy and multilateralism have become the standard discourse of Chinese foreign policy. Beijing has participated actively in multilateral diplomacy at both the regional and global levels. Further, instead of simply reacting to the multilateral initiatives of other countries, Beijing has become more proactive, advocating and promoting regionalism and multilateralism both economically and for security reasons by launching regional international organizations such as the Shanghai Cooperation Organization (SCO) and the Asian Infrastructure Investment Bank (AIIB). China's strong advocacy of multilateralism reached its zenith in 2017 after Donald Trump's election as President of the United States. When Trump spared no effort to push American unilateralism by withdrawing from a series of multilateral international treaties and bodies, China presented itself as the champion of multilateralism and globalism ("Full Text of Xi Jinping Keynote at the World Economic Forum" 2017). It is ironic that Chinese multilateralism and American unilateralism/bilateralism are now frequently and sharply contrasted in both discourse and practice.

Chinese multilateralism displays some characteristics that are different from the conventional understanding of that approach to foreign policy. These can be understood best in terms of relational sociology, which emphasizes the primacy of interactions, social ties, or relations and networks, both ontologically and epistemologically (Crossley 2015: 66). The relational argument runs counter to conventional individualism in which networks and interactions presuppose that actors are primordial and therefore should be afforded primacy ontologically and methodologically. The relational perspective contends instead that, both individually and collectively, all human actors are shaped by and become social beings via relational interactions. Actors, including states, cannot be understood atomistically; rather, the isolated individual is an abstraction, since human beings always live in groups, are intertwined with others, and remain embedded in numerous relationships. Overall, the relations themselves matter in ways that cannot be reduced to the interests and desires of individual actors (Crossley 2015: 67).

Relational thinking entails reconsideration of international studies at the most fundamental level (Qin 2016). In this regard, a debate has emerged between substantialism and relationalism over the ontological basis of international relations. The former holds that ontological primitives are entities that exist before interactions and that all relations are between such predefined entities. This conventional approach contrasts with relationalism, which treats the relational ties between various social aggregates as the most essential focus of attention. Relational thinking thus subscribes to relational rather than substantive ontology. In other words, the relational totality constitutes a social context that shapes and is shaped by, enables and is enabled by, and constrains and is constrained by the actors therein (Qin 2016: 38). Because such social ties are not static, but rather dynamic and ongoing, analysis must be based on processes and relations. In this relational process, various factors are interrelated with one another. It is neither necessary nor possible to differentiate independent and dependent variables, because these are inherently interdependent. In terms of epistemology, therefore, relational thinking takes an interpretive approach to understanding, not explaining, the empirical world.

According to relational theory, states as social beings have always lived in groups with numerous social ties of varying densities and intimacies. Indeed, the very existence of a state relies on its interactions with other actors. Without its relationships with other actors, no state could maintain its existence. It follows from this observation that issues like national interests, international prestige, the international outlook, and corresponding state behaviors are inexorably interwoven with those of other actors and cannot be defined independently from them. Interactions can take on various forms such as dialogues, activities, events, and projects. Always embedded in numerous relations (which approximate social networks), the behaviors of international actors are enabled and constrained by these relations (Qin 2016: 38). Actors-in-relations thus make active use of their relational circles for instrumental purposes. It often happens, for example, that actors make decisions according to the degree of intimacy and/or importance of their relationships with specific others, with the totality of their relational circles as the background (Qin 2016: 37).

Yet it is unclear how relational thinking can be operationalized in empirical analysis. Relational thinking has spurred scholarly endeavors to develop various analytical tools for real world politics. Among them, an interpretive version of the Social Network Analysis (SNA) stands out (Crossley 2015). As a research paradigm, the interpretive approach is based on the assumption that social reality is not a singular and objective ontology but is shaped by human experiences and embedded in social contexts. Therefore, it is better to study international relations within a social–historical context by interpreting the meanings within the contexts rather than by following a positivist approach of hypothesis testing (Lynch 2014: 12–18). From an interpretive perspective, an SNA is particularly amenable to analysis of cultural and ideational factors. In reality, all states live in an interactive social network of state and non-state actors. Bilateral relations between two states are the most simplified version of social ties in international relations. Multilateral relations are more complicated modes of social interaction. States, like "nodes," interact with one another within various social networks. Those with more substantial ties usually have more influence and serve as "hubs." Ties and networks can exist in various forms. Some are more institutionalized as members of the same organization. Others are aggregated more closely due to geographic proximity, cultural affinity, or religious beliefs. These numerous ties and bonds vary in intimacy, as states may be friendly allies, cooperative partners, business competitors, or strategic rivals. They also differ in the density of exchanges and activities within the political, social, economic and cultural spheres such as trade, migration, and religion. It is through these kinds of dynamic interactions and networking that norms, rules, and values arise among international actors. Through social interactions they further diffuse across other members within certain social networks.

This chapter relies on the above-elaborated relational perspective to understand and interpret China's practice of multilateralism in the regional context. Relationships and connections occupy an important position in the Chinese philosophical worldview and cultural identity (Qin 2016). Although China used to be more comfortable in cultivating relationships and interacting with other nations in a bilateral fashion, multilateral diplomacy has become an increasingly important and effective instrument of Chinese foreign policy. Beijing's diplomatic practice in recent years has shown that Chinese leader Xi Jinping is particularly fond of using multilateral platforms to promote and disseminate his ideas of common interests, identities, and destinies. Domestically, cultivating relationships/connections through interactions has been a prevailing characteristic of Chinese politics. However, that tendency is now reflected in its interactions with other countries, particularly with its neighboring countries.

Given some practical constraints, this study narrows the scope to investigate China's relational multilateral diplomacy with Central Asia and Southeast Asia. This choice of focus is based on reasonable grounds. Multilateral diplomacy with the two regions has been among China's foreign policy priorities, where its good neighbor policy and relations with developing countries have merged. China's multilateral endeavors have been deliberate and intensive, and Central Asia and Southeast Asia have stood out in its overall foreign strategy. China's current high profile in the Belt and Road Initiative (BRI) was inspired by its experiences and engagement with the two sub-regions.[1] Thus, China's regional engagement with Central Asia and Southeast Asia provides an ideal showcase to demonstrate how the country has implemented its multilateral diplomacy from the relational perspective.

China's multilateral diplomacy in Central Asia

China's engagement with the Central Asian countries has been largely undertaken through the Shanghai Cooperation Organization process. The creation and evolution of the SCO reveals the social actors' needs and desire to interact. Established in 2001, the history of the SCO can be traced back to the "Shanghai Five" process of the mid-1990s. Despite the legendary "Silk Road" historical romance, relations between China and the Central Asian countries began with marked alienation after a long period of isolation in bilateral relations. Not until the early 1990s did the two sides feel that the time was ripe for them to enter into direct contact with each other. It was in those years, of course, that the Central Asian republics declared their independence after the Soviet Union imploded. That unexpected political change occasioned direct contact between China and its Central Asian neighbors, originally with the aim of demarcating their borders. However, these boundaries turned out to be not only spatial, but temporal and normative. Barriers to smooth interactions between China and its Central Asian partners grew out of cultural alienation based on religious and civil differences, historical separation, and linguistic obstacles.

It is widely believed that the SCO largely has been a Chinese networking initiative with the Central Asian states. Analysts have asserted that China was the "major impetus" behind the SCO's formation based on multilateral security cooperation with Central Asia (Lanteigne 2006/2007: 607). "China's enthusiasm for helping to establish, develop and structure this regional multi-lateral organisation" has been obvious (Chung 2006: 5). In the process of constructing a regional social network, each nation has been represented by a "node," and both China and (to a lesser extent) Russia have acted as the "hubs," given their resources and linkages. China has made major efforts to cultivate the growth of this network. To quote a senior Chinese analyst on the issue, China's driving role in forming multilateral relations through the SCO largely has been in three areas: formulating the theoretical guidelines, driving institutionalization forward, and giving direct support to major projects (Pan 2008/2009). From the relational perspective, these three areas involve the normative basis, institutional ties, and interactions, respectively. Of these, institutional ties are the most basic, because they provide infrastructure, whereas interactions occur among the nodes of the network in various forms, including events, issues, and activities. Forming a normative basis for future relations is more of a long-term objective because it usually takes a great deal of time to disseminate and absorb commonly shared values and rules throughout the network.

Drawing on relational theory, we assert that ties gradually have been created and strengthened in the process of SCO institutionalization. Although China endeavored to create the SCO out of its strategic ambition to engage Central Asian countries, the Chinese initiative generally has been welcomed by the Central Asian states, which have been eager to promote their international visibility in addition to meeting their practical need for social contacts. The SCO has provided institutional support conducive to the formation of a social network among countries in the region.[2] Thus far, the SCO has witnessed several major developments in the formalization process: the establishment of a basic institutional framework in the first period from 2001 to 2006; the furthering of institutional arrangements in the second period from 2007 to 2011; and the exploration of new areas for institutional improvement in the third period from 2012 to the present. It is worth mentioning that the first SCO summits in 2001 and 2002 produced two important documents: its founding declaration and an SCO Charter that legalizes the principles and mechanisms developed since the Shanghai Five. These have provided a legal framework for further institutional development. In this way, the Charter has defined the SCO as an ensemble of major institutional organs, including the two permanent ones, the Regional Anti-Terrorist Structure/ Regional Counter-Terrorist Structure and the SCO Secretariat. The SCO has been institutionalized further by routines such as annual summits of state leaders and heads of government. SCO cooperation covers a wide range of issues, including politics and security, economics and functional, cultural, and educational matters.

Social networks operate only when members interact with one another. Such interactions take place through cooperation in multilateral diplomacy. Cooperation within the SCO framework covers a wide range of issues related to security, economics, energy, various functional areas, education, and culture. Institutional arrangements likewise have been developed for external relations and interactions with non-governmental organizations (NGOs). Regional security is at the top of the SCO agenda. Cooperation in the security field and particularly the struggle against international terrorism have comprised the main areas of SCO activity since its establishment (Lukin 2007: 142). Hence, strengthening security cooperation was the priority when the member states developed the SCO's institutional architecture. The security cooperation framework is supported by several institutional mechanisms. As a special security mechanism, the SCO's joint anti-terrorism military exercises have become routine means to improve member states' anti-terrorism capacities. The six member countries of the SCO signed a communiqué in 2006, agreeing to stage a joint anti-terror military exercise in Russia the following year.[3] As a concrete step, the joint anti-terrorism military exercise known as the Peace Mission has been held almost annually. Overall, security cooperation has been acclaimed as the hallmark of the SCO.

Apart from the security sphere, the SCO has gradually intensified its cooperation in economic areas. An institutional framework has been set up comprising both official and non-official participants from the member states. These include relevant governmental ministries as well as two government-sponsored NGOs:

the Business Council, which serves as a platform for enterprises from the SCO member states to establish links and dialogues, and the Interbank Consortium, which provides financial support to cooperating programs under the aegis of the SCO network. Although many ambitious goals for trade and economic cooperation have been proclaimed, the SCO member states have made only modest progress in matters touching on trade and the facilitation of investment. Most of the work in the economic sphere has involved discussion and some symbolic or exploratory projects. Only in energy cooperation has there been more substantial activity; however, that has been achieved on a bilateral basis in the guise of the SCO's multilateral framework. For example, in the transportation sector, several projects on highway construction have been implemented in Kyrgyzstan, Uzbekistan, and Tajikistan, largely due to China's financial support (Liu 2011: 39–41). Nonetheless, overall, the evidence shows that economic and trade cooperation in the SCO have followed a trajectory of cheap talk and little work.

The contrast between security and economic cooperation within the SCO stems from differences in the way the parties' interests are understood. In this regard, "focus" has been an important element in the SNA framework, which can account for more successful cooperation in the security spheres than in the economic sphere. It refers to something that catches the actors' attention or interest, bringing them together and allowing them to meet, form ties, and mount collective actions that in turn create a social space (Crossley 2015: 78). The evolution of the SCO has been characterized and triggered by a series of such "foci," particularly state-building and regime stability. When Central Asian leaders declared their independence in the aftermath of the Soviet collapse, they were ill prepared to handle the daunting task of state- and nation-building, which became the issue of focus. In international relations, the new situation necessitated border demarcation with China. National boundaries previously had been negotiated with the Soviet Union in the late 1980s with the aim of settling their shared border on China's Northwest frontier. The Shanghai Five came into being in 1996, inspired by this practical problem, and China seized the opportunity to institutionalize ties with its long-lost Silk Road neighbors. The newly independent states also were prone to various challenges, both internally and externally. A more acute issue was the so-called "three evils" as defined by China: transnational terrorism, ethnic separatism, and religious extremism. Inroads by the United States in the region in the wake of the Afghanistan war that began in 2001 were interpreted as major threats to the stability of regimes in the smaller and weaker Central Asian countries. Based on these issues or foci, and in response, China and eventually the other members of the SCO, including Russia, began to feel the need to forge closer ties of mutual cooperation.

Such ties are social relationships centered around, but not limited to, the SCO. According to relational thinking, all countries are embedded in numerous relations in the international arena, subject to international and external normative influences. China and the Central Asian countries are shaping and being shaped in their interactions with other actors. The SCO social network has been extended institutionally through the methods of the observer states and dialogue partnerships. The former status is currently being extended to Mongolia and Afghanistan, two countries in the region with the potential to join the club. India and Pakistan were granted the same status before they became full members in 2017. Countries interested in becoming affiliated with the SCO but with little chance to join as full members either due to geographical distance or political sensitivity have the opportunity to link up with the SCO as dialogue partners. The list of such countries currently includes Iran, Turkey, Sri Lanka, and Belarus. According to relational theory, actors are embedded in complicated webs of relationships. Therefore, this list of extended social networks is far from exhaustive. Other actors that have notable relations with the SCO members and the region as a whole may include the US, Japan, the EU and its member states, and other former Soviet republics.

China's engagement with the Central Asian states, together with other SCO members, has not taken place in a vacuum. To the contrary, relations have flourished in the international arena where networks of states interact with other states, both individually and collectively, and one state can belong to a variety of networks simultaneously. This multiplicity of relational networks has intensified and burgeoned as time has gone by. In Central Asia, either as a region in itself or as part of a wider region, there are several multilateral organizations that largely have been operating in parallel with the SCO. These have included the Commonwealth of Independent States (CIS), the Collective Security Treaty Organization (CSTO), and the Eurasian Economic Union (EAEU or EEU). Despite numerous obstacles and divergences, self-initiated multilateralism also has been underway in the region. Driven by the vision of Central Asian regionalism, states there have resumed the process of launching a prospective Central Asian Union. In addition, the idea for a Conference on Interaction and Confidence-Building Measures in Asia was proposed by Kazakhstan as a forum for dialogue and consultation on regional security issues in Asia. Activities around these multilateral regional initiatives have contributed to social networking efforts of varying scope, form, and focus. Together with the SCO, they have converged with, complemented, or competed with one another.

The core normative consensus that China has strived to promote via the SCO is known as the "Shanghai Spirit." It boasts that cooperation within the organization is distinguished by the norms of "mutual trust, mutual benefit, equality, mutual consultations and respect for cultural diversity and aspiration for common development" (SOC 2007). This has been mainly a Chinese project, which has been intellectually innovative in creating and promoting a number of concepts, including the Shanghai Spirit, the "New Outlook on Security," and the "Harmonious World." Pan (2008/2009: 59) asserted that China has played the leading role in "formulating the theoretical guidelines" of the SCO. The three institutional norms derived respectively from the three major sources diverge in some ways from existing international norms, having been inspired by scholarly work and derived from domestic norms. The primary purpose of China's effort to promote norms was mainly to encourage solidarity among SCO members by providing institutional guidelines and values. Compared with international organizations in the West, the SCO is less legalistic and more normative in nature, with members sharing common perceptions (Aris 2009: 479). Although the norms and values originally were formulated to foster organizational solidarity, they also can be used as balancing weapons against perceived threats when necessary. Both strategies are conducive to stabilizing the still-evolving social network of the SCO.

China and Russia (as "critical states") have spared no effort to promote the Shanghai Spirit in the SCO process, with an emphasis on "stability" and "diversity" (Ambrosio 2008). At the Bishkek summit held on August 16, 2007, the Council of Heads of State adopted the Treaty on Long-Term Good-Neighborliness, Friendship, and Cooperation between the Member-States of the Shanghai Cooperation Organization. According to the treaty, the member states of the SCO were

> convinced that strengthening and deepening relations of goodneighbourliness, friendship, and cooperation between the member states of the organization corresponds to the fundamental interests of their peoples and contributes to peace and development in the SCO space and in the whole world.
>
> *(SCO 2007)*

Together with the SCO Charter, the treaty stressed that the principles upheld by SCO members fundamentally underpinned the organization. More importantly, it elaborated the organization's values and norms, known collectively as the Shanghai Spirit. Thus, the Shanghai Spirit in essence has merged with the age-old Five Principles long upheld by the Chinese government. In other words, the Shanghai Spirit is the incarnation of the Five Principles in the context of Central Asia. As an adaptation to local conditions there, it is complemented by "respect for cultural diversity and aspiration for common development" (SCO 2007) highlighting the major religious and cultural gaps between China and its Central Asia partners.

Chinese and Russian leaders have drawn criticism from governments and NGOs in the West for promoting norms through the SCO process. The Shanghai Spirit has been denounced as an authoritarian effort to counteract the promotion of Western norms (Ambrosio 2008). There has been a kind of normative competition in the region. Efforts have been made by Western governments and Western-based NGOs to support democracy promotion activities and the rule of law. However, these activities have been viewed by the two hub countries (China and Russia) as threatening the stability of the SCO members and the region as a whole. On this normative issue, there has been a high level of consensus among all SCO members. Leaders of the Central Asian SCO states have shared similar perceptions of US intentions behind the Color Revolutions (Song 2013: 674–76). They have given a higher priority to counterbalancing American and Western efforts to promote democracy in their countries. China's soft balancing through norm promotion has tended to be less problematic. Within the SCO, China has been relatively successful at adopting relevant discourses to bind together other members of the organization, rebut criticism from the United States and other Western governments, and defend its positions. Promoting certain norms can be a major instrument for soft balancing purposes, as long as the norms are shared among the members of the relevant international institution.

Although the norm of regime stability enshrined in the Shanghai Spirit has been successfully shared within the SCO framework, China's efforts to promote economic cooperation and its own development model have been less successful. Despite China's years-long campaign, a multilateral free trade agreement has proved elusive. The issue has not become a focus because states' interests and priorities have diverged considerably. As an alternative, economic cooperation, mostly in the energy sector, has taken place bilaterally between what we have called the nodes. However, the norms of trade liberalization and economic cooperation have been invoked rhetorically in the SCO. In the context of the American Trump administration's policies on global trade and the economy, SCO members recently declared that they jointly stood for strengthening "an open, inclusive, transparent, non-discriminatory, and multilateral trade system based on rules, as well for the prevention of the fragmentation of international trade relations and rejection of any forms of trade protectionism" (SCO 2018: 6). China clearly has been the prime target of the US-initiated trade war and has had major concerns about trade protectionism compared to the other SCO members. The inclusion of rhetorical support does not mean that the norm of free trade has been widely shared by the members, but it has been helpful to the unity of the organization as a social network.

The evidence suggests that if successful, major issues or foci give rise to "value homophily," referring to the social actors' tendency to associate with counterparts who share similar beliefs, values and norms (Crossley 2015: 78). It can be argued that the term "normative space" should be used here to capture the situation in which the normative framework of the Shanghai Spirit has been generally integrated into the social network. The formation of normative space within the SCO cannot be attributed to the China factor alone, although its influence has been considerable. The SCO partners as social actors have shared the norms surrounding the Shanghai Spirit by following the accepted standards of mutual respect for the sovereignty and civil/cultural traditions of the other participants in their relationship. The actors often have enjoyed multiple types of ties with the same alters/others that are nodes to whom ego/oneself is directly connected, making their relationships "multiplex" (Crossley 2015: 73). Thus, connecting to certain alters may be limited to particular types of ties, such that there is one type of relationship with one alter or set of alters and another type with a different set of alters. Multiplex relations have occurred in the SCO: China and Russia have been quasi-allies when facing the common US challenge, but competitors for regional influence in Central Asia. The admission of India and Pakistan into the SCO in 2017 has brought more volatility to the relationships within the social network, centered around the Central Asia region. The dynamic has gone beyond the complicated relations between India and Pakistan. India has been the only SCO member state not to endorse China's BRI program. At the SCO summit, Indian Prime Minister Narendra Modi stressed the obligation to "respect sovereignty" in selecting and building projects. However, he also said that "connectivity with SCO and neighbors is a priority for India" ("India Only SCO Member to Oppose China's BRI" 2018).

China's interactions with the Central Asian states, which have largely focused on but not been limited to the SCO process, have been conducive to the formation of social networks encompassing these countries and some others. The SCO has become an important venue for international relations. At the 2013 SCO summit in Bishkek, President Xi proposed the "Silk Road Economic Belt" based on a speech delivered at Nazarbayev University in Astana during his visit to Kazakhstan, which marked the beginning of the "One Belt, One Road" initiative. The Central Asian states were interested in the initiative because they hoped it would offer an opportunity to receive Chinese investment and hasten infrastructure improvements (Chen 2014: 25–26). To summarize, China's engagement with the Central Asian states, centered around the SCO, has been helpful to international social networking in a number of ways, including establishing institutional ties, defining the scope of cooperation, and transmitting shared norms. These institutional ties have been essential to facilitating interactions among the members and beyond. They have been flexible enough to enable the states involved to develop relations multilaterally and bilaterally with other members, but without inhibiting the states from developing relations with countries outside the organization. The scope of cooperation has been defined so that members can carry out various activities as the substance of social interactions. In general, China has been more successful at developing cooperation on non-traditional security issues and less so on trade and economics, due to the states' divergent interests. The normative values and principles known as the Shanghai Spirit have dominated the SCO network because they have been shared by the members who jealously guard state sovereignty and protect regime stability. However, they have been less attractive when China has strongly promoted norms of mutually beneficial economic cooperation.

China's multilateralism in Southeast Asia

China's multilateral diplomacy started much earlier in Southeast than in Central Asia. Furthermore, it has undergone significant change and demonstrated different characteristics as compared to Central Asia. Unlike Central Asia, where China took the lead in creating a multilateral institution, in Southeast Asia there long has existed a multilateral regional organization: namely, the Association of Southeast Asian Nations (ASEAN). As a result, instead of setting new identities and norms for ASEAN, China initially needed to interact with and respond to the ASEAN model of multilateralism. Then it could attempt to reshape and mutually constitute a common identity among the ASEAN countries through dynamic interactions and the cultivation of formal and informal relations. In this regard, China could find more common ground with the ASEAN countries based on shared historical experiences and cultural values than it did with the republics of Central Asia. For example, the ASEAN model of multilateralism, which includes consensus-building, openness, and inclusiveness, accommodates the respective comfort levels of the member countries and insists on non-interference in others' domestic affairs. All those practices are highly compatible with Chinese norms for managing international relations, such as diversity in harmony, finding common ground while respecting differences, and maintaining a "don't do to others what you don't want others to do to you" approach.

China started to normalize its relations with the Southeast Asian countries in the 1990s. It should be acknowledged that the initial motivation behind Beijing's diplomatic move was more instrumental than normative. To break its post-Tiananmen diplomatic isolation after 1989, China launched "peripheral diplomacy" to counter Western pressure for diplomatic sanctions, mainly by improving relations with the Southeast Asian countries. The initial tactical measure, however, soon took on strategic significance for Chinese foreign policy. Although in its early stages the diplomatic initiative was undertaken on a bilateral basis with individual ASEAN countries, multilateralism gradually gained salience in China's peripheral diplomacy. In other words, Beijing's increasing embrace of multilateralism emerged as it interacted with the ASEAN countries. Subsequently, intensive relationships have been established between the two sides. During the process, China has shaped and been shaped, constrained and been constrained by the ASEAN countries. As a result, China's pre-national identity and interest in multilateralism has evolved. Soon after its overtures to ASEAN, a consensus emerged in the Chinese foreign policy community that multilateralism might be the most effective way to mitigate suspicions of China among the ASEAN countries, maintain good relations with them, and increase China's influence in the region. In this regard, some scholars have suggested that China should adopt so-called "flexible multilateralism" (Pang 2001), meaning that China would pursue not a single model of multilateralism in the region but rather multiple forms of multilateralism depending on the degree of intimacy and importance of China's relationship to the ASEAN actor in question.

China established official relations with ASEAN in 1991 by becoming a consultative partner, and it became a full dialogue partner of ASEAN in 1996. In 1997, the first informal China–ASEAN summit was held, establishing a new mechanism for consultation (10+1). Since then China gradually has established a multilayered, multilevel network for dialogue and consultation with ASEAN, including ASEAN PMC, the ASEAN Regional Forum, ASEAN-1, and ASEAN+3. It can be said that China's regional multilateral diplomacy started with its ASEAN interactions. The institutionalized interactions between China and ASEAN have enabled both sides to form a relational social network featuring a dynamic process in which each partner helps constitute the others' identity, interests, and policy agendas, all on the basis of mutuality. Although in the early stages of its relations with the ASEAN countries China was more on the receiving side, adapting to ASEAN's norms and rules, gradually China has become more proactive in promoting new norms and rules in its relations with the ASEAN countries.

To cite one political example, ASEAN long had hoped that China would accede to the Treaty of Amity and Cooperation in Southeast Asia (TAC), signed in 1976 as a normative document for ASEAN countries to handle conflicts. In June, 2003, China's highest legislative body, the National People's Congress (NPC), approved China's accession to TAC. In October 2003, China formally joined the TAC treaty, becoming the first non-Southeast Asian major power to accede to it. Thereafter, other major powers, including India, Japan and South Korea, followed China's example ("China Joins Treaty of Amity, Cooperation in Southeast Asia" 2003). In adopting the treaty, China and the ASEAN countries agreed not to "participate in any activity which shall constitute a threat to the political and economic stability, sovereignty, or territorial integrity of other signatory states" (Boyd 2003). In turn, China tried to shape the relationship discursively by signing an historical document to forge "a strategic partnership for peace and prosperity" with the ASEAN countries. This "strategic partnership" is comprehensive and forward-looking. It includes cooperation in politics, the economy, social affairs, security, and international and regional affairs. Once again, China has become the first strategic ASEAN partner to upgrade their mutual political and strategic relations ("China joins Treaty of Amity, Cooperation in Southeast Asia" 2003). This strategic partnership is another example of what China has called a new type of interstate relations. It is a new norm that China consistently has advocated in recent years. It is "non-aligned, non-military and non-exclusive, and does not prevent the participants from developing their all-directional ties of friendship and cooperation with others" ("ASEAN, China forge strategic partnership" 2003). In 2008, China appointed its first ambassador to ASEAN against the background of the organization's ongoing political and economic integration. At around the same time, the ASEAN Charter came into force, lifting the China–ASEAN relationship to a more institutionalized level. At the 21st China–ASEAN leaders' meeting in 2018, the China–ASEAN Strategic Partnership Vision 2030 was adopted, providing a roadmap for the future of the relationship ("Premier Li's Speech at 21st China–ASEAN Summit" 2018). Many of the common identities and norms shaped during the dynamic interactions between China and ASEAN are reflected in that document (*ASEAN–China Strategic Partnership Vision* 2018).

In the economic domain, China has begun to take the lead in setting a new agenda for the liberalization of multilateral trade and economic integration. In 2000, then-Chinese Premier Zhu Rongji proposed the establishment of a China–ASEAN free trade area. This was the first time China had taken the initiative to advocate for a multilateral free trade agreement (FTA) with other countries. In 2001, China and ASEAN formally committed to establishing such a zone within 10 years. This initiative surprised many people and caught ASEAN's other regional partners such as Japan, South Korea, and the United States off-guard. These countries, together with India and Russia, suddenly began to talk about establishing an FTA with ASEAN, thereby triggering a new wave of negotiations to liberalize trade in East Asia. During the negotiation process, China came up with new schemes for differential trade liberalization by offering preferential treatment to some economically less-developed ASEAN members under the "early harvest package." For example, China gave Laos, Cambodia, and Myanmar preferential tariff rates and granted most favored nation status to ASEAN nations that were not WTO members. By offering a preferential trade policy to various ASEAN countries, China to some extent was committing to unilaterally opening its market to these countries. As Long Yongtu, the chief Chinese negotiator for WTO accession, put it, China's policy was to make its neighbors richer by letting them share in the benefits of China's development ("Forum Set to Promote Regional Integration" 2003). China's preferential trade policy toward ASEAN also increased mutual trust that had often been lacking in the relationship in the past. Promoting sub-regional economic integration subsequently has laid a more solid foundation for political stability and security, among other functional relations between China and ASEAN. Taking advantage of its economic resources and consequent influence, China in a way has served as an economic hub to intensify social ties and networking in the region.

The ASEAN–China Free Trade Agreement (ACFTA) was completed in 2010. It created the largest free trade area in the world in terms of population and the third largest in terms of GDP at that time. By January, 2010, the average tariff rate on Chinese goods sold in ASEAN countries had decreased from 12.8 to 0.6 percent, and the average tariff rate on ASEAN goods sold in China had decreased from 9.8 to 0.1 percent (Coates 2009). As a result, the volume of bilateral trade increased almost nine-fold, from $54.8 billion US in 2002 to $480.4 billion in 2014. In 2015, China and ASEAN signed a new protocol to upgrade the existing FTA, the so-called 2.0 version, covering a wide range of sectors including goods, services, investments and economic and technological cooperation, with both sides committed to further improving and opening their service sectors ("ASEAN, China Signs FTA Upgrade Protocol" 2015).

China's goal of achieving "win/win" economic benefits for all has not been limited to its FTA with ASEAN. Indeed, that was only the first step toward the broader and larger economic integration of East Asia and the Asia–Pacific region. For example, China has been the main driving force behind the Regional

Comprehensive Economic Partnership (RCEP), aimed at liberalizing trade between ten ASEAN countries and six other countries that have already signed FTAs with ASEAN. In August 2012, the ministers of economics from the 16 participating countries endorsed the Guiding Principles and Objectives for Negotiating the RCEP. The negotiations were formally launched in November of 2012 and commenced early the following year. However, the progress of the negotiations has been slow, due to a wide range of factors, including the differing political systems and historical and cultural backgrounds of the countries involved; the varying development levels of the 16 participating states; competition from other free trade initiatives such as the Trans-Pacific Partnership (TPP) and the Comprehensive and Progressive Agreement for Transpacific Partnership (CPTPP); and the geopolitical complexity of the region. Nevertheless, China has spared no effort to remain the main driving force behind it. Chinese leaders have tried very hard to set a target date to conclude the negotiations. For instance, at the Boao Forum in April of 2014, Chinese Premier Li Keqiang expressed the hope that RCEP could reach an agreement in 2015 ("Full Text of Premier Li's Speech at Boao" 2014). When that deadline was not met, he once again called for the end of RCEP negotiations in 2016 ("Premier Li calls for an end to RCEP talks by next year" 2015). Yet the talks have dragged on. At the East Asia Summit in 2018, premier Li urged the leaders of the countries involved to use their political resolve to conclude the negotiations as quickly as possible ("Premier Li's Speech at 21st China–ASEAN Summit" 2018) and unleash a strong "finishing kick," striving to complete the deal by 2019 ("Chinese Premier Calls for Strong 'Finishing Kick' of RCEP Talks" 2018). His view was echoed by Singapore's Prime Minister Lee Hsien Loong, who warned that "further prolonging negotiations puts the RCEP at risk of losing credibility and support from our stakeholders" ("China-backed RCEP Trade Pact in 'Final Stage,' Deal Eyed in 2019, Singapore" 2018). If it is ever consummated, RCEP will become one of the world's largest and most diverse trade blocs, accounting for almost half of the world's population and about one third of the global GDP.

With regard to security, China initially was more cautious and reactive. Its changing attitude toward the only region-wide multilateral security mechanism, the ASEAN Regional Forum (ARF), is a telling example of how China's security multilateralism has evolved through mutual interactions and the cultivation of relationships. ARF was established in 1994 to discuss security issues between ASEAN and other concerned countries in the region in an informal setting. It marked the beginning of regional security multilateralism at the official level. Beijing at first harbored reservations about ARF and was somewhat "dragged into" it, reflecting Chinese uneasiness with security multilateralism. Gradually, however, China became accustomed to participating in this security consultation mechanism and began to view ARF in a more positive way. Thereafter, China, which also has been fully involved in other auxiliary security mechanisms either derived from ARF or related to other regional groups, started to sponsor and hold multilateral security dialogues and consultations in Beijing. China also tried to use ARF to counterbalance the US military alliance in the Asia–Pacific region and to ensure that ARF would not turn into a similar institution that could be used by dominant powers to deal with a perceived enemy.[4] For the development and operation of ARF, China advocated for the so-called "ARF approach," which featured norms such as "equal participation, consensus-building, seeking common ground while shelving differences, and incremental progress" (Tang 1998). In addition, China tried very hard to promote its own security norms to ARF. In 1996, at an ARF foreign ministers' meeting, China called for the first time for the abandonment of the "Cold War mentality" and introduced a new security concept based "neither on military build-up nor on military alliances," but grounded in "mutual trust and common interests" (Qian 1997). This was obviously an attempt to offset the perceived security philosophy of the United States and to shape new norms and a discourse in favor of security multilateralism in the region. In 2002, China submitted a position paper on its new security concept to the ARF foreign ministers' meeting, systematically articulating its views on international security affairs. Such an effort to shape the conceptual and normative underpinnings of a regional security mechanism has been quite new in Chinese diplomacy. However, it also can be discerned in China's practice in the Shanghai Cooperation Organisation in Central Asia, as discussed earlier.

In contrast to its economic multilateralism, China has remained more cautious and conservative about security multilateralism in Southeast Asia. Security multilateralism could interfere with China's vital national interests of sovereignty and territorial integrity. For a long time, China was highly reluctant to allow the multilateral security consultation mechanism (ARF) to discuss security issues directly involving China's vital interests, even though they also could have implications for regional peace and stability. China participated in ARF meetings but did not want the ASEAN countries to dictate the agenda.

The stickiest issue in Beijing's relationship with ASEAN has been the South China Sea dispute. On this issue, most ASEAN countries have formed a united front against Chinese claims. Realizing ASEAN's intention to use ARF to tie Beijing up on the issue, China has discouraged discussions of the South China Sea by ARF. Instead, it has tried to shape the ARF agenda by putting forward its own proposals and focusing on less controversial security issues, such as confidence-building measures. However, one important objective of China's engagement with ASEAN has been to ease tensions over the South China Sea by cultivating a more amicable relationship with ASEAN. Beijing's territorial claims overlap the claims of many ASEAN countries. Thus, although China had routinely refused to discuss security concerns over the South China Sea in its annual dialogue with ASEAN, in 1997 that began to change. During the mid-April China–ASEAN dialogue held in China's Anhui province, Beijing agreed for the first time to discuss ASEAN members' claims in the South China Sea and offered to frame a code of conduct governing ties with ASEAN (Vatikiotis 1997). Unfortunately,

China and the ASEAN countries have continued to disagree on how to handle the issue. The ASEAN countries have preferred to address it in a multilateral fashion, whereas China has insisted that the dispute must be dealt with bilaterally. As Chinese senior officials put it, disputes over the South China Sea should be solved by the sovereign states directly affected through bilateral consultation and negotiations ("Wen Jiabao Attends Meetings of East Asia Leaders: For peace and prosperity in East Asia" 2011). Beijing has strongly opposed the so-called "internationalization" and "multilateralization" of the South China Sea because taking such a step supposedly would only make matters worse ("Foreign Minister Yang Jiechi Refutes the Fallacy on the South China Sea" 2010).

Starting in 2014, however, China's insistence on a bilateral approach to the South China Sea issue has softened. Senior Chinese officials such as Premier Li Keqiang and Foreign Minister Wang Yi have begun to recognize—at least in part—the legitimacy and relevance of managing the maritime dispute through a multilateral approach. In 2014, at the China–ASEAN (10+1) Foreign Minister's Meeting, Wang Yi suggested a "dual-track" approach to resolving the issue, which originally had been put forward by Brunei. Under this approach, relevant territorial disputes over the South China Sea would still be addressed by the countries directly concerned through consultations and negotiations; however, peace and stability in the South China Sea as a whole would be jointly maintained by China and the ASEAN countries. Obviously, this "dual-track" approach combined bilateral and multilateral diplomacy. Wang elaborated on its rationale: consultations and negotiations by the countries directly concerned were the most effective and viable way to resolve disputes, and thus constituted one of the most important provisions in the Declaration on the Conduct of the Parties in the South China Sea (DOC). Nonetheless, peace and stability in the South China Sea concerned the real interests of all littoral countries, and therefore both sides were obligated to work together to uphold peace and stability there (Wang 2014). This approach was further endorsed by Chinese Premier Li Keqiang a few months later at the East Asia Summit, another multilateral forum in the region. It was the first time that China officially and clearly endorsed the dual-track approach and, more importantly, acknowledged the legitimacy of multilateralism in establishing a peaceful order in the South China Sea. The dual-track approach can be seen as a compromise between China's traditional hard-core bilateral stance and ASEAN's preference for a multilateral approach to managing this thorny issue. This is a clear indication that China's behavior has been constrained by its relational social networking with the ASEAN countries. To some extent, that new approach has improved China's image as a country that adheres strictly to tough, rigid bilateralism on the South China Sea issue, mitigating the impression that China attempts to bully small countries in bilateral diplomacy (Sun 2014).

Within this context of accepting multilateralism to deal with the South China Sea, China has become more proactive at working with ASEAN countries to produce a code of conduct (COC) on the South China Sea. This is not the first time

China has cooperated with the ASEAN countries on the South China Sea issue in a multilateral way. In 2002, China signed the DOC after years of prolonged negotiations. However, the DOC was merely a declaration of consensus, not a legally binding document. After it was signed, numerous discussions between China and ASEAN followed regarding its implementation, which proved difficult. China insisted that the South China Sea issue did not concern the whole of ASEAN, but only a few of its member countries. Accordingly, China preferred to discuss the issue with the "relevant parties," not ASEAN collectively. This indicated the limited nature of China's multilateralism on the implementation of the DOC, a position that later was modified. Both sides agreed to conclude the DOC implementation guidelines in 2011.

The DOC mandates that the parties concerned adopt a more concrete and binding COC in the South China Sea. This certainly has been the norm-building process for the China–ASEAN social network. In 2001, Chinese then-premier Wen Jiabao expressed China's willingness to discuss the drafting of a COC. However, ASEAN initially tried to work out its own draft without China's participation, reflecting the fact that it continued to regard its relationship with China on the South China Sea issue as more bilateral than multilateral. Even though China was not happy with this position, it was still willing to talk to ASEAN about a COC. In 2013, the first China–ASEAN Senior Officials' Meeting on the COC was held. However, progress has been slow (Li 2014), and tensions in the South China Sea have surfaced from time to time, particularly with China's island reclamation efforts and its intensified disputes with the Philippines and Vietnam. In recent years, China has become more actively involved with the COC and has pushed for an early conclusion to the accord. In May of 2017, China and ASEAN agreed to a negotiating framework for the COC ("China, ASEAN Countries Agree on COC Framework" 2017). By June of 2018, both sides had created a single draft text to serve as a basis for future negotiations. During his visit to Singapore in November, 2018, Chinese Premier Li Keqiang said that China hoped to complete COC negotiations within 3 years ("China Hopes to Complete Talks on S. China Sea COC in 3 Years" 2018). This was the first time that a senior Chinese leader had set a clear deadline to conclude the COC. Of course, meeting the Chinese deadline will still be very challenging. One sticking point in the negotiations could be the extent to which the COC should be legally binding. China reportedly prefers the document to be less legally binding, whereas the ASEAN countries want a legally enforceable document ("Philippines Says China Wanted Non-legally Binding South China Sea Code" 2017): a fact that will determine the effectiveness of the COC's implementation and the differences between the DOC and the COC.

Conclusion

Although China's multilateral diplomacy in Central Asia and Southeast Asia share many features in common as integral parts of China's overall foreign policy, some interesting differences have come to light in respect to China's position, role, and strategy, which are largely the result of disparate circumstances.

First, China has taken more of a driver's seat approach to promoting multilateralism in Central Asia than in Southeast Asia. In Central Asia, both China and Russia have served as hubs, whereas other members of the SCO have served as nodes. From the very beginning, China played a leading role in the creation, institutionalization, and practical implementation of the SCO. This can be seen in the very name of the organization. Conversely, in Southeast Asia ASEAN has been more of a hub, and China has endorsed the ASEAN-centred approach to promoting multilateralism and managing various political, economic, and security issues in the region. Of course, China has not just been an insignificant node; for some focal issues, such as trade liberalization, it also has played a hub role.

Second, related to the first point, China's role in forming and promoting norms has been different in Central Asia than in Southeast Asia. China has been the main driving force behind the normative agenda of the SCO as exemplified by the Shanghai Spirit, the preoccupation with regime stability against "color revolutions," and fighting the "three evils." In other words, China has been the leading advocate for generating shared norms in Central Asia. Compared to that in the SCO, China's normative influence in the China–ASEAN network has been more of a two-way process, characterized by mutual consultation. Particularly in the early stages of China–ASEAN interactions, China responded to and accepted ASEAN norms such as the ASEAN Way, TAC, DOC, and COC rather than formulating its own. In other words, China has been shaped by its ASEAN partners in the process of interacting with them, as much as it has shaped their perceptions and behavior.

Third, China's multilateral diplomacy has been both successful and unsuccessful in different ways and sequences in the two sub-regions. In Central Asia, China started with security multilateralism, aimed at settling border disputes between SCO members. For that purpose, the SCO was successful at creating a quasi-security community among the member states. Relatively successful security multilateralism, however, was not enough to sustain the growth of the SCO. Therefore, China tried to turn the momentum from security multilateralism into economic multilateralism. Largely due to developmental and cultural gaps in the region, China to date has been less successful at promoting multilateral economic cooperation. Conversely, it has been more successful at economic multilateralism than security multilateralism in Southeast Asia. Economic FTA diplomacy has given China leeway to bypass the security dilemma resulting from territorial disputes over the South China Sea. Yet China's practice has shown that it remains difficult, if not impossible, to convert economic benefits into security incentives for conflict resolution.

From the cursory analysis offered here, we can see that relational thinking can bring new insight into understanding China's multilateralism and regionalism in Central and Southeast Asia. Relational theory argues that we should understand nation-states not just as predefined and predetermined entities with fixed dispositions and features, but rather as agents constantly involved in dynamic interactions with other actors in the system, through which their identity, interests, norms, and discourse can be redefined and changed. This relational perspective can also apply to China. The conventional Western analysis of Chinese diplomacy frequently has started with preconceptions such as the view that China is a rising superpower, authoritarian state, or Communist regime. It has frequently neglected or paid insufficient attention to China as a social entity, and has failed to consider how China's policies and behavior could change through its interactions with other countries. As a result, the narratives on Chinese diplomacy have often been incomplete and biased. Over the years, China has created strong institutional ties and social networks with its neighbors, through which their interactions have become regular and routine. Transnational norms and rules have spread across the actors within the institutional framework through various activities and events in a range of sectors and spheres. This chapter has attempted to highlight the importance of these relational interactions to China's diplomatic transformation, especially its growing commitments to multilateralism and regionalism. It has demonstrated that adopting a relational perspective in analyzing China's multilateral diplomacy in Central Asia and Southeast Asia can yield more accurate and balanced findings.

Notes

1. The BRI was officially announced by Chinese President Xi Jinping during his visits to Kazakhstan and Indonesia in 2013.
2. In addition to China and Russia, all former Soviet republics in Central Asia except Turkmenistan are SCO member states. They are: Kazakhstan, Kyrgyzstan, Tajikistan, and Uzbekistan. In 2017, India and Pakistan were admitted as the newest members. In addition, Mongolia and Afghanistan are SCO observers and Iran, Turkey, Sri Lanka, and Belarus are its dialogue partners.
3. For SCO staging of joint anti-terror military exercises, see www.gov.cn/misc/2006-04/26/content_266272.htm.
4. Chinese Vice Premier Qian Qichen made it very clear that the purpose of ARF "is not to defuse a common threat, but rather to achieve a common goal, that is, regional peace and stability." See Qian 1997.

References

Ambrosio, T. 2008. "Catching the 'Shanghai Spirit': How the Shanghai Cooperation Organization promotes authoritarian norms in Central Asia." *Europe-Asia Studies* 60(8): 1321–44

Aris, S. 2009. "The Shanghai Cooperation Organization: Tracking the 'three evils', a regional response to non-traditional security challenges or an anti-Western bloc." *Europe-Asia Studies*, 61(3): 457–82

"ASEAN, China Forges Strategic Partnership." *People's Daily*, October 9, 2003

"ASEAN, China Sign FTA Upgrade Protocol." *Financial Express*, November 23, 2015. Available at www.bilaterals.org/?asean-china-sign-fta-upgrade&lang=fr

ASEAN–China Strategic Partnership Vision 2030. November 14, 2018. Available at https://asean.org/storage/2018/11/ASEAN-China-Strategic-Partnership-Vision-2030.pdf (accessed March 8, 2019)

Boyd, A. 2003. "South China Sea: Pact won't calm waters." *Asian Times*, July 2, 2003

Chen, Y. 2014. "2013nian Shanghai hezuo zuzhi yuanshou lishihui huiyi" ['The 2013 meeting of the Council of Heads of State of the SCO"]. In L. Jinfeng, W. Hongwei, & L. Wei (eds.), *Annual Report on the Shanghai Cooperation Organization 2014*. Beijing: Social Sciences Academic Press, pp. 19–27

"China, ASEAN Countries Agree on COC Framework." *Xinhua News Agency*, May 18, 2017. Available at www.xinhuanet.com//english/2017-05/18/c_136295814.htm (accessed March 19, 2019)

"China-backed RCEP Trade Pact in 'Final Stage,' Deal Eyed in 2019, Singapore." *Reuters*, November 14, 2018. Available at www.reuters.com/article/us-asean-summit-trade/china-backed-rcep-trade-pact-in-final-stage-deal-eyed-in-2019-singapore-idUSKCN1NJ1DW (accessed March 6, 2019)

"China Hopes to Complete Talks on S. China Sea COC in 3 Years." *Xinhua News Agency*, November 13, 2018. Available at www.xinhuanet.com/english/2018-11/13/c_137603619.htm (accessed March 19, 2019)

"China Joins Treaty of Amity, Cooperation in Southeast Asia." *People's Daily*, October 9, 2003. Available at http://en.people.cn/200310/08/eng20031008_125556.shtml (accessed March 19, 2019)

"Chinese Premier Calls for Strong 'Finishing Kick' of RCEP Talks." *Xinhua News Agency*, November 14, 2018). Available at www.xinhuanet.com/english/2018-11/14/c_137606226.htm (accessed March 6, 2019)

Chung, C. 2006. "China and the institutionalization of the Shanghai Cooperation Organization." *Problems of Post-Communism* 53(5): 3–14

Coates, S. 2009. "ASEAN-China open free trade area to rival world's biggest." *Agence France-Presse (AFP)*, December 30. Available at www.smh.com.au/world/aseanchina-open-free-trade-area-to-rival-worlds-biggest-20091230-ljf8.html (accessed March 1, 2019)

Crossley, N. 2015. "Relational sociology and culture: A preliminary framework." *International Review of Sociology* 25(1): 65–85

Emirbayer, M. 1997. "Manifesto for a relational sociology." *American Journal of Sociology* 103(2): 281–317

"Foreign Minister Yang Jiechi Refutes the Fallacy on the South China Sea." Foreign Ministry of the PRC, July 25, 2010. Available at www.fmprc.gov.cn/ce/celt/chn/xwdt/t719371.htm (accessed March 8, 2019)

"Forum Set to Promote Regional Integration." *China Daily*, November 1, 2003, p. 4

"Full Text of Premier Li's Speech at Boao." *Xinhua*, April 11, 2014. Available at www.china.org.cn/business/2014-04/11/content_32062531.htm (accessed March 7, 2019)

"Full Text of Xi Jinping Keynote at the World Economic Forum," January 17, 2017. Available at www.china.org.cn/node_7247529/content_40569136.htm

"India Only SCO Member to Oppose China's BRI." *The Times of India*, June 10, 2018. Available at https://timesofindia.indiatimes.com/india/india-stays-out-of-move-to-support-chinas-bri-at-sco-meet/articleshow/64533390.cms (accessed October 2, 2018)

Lanteigne, M. 2006/2007. "In Medias Res: The development of the Shanghai Co-operation Organization as a security community." *Pacific Affairs* 79(4): 605–22

Li, M. 2014. "Managing security in the South China Sea: From DOC to COC." *Kyoto Review of Southeast Asia* 15. Available at https://kyotoreview.org/issue-15/managing-security-in-the-south-china-sea-from-doc-to-coc/ (accessed March 4, 2019)

Liu, H. 2011. "Shanghai Hezuo Zuzhi de Quyu Jingji Hezuo" ["Regional Economic Cooperation in the Shanghai Cooperation Organization"]. In E. Wu & H. Wu, (eds.), *Shanghai Hezuo Zuzhi Fazhan Baogao 2011 [2011 Annual Report on the Shanghai Cooperation Organization]*. Beijing: Shehui Kexue Wenxian Chubanshe, pp. 36–52

Lukin, A. 2007. "The Shanghai Cooperation Organization: What next?" *Russia in Global Affairs* 5(3): 140–56

Lynch, C. 2014. *Interpreting International Politics*. Abingdon, UK: Routledge

Pan, G. 2008/2009. "A new diplomatic model: A Chinese perspective on the Shanghai Cooperation Organization." *Washington Journal of Modern China* 9(1): 55–72

Pang, Z. 2001. "China's Asian Strategy: Flexible multilateralism." *World Economy and Politics* 10: 30–35

"Philippines Says China Wanted Non-legally Binding South China Sea Code." *Reuters*, August 8, 2017. Available at www.reuters.com/article/us-asean-philippines-southchina-sea-idUSKBN1AO1LW (accessed March 1, 2019)

"Premier Li calls for an end to RCEP talks by next year." November 22, 2015. Available at http://english.www.gov.cn/premier/news/2015/11/22/content_281475239823043.htm

"Premier Li's Speech at 21st China–ASEAN Summit." *China Daily*, November 15, 2018. Available at www.chinadaily.com.cn/a/201811/15/WS5becd1c2a310eff303288d5c.html (accessed March 6, 2019)

Qian, Q. 1997. "Opening Statement by H. E. Mr. Qian Qichen, Vice Premier and Minister of Foreign Affairs, People's Republic China." ASEAN Regional Forum, Subang Jaya, July 27. Available at https://asean.org/?static_post=opening-statement-by-he-mr-qian-qichen-vice-premier-and-minister-of-foreign-affairs-of-china (accessed March 19, 2019)

Qin, Y. 2016. "A relational theory of world politics." *International Studies Review* 18(1): 33–47

SCO, 2007. "Treaty on Long-Term Good-Neighbourliness, Friendship and Cooperation between the Member States of the Shanghai Cooperation Organisation," http://en.pkulaw.cn/display.aspx?cgid=0b38322f2c86af29cdfd7af72f653b0cbdfb&lib=tax (accessed November 4, 2019)

SCO, 2018. "Qingdao Declaration of the Council of Heads of State of Shanghai Cooperation Organization." Secretariat of Shanghai Cooperation Organization. Available at http://eng.sectsco.org/documents/ (accessed October 2, 2018)

Song, W. 2013. "Feeling safe, being strong: China's strategy of soft balancing through the Shanghai Cooperation Organization." *International Politics* 50(5): 664–85

"Speech by H.E. Li Keqiang, Premier of the State Council of the People's Republic of China at the 13th East Asia Summit." *China Daily*, November 15, 2018. Available at www.chinadaily.com.cn/a/201811/16/WS5bee1a9ea310eff3032890d5.html (accessed March 6, 2019)

Sun, X. 2014. "To use the 'dual-track' approach to solve the South China Sea issue." August 16. Available at http://qiusuoge.com/12013.html (accessed March 7, 2019)

Tang, J. 1998. "Address by H.E. Mr. Tang Jiaxuan Minister of Foreign Affairs of the People's Republic of China at the 5th ARF ministerial meeting, Manila, July 27." Available at https://asean.org/?static_post=statement-by-foreign-minister-tang-jiaxuan-of-the-people-s-republic-of-china-at-the-post-ministerial-conference-manila-28-july-1998 (accessed March 19, 2019)

Vatikiotis, M. 1997. "Friends and fears." *Far Eastern Economic Review*, May 8, p. 15

Wang, J. 2005. "China's multilateral diplomacy in the new millennium." In Y. Deng & F. Wang (eds.), *China Rising, Power and Motivation in Chinese Foreign Policy*. Lanham, MD: Roman & Littlefield, pp. 159–200

Wang, Y. 2014. "Handle the South China Sea issue through the 'dual-track' approach." August 9. Available at www.china-un.ch/eng/wjyw/t1181523.htm (accessed March 1, 2019)

"Wen Jiabao Attends Meetings of East Asia Leaders: For peace and prosperity in East Asia." November 20, 2011. Available at www.china-embassy.org/eng/zgyw/t879898.htm (accessed March 9, 2019)

"Xi Jinping participating in the central conference on work relating to foreign affairs and delivering an important speech." *Xinhua News Agency.* Available at www.xinhuanet.com/politics/2014-11/29/c_1113457723.htm (accessed September 22, 2018)

9
SOUTH ASIA BETWEEN NATIONALISM AND REGIONALISM

Ummu Salma Bava

In the South Asian context, politics recently has been marked by an emphasis on the state, identity, and borders. In spite of their shared past, India, Pakistan, and Bangladesh, especially, have sought new and distinct political identities in the post-colonial era, and that has posed a new set of challenges. Political developments in the immediate aftermath of Indian independence have had a lasting impact on the region.

While it is true that history connects the peoples of the region, contemporary political history continues to divide them. The discourse has privileged identity as a marker of distinctions among the states of South Asia. Political history and the construction of an identity powerfully defined by borders have been impediments to cooperation in a region that prefers to understand itself in terms of sovereignty. South Asia as a geopolitical unit is located in a larger geographical space connected to other regions. In the past three decades, regional cooperation and integration have grown by fits and starts, leading to the search for other regional or sub-regional arrangements. The impact of globalization and the connectivity factor likewise have induced several states to put forward sub-regional schemes.

Although the South Asian Association for Regional Cooperation (SAARC), which dates back to 1985, has attempted to build up regional networks and identity, it usually has come to grief over traditional sovereignty issues. The huge trust deficit among the participating states has reduced their capacity for cooperation. In the three decades of its existence, SAARC has been unable to deliver a strong regional platform, largely due to bilateral rivalries between India and Pakistan. In that context, this chapter will examine the impact of decolonization on South Asia and the processes of national identity-formation. Furthermore, it will try to shed light on the relations between the states and gauge the degree of regional cooperation embodied in SAARC. Finally, it will analyze India's response to regional cooperation and multilateralism.

The impact of decolonization in South Asia and the creation of national identities

For purposes of this study, South Asia includes India, Pakistan, Bhutan, Nepal, Bangladesh, Sri Lanka, and the Maldives. With a combined population of 1.8 billion, they constitute about 25 percent of the world population. A substantial section of the region was part of the British Empire. The end of World War II hastened the demise of colonialism on the Indian subcontinent, an event that resulted in the creation of the Union of India and the Dominion of Pakistan, which at the time consisted of East and West Pakistan. British rule, however, left a lasting impact on state-formation on the Indian subcontinent. Religion and identity played crucial roles in the establishment of Pakistan by the British, since that country was meant to be a secure homeland for the Muslim population of India. However, the partition of India did not result in an exodus of all Muslims from India into Pakistan. The remaining Muslim population in India has continued to spark identity conflicts between the two states. The year 1947 can be read as a watershed of new identity markers for India and Pakistan. In particular for India, Pakistan, and Sri Lanka, colonialism "represents the displacement of one form of interconnection by another" (Gupta & Ferguson 1992: 7). While India established a secular democratic republic, Pakistan struggled with language-based identity politics between its Eastern and Western components. Meanwhile, its nascent democracy eroded until military rule was imposed in 1958. Thereafter, Pakistan endured long cycles of military rule interrupted by short periods of (aspirational) democratic governance. Nepal was never colonized; nevertheless, with its monarchical government it had acted as a buffer zone between British India and imperial China. In 1990, absolute monarchy there gave way to constitutional monarchy. However, during this same period the Himalayan kingdom also went through a civil war. The abolition of the monarchy in 2008 resulted in the creation of a democratic republic. Bhutan, another tiny Himalayan kingdom, was never colonized and in 2008 transitioned from an absolute to a constitutional monarchy. Sri Lanka (formerly Ceylon), a small island state located in the Indian Ocean, emerged from British colonial rule in 1948 and eventually endured a 26-year-long civil war that ended in 2009. At this writing, Sri Lanka's government continues efforts to rebuild the war-torn country. The Maldives, once a British protectorate, gained independence in 1965.

Anderson (2006) suggestively describes nations as "imagined communities." However, the British colonial authorities' attempt to construct such communities ended up pitting Indians vs. Pakistanis. In the post-1945 period, the formation of new national identities in South Asia was strongly linked to territory. Thus, boundaries and sovereignty became defining aspects of identity in each of the countries. The end of colonial rule on the subcontinent not only led to independence; it also resulted in geographical and political fragmentation through the partition of India along religious lines. Affecting over a billion people, this territorialization of identity, with its attendant historical issues and complex political relations, impacted the subsequent evolution of political and cultural life in both Pakistan and India and the prospects for cooperation.

Speaking more generally, while the countries of South Asia display certain cultural affinities, the process of nation-building in the region has been diverse and rooted in the unique political tradition of each of them. Thus, all states in the region have sought their own idiosyncratic routes to building new political identities, emphasizing their political and socio-cultural distinctiveness rather than their similarities. In post-colonial India, the government began reconstituting political identity based on the idea of the secular state. That goal found expression in the adoption of a constitution firmly rooted in European political values. The latter would influence both the forms that the nascent Indian democracy would take and the political institutions that framed it. The identity-building process in Pakistan faltered, because the new state was unable to establish a narrative that did not involve India. Moreover, the internal political upheaval caused by military rule damaged the process of democratization and institutional consolidation. The 1971 war between India and Pakistan led to the creation of Bangladesh, fashioned out of the former East Pakistan. That new state also has sought to build its identity around language and religion. Nepal and Bhutan, for their part, evolved politically over time, becoming more democratic. However, the strategic locations of these tiny landlocked countries on the borders of India and China has tempted both major powers to use them as leverage in their longstanding rivalry. India is undoubtedly the preponderant power in South Asia, overshadowing all the others. Despite their different political trajectories, the one factor that all of those countries share is a strong commitment to the Westphalian idea of the state and political sovereignty, with all its implications.

During the Cold War period, the South Asian countries also experienced the pull and push of global politics. While India in 1961 spearheaded the non-aligned movement along with Egypt and Yugoslavia, Pakistan joined Southeast Asia Treaty Organization (SEATO) and Central Treaty Organization (CENTO), two collective defense organizations strongly anchored by the United States. It is significant to note that the political dynamics in the region shifted further with the Indo-Soviet Treaty of Peace, Friendship, and Cooperation signed in August, 1971 against the backdrop of growing unrest in East Pakistan, which finally resulted in the Bangladesh War in December of that year. The Indo-Soviet Treaty demonstrated that New Delhi was willing and able to reach beyond the region in addressing the growing challenges in its neighborhood and even to partner with the Soviet Union, given that the US was extending support to Pakistan. The superpowers' engagement in the region also affected New Delhi's relations with Washington and Beijing. After SEATO was disbanded in 1977, Pakistan joined the Non-aligned Movement (NAM) 2 years later, a decision that brought all South Asian countries onto a single body operating at the global level. Nevertheless, bilateral tensions between India and Pakistan continued. This period also witnessed America's opening to China beginning with Nixon's historic visit to Beijing in 1972. The outbreak of war in Afghanistan in 1979 resulted in both superpowers involving themselves more deeply in the region, which cast a long shadow over South Asia that lingers to this day.

South Asia did not attract much attention from policymakers in the West during the Cold War, except during the outbreak of the conflicts between India and Pakistan in 1947, 1965, and 1971, the Indian–Chinese hostilities of 1962, and the nuclear test by India in 1974. Given the region's low level of economic development and its growing population, it did not figure heavily in the West's strategic calculus. Although Pakistan was a member of SEATO and CENTO, India was not interested in joining existing security blocs. Rather, the building of national identity around territorial self-assertion led to contestations over territory and borders.

It should be emphasized that all national identity-building is contextual and historical. While certain countries may share a number of similar features, the outcomes of their respective quests for a consciousness of national identity may not take them down the same paths. For example, after World War II, Western Europe was exhausted from the excess of nationalism that had helped to spark the conflict. By contrast, South Asia and in particular India and Pakistan emerged from colonialism fervently embracing nationalism. In addition, the cultural displacements that occurred following the partition of colonial-era India in both its Eastern and Western regions and the consequent redrawing of boundaries led both countries to invent and/or reconstitute their political identities. Because ideas had flowed from the West to South Asia during the colonial era, the Westphalian idea of the state, which links sovereignty to territory, had acquired prominence in that region. This was especially true of the newly independent India and Pakistan. In both countries national identity was visualized in territorialized terms, and this led the rivals to make and contest territorial claims.

Nation-building in Pakistan and India also involved the construction of versions of national identity in which the one state's self-concept provoked hostility toward the other. In the predominantly bilateral standoff between India and Pakistan, this entanglement was reflected in increased defense spending on both sides, which each justified as a way to address its perceived "security dilemmas." In 1957, India and Pakistan respectively spent 2.5 percent and 4.2 percent of total GDP on defense; by 1987, these figures had jumped to 4.2 percent and 7.0 percent. Similarly, the defense budget of Sri Lanka saw an increase from 0.9 percent of GDP in 1957 to a peak of 4.6 percent in 1997, during its civil war. This growing investment in military defense not only profoundly impacted how nations were constructed in South Asia; it also prevented the crystallization of a robust regional identity. Clearly, the perceived security dilemmas of India and Pakistan saw to it that regional aspirations would take a back seat to strategic considerations. The nationalistic discourse of the 1950s, 1960s and 1970s emphasized the differences between the two and diminished the space available for developing any political vision of a common future. Furthermore, while all South Asian countries belonged to one or another multilateral groups, they took few initiatives toward constructing any regional multilateral bodies. Thus, although all the countries occupied the same South Asian space, post-colonial identity-building—particularly in India, Pakistan, and Sri Lanka—exhibited different ways of being "modern." Moreover, all of them followed divergent political, cultural, and economic trajectories at the internal and external levels (Shastri & Wilson 2001).

Relations among the states of South Asia

Even though the countries of South Asia have similar cultural backgrounds, that common starting-point has not translated into the endorsement of shared political values, especially given the challenges of modern identity-building after independence, the complex political relations between states, and the recent history that has shaped the region. There have been four wars between India and Pakistan; furthermore, the issue of Kashmir has shaped the political relations between the two countries and continues to do so even at present (Ganguly 1993; Ahmed & Bhatnagar 2008). As landlocked countries, Nepal and Bhutan share a border with India and had an India-first policy from 1947 until the 1990s. Access to transit routes and the maintenance of good political and economic relations with New Delhi were vital for Thimpu and Kathmandu.

As the largest country in South Asia, India has dominated the region, asserting its influence especially over Nepal and Bhutan in the North and the Maldives in the South. This assertion of supremacy has not been accepted by all countries. Pakistan, especially, has contested it vigorously, since it regards itself as a power or contender for power equal to India. While globalization can be seen as creating a borderless world, in South Asia the salience of borders has dictated the hierarchies between countries; indeed, contestation over the borders still remains a live issue, especially between India and Pakistan.

In this context, relations among the component countries have been mixed, shaped not only by political, economic, and socio-cultural differences but also by the legacies of the past. Shared history has played a role here, as have more recent regional and global events. Thus, past and present flow together into an interesting amalgamation of factors influencing interstate affairs. India, as the region's dominant country, has had both cordial and conflictual relations with its neighbors. Conflict has been the defining word in the India–Pakistan relationship, whereas Bhutan has had no conflicts with any of its neighbors. Nepal's transition from an absolute to a constitutional monarchy and then to a parliamentary democracy has caused friction with India. Nepal moved from a pro-India position toward greater willingness to engage with China and thereby to reduce India's influence.

Bangladesh was created in 1971 as a result of the quest by then-East Pakistan for an identity based on language and religion. That quest led to its separation from Pakistan, a schism that has exerted a continuing influence on the relations between Dhaka and Islamabad. As Devin Hagerty (2005) points out, the strategic landscape changed after the creation of Bangladesh. New Delhi's relations with Dhaka and Sri Lanka also have undergone their fair share of both cooperation and competition. Relations between Sri Lanka, Bhutan, and the Maldives, and the other South Asian countries largely have been peaceful and cordial.

However, in the post–Cold War era, the growing presence of China in South Asia also constitutes a factor that needs to be acknowledged in any analysis of the transformation of the region's dynamics. Not only has the Pakistan/China nexus grown, but Chinese influence applied through political outreach and economic participation also has been crucial, especially when viewed from India's perspective. The military modernization of China and the standoff between New Delhi and Beijing over still-unsettled border issues also have impacted the broader dynamics of the region and continue to transform the regional equations.

India is the only country in the region to have had a strong democratic framework and a functioning democracy since independence. During the post–Cold War period, the process of democratization has proceeded apace across the region, although not all of its countries as yet have laid solid foundations for resilient democratic systems. The evolution toward democracy augurs well for collective action and for building a community in the region.

The status of regional cooperation in South Asia

A cursory glance at South Asia shows an asymmetric power balance. India straddles the region in all possible ways and its preponderance weighs heavily on regional arrangements. Leaving aside the Maldives and Sri Lanka, India shares a border with all the other South Asian countries: Pakistan on the West, Nepal and Bhutan in the North, and Bangladesh in the East. Distrust has dominated the relations between these states, especially India and Pakistan. In such a context, proposals to construct a regional identity and a scheme of cooperation have not been well received, since the dominant discourse in the subcontinent has emphasized the uniqueness of each country, not solidarity among them. National security and interests also have shaped bilateral relations; consequently, any attempt at creating a regional multilateral platform generally has taken a back seat due to the prioritizing of the national agenda. Transactions between states, whether formal or informal, create a web of relations that help to engender the "we feeling" characteristic of a community. According to Karl Deutsch, building a political community requires changes in political behavior and attitudes. In South Asia, this kind of political community-building process that in Deutsch's terms displays a "mutual compatibility of main values" (Deutsch 1957) never has existed. It took four decades since the end of colonial rule on the subcontinent in 1947 for the political climate to be transformed enough that people even could imagine a scheme of regional cooperation. Part of the problem was that South Asia was basically a geographical construct dreamed up by the external actors. For the countries of the region, South Asia had never existed in the past as a political reality.

Thus, the creation of the South Asian Association for Regional Cooperation (SAARC) in December of 1985 was "hailed as a diplomatic breakthrough for South Asia" (Dash 1996: 185). Bangladesh first proposed the establishment of a scheme of regional cooperation 1979. It should be noted that there had been previous proposals to initiate such a body even as early as 1947, 1950, and 1954. Reluctance to engage in regional cooperation was expressed by both India and Pakistan, since each feared that the platform would be used against it. The process of institutionalizing cooperation did bear modest fruit when the SAARC secretariat was established in Kathmandu, Nepal, in 1987. SAARC created a regional platform for all the leaders to meet periodically, but this did not translate into building a common identity or a vision for the future, as had been the case in Western Europe in 1957. SAARC did not arise due to external stimuli or catalytic shocks comparable to the onset of the Cold War and the division of Europe, both of which provided strong impulses for regional integration (Haas 1958). In the absence of a common external catalytic factor, the growth of SAARC has been slow, and it has come to be identified globally as the most lackluster laggard of regional integration. Attempts at building a regional identity have faltered due to the existence of strained bilateral relations, interstate and intrastate conflicts, and a lack of political will (Reed 1997; Breslin & Higgot 2000; Mattli 2000).

According to the SAARC charter, the organization's stated objectives are to promote the welfare of the peoples of South Asia and improve their quality of life; to accelerate regional economic growth, social progress, and cultural development; to provide all individuals the opportunity to live in dignity and to realize their full potentials; to promote and strengthen collective self-reliance among the countries of South Asia; to contribute to mutual trust, understanding, and appreciation of one another's problems; to promote active collaboration and mutual assistance in the economic, social, cultural, technical, and scientific fields; to strengthen cooperation with other developing countries; to strengthen cooperation among themselves in international forums on matters of common interest; and to cooperate with international and regional organizations with similar aims and purposes.

Decision-making in the SAARC has been based on unanimity, and it excludes all bilateral and conflictual issues from discussion. The main areas identified for cooperation include Human Resource Development and Tourism; Agriculture and Rural Development, Environment, Natural Disasters, and Biotechnology; Economics, Trade, and Finance, Social Affairs, Information, Poverty Alleviation; Energy, Transport, Science and Technology; and Education, Security, and Culture.

The diverse sectors identified for cooperation are indicative of the aspiration to create a regional community in which trust-building sets the stage for jointly addressing common challenges. India did not welcome the idea of regional cooperation, viewing the scheme as an attempt by smaller states to bandwagon against it. The region was not conducive to norm diffusion from Western Europe. Seen from the vantage point of today, although the SAARC grew to incorporate new sectors of cooperation, promote robust exchanges, and enhance welfare, none of those benefits helped much to defuse the security dilemmas of India and Pakistan. Regional cooperation also fosters interdependence, and economic ties have the potential to assuage conflict by generating new equations between actors as they weigh the costs and benefits of conflict.

Nor has it been easy for the states of South Asia to re-imagine their conceptions of the political unit. Similarly, it has been difficult for the region's countries to rethink cooperation across a larger regional geography. The severe trust deficit that has plagued bilateral relations between India and Pakistan (among others) has hampered the regional practice of cooperation. The very diverse "socio-cultural milieus" that characterize South Asia have produced different degrees and kinds of regional integration (Muni & Muni 1984). There is no escaping the history of a particular geography and the impact it continues to have on the level of cooperation among countries. Borders are also powerful symbols of state power. Plans for regional integration that would transcend borders generally are regarded as hampering rather than assisting broader cooperation.

In the much-quoted idiom of John Ruggie (1993), globalization allegedly has led to the "unbundling" of the relationship between states, territoriality, and sovereignty and, we could add, identity. There supposedly has been a reconstitution of political boundaries above or beyond nation-states, and a parallel reconstitution of political and cultural identity beyond political boundaries. The tedious process of forging cooperative intraregional ties can be viewed as sidestepping the limits of the political, especially the conflicts over territory and borders that have defined the bilateral relation between India and Pakistan. The sub-optimal output of cooperation in South Asia underscores the point that world politics is characterized by diversity, and that varied, multiple modernities and regional orders are evolving along different historical trajectories.

This fast-transforming region has the dubious distinction of boasting two states with nuclear weapons: India and Pakistan. In that same geographic space, the unprecedented growth of the Indian economy has transformed it into the fifth largest in the world. Yet at the same time the country's huge population retards its efforts to overcome poverty and spur development. Nevertheless, India now has the scientific capability to launch a moon or Mars mission. These contrasts highlight not only the diversity but also the problems and opportunities that this region embodies. "The challenge for South Asia has been the absence of any rallying point for cohesion be it an external security threat or economic concern" (Bava 2010b: 13). South Asia is also caught up in the transition from efforts to address traditional security threats while simultaneously coping with the rise of non-traditional menaces such as terrorism that impose costs on all states, but more importantly require a coordinated effort by all countries in the region.

Transcending the existing status quo of conflict and moving toward cooperation would enhance the welfare of the people of the region by providing more shared regional public goods. Moving from competition to cooperation would produce a win/win situation for all the countries of South Asia. Regional public goods (such as climate change impact-mitigation, or food and energy security) require strong "regionalism" (Rahman et al. 2012: xiii). As Dubey notes, "most of the decisions made by SAARC are of the nature of public relations campaigns designed to impress domestic audiences and foreign powers. Thus, the entire SAARC process is an exercise in competitive deception" (Dubey 2010: 60). So, if regionalism has not transformed the region, then what other modes of cooperation can bring about change?

India, regional cooperation, and multilateralism

"The politics of division are prevalent in South Asia, where cross-border cooperation has become hostage to political divisions and ambitions. What geography unites, politics divides, and so promoting regionalism in South Asia requires leadership and vision" (Bava 2010b: 49). This remark draws attention to regional diversities that exist because states do not find themselves at the same intersecting points of history, politics, and culture, which are the main factors influencing how regional integration has evolved around the globe. While the excess of nationalism delivered Europe to the post-national moment that would facilitate regional cooperation and the idea of pooled sovereignty, South Asia embraced the national identity project with a vengeance, recalling the Europe of the 1930s, when nation was pitted against nation. Thus, conditions that affect prospects for political and economic cooperation were much less favorable, even "disabling," in the former than in the latter (Mehta 2012; Mishra 2014).

According to Katzenstein, "All regional orders are indissolubly linked to both the larger international and global systems and the various national and sub-national systems of which they are a part, and which they help to constitute" (Katzenstein, Chapter 1). As he emphasizes, distinctive regional orders are important in shaping national politics, policies, and practices, a circumstance that fosters even more diverse outcomes. All cases of regional cooperation create different public goods, underscoring the point that integration is a process unique to each region, one that lacks any single common objective. Thus, although the European Union is one form of integration, it cannot serve as a model for all regions (Lindberg & Scheingold 1970).

India's growing political confidence, manifested in an assertive foreign policy driven by economic strength, has drawn attention to the ways in which it is molding its neighborhood and even places much farther away. With a growing ability to make and shape global rules, it is modifying the multilateral order, moving it beyond the hegemony of a few states. How are other emerging powers responding to the post-hegemonic space? China has become far and away the principal actor in trying to create a parallel structure and assume a leadership role. That much is evident from its Belt and Road Initiative (BRI). Yet India has vehemently rejected the new framing of order that Beijing has launched. As India's ambassador to China Vikram Misri has stated, "No country can participate in an initiative that ignores its core concerns on sovereignty and territorial integrity" (Wenting & Yunyi 2019). Accordingly, in April of 2019, India declined for the second time to participate in the BRI Forum.

The ancient silk route that symbolizes and forges connections within the new venture has brought Chinese investment, infrastructure, and ideas to far-away places, but these new networks all have been driven by Beijing. The BRI has provoked other concerns as well, including its commitment to inclusivity, financial and environmental sustainability, and what seems to be its unilateralism. Growing debt in the participating states has begun to turn relations with Beijing sour even as Italy has succumbed to the investment bait put out by China, becoming the first Western European country to overcome the region's resistance to joining the BRI. This break in Western European cohesion does not augur well for the EU, an organization that already faces severe internal strains over the refugee crisis, a growing identity problem on the nature of the liberal values that it collectively endorses, and an inability to hold member states aloof from Chinese influence.

China's growing presence in and engagement with the countries of South Asia and the extended region, especially given its immense economic capability and capacity, pose a direct threat to what India considers its own backyard. While India has ambitions to shape the region, it is in no position to compete with or even balance China, and therein lies the difference between the region-shaping capabilities of both actors. The Indian response has been to propose the Asia Africa Growth Corridor as a way to offset growing Chinese political influence, economic outreach, and security encirclement. More recently New Delhi has created a desk of Indo-Pacific Affairs, tacitly acknowledging the shift in the larger region of the Indo-Pacific and thus attempting to escape the constraints of South Asia. In the region and beyond there is a growing perception of the realist turn in Indian foreign policy and its rise as a strategic actor that seeks to shape existing multilateralism (Bava 2010a: 125).

Conclusion

In a fast-globalizing world, as traditional power and structures start to break down, the foundations of state authority have been shaken. For South Asian states, the challenge is twofold. First, the region needs to overcome historical animosities so it can realize the collective potential of cooperation that will drive economic growth and connectivity and enhance the welfare of its people. Second, the region must come to terms with the rapidly transforming economic capacity of India as it surges ahead of its neighbors and seeks to augment its political role as well. India's growing foreign policy ambitions have seen it expand its engagement around the world, a trend that also has been reflected in the spread of its strategic partnerships.

As Rahman, Khatri, and Brunner have noted, "Asia is experiencing a transformation in how business is conducted, resulting in increased specialization and cross-border production networks" (Rahman *et al.* 2012:xiv). The huge trust deficit among the states has reduced their capacity to cooperate. In the three decades of its existence, SAARC has been unable to deliver a strong regional platform, largely due to the bilateral rivalry between India and Pakistan. Will South Asia as a region be able to transcend conflict and national identities and address collective concerns? That is a question that all concerned in the region will have to answer.

References

Ahmed, Z. & S. Bhatnagar, 2008. "Interstate Conflicts and Regionalism in South Asia: Prospects and challenges." *Perceptions: Journal of International Affairs*, Spring/Summer: 1–19

Anderson, B. 2006. *Imagined Communities: Reflections on the origins and spread of nationalism.* London: Verso

Bava, U. 2010a. "India: Foreign policy strategy between interests and ideas." In D. Flemes (ed.), *Regional Leadership in the Global System: Ideas, interests, resources, and strategies of regional powers.* Burlington, VT: Ashgate, pp. 113–25

Bava, U. 2010b. "Regional Integration: Lessons for South Asia from around the world." In R. Dossani *et al.* (eds.), *Does South Asia Exist? Prospects for regional integration.* Baltimore, MD: Brookings, pp. 37–52

Breslin, S. & R. Higgott, 2000. "Studying Regions: Assessing the new, learning from the old." *New Political Economy* 5(3): 333–53

Dash, K. 1996. "The Political Economy of Regional Cooperation in South Asia." *Pacific Affairs* 69(2): 185–209

Deutsch, K. 1957. *Political Community and the North American Area.* Princeton, NJ: Princeton University Press

Dubey, M. 2010. "Regional Economic Integration in South Asia: The development of institutions and the role of politics." In R. Dossani *et al.* (eds.), *Does South Asia Exist? Prospects for regional integration.* Baltimore, MD: Brookings, pp. 53–81

Ganguly, S. 1993. "The Prospects for SAARC." In H. Malik (ed.), *Dilemmas of National Security and Cooperation in India and Pakistan.* London: Palgrave Macmillan, pp. 273–91

Gupta, A. & J. Ferguson, 1992. "Beyond 'Cukture': Space, identity, and the politics of difference." *Cultural Anthropology* 7(1): 6–23

Haas, E. 1958. *The Uniting of Europe.* Stanford, CA: Stanford University Press

Hagerty, D. 2005. *South Asia in World Politics.* Lanham, MD: Rowman & Littlefield

Lindberg, L. & S. Scheingold (eds.), 1970. *Regional Integration: Theory and research.* Cambridge MA: Harvard University Press

Mattli, W. 2000. "Sovereignty Bargains and Regional Integration." *International Studies Review* 2(2): 149–80

Mehta, P. 2012. "SAARC and the Sovereignty Bargain." In K. Dixit (ed.), *The Southasian Sensibility: A Himal reader.* Delhi: Sage Publications, pp. 189–97

Mishra, B. 2014. "The Nation State Problematic in Asia: The South Asian experience." *Perceptions: Journal of International Affairs* 19(1): 71–85

Muni, D. & A. Muni, 1984. *Regional Cooperation in South Asia*. New Delhi: National Publishing House

Rahman S.H., S. Khatri, & H-P. Brunner (eds.), 2012. *Regional Integration and Economic Development in South Asia*. Northampton, MA: Edward Elgar Publishing House

Reed, A. 1997. "Regionalization in South Asia: Theory and praxis." *Pacific Affairs* 70(2): 235–51

Ruggie, J. 1993. "Territoriality and Beyond: Problematizing modernity in international relations." *International Organization* 47(1): 139–74

Shastri, A. & A. Wilson (eds.), 2001. *The Post-Colonial States of South Asia*. New York: Palgrave Macmillan

Wenting. X. & B. Yunyi, 2019. "Cooperation Trumps Coordination between China and India: Envoy." *Global Times* (Beijing), March 19

10
MULTILATERALIZING REGIONALISM IN EAST ASIA

Moonsung Kang

Multilateral trade talks

Since the multilateral trade negotiations under the Doha Development Agenda (DDA) have stalled and the Trump administration in the United States has started to adopt protectionist measures against its trading partners, countries in East Asia have a strong incentive to focus on bilateral and regional trade talks, rather than multilateral ones, in order to secure their export markets and to strengthen economic ties with their major trading partners.

The DDA, the first multilateral trade negotiation since the advent of the World Trade Organization (WTO), has not been very successful so far, even though the WTO had seven Ministerial Conferences (MCs), from MC 5 in Cancún, Mexico in 2003 to MC 11 in Buenos Aires, Argentina in 2017, and expects to hold MC 12 in Astana, Kazakhstan in 2020. As shown in Table 10.1, multilateral trade negotiations have taken more time to conclude as more countries have been participating. So far, WTO members have failed to bridge the broad gaps between their positions over market access and domestic supports in the agricultural sector; non-agricultural market access; and market access and domestic regulations in the service sectors. After holding eight rounds of multilateral trade negotiations, the multilateral trading system has worked to lower various trade barriers, but the DDA faces thorny issues, including agricultural markets, non-tariff trade barriers in manufacturing sectors, and services markets.

In addition, the Trump administration takes a negative view of the multilateral trading talks and system. The United States Trade Representatice (USTR) stated that it resists "efforts by other countries—or members of international bodies like the World Trade Organization (WTO)—to advance interpretations that would weaken the rights and benefits of, or increase the obligations under, the various

TABLE 10.1 Multilateral trade negotiations

	Negotiation	Year	Number of months	Number of participating countries
1	Round 1 (Geneva)	1947	7	23
2	Round 2 (Annecy)	1949	5	29
3	Round 3 (Torquay)	1950–51	8	32
4	Round 4 (Geneva)	1955–56	5	33
5	Dillon Round	1960–61	11	39
6	Kennedy Round	1964–67	37	74
7	Tokyo Round	1973–79	74	99
8	Uruguay Round	1986–94	87	117
9	Doha Development Agenda	2001–present	?	164

Sources: Hoekman & Kostecki (2009: 133–35) and World Trade Organization (www.wto.org)

trade agreements to which the United States is a party" (USTR 2017: 2). There are two reasons for its negative view: (1) the Trump administration believes that the WTO has been ineffective in regulating the unfair trade practices of its trading partners, mainly China; and (2) the US has been *unexpectedly* requested to change its trade policy after losing cases under the WTO's dispute settlement procedures and hence considers the WTO to be infringing on its sovereign right to protect its domestic producers and markets.

US trade policy under the Trump administration

Since the start of the Trump administration, protectionism has spread from the United States to other countries around the world. The US–China tariff war is worsening, and trade conflicts with countries that have exported washing machines, solar batteries, steel, electronics and automobiles to the US market are intensifying. The Trump administration has set "America First" as its top trade policy goal, and has imposed safeguard measures under the slogan, "Buy American, Hire American."

This policy has also been reflected in the US position on free trade agreements (FTAs). Trump prefers bilateral negotiations, allegedly to ensure that US interests prevail and to reduce the country's trade deficits. The operative assumption is that the United States can maximize its negotiating power and gain its objectives by making bilateral deals. That strategy is supposed to replace the more traditional kind of trade negotiations that were intended to systematically reduce trade barriers and make global trade freer than before. In other words, the Trump administration places priority on bilateral trade negotiations with individual trading partners rather than multilateral trade negotiations or trade negotiations with specific regions. It prefers a framework for trade negotiations in which it can actively utilize US political power, especially against smaller and weaker countries, to achieve its goal of putting America First. That is largely the reason that bilateral trade negotiations take priority over multilateral or regional trade deals involving a relatively large number of countries. In short, the Trump administration's basic "power politics" philosophy is that the trade negotiation framework best suited to take full advantage of the clout of the United States is a bilateral one. This reflects President Trump's longstanding personal style of carrying on business negotiations. He wants to focus more on reducing bilateral trade deficits, creating jobs, and spurring domestic production than on freeing up trade, even though free markets are more efficient than protectionism.

The first action taken by the Trump administration in the field of trade policies was to withdraw from the Trans-Pacific Partnership (TPP), a move that was announced in the form of a Presidential Memorandum on January 23, 2017. Following this decision, 11 TPP members, excluding the United States, were confused and, at least for a while, did not know exactly what the future of the TPP might be. Some countries, including Japan and Vietnam, could not accept the TPP without the participation of the United States, while others (such as Canada and Australia) argued in favor of launching the TPP without the United States. Finally, the TPP-11 members met in Santiago, Chile on March 8, 2018 to agree on the Comprehensive and Progressive Trans-Pacific Partnership (CPTPP). That agreement entered into force on December 30, 2018 after six countries—Australia, Canada, Japan, Mexico, New Zealand, and Singapore—were successful in securing domestic ratification.[1] However, it seems that the CPTPP member countries have not given up hope that the United States will return to the TPP in the near future. Even President Trump recognized the value of the TPP as a political boon for China and its containment policy.

Another critical FTA policy of the Trump administration soon followed: the renegotiation of the North American Free Trade Agreement (NAFTA), which took effect in January, 1994 and was called a "catastrophe" by Donald Trump during his presidential campaign. More specifically, he blamed Mexico for a big chunk of the overall US trade deficits, since its deficit with its southern neighbor alone amounted to $634.4 billion in 2015, three times more than that with Canada ($213.6 billion).[2]

The Trump administration also has suspended negotiations on the Trans-Atlantic Trade and Investment Partnership (TTIP) with the European Union (EU), a deal that had been under consideration since July, 2013. There has been no progress since the 15th round of negotiations in October of 2016, although discussions on a mini-version of the TTIP have gotten underway in recent months. These would greatly reduce its scope and the level of economic integration contemplated.

Responses of US trading partners in the multilateral trading system

After experiencing protectionist measures under the Trump administration, US trading partners actively started to complain about them in the multilateral trading system, more specifically by bringing cases to the WTO's dispute settlement mechanism. During the Trump administration, the number of cases in which US trading partners have lodged complaints against US trade measures reached 24 as of March, 2019, as shown in Table 10.2. Until recently, most US trading partners had tried to resolve trade conflicts with the United States within the multilateral trading system because they believed that this rules-based, rather than political-power-based, system would help solve conflicts in a more peaceful way. China has brought five cases to the WTO's dispute settlement mechanism, followed by Canada (four cases), Korea (three cases), European Union (two cases), Turkey (two cases), and Vietnam (two cases).

TABLE 10.2 WTO dispute cases with the US as a respondent during the Trump administration (as of March, 2019)

Complaint	Number of Cases	Issues
China	5	DS543 (Tariff Measures), DS544 (Steel and Aluminum), DS562 (Safeguard Measures on Crystalline Silicon Photovoltaic Products), DS563 (Renewable Energy), DS565 (Tariff Measures)
Canada	4	DS533 (Countervailing Measures on Softwood Lumber), DS534 (Anti-Dumping Measures on Softwood Lumber), DS535 (Trade Remedy Measures), DS550 (Steel and Aluminum)
Korea	3	DS539 (Anti-Dumping and Countervailing Duties), DS545 (Safeguard Measures on Crystalline Silicon Photovoltaic Products), DS546 (Safeguard Measures on Residential Washers)
European Union	2	DS548 (Steel and Aluminum), DS577 (Anti-Dumping and Countervailing Duties on Ripe Olives from Spain)
Turkey	2	DS523 (Certain Pipe and Tube Products), DS564 (Steel and Aluminum)
Vietnam	2	DS536 (Anti-Dumping Measures on Fish Fillets), DS540 (Seafood Products)
India	1	DS547 (Steel and Aluminum)
Mexico	1	DS551 (Steel and Aluminum)
Norway	1	DS552 (Steel and Aluminum)
Russia	1	DS554 (Steel and Aluminum)
Switzerland	1	DS556 (Steel and Aluminum)
Venezuela	1	DS574 (Measures relating to Trade in Goods and Services)

Source: World Trade Organization (www.wto.org)

Responses of US trading partners in RTAs

Since the uncertainties in the international trade environment have increased with the spread of US unilateral trade protectionism as well as stalled multilateral trade talks, many countries have started to actively participate in regional or bilateral trade talks and to speed up such negotiations on those talks in order to secure their foreign markets. As of March, 2019, 471 regional trade agreements (RTAs) have been registered with the WTO, and 37 more RTAs have been listed as early announcements. In addition, 12 RTAs entered into force during the Trump administration, as shown in Table 10.3. All this implies that, in an environment where protectionism is spreading all over the world, individual countries are actively utilizing RTAs to secure overseas markets and jointly respond to protectionism.

This trend can be divided roughly into three categories. The first category includes RTAs between relatively big economic blocks. For example, an RTA under the Enabling Clause[3] between the MERCOSUR[4] and the South African Customs Union (SACU)[5] entered into force in April, 2016. Another example is the bilateral FTA between the EU and the South African Development Community (SADC),[6] which took effect in April, 2017.

TABLE 10.3 New regional trade agreements since the Trump administration took office

RTA	Date of Entry into Force	Coverage	Notification
MERCOSUR-Chile	Mar. 10, 2017	Goods	Enabling Clause
Canada-Ukraine	Aug. 1, 2017	Goods	GATT Art. XXIV
EFTA-Georgia	Sept. 1, 2017	Goods/Services	GATT Art. XXIV & GATS Art. V
MERCOSUR-Egypt	Sept. 1, 2017	Goods	Enabling Clause
EU-Canada	Sept. 21, 2017	Goods/Services	GATT Art. XXIV & GATS Art. V
Hong Kong-Macau	Oct. 27, 2017	Goods/Services	GATT Art. XXIV & GATS Art. V
El Salvador-Ecuador	Nov. 16, 2017	Goods	Enabling Clause
China-Georgia	Jan. 1, 2018	Goods/Services	GATT Art. XXIV & GATS Art. V
EFTA-Philippines	June 1, 2018	Goods/Services	GATT Art. XXIV & GATS Art. V
CPTPP	Dec. 30, 2018	Goods/Services	GATT Art. XXIV & GATS Art. V
EU-Japan	Feb. 1, 2019	Goods/Services	GATT Art. XXIV & GATS Art. V
Hong Kong-Georgia	Feb. 3, 2019	Goods/Services	GATT Art. XXIV & GATS Art. V

Source: RTA Database of the WTO (http://rtais.wto.org/; accessed on March 4, 2019)

The second category includes existing RTAs that increase their size by inviting new members to join. For example, the EU has invited Ecuador to join its existing FTA with Colombia and Peru.

The third category includes RTAs under the so-called hub-and-spoke strategy, in which a country becomes a hub within its FTA network, expanding more bilateral FTAs with its trading partners. For example, the EU entered into a bilateral FTA with Ghana in December, 2016, reflecting its efforts to expand its FTA networks with African countries. In addition, the European Parliament agreed on the Comprehensive Economic and Trade Agreement (CETA) with Canada in February of 2017, an agreement that will be fully implemented when all EU members have completed their domestic ratification. Likewise, the EU concluded an Economic Partnership Agreement (EPA) with Japan in December, 2017. This EPA will be sent to the European Parliament and member states after the legal verification and translation processes are finished. In addition to these agreements, the EU has multiple bilateral negotiations going on with seven ASEAN countries: Singapore and Malaysia in 2010; Vietnam in 2012; Thailand in 2013; the Philippines and Indonesia in 2016; and Myanmar (investment chapter only) in 2015. More FTA negotiations by the EU have been underway, including FTAs with Mexico (June, 2016), Chile (November, 2017), Australia (June, 2018), and New Zealand (June, 2018), in order to expand its FTA network under its hub-and-spoke strategy.

The EU's EPA with Japan has another interesting aspect. In addition to issues such as trade in goods and services, investment, and intellectual property rights, the EPA states that the two parties need to commit themselves to implementing the core environmental standards of international environmental agreements, including the UN Framework Convention on Climate Change and the Paris Climate Agreement. This can be interpreted as a measure to exert subtle pressure on the United States, which has declared its withdrawal from the latter agreement. The EU tries to work with Japan, an environmentally advanced country, to change the position of the Trump administration in relation to climate change.

In East Asia, a total of 16 countries have been negotiating the Regional Comprehensive Economic Partnership (RCEP) since May, 2013. These 16 countries, including Korea, China, Japan, 10 ASEAN member countries, Australia, New Zealand, and India, participated in the talks, and a total of 23 rounds of negotiations were held. According to the Association of Southeast Asian Nations (ASEAN) (2012), RCEP negotiations are guided by eight key principles, as follows: (1) consistency with the WTO; (2) broader and deeper engagement with significant improvements over existing ASEAN+1 FTAs; (3) facilitation of trade and investment, and transparency in trade and investment relations; (4) flexibility, including special and differential treatment; (5) continuation of existing FTAs, including ASEAN+1 FTAs and bilateral/plurilateral FTAs; (6) an open accession clause; (7) technical assistance and capacity building; and (8) parallel negotiation to ensure a comprehensive and balanced outcome. However, it has become apparent that participating countries have different views regarding the scope and the level of economic integration at which the RCEP should aim. In the last analysis, the impact of RCEP on the global trade order is expected to be significant since it has the largest population among regional trade blocs, with about 3.4 billion people, and its market size will be comparable to that of the EU.

In addition, a trilateral trade agreement among China, Japan, and Korea is still under negotiation. The three countries have gone through 13 negotiation rounds since March of 2013, but it seems that the negotiation may begin to lose momentum due to ongoing territorial disputes among partner countries. In the RCEP negotiations, these three states are also key players because they have 73.8 percent of the total GDP, 44.1 percent of the total population, and 63.9 percent of the total trade volume among participating countries.

Despite this global trend, the United States has stopped at 14 RTAs since the bilateral FTA with Panama, which went into effect in October of 2012, and has not negotiated any more RTAs since that time. The United States has been excluded from the FTA talks unintentionally because the negotiations between the TPP and TTIP, which were actively promoted by the Obama Administration, were halted and then scrapped.

Future prospects

How, then, will the international trade order be reorganized? First of all, it is likely that the multilateral trading system will get weaker and regionalism will expand further as countries demand more FTAs to secure their foreign markets and collectively respond to protectionism. The weakening of the multilateral trading system has been expected since the beginning of the Trump administration, given its negative view of the multilateral trading system. The United States, which complains that the WTO has been ineffective at controlling China's unfair trade practices since that country joined the organization in 2001, actually has lost most of the dispute cases to which it was asked to respond in the WTO's Dispute Settlement Procedure (DSP). These losses, among other factors, have led the US to call into question both the effectiveness and the fairness of the multilateral trading system. Due to its many defeats, the United States has been asked to change its trade regime and policy. It has tended to reject those requests, regarding them as implying an encroachment on its sovereign authority to set its own trade policies. As the US's negative perception is reflected in its policy since the inauguration of the Trump administration, the future of the DDA negotiations launched in 2001 has become more uncertain. Likewise, the WTO regime also faces challenges. It seems, however, that the United States does not have any alternative to the multilateral trading system, nor has it put forward a reform plan. All this suggests that the future direction of the WTO remains uncertain.

On the other hand, despite the United States' passive approach to FTA negotiations, other countries are expected to participate actively in regional and bilateral FTA negotiations. As US protectionist policies raise uncertainty in regard to trade, countries' desire to secure foreign markets will increase demand for FTAs and the FTA networks that may emerge from them. In addition, countries also are looking for institutional frameworks provided by FTAs that may help them to respond collectively to protectionism with other member countries.

In addition, trade disputes among major trading partners are likely to be prolonged and permanent in the future. In 2018, some people speculated that the trade conflict between the United States and China was just theater, conjured up for the US midterm elections in November, 2018. However, the conflict actually has grown worse since that time, implying that it would be more plausible to see it as a prelude to the hegemonic war over the future technology industry. The election results did not change the direction of the US–China trade war, because it turned out that trade policies themselves were not a key factor influencing the election results. Immigration, child detention issues, Russian attempts to influence US domestic politics, and the Special Counsel investigation had been more important issues for US voters.

The key target of US trade policy seems to be "China Manufacturing 2025," which is a strategic plan by China to transform the Chinese economy from a labor- and resource-intensive industrial structure to a technology-intensive one. In April, 2017 President Trump ordered a review of aluminum imports and threats to national security under the Trade Expansion Act of 1962, and then signed an order to impose the tariffs on steel and aluminum under Section 232 of the Act, citing "national security" grounds. The Trump administration has argued that the United States has a right to use Section 232 under Article XXI (Security Exceptions) of the General Agreement on Tariffs and Trade (GATT). Therefore, the key strategy of the Trump administration, where it tries to link trade issues with security ones, is not designed to achieve short-term political goals; instead, it aims to be a pre-emptive move to maintain and enhance competitiveness in the future technology industry.

What East Asia needs to do

Once a late-comer to the RTA world, East Asia by now has become the place where regionalism is growing fastest. However, Estevadeordal *et al.* (2009) have argued that Asian RTAs, together with their African counterparts, have the most divergent rules in the world: the system of rules is a confused mess, a "spaghetti bowl" or "noodle bowl," as it is known in East Asia. It is also worth noting that East Asia is the region of the world in which the fragmentation of the international production process has gone farthest. For example, the vast majority of trade among ASEAN countries is in parts and components (Ando & Kimura 2005).

The first thing for East Asia to do is to multilateralize RTAs in the region. Multilateral regionalism could help overcome the so-called spaghetti bowl effects of crisscrossing rules on trade practices. This process of multilateralizing regionalism would be promoted through the non-discriminatory extension of trade preferences to additional partners. There are too many bilateral, plurilateral, and regional free trade agreements in East Asia, including bilateral and plurilateral FTAs among countries in East Asia, and multiple ASEAN+1 FTAs, even though the RCEP, including ASEAN+6 countries involved, has been under negotiation. The current trading system in East Asia has been too complex and redundant, generating quite burdensome administrative tasks for governments and businesses. The process of multilateralizing regionalism in East Asia can be achieved either through the inclusion of new members in existing RTAs or by replacing existing RTAs with new ones that extend to new members. Ultimately, the RCEP would cover all existing RTAs in this region and would have to be designed so as to multilateralize all the existing RTAs of the countries involved. Then, those member countries need to consider adding potential new members, such as Chinese Taipei, Mongolia, and even North Korea, to the RCEP in order to broaden its membership.

Second, the process of multilateralizing regionalism in East Asia must be done in a manner that is friendly to the Global Value Chain. As discussed before, East Asia, including the ASEAN countries, has been successful in integrating its economies, even without having an institutional framework of economic integration, by establishing a regional production network. By trading parts and components within the region, East Asia has been able to fully utilize production factors in this region and to produce commodities more efficiently. This network has provided more benefits to all countries involved. Therefore, the process of multilateralizing regionalism should continue in order further to develop, deepen, and widen the regional production network. This process will encourage multinational corporations in this region to invest more in countries in East Asia because they will want to develop and strengthen their own production networks in this region by establishing factories in developing countries where labor costs are still relatively low.

Third, the process of multilateralizing regionalism must be designed in a development-friendly manner. Developing countries in East Asia have been eager to boost their economies by fully capitalizing on their export opportunities, and have chosen their own development strategies focused primarily on export-oriented industrialization. More specifically, although rules of origin stipulated in East Asia RTAs could act as protectionist devices, the legitimate reason for rules of origin is the need to avoid trade deflections: to prevent firms in a third country from exploiting a bilateral RTA by transshipping their products via one of the RTA member countries. Reflecting upon the logic of these rules, we can imagine some innovative approaches to multilateralizing regionalism in a way that still would be development-friendly. In short, the whole process must attend to the needs of the less-developed countries in the region, which have been actively designing their development policies in a more export-oriented way.

Summing up, we have examined and clarified trends in regionalism and regional production networks in East Asia, arguing that East Asian countries, in order to achieve shared prosperity, need to multilateralize regionalism and thereby promote global value chains while remaining development-friendly.

Notes

1. On January 14, 2019, CPTPP entered into force for Vietnam after it finished its domestic ratification process on November 15, 2018.
2. The US bilateral trade deficits with Canada and Mexico widened in 2017 when the NAFTA renegotiation was underway. By then, the US trade deficit with Mexico ($738.9 billion) was 3.13 times higher than that with Canada ($236.4 billion).
3. The so-called "Enabling Clause" was adopted in the Tokyo Round of 1979, in which developed countries are enabled to grant preferential tariffs to developing countries [paragraph 2(a)] and developing countries are also enabled to establish a trade agreement with other developing countries by granting mutual preferential tariffs [paragraph 2(c)]. Especially for RTAs under paragraph 2(c), the requirement of RTAs provided in Article XXIV of the GATT Agreement shall be waived.
4. The Southern Common Market, which included Argentina, Brazil, Paraguay, Uruguay, and Venezuela, was established in 1991. However, the membership of Venezuela has been suspended since December of 2016.
5. Established in 1910, the SACU is a customs union among five countries in Southern Africa: Botswana, Lesotho, Namibia, South Africa, and Swaziland.
6. The SADC is an intergovernmental organization that was registered as an FTA to the WTO in 2008. It has 16 Southern African countries as members, including Angola, Botswana, Comoros, Democratic Republic of Congo, Lesotho, Madagascar, Malawi, Mauritius, Mozambique, Namibia, Seychelles, South Africa, Swaziland, Tanzania, Zambia, and Zimbabwe.

References

Ando, M. & F. Kimura, 2005. "The Economic Analysis of International Production/Distribution Networks in East Asia and Latin America: The implication of regional trade arrangements." *Business and Politics* 7(1): 7–17

Estevadeordal, A., J. Harris, & K. Suominen, 2009. "Harmonizing Preferential Rules of Origin Regimes around the World." In R. Baldwin & P. Low (eds.), *Multilateralizing Regionalism*. Cambridge, UK: Cambridge University Press, pp. 262–64

Hoekman, B. & M. Kostecki, 2009. *The Political Economy of the World Trading System*. Oxford, UK: Oxford University Press

USTR 2017. *2017 Trade Policy Agenda and 2016 Annual Report of the President of the United States on the Trade Agreements Program*. Washington, DC: United States Trade Representative

11

THE ASIA–EUROPE MEETING (ASEM)

Multilateral interregionalism beyond trade relations

Evi Fitriani

Since the Renaissance, the advent of European colonialism, and the onset of the industrial revolution, Western modernity has spread around the world and shaped the international system. Indeed, after World War II, global governance was supported by what we often call the liberal order, which was imposed and upheld by North American and Western European countries ("the West"). However, the end of the Cold War and its aftermath have entailed not merely the perception that a power shift in international politics is underway but also various challenges to global governance. Western countries' domination of international politics and the world economy has been eroded by the emergence (or re-emergence) of alternative centers of development in East Asia and elsewhere. In addition, given the complex interaction of human and natural systems, one scholar was moved to ask a provocative question: whether "a globalized or globalizing world can actually be governed" (Whitman 2005: i). Those who do believe that global governance works may point to the continuing operation of international finance, global trade, the free movement of people all over the world, and other such factors. By contrast, their opponents higlight the failure of the World Trade Organization's (WTO) Doha Round, trade wars, the ill-fated Kyoto Protocol, refugee crises, and continuing wars or conflicts in many part of the globe. Meanwhile, some of the authors represented in this volume argue that global governance (at least in its ideal form of multilateralism) is now threatened by political authoritarianism, religious and political fundamentalism, and neo-populism. In short, we now are living in a much more complicated and problematic world than we were just a few years ago.

Under such pressing circumstances, multilateralism seems to have remained the vital pillar of global governance. As opposed to unilateral approaches, multilateral ones are better suited to address the complexity of many increasingly global issues by—among other advantages—allowing greater inclusion of less powerful participants in the center of the process or action (Sen 2007: 110–12). Nevertheless, multilateral frameworks have become increasingly difficult to apply at the global level due to the intricacy of the issues and the predominance of big power politics. Thus, although it consistently seeks a global multilateral framework, multilateralism sometimes may display different configurations (e.g., only partial governance of particular issues and/or geographical spaces). The challenge is to determine whether partial multilateralism, as embodied in regionalism, transregionalism, or interregionalism, can sustain multidimentional cooperation.

In this context, we may be able to shed some light on regionalism within Asia and Europe, as well as interregionalism between those two continents. The Association of Southeast Asian Nations (ASEAN) is generally regarded as the second longest-lived regional institution after the European Union (EU). The two regional institutions, together with other regional bodies, have engaged in interregional cooperation under the aegis of the Asia–Europe Meeting (ASEM) since 1996. Currently involving 53 partners[1]—51 states in Asia and Europe, plus two regional institutions, the Secretary General of ASEAN and representatives of the EU—ASEM has developed forms of multidimensional cooperation ranging from political dialogue and economic collaboration to social-cultural interactions between officials and peoples from the two regions. The underlying question is whether ASEM's interregionalism can serve as an alternative to global multilateralism or a possible model for a new and better kind of multilateralism.

Previous studies have responded to that question by treating ASEM as a strategy adopted by certain nation-states to insure their survival and secure their interests against globalization. Some observers argue that ASEM supports international governance (Maull *et al.* 1998; Richards & Kirkpatrick 1999), whereas others assert that ASEM supports multilateral systems (Dosch 2001; Dent 2004; Bersick 2004). Still others have interpreted the emergence of interregional cooperation pioneered by ASEM as one outcome of the post-Cold War era, when regional forms of order replaced bipolar strategic competition with cooperation and discord among regional networks (Fawcett & Hurrell 1995; Katzenstein 2000). When ASEM entered its second decade, a group of leading scholars urged that the ASEM process marked the start of a new style of multilateralism known as multiregionalism, representing a desperately-needed opportunity to create a more balanced global order (Bersick *et al.* 2006). Recently, Fitriani (2015) has highlighted some difficulties in ASEM processes, many of which can be traced to differences in Asian and European countries' cultures of cooperation. Those differences have hampered the development of more genuine relations between ASEM partners and its more active participation in the multilateral world. However, Yeo (2017) observes that people-to-people connectivity in the ASEM process can contribute to broadening ASEAN–EU relations and to stimulating discussions of how multilateral investments might be developed within the ASEAN framework. More optimistic than Yeo, Rüppel (2018) seems convinced that ASEM can serve as an instrument of the rules-based multilateral order, provided that ASEM not only can address its inherent dilemmas but also can emphasize the benefits it brings. We need further studies on ASEM as a novel form of multilateralism, especially one that goes beyond trade. Taking into consideration ASEM's current developments, this chapter will explore the ways in which it has served as a partial multilateral forum and inquire whether it may have evolved beyond trade so as to include multidimensional cooperation between Asia and Europe at all levels.

This chapter is divided into four main parts. First, we will survey ASEM as a form of interregional multilateralism and a multidimensional framework able to build bridges between Asia and Europe. Second, we will describe ASEM's unusual type of multilateralism, involving not just states but also non-state actors. Third, we shall see that the 2016 launch of connectivity as the focus of ASEM's future cooperation presages some new developments in the ASEM process. It reveals that, despite interregional efforts to move ASEM beyond trade, material interests remain the main drivers in this phase of interregionalism. Nevertheless, we shall notice that ASEM offers hope that even the partial multilateralism between Asia and Europe might be able to circumvent the unilateralism that potentially always accompanies regional politics dominated by major powers. The final section addresses issues posed by ASEM as a multilateral forum. The conclusion to the chapter summarizes the key findings of this analysis as it attempts to answer our central question: Can Asian and European regional entities, originally the expression of the power and interests of regional states, strike a balance among their national, regional, and global interests and amicably deploy their power to safeguard multilateralism and support global governance?

The ASEM process: a multilateral and multidimensional forum between Asia and Europe

Ever since ASEM's establishment, economic issues, especially trade, have been the major preoccupations of the interregional forum. Indeed, the dynamism of the economies in East and Southeast Asia largely has shaped European countries' interests in the region. This material motivation is an indispensable factor in the ASEM process. Without it, ASEM would not be the multidimensional, multilateral organization that it has become over the last few decades.

It goes without saying that Asia's miraculous growth during the 1980s and early 1990s encouraged East Asian countries and EU member states to use the occasion of their first summit in Bangkok in 1996 to establish ASEM. Both parties appeared to take advantages of economic opportunities and try to ease tensions between ASEAN and the EU by involving major countries in East Asia—namely, Japan, Korea, and China—in their dealings (Fitriani 2014). Given the fact that trade is the EU's core value (Yeo 2017), European countries had been observing

Asia's phenomenal economic growths rate (Richards & Kirkpatrick 1999). In response, the European Commission launched its so-called "New Asia Strategy" in 1994 to enhance interregional relations. Similarly, the Asian countries perceived Western Europe as a rich market that could bring them economic benefits and, perhaps, strategic gains that might free them somewhat from the pressures of American unilateralism.

Since trade was the main justification for the creation of ASEM, it is hardly surprising that European optimism about the new organization diminished when the Asian financial crisis devastated much of that continent at the end of 1990s. In addition, the EU's criticism of the decision to accept Myanmar as the newest member of ASEAN in 1999 roiled Asia–Europe relations in the ASEM process. For almost a decade, ASEM moved slowly, kept a low profile, and did its business almost unnoticed, but it managed to survive, largely on account of its strategic values and by the conception of its mission held by many Asian countries. The latter regarded the ASEM process not merely as a platform for interregional ties to the European Union but also as an indispensable forum for intra-Asian cooperation and trust-building (Fitriani 2014). European interest in ASEM seemed to revive in 2003 when the European Commission issued a policy paper entitled "A new partnership with Southeast Asia." But this comity was short-lived, as ASEAN and the EU countries continued to bicker about Myanmar's membership in ASEM at the 2004 ASEM summit in Hanoi. Their quarrels marked the nadir of the ASEM process. The situation seemed to turn around in 2007, when the World Bank reported that East Asian countries had been growing even more strongly than before the financial crisis (Gill & Kharas 2007). The dynamic economic growth in East Asia, including Southeast Asia, has motivated European countries to upgrade trade relations with that region as well as to scout out possible investments there.

ASEM defines itself as a multilateral forum on trade and investment. Taken together, ASEM's partner countries account for 60 percent of the world's population, 65 percent of the global economy, and 55 percent of global trade (ASEM Infoboard 2018). The most recent meeting among the partners was the 12 ASEM Senior Officials' Meeting on Trade and Investment on December 2, 2017, in Seoul, South Korea. The meeting reaffirmed the officials' support for the multilateral trading system upheld by the World Trade Organization. However, the ASEM partners also recognized growing uncertainty in the global trade and investment environment. Previously, they had adopted ASEM's Trade Facilitation Action Plan as well as the Investment Promotion Action Plan. ASEM also provides a platform for the business community. In parallel with the leaders' meeting at the 12th ASEM conference in Brussels, held in October of 2018, ASEM also organized the 16th Asia–Europe Business Forum and the Asia–Europe Economic Forum.

Despite the fact that trade issues dominate its agenda, ASEM has evolved into a multidimensional, multilateral forum. For many years, the ASEM process was dominated by meetings, task forces, and working groups devoted to economic and financial relations. That began to change with the first Environment Ministerial Meeting in January of 2002 and the first Culture Ministerial Meeting in December of 2003, both of which took place in Beijing. Those two conferences were followed by the ASEM Labor Ministers' Meeting in Berlin in September, 2006; a meeting on migration held in Kuopio, Finland in December, 2006; and the first ASEM Social Partners' Forum in Brussels in June, 2008. The ASEM process then expanded to embrace a host of fields, including education, small and medium-sized enterprises, global governance, employment and social issues, mutual learning, interfaith dialogue, piracy at sea, forest governance and forest products, green growth, intellectual property rights, development, counter-terrorism, employment, sustainable food security, human rights and gender equality, climate change, parliamentary relations, social protection and the informal economy, popular forums and civil society, and journalism, among other topics. At the last summit, ASEM leaders sought to enhance cooperation and dialogue between the two regions on a wide range of areas, but with special emphasis on four of them: trade and investment, connectivity, sustainable development and climate, and security challenges. The theme of the 12th summit was "Europe & Asia: Global partners for the global challenge." Here, leaders tried to address issues of international politics and the global economy that had affected people and countries in Asia and Europe.

The development of ASEM cooperation reflects the priorities of both the EU and ASEAN. These consist of three pillars: the political; the economic and financial; and the social, cultural, and educational. ASEM's political pillar encourages a dialogue on the main political issues of concern to ASEM partners. This pillar has developed slowly due to the delicate relations between Asian and European countries, especially on the issues of human rights, civil rights, and democratization. Currently, the ASEM political pillar serves as an indispensable framework for discussing major global and regional concerns without having to involve the United States and mollify its superpower pretensions to unilateralism. From the very outset, the economic and financial pillar has been crucial in moving the ASEM process forward. Despite the lack of binding mechanisms in ASEM, this pillar has grown, providing an appropriate forum to bolster the economic partnership between Asian and European countries. Essentially, it provides for the growth of avenues for trust, which is the precondition for expanding business ties. The final pillar, concentrating on social, cultural, and educational matters, is vital to counterbalance the more purely materialistic motives behind the other two. After all, efforts to enhance relations between Asia and Europe can be justified ultimately on the grounds that they improve the lives of ordinary citizens. While maintaining ASEM as an informal forum for political dialogue, ASEM's partners treat cooperative initiatives in the economic and socio-cultural fields as the true cornerstone of their partnership, as stated in the Ulaanbaatar Declaration of 2016.

ASEM's multilateralism: multiple actors from state and non-state partners

The ASEM process has also been broadened to include forums for different kinds of actors. Despite being an intergovernmental institution, ASEM has involved both state and non-state actors since its inception. At the first summit in March, 1996 in Bangkok, ASEM leaders also launched the Asia–Europe Business Forum to facilitate dialogue among members of the business community from all of ASEM's partners and to enhance the relations between business and ASEM's government sector. Another important organ of ASEM, the Asia–Europe Foundation (ASEF), was established in February of 1997 to generate and facilitate people-to-people contacts among ASEM partners. Until recently, ASEF played an indispensable role in storing and cataloguing ASEM documents and information (via the ASEM Infoboard). Additionally, it has been prominent in managing ASEM's multi-actor forums. ASEF activities and programs reach out to scholars, artists, journalists, dancers, painters, social workers, writers, environmentalists, and young politicians and diplomats, as well as human rights activists; programmatically, it promotes gender equality, female empowerment, and civil rights across ASEM countries. In short, ASEF has worked with a wide range of actors in Asia and Europe and continues to do so.

The ASEM process features three "tracks": one for government officials, a second for the business community, and a third for people-to-people interactions. Another distinctive aspect of the ASEM process is that it offers forums that involve state officials and non-state actors, such as entrepreneurs, scholars, and/or civil society organizations. This hybrid fourth track is an important mechanism for fostering communication among people with different jobs who are employed in the same fields or deal with similar issues. The point is to enable them to work together to solve their common problems, or at least to listen to perspectives that differ from their own. The development of these four tracks in the ASEM process reveals that ASEM is much more than a multilateral institution composed of 51 Asian and European countries, both large and small. It is also a multi-actor platform that provides important opportunities for dialogue and interaction across a range of partners and participants.

ASEM has endured for more than three decades amid criticism directed against its seemingly unproductive forums. Critics point to ineffective meetings, lack of binding commitments, and the absence of properly functioning institutions. What these flaws add up to, the critics allege, is that ASEM holds meaningless forums that fail to yield concrete benefits (Yeo 2000; Dent 2001; Loewen 2007). In addition, ASEM forums generally do not attract much attention from the media; hence, ASEM suffers from low visibility except from media in countries that host its meetings. However, we should treat ASEM as a platform in which a meeting of minds takes place. Since the two regions have different cooperative cultures (Fitriani 2015), ASEM provides a platform to articulate the partners' interests and expectations, as well as their concerns. The soft-institutional character of ASEM's mechanism, especially the paucity of binding commitments that it requires and its overall informality and flexibility, allows Asian and European partners who have distinctly different approaches to many issues to talk and listen to each other. In the era of competitive global economy and aggressive politics, when tensions can accelerate quickly, venues of the sort offered by ASEM are rare and valuable. They help to clarify suspicions, unravel misunderstandings, and dispel stereotypes not only among states but also between state and non-state actors. Indeed, the informality and flexibility of ASEM institutions, together with its multi-actor forums, have created numerous opportunities for its Asian and European participants to cooperate in tackling common problems such as environmental degradation, violent extremism, and trade protectionism. In welcoming ASEM's third decade of existence, the EU's High Representative for Foreign Affairs and Security Policy, Federica Mogherini, wrote that Asia and Europe matter to each other not only for economic reasons but also for the security of the two continents and the world at large. She noted that ASEM represents one of the most crucial forces for cooperation in the global political system (Gaens 2015).

Several examples will reveal the benefits of ASEM's mixed-actor informal forums. To start with, the ASEF has organized many informal human rights forums, political talks, and environment seminars that have involved government officials, civil society groups, activists, and scholars from many of the Asian and European partners, all of whom were offered an opportunity to speak freely with one another. This kind of platform encourages discussion of sensitive issues that could not happen in formal intergovernmental settings. Although forums held just once or twice may not make much of a dent in long-established suspicions and negative stereotypes between Asian and European countries, they do introduce the benefits of habitual dialogue to the ASEM partners. In addition, since the early 2000s ASEF has brought together several young political leaders from Asia and Europe partner countries. This project has created a platform in which future leaders of the two regions might establish communications or even networks. One observer of this kind of program found tensions among the young participants and noticed a tendency for Asians and Europeans to associate with others from their own continent (Fitriani 2014). However, the opportunity to meet peers and be introduced to different perspectives provided future leaders of the two regions with an extraordinary experience. This kind of program, together with the long-established ASEF summer university that targets students and the ASEF mobility fund for artists, have all become indispensable activities to connect Asians and Europeans. Moreover, one item on ASEF's 2019 agenda is a training program on the protection of human rights and prevention of violent extremism. This last case shows how ASEM can make it easier to solve a problem that vexes all participants—one that is exceedingly complex, since it overlaps state security and human security as well as domestic and global security. Furthermore, in 2018 ASEF invited proposals for a seminar on human rights and disabilities. This forum could serve as a spotlight on domestic issues that rarely get serious attention from governments. Because an ASEF seminar will highlight the issues, Asian and European governments will be encouraged (if not exactly educated) to pay attentions to people with disabilities.

Thus, despite the pessimism mentioned earlier, ASEM has acted as an important bridge between people and countries in Asia and Europe and as an indispensable multilateral platform for dialogue and cooperation. In track one, ASEM has become a mechanism not only to discuss international politics, security, and the global economy but also to enable small countries, whether in Asia or Europe, to get help in solving their problems. Those may include everything from environmental degradation and economic weakness to security issues. All now can be considered jointly with some of the larger Asian and European countries that, incidentally, may not have been aware that they had a hand in creating such problems in the first place. In tracks two and three, ASEM has made it easier for Asian and European businesses and individuals to seek common ground. Programs for youth and on mobility are just two of ASEM's valuable contributions to forging links between future generations from Asia and Europe. In cross-track forums, in which multiple actors meet and converse, ASEM has encouraged discussion of sensitive but important issues from different perspectives. Furthermore, it has provided forums for hitherto neglected topics. As a scheme of cooperation, ASEM functions as a kind of hub. Since its Asian and European member countries face similar problems, they can pool expertise, experience, and resources to tackle the problems together.

ASEM connectivity: multilateralism beyond trade

The aforementioned examples of ASEM programs involve activities that go beyond trade, ones that somehow have survived in ASEM and demonstrate that it is a functioning multilateral platform. Nevertheless, despite the political supports that such programs have received from ASEM's partners, they have attracted insufficient concrete sponsorship; consequently, they have come to rely on resources from the EU and a few Asian countries. Of course, material benefits usually generate interest in cooperation. Thus, it is understandable that ASEM officials recently tried to define and strengthen ASEM's relevance through concrete cooperative frameworks that involve both material as well as ideational advantages. In this context, ASEM leaders launched a program called ASEM connectivity at the 11th summit in Mongolia in 2016 under the rubric, "20 Years of ASEM: Partnership for the future through connectivity."

The idea of ASEM, which was launched at the Ulaanbaatar summit, was intended to be the focus of ASEM's upcoming third decade. ASEM weighed its options carefully before finally selecting connectivity as the optimal way to enhance the relevance of the interregional platform. The idea of focusing on connectivity was justified in a seminar on "ASEM at 20: The challenge of connectivity," which was held in Brussels in 2015, As Prakash notes, "Placed within global developments of social and economic importance, a consensus outcome was to give ASEM a more responsive and significant agenda in bringing Asia and Europe closer through people, institutions, and even physical infrastructure" (Prakash 2016: vi). Supported by the Economic Research Institute for ASEAN and East Asia, the Government of Mongolia, the host of the 11th ASEM summit, prepared a document entitled "Asia–Europe Connectivity, Vision 2025: Challenges and Opportunities." The document, which was presented and accepted at the summit, envisions the development of a plan and agenda for ASEM connectivity in future decades. It is important to stress that the document conceptualizes ASEM connectivity in a physical sense and also as a goal that involves institutional and human aspects. It was inspired by the Master Plan of ASEAN Connectivity, adopted in Hanoi in 2011, which encompasses connectedness and community-building through economic integration. In the context of ASEM, physical connectivity and infrastructure are emphasized not because of inadequate infrastructure funding but due to deficiencies in enforcement mechanisms for transnational infrastructure projects in which countries consider both costs and benefits (Prakash 2016). Thus, it is vital that ASEM partners reconcile the alignments of both economic and non-economic costs and benefits for their infrastructure connectivity. The institutional dimension of ASEM connectivity focuses on the development of agreements, procedures, norms, and mechanisms to foster economic connection and people-to-people interactions. ASEM connectivity in its people-to-people dimension aims to enhance interactions at the human level, especially among the youth of Asia and Europe. The ultimate goal is to deepen mutual understanding and overcome bitter historical experience so that participants eventually can take part in a cooperative world order.

The leaders' agreement on ASEM connectivity was confirmed by the official protocols of the summit. In the 2016 Ulaanbaatar Declaration, ASEM leaders emphasized the importance of mainstreaming connectivity so as to encourage closer relations and deeper cooperation among people and countries from Asia and Europe. In the Chairman's "Statement of the Summit," ASEM leaders agreed to enhance every dimension of connectivity. As a follow-up to that decision, the EU launched an initiative to strengthen the ASEM connectivity agenda. In 2017 the EU hosted the ASEM Pathfinder Group on Connectivity (APGC), an organization that includes all ASEM partners and the ASEF. In the protocols of its meeting in Nay Pyi Taw, Myanmar, the APGC highlights key aspects of ASEM connectivity:

> ASEM connectivity covers all the three pillars of ASEM—economic, political and sociocultural. It should be result-oriented, and in support of the following key principles: level playing field, free and open trade, market principles, multi-dimensionality, inclusiveness, fairness, openness, transparency, financial viability, cost-effectiveness and mutual benefits. It

should also contribute to the materialisation of the principles, goals and targets of the 2030 Agenda for Sustainable Development. Sustainability is one of the important quality benchmarks for the connectivity initiatives in the ASEM context.

(APGC 2017)

Subsequently, the European External Action Service organized a series of workshops designed to include both Asian and European experts who were to prepare more concrete proposals on ASEM connectivity in 2018. Prior to the ASEAN summit, the EU also issued a "Joint Communication on Connecting Europe and Asia – Building blocks for an EU strategy" in September of 2018. The 12th ASEM summit was held in Brussels in 2018 with the theme, "Europe & Asia: Global Partners for Global Challenges." On that occasion, Asian and European leaders enhanced dialogue and cooperation on a wide range of issues, especially trade and investment, connectivity, climate change and environment, and security challenges. As the host, the EU also created an online tool to socialize connectivity links and sustainability performance in ASEM: namely, the ASEM Connectivity Portal (https://composite-indicators.jrc.ec.europa.eu/asem-sustainable-connectivity/). The portal displays a report entitled Exploring ASEM Sustainable Connectivity whose key findings are as follows.

> (i) [C]onnectivity can help achieve Sustainable Development Goals, but challenges lie ahead; (ii) political and institutional links can make a significant and cost-efficient contribution to enhanced connectivity outcomes; (iii) every country has something to offer and to learn from each other; and (iv) ties within ASEM are stronger than with the rest of the world, but opportunities exist to further strengthen Asia-Europe cooperation.
>
> *(Becker et al. 2018)*

The report shows not only that connectivity has existed among ASEM partners but also that it expanded substantially in the ASEM network between 2014 and 2018. The official connection launched by ASEM leaders since 2016 aims to reinforce further connectivity development effectively and efficiently by avoiding overlaps and negative setbacks. This initiative indicates that ASEM has maintained substantial networking and cooperation beyond trade.

ASEM connectivity is a reflection of the ASEM partners' efforts to focus their cooperation so as to reap concrete, tangible benefits. However, the most recent trends in ASEM also show that the organization's Asian and European partners have sought alternatives to building infrastructure to support national economic development and expand regional links. Their efforts are understandable given the fact that, since 2013, Asian countries have been invited to join the Belt and Road Initiative (BRI)[2] by China. According to one prominent ASEM scholar,

ASEM connectivity provides alternatives to infrastructure financing (Yeo 2017). Indeed, that connectivity has both financial and political significance for ASEM partners. The motives behind the BRI as well as its methods suggest a strong unilateral dimension. After all, so far it has been designed, determined, and dominated exclusively by China (Greer 2018; Jiang & Shi 2018). In addition, the aforementioned process on connectivity has featured a series of workshops, seminars, and dialogues that involved the first three tracks identified by ASEM's Asian and European partners. This process reflects multilateral mechanisms in place for planning, designing, and executing connectivity. This process contrasts sharply with that of the BRI, which was created, decided, and executed by a single country. Moreover, by emphasizing the importance of sustainability as a crucial aspect of ASEM connectivity, the ASEM partners also set a high environmental standard that differs from prevailing practices in other connectivity schemes. Thus, ASEM demonstrates the value of multilateralism over unilateralism.

Challenges to ASEM multilateralism

Previous sections described ASEM's format as one that creates partial multilateralism through establishing interregional ties between Asia and Europe. This regional partnership offers an indispensable alternative framework that enables countries and individuals to sidestep the currently conflict-laden relations among the major powers. As leaders claimed at the Ulaanbaatar summit, ASEM had contributed to promoting effective multilateralism and strengthening other multilateral processes. In short, a partnership between Asia and Europe in the form of ASEM can lay a solid foundation upon which to build a cooperative world order. However, ASEM also has to deal with several challenges to its commitment to multilateralism. These include the continuing predominance of materialistic motives, domination by the large countries, and striking the right balance among national, regional, and global interests.

Recently, ASEAN–EU interregionalism under the aegis of ASEM seems to have found ways to manage the two regions' cultural diversity and defensive identities, mainly because of the partners' powerful economic motivation to make advantageous trade deals. Observing the ASEM from Southeast Asia, one can identify the European economic interests that have driven their accommodation and adjustment to the distinctive cooperative culture that Asian countries have brought to ASEM. Let it also be noted that EU countries typically change their minds about interregional cooperation when the Asian countries pass through different economic phases, ranging from "Asian miracles" to Asian financial crises to East Asian economic growth. Their moods swing from enthusiasm to disillusionment and back to enthusiasm. For that reason, trade and other economic interests become the impetus that moves interregional relations forward. Arguably, ASEM's multidimensional cooperation flourishes only when economic incentives are available. This phenomenon was, and still is, reflected in insufficient support during the past few years for non-economic engagements and activities, especially those organized by ASEF. Under the circumstances, we must ask how long ASEM's form of interregionalism will last in the absence of attractive trade prospects.

In addition, due to economic divergences among ASEM member countries, ASEM activities and programs tend to be supported by rich countries in Asia and Europe. There are also differential resource levels across ASEM member countries. The availability of such resources, or the lack thereof, can lead to different degrees of engagement and involvement from one partner to another. This resource disparity can lead to domination by countries that are stronger and wealthier over ASEM programs and decision-making processes. ASEM's version of multilateralism will be under serious threat if it becomes a battleground for the big countries' power politics and economic interests.

Moreover, as in the EU and ASEAN, ASEM's fundamental challenge—namely, the competition between national interests and regional or transregional commitments—remains unresolved. The challenges of populism nowadays also affect people in the ASEM member countries. Sometimes, national governments may have to demonstrate their commitments to national interests so forcefully that ASEM interregionalism will take a back seat. This is one of the reasons for relative ASEM invisibility over the first two decades of its existence.

Conclusion

Beset by big-power competition and the challenge of unilateralism to the current liberal global order, ASEM exemplifies partial multilateralism. This transregional platform binding together the countries and peoples of Asia and Europe has survived for more than two decades. Despite the predominance of economic motives in its founding, the ASEM process has given rise to multidimensional and multi-actor forums. Over time, these have evolved into activities that go far beyond trade. As an informal and flexible institution, ASEM has provided valuable multilateral forums for informal political dialogue, economic cooperation, and people-to-people interactions that involve not only government officials but also non-state actors. The multilateral characteristics of ASEM are evident on many levels: the number of states involved; the many different types of actors; the broad spectrum of issues; the free, informal character of interactions; and finally, the flexible, open expression of opinions and positions—if not of the decision-making process itself.

The most recent ASEM initiative on connectivity indicates how strongly many actors are engaged in trying to maintain ASEM's relevance and build stronger bridges between Asia and Europe. The planning and designing of the ASEM connectivity project also reflect multilateralism in the sense that it offers alternatives to other connectivity schemes. Nevertheless, as an international institution, ASEM's version of multilateralism also has to face problems such as domination by the big powers and insufficient resources for programs that do not necessarily produce economic gains.

Notes

1. ASEM has expanded from 26 to 53 partners in two decades. Its member institutions are ASEAN and the EU. The 51 member states include Australia, Austria, Bangladesh, Belgium, Brunei, Bulgaria, Cambodia, China, Croatia, Cyprus, the Czech Republic, Denmark, Estonia, Finland, France, Germany, Greece, Hungary, India, Indonesia, Ireland, Italy, Japan, Kazakhstan, Korea, Lao PDR, Latvia, Lithuania, Luxemburg, Malaysia, Malta, Mongolia, Myanmar, Netherlands, New Zealand, Norway, Pakistan, Philippines, Poland, Portugal, Romania, Russian Federation, Singapore, Slovakia, Slovenia, Spain, Sweden, Switzerland, Thailand, the United Kingdom, and Vietnam.
2. Previously called One Belt One Road (OBOR).

References

APGC. 2017, ASEM Connectivity – Annex 1, source: d333mq0i40sk06.cloudfront.net/documents/Annex_I.pdf

ASEM Infoboard. 2018. https://aseminfoboard.org/

Becker, W., M. Dominguez Torreiro, A. Fragoso Neves, M. Saisana, & C. Tacao Moura, 2018. *Exploring ASEM Sustainable Connectivity: What brings Asia and Europe together?* EU and ASEM Publication. https://ec.europa.eu/jrc/en/publication/eur-scientific-and-technical-research-reports/exploring-asem-sustainable-connectivity-what-brings-asia-and-europe-together

Bersick, S. 2004. "China and ASEM: Strengthening multilateralism through inter-regionalism." In W. Stockhof, P. Velde, & L. Yeo (eds.), *The Eurasian Space: Far more than two continents.* Leiden, The Netherlands: IIAS

Bersick, S., W. Stockhof, & P. Velde, 2006. *Multiregionalism and Multilateralism.* Amsterdam: Amsterdam University Press

Dent, C. 2001. "ASEM and the 'Cinderella Complex' of EU–East Asia Economic Relations." *Pacific Affairs*: 70(4): 495–516

Dent, C. 2004. "The Asia-Europe Meeting and Inter-regionalism: Toward a theory of multilateral utility." *Asian Survey*: 44(2): 213–36

Dosch, J. 2001. "The ASEAN-EU Relations: An emerging pillar of the new international order?" in S. Chirathivat, F. Knippping, P. Lassen, & C. Yue (eds.), *Asia-Europe on the Eve of the 21st Century.* Bangkok: Centre for European Studies, Chulalongkorn University

Fawcett, L. & A. Hurrell, 1995. "Introduction." In L. Fawcett & A Hurrell (eds.), *Regionalism in World Politics: Regional organization and international order.* Oxford, UK: Oxford University Press, pp. 1–8

Fitriani, E. 2014. *Southeast Asians and the Asia-Europe Meeting (ASEM): States' interests and Institutions' Longevity.* Singapore: Institute of Southeast Asian Studies (ISEAS)

Fitriani, E. 2015. "ASEAN and EU Cooperative Culture in the Asia-Europe Meeting." In M. Telò, L. Fawcett, & F Ponjaert (eds.), *Interregionalism and the European Union: A Post-revisionist approach to Europe's place in a changing world.* London: Ashgate

Gaens, B. (ed.), 2015. *The Future of Asia Europe Meeting (ASEM): Looking ahead into ASEM's third decade.* ASEM & EU Project. Available at www.eeas.europa.eu/archives/docs/asem/docs/20150915-final-future-of-the-asem_website_en.pdf

Gill, I. & H. Kharas, 2007. *An East Asian Renaissance: Ideas for Economic Growth.* Washington, DC: The International Bank for Reconstruction and Development (World Bank)

Greer, T. 2018, "One Belt One Road One Big Mistake." *Foreign Policy*, December 8. https://foreignpolicy.com/2018/12/06/bri-china-belt-road-initiative-blunder/

Jiang, J. & W. Shi, 2018. "Substance or Show? The Belt and Road Forum." *Global Asia* 14(4): 54–58

Katzenstein, P. 2000. *Asian Regionalism*. Ithaca, NY: East Asia Program, Cornell University

Loewen, H. 2007. "East Asia and Europe – Partner in Global Politics?" *Asia-Europe Journal*: 5(1): 23–31

Maull, H., G. Segal, & J. Wanandi, 1998. "Preface." In H. Maull, G. Segal, & J. Wanandi (eds.), *Europe and the Asia Pacific*. London: Routledge, pp. ix–xv

Prakash, A. (ed.), 2016. *Asia–Europe Connectivity Vision 2025: Challenges and opportunities*. Jakarta: ERIA & Government of Mongolia Document

Richards, G. & Kirkpatrick, C. 1999. "Reorienting Interregional Cooperation in the Global Political Economy: Europe's East Asia policy." *Journal of Common Market Studies*: 37(4): 683–710

Rüppel, P. 2018. "Is Europe's Future in Asia? The Asia Europe Meeting as an instrument of the rules-based multilateral order." *International Report* 4. Singapore: Konrad-Adenauer-Stiftung, pp. 21–32

Sen, A. 2007. "Multilateralism and the International Order." In A. Sen (ed.), *Peace and Democratic Society*. Cambridge: Open Book Publisher, pp. 109–22. https://books.openedition.org/obp/145

Whitman, J. 2005. *Limits of Global Governance*. London: Routledge

Yeo, L. 2000. "ASEM: Looking forward." *Contemporary Southeast Asia* 22(1): 113–44

Yeo, L. 2017. "ASEAN's Cooperation with the European Union: ASEM and beyond." *Panorama* Special Edition, *ASEAN at 50: A look at its external relations*. Singapore: Konrad-Adenauer-Stiftung. Available at www.kas.de/einzeltitel/-/content/asean-at-50-a-look-at-its-external-relations

12
IS THE WORLD READY FOR COOPERATIVE MULTIPOLARITY?

Antonio de Aguilar Patriota[1]

The past few years have generated a widely shared perception that multilateralism may be under threat. As the bipolar environment of the Cold War gave way to a "unipolar moment," it seemed that the systemic safeguards against unilateralism enshrined in the United Nations Charter and other instruments were no longer performing their intended roles. Thus, the unilateralist impulse, which has come to manifest itself with renewed intensity, should not be seen as anything new in itself. The military intervention by the United States and some of its allies in Iraq in 2003 may have been its most unequivocal manifestation.

As Amitav Acharya pointed out in *The End of the American World Order*, disregard for multilateralism may have had the unintended effect of accelerating the end of the unipolar moment rather than prolonging it (Acharya 2014). The intervention in Iraq illustrated the fact that a geopolitical shift was underway in which individual actors, independently of their economic and military power, were at pains to determine outcomes singlehandedly and in defiance of international law. The global disarray brought about by the 2008 economic crisis further contributed to the realizations that not only were a number of established powers playing a decisive role in shaping decisions and proposing solutions to existing or new challenges, but several emerging powers had come to wield more than regional influence. This was the logic behind the transformation of the G-7 into a G-20 as the premium locus for coordination on economic and financial affairs.

If the Cold War had created what former Brazilian Foreign Minister Araújo Castro termed a "freezing or power" along an ideological East–West axis, the end of the unipolar moment seemed to herald a certain "melting of power." While significant military muscle remained in the hands of those in possession of nuclear weapons and other weapons of mass destruction, economic power became less concentrated in the North Atlantic developed world. Meanwhile, diplomatic influence grew even more widely dispersed. This new situation has been described broadly as a trend toward multipolarity. United Nations (UN) Secretary-General António Guterres has recently spoken of a "multidimensional multipolarity."

The expression implies that the poles are not necessarily in equilibrium and that the main players may vary according to the issues at hand. Zbigniew Brzezinski pointed out in a presentation at the United Arab Emirates in 2016 that—in military terms—the current situation may be without historic precedent, with none of the three major powers (US, Russia, and China) in a position to assume a hegemonic role. In this sense, and at least in theory, an opportunity for post-hegemonic multilateralism may be at hand. This is certainly the inspiration behind the brilliant book *Good-bye Hegemony!* by Simon Reich and Richard Ned Lebow (2014).

If one examines the distribution of economic weight, with China soon to assume the number one position and several established and emerging players retaining or acquiring additional wealth, the current process of power redistribution is generating even more polycentric dynamics. A broader range of actors may be setting the stage for multipolarity in the political or diplomatic sphere, as the international agenda is shaped or reoriented by an increasing number of players. The fact that not only governments, but civil society, the private sector, and intellectuals have found new ways to make themselves heard adds yet another layer of complexity and pluralism to the current panorama.

It is therefore appropriate to envisage a "multilayered multilateralism" for an era of multidimensional multipolarity, whether post-hegemonic or not. In reality, whereas one can find examples of governance mechanisms that have become more inclusive as a reflection of today's evolution toward a multipolar international reality, such as the G-20, it is also undeniable that in other existing structures, such as that of the United Nations Security Council, reform remains elusive. While there has been a consensus since the 1990s to expand the Council so as to render its composition more equitable and in tune with the times, in practice a certain hegemonic entrenchment on the part of the five permanent members has taken hold.

At the same time, cooperative and increasingly inclusive forms of interaction among states are happening every day on important issues. The consensus adoption of the 2030 Agenda on Sustainable Development is a telling example of successful multilateralism at work. Since the Agenda's adoption in 2015 it has become impossible to discuss economic growth independently of social and environmental variables. The universal applicability of the 2030 Agenda is groundbreaking and underlines the idea that certain global challenges cannot be handled by individual countries acting alone in an era of interdependence and global constraints. At the UN General Assembly, where no country wields a veto, decisions are arrived at through a negotiating process that indeed defies attempts at hegemonic behavior. All participants, irrespective of their size, can exercise leadership—individually or in coalitions—through competent persuasion.

In this sense, the current multilateral institutions, in spite of persistent manifestations of unilateralism, provide a basis for all of those intent on improving international cooperation to work together. Indeed, it seems inappropriate to describe the current system as led or owned by a single country or region. The time has come for those who wish to preserve it to uphold the system as "our" collective property. And the pronoun "our" is used here deliberately to describe the vast majority of the international community's members, who—if given a chance to express their preferences—undoubtedly would side with the stability and predictability offered by multilateralism.

Thus, I arrive at a call for the creation of a coalition of government officials, academics, civil society organizations, and individuals to uphold the notion that, in spite of the tensions generated by a shifting geopolitical chessboard, unresolved or new challenges, and explicit unilateralism, the advancement of an agenda for cooperative multipolarity is possible. At least three core considerations need to be borne in mind in this regard.

1. We must work together to preserve the undeniable accomplishments of the past 75 years. As the Advisors to the President of the General Assembly stated in their 2017 report, the erosion of respect for the rules embodied in the UN Charter, at a time of persisting security risks, can have profoundly destabilizing consequences. Particular importance resides, in this context, in the rules enshrined in Chapter VII governing the use of force.
2. We must not sidestep a critique of the contradictions, asymmetries, and weaknesses that affect the functioning of the multilateral system as it exists today. This critical attitude should go in tandem with a clear rejection of unilateralism and exceptionalism as intrinsically incompatible with a law-based international world order.
3. It is not sufficient to preserve the essential tenets of the system and denounce its imperfections or decry violations. We must work creatively, proposing ideas and solutions that contribute to improved governance mechanisms and seriously tackle new challenges. An agenda for cooperative multipolarity capable of contributing to a world of improved multilateralism only will succeed in neutralizing destructive hegemonic forces if it demonstrates an ability to modernize and adapt the system to make it more functional.

With these points in mind, I seek to outline below both the shortcomings in our response to a new historic opportunity for multilateralism as well as the areas of relative success from which to derive some encouragement. It is impossible to engage in a conversation about the geopolitical changes the world is currently undergoing without stumbling on the idea of multipolarity. Beyond the fascination exerted by topics such as a rising China, Europe after Brexit, BRICS (Brazil, Russia, India, China, and South Africa), or the relative decline of the United States, the twenty-first century has ushered in a renewed appetite for discussions on the international configuration of power. As a transition seems to be happening before our very eyes, geopolitical commentary has become a growth industry. If indeed the world is entering a multipolar era, what insights can we draw from international relations theory? What are the relevant lessons of history? What are the specific features of our situation? How can we work together to ensure that multipolarity becomes a vehicle for sustainable development and durable peace? To start examining these questions, we need an inclusive, multipolar debate. The following thoughts are presented in this spirit.

A glimpse at international relations theory and the lessons of history[2]

Before we consider the specificity of our geopolitical context, it is worth looking at some theoretical insights and historical precedents most relevant to our situation. To begin with, it is interesting to note that there is no consensus when it comes to the debate on whether multipolarity is inherently more unstable than bipolarity or unipolarity. In 1964, at the height of the Cold War, Kenneth Waltz presented one set of arguments upholding the "Stability of the Bipolar World." In that same year, Karl Deutsch and David Singer argued in favor of the greater stability of multipolarity in an article entitled, "Multipolar Systems and International Stability" (Deutsch & Singer 1964).

More recently, and from a different angle, Amitav Acharya in *The End of the American World Order* (2014) dismisses the fears—attributed to some scholars in the West—associated with the end of a unipolar US hegemony. Simon Reich and Richard Ned Lebow, in *Good-bye Hegemony!* (2014), also question the belief, held by both realist and liberal US academics, that a global system without a hegemon would become unstable and more likely to generate wars.

A distinction perhaps could be made between two unipolar attitudes: one that is favorably inclined toward multilateralism, the other more blatantly unilateralist. George H.W. Bush might represent the first, and his son George W. Bush the second. Acharya (2014) notes with irony that the neo-conservative worldview typical of the latter may have hastened the end of the unipolar moment by pushing for an aggressive Pax Americana that viewed the unilateral resort to the use of military force as a natural US prerogative.

Another set of distinctions worth considering pertains to the durability of orders and power configurations, the role of hegemonic wars, and types of transitions. The Westphalian system dating to 1648 has organized world politics on the basis of relations among sovereign states for more than three and a half centuries, as successive world orders and configurations of power came and went— frequently in the aftermath of hegemonic wars. Robert Gilpin's classic study, *War and Change in World Politics* (1981), remains an important reference work on these questions, having given rise to a recent set of essays by a group of American scholars edited by John Ikenberry under the title of *Power, Order and Change in*

World Politics (2014). This compilation can be a useful guide to current perceptions among US specialists.

As emerges from these texts, changes in the world order and in the distribution of power have taken place all the way up to the present day without destabilizing the essence of the Westphalian paradigm. At the same time, nuclear weapons and the specter of mutually assured destruction set the stage for transitions that do not necessarily involve wars. Indeed, in spite of some destructive proxy conflicts, which victimized several developing countries during the Cold War, the transition from bipolarity to unipolarity after the fall of the Berlin Wall did not involve a large-scale hegemonic war, and took place within a world-order continuum (the most notable institutional adjustment being the replacement of the Soviet Union by the Russian Federation as a permanent member of the UN Security Council in 1992).

The current transition toward multipolarity is perhaps of a more structural nature. In terms of governance, it has already entailed the incorporation of the BRICS, among others, into the G-20 informal group of leading economies. Although agreement has yet to be reached on an expansion of the membership of the UN Security Council, a consensus has existed since the end of the Cold War that its composition is not sufficiently representative of contemporary geopolitical realities. At the same time, it is possible to argue that such adjustments to multipolarity—some already happening, others yet to take place—will not necessarily involve a challenge to the prevailing world order as shaped over the past 70 years, with the UN Charter and the Bretton Woods institutions at its core. The so-called "American-led world order" in fact is likely to survive the end of the unipolar moment and seems well suited to form the basis for a new multipolar order.

It would be a mistake to suggest that the rising powers intend to create a new or different world order. Visibly, for the majority of the international community, rising powers included, the real issue is one of compliance by all countries with the existing rules, without unilateralism and with expanded opportunities for participation in decision-taking. In this respect, Marcos Tourinho presents an interesting view of the current world order. He argues that "the universal international society is a fundamentally syncretic society, since neither from an institutional nor a normative point of view was it shaped by Western powers alone." According to this view "parties have consistently found effective strategies to participate in international rulemaking by regulating the behavior of the most powerful and enhancing their own position in the hierarchy" (Tourinho 2015: 303).

From this viewpoint it is possible to affirm that the contemporary world order, rather than being American led, already reflects a plurality of influences and is not single-handedly led by anyone. Clearly, rising powers are more attached to it than those who might feel nostalgia for unipolar unilateralism. If we are to believe, as suggested by Ikenberry, that "world orders do not just rise and decline, they also evolve" (Ikenberry 2014: 105), it is fair to conclude, as he does, that the forces of democracy and modernity can push and pull history in new, more cooperative, directions.

Historically, several situations provide lessons or insights for a world in transition such as ours. Two centuries ago a unipolar period came to an end and gave rise to a multipolarity of sorts, after the defeat of the Napoleonic army by the combined strength of Russia, Great Britain, Austria, and Prussia. At the Congress of Vienna, a diplomatic effort aimed at reorganizing the European geopolitical landscape can be said to have brought about several decades of relative stability based on new forms of cooperation. The Concert of Europe was the precursor of the high-level conferences to which world leaders and diplomats became accustomed. The Holy Alliance represented a pioneer exercise in preserving peace. Equally noteworthy was the fact that France, although defeated on the battlefield, was not subjected to humiliating treatment by the victors.

It was clear from the outset that the objective of thwarting a return to unipolarity constituted a strong unifying factor among the victorious powers as they engaged in groundbreaking forms of cooperation in the aftermath of Napoleon's defeat. Still, the experiment involved a narrow thematic scope and limited inclusiveness, even within a non-universal, European context. The exclusion of the Ottoman Empire from the negotiating table, for example, sowed the seeds of the Crimean War, which marked the beginning of the prelude to the Great War of 1914–18. It must also be recognized that, more often than not, cooperation was put in the service of the repression of political dissent and nationalist popular uprisings. In other words, multipolarity can be reactionary rather than progressive; hegemonic rather than democratic.

The Versailles Treaty was notoriously less successful than the Vienna settlements in advancing stability. The most obvious reason for its disappointing outcome was the punitive treatment accorded to a defeated Germany. By contrast, the agreements emerging from World War II provided a new example of magnanimity toward the defeated.

Notwithstanding the hierarchical design of the Security Council established in the UN Charter, the Chapter VII provisions limiting the use of force required self-restraint on the part of the victorious powers, and can be described as a step forward for international relations. Thus, it appears that a learning process is possible within a power-sharing system such as the one that came into being after the Allied victory in 1945. It is obvious that the strategic choices made in the 1990s that led to NATO expansion after the demise of the Soviet Union and, soon after, of the Warsaw Pact did not draw inspiration from the reasoning of 1945.

Tragically, a new type of threat from a non-state source made its appearance on the geopolitical scene with the terrorist attacks on the World Trade Center and Pentagon in 2001. This threat metastasized into a non-state movement seeking to impose its rule over large swaths of territory in Iraq and Syria, following the instability that resulted from the military intervention against Saddam Hussein in 2003. As described by Henry Kissinger in the *Wall Street Journal* (2015), the geopolitical order in that region is now "a shambles," with several states facing serious threats to their sovereignty. Thus, Islamic fundamentalist terror, the "unrelenting foe of established order," has come to represent a historically unprecedented challenge to the Westphalian paradigm itself, as elaborated by Kissinger in his book *World Order* (2014).

The declaration of a "war on terror" after the September 11 attacks inaugurated a new chapter in international relations, one that was fraught with unintended consequences. Rather than being defeated or held in check by the most powerful military in history, terrorism assumed more radical features and expanded geographically.

We thus arrive at the latest transition, which seems to have been accelerated by a transgression of the established rules on the use of force deliberately undertaken by the very power that was the alleged custodian of the prevailing order. The unique character of this new situation seems to defy our existing vocabulary as it includes elements of unipolarity and multipolarity, and combines more traditional forms of geopolitical tension with a new threat to the very system within which world orders have evolved since 1648.

What are the specific features of twenty-first century polarity?

In certain respects, the transition underway should not cause anyone to jump to the conclusion that material capabilities, whether economic or military, are less relevant than before. Traditional forms of competition for hegemonic influence, e.g., through arms buildups and the search for territorial advantage, will continue to shape rivalries at the regional and global levels. In parallel, the strategic constraint on all-out war created by nuclear weapons now will be compounded by the proven limitations of military power as a means to combat terrorism.

One of the most original features of the new configuration of power is the unprecedented fact that a non-European, non-Western power will become the leading world economy during the decades ahead. China's economic growth is destined to translate into increased diplomatic influence. The same will apply to other regional powers from the South as they enhance their global outreach, admittedly in non-linear ways. A resurgent Russia will continue to wield considerable military might. A highly developed Europe may find a renewed sense of cohesion with Germany at its center. Japan will be faced with new strategic dilemmas, whether the US–China relationship becomes more cooperative or adversarial. How the United States responds to a new situation of relative loss of influence will be of major relevance to the rest of the international community: The Obama legacy with respect to Iran or Cuba points in one direction, while the "exceptionalist" mindset still prevalent among many in the US points in another.

It is not clear whether this new environment amplifies the space for multilateralism, diplomacy, and cooperation. But a number of characteristics that were absent from previous transitions, and seem to be peculiar to the early twenty-first century, create a distinct framework for opportunity alongside and beyond the obvious pitfalls. Certain factors that were not present at other turning points can play—and indeed already are playing—a unifying role.

An important cross-cutting factor in the reshuffling of international hierarchies is the higher degree of global interconnectedness among governments, economies, and societies through trade, investment, telecommunications, the media, and people-to-people contacts. The flip side of this coin is the fact that an increase in connectivity also may be placed in the service of destabilizing agendas.

Among the most notable unifying elements is the challenge posed by global warming and climate change. This is a situation that, for the first time in human history, is forcing the community of nations to confront the stark reality that there will be no salvation without cooperation. The problem affects countries large and small independently of their level of development and cannot be mitigated without the active engagement of the biggest emitters. As the resolution that adopted the Paris Agreement in December of 2015 acknowledges, "climate change represents an urgent and potentially irreversible threat to human societies and the planet and thus requires the widest possible cooperation by all countries" (United Nations 2015a: 2).

Violent extremism, the gateway to terrorism, is increasingly perceived as a global threat requiring comprehensive, coordinated international efforts. The failure of the so-called "war on terror" has gradually given way to a heightened awareness of the need for harmonized, multilaterally agreed approaches to curtail the phenomenon. A recent UN report on the subject was particularly direct when it stated that "we must take action now to save succeeding generations" (United Nations 2015b).

The Ebola outbreak in 2014, which caused thousands of preventable deaths, demonstrated that the world is ill prepared to address the threat posed by epidemics. Although not a new threat in itself, the potentially devastating social and economic effects of health crises in an age of unprecedented human mobility have put the world on heightened alert. The global drug problem is now considered a "common and shared responsibility," as nations at different points in the production and consumption chain acknowledge the unsatisfactory results of the "war on drugs" and seek more effective solutions through multilaterally concerted efforts.

Moreover, it is possible to affirm that civil society has assumed an increasingly important role in influencing international debates and agendas, in contrast with previous eras or transitions. To a certain degree, the appearance on the world stage of a myriad of non-governmental organizations promoting causes which range from gender equality to disarmament and non-proliferation represents a historical evolution that cannot be ignored.

As distinct from the nineteenth century's Eurocentric multipolar experiment, a twenty-first century multipolar world order will be universal in scope. In other respects, however, the two periods may yet come to share certain similarities.

It is not unlikely that the new multipolar world order will give rise to coordinated attempts at thwarting a return to unipolar hegemony. It is conceivable that rivalry and competition involving the main military powers will degenerate into increased tensions that could lead to widespread instability and even war. It is also possible to imagine other bleak scenarios unique to the twenty-first century involving the possession of weapons of mass destruction by non-state actors. The pressures resulting from large groups of refugees fleeing conflict and of migrants searching for economic opportunity represent new challenges with unpredictable domestic and international repercussions.

Are we dealing constructively with the new situation?

These imaginable and other as yet unimagined pitfalls could be avoided or circumvented if we had more enlightened leadership and effective diplomacy. And there are reasons to feel encouraged by some of the responses to shared challenges that are already being articulated, in regard to both multilateral governance structure and the challenges themselves.

International governance mechanisms have begun to incorporate a larger number of participants, as they adapt to a multipolar context. One of the first examples of this trend was the disappearance of the "Quad" group, composed of the US, the EU, Japan, and Canada, from the GATT/WTO negotiating praxis. Since the Cancún Ministerial Conference in 2013, developing countries with a special stake in negotiations on agriculture started making their way into the inner decision-making circles of the WTO, with India and Brazil often taking the lead. The informal group of larger economies known as the G-7 (and then G-8, as it temporarily reached out to Russia) was enlarged in the wake of the 2008 economic crisis due to the perception among its founders that the group should include other players, in particular the BRICS. Quota reform at the IMF and World Bank is starting to redress the asymmetries in voting rights at the International Financial Institutions (IFIs), bringing these more in line with the real economic weight of member states.

Within the United Nations system, small steps are being taken to respond to a widespread demand for greater inclusiveness. The procedures for the selection of a new Secretary General now contemplate public hearings with the official candidates and include the possibility of participation by civil society. Following a recommendation by the Rio+20 Conference, the membership of the Governing Council of the United Nations Environment Program became universal. The High-Level Plenary of the UN General Assembly on Migration and Refugees incorporated the International Organization for Migration into the UN family, a development that many hope will help to improve international coordination in response to the plight of migrants worldwide.

But the picture is not an entirely encouraging one, with many anachronistic institutional arrangements still in place in spite of the pressure for change. The IFIs continue to be headed by nationals of developed countries. Key positions in the UN Secretariat tend to be monopolized by the five permanent members of the Security Council. The unchanged composition of the Security Council itself reveals an incapacity on the part of the organization to adapt to the geopolitical realities of the new century. When the membership of the UN doubled from the original 51 signatories of the Charter in 1945 to approximately 100 members in the early 1960s, the Council's composition was increased from 11 to 15, with all new seats being in the non-permanent category. Today the UN has 193 members, a majority of which favor an expansion in the permanent and non-permanent categories. As Bruce Jones from the Brookings Institution points out in a recent paper, the Organization needs to engage a wider set of states more directly in the promotion of international peace and security and re-position itself for the new realities of geopolitics (Jones 2016).

On the substantive front, the record is also mixed, with an array of unresolved problems and a few brighter spots. On the positive side, 2015 was hailed as a good year for diplomacy and multilateralism on account of the consensus reached on the 2030 Agenda for Sustainable Development, the adoption of the Paris Agreement on Climate Change, and the successful negotiations on the Iranian nuclear program. These are not minor accomplishments and represent a victory for patient dialogue and persuasive diplomacy.

The 2030 Agenda for Sustainable Development is an innovative, transformative, universally applicable platform that seeks to combine economic growth with social progress and environmental awareness. With poverty eradication at its center, the Agenda is the most ambitious and comprehensive program of action ever adopted by the UN membership with its 17 goals and 169 targets. Development henceforth will be inextricably linked to sustainability.

The Paris Agreement under the Framework Convention on Climate Change adopted in December of 2015 lays the groundwork for holding the increase in the global average temperature to well below 2 degrees Celsius above pre-industrial levels, and to pursue efforts to limit the temperature increase to 1.5 degrees. With all major emitters on board, the agreement proved the skeptics wrong, notwithstanding the technical complexity and political sensitivity of the matter.

Three recent reports brought to the attention of the UN membership the related topics of peace operations, post-conflict peace-building (or "sustaining peace," under the new terminology), and the role of women in the promotion of international peace and security. All three emphasized prevention and underlined the primacy of politics and diplomacy. The message was clear: Military action should always be a measure of last resort, and carried out in full compliance with UN Charter provisions. This message can be seen as a polite rejection of the more militaristic and interventionist mindsets of the first years of the century. The agreement reached by the P5+1 and Iran, with a view to ensuring that its nuclear capability is applied for peaceful purposes alone, should be appreciated through a similar logic. It stands as an example of a preventive measure secured through effective diplomacy and political leadership on an issue of obvious relevance for world peace.

The Human Rights Council, which came into being as a result of a decision by the General Assembly meeting at summit level in 2005, created a more equitable framework for the promotion and protection of human rights through innovative mechanisms such as the Universal Periodic Review of all UN members' policies and practices. It also had provided a venue for breaking new ground in responding to contemporary challenges, such as those related to the Edward Snowden revelations on mass surveillance, with the appointment of a Special Rapporteur on the Right to Privacy in the Digital Age. Another significant recent development was the appointment of an independent expert on protection against discrimination and violence based on sexual orientation and gender identity.

On the negative side, a longer list no doubt could be drawn up comprising the many unresolved international challenges with respect to which a constructive way forward is yet to be found. These are predominantly in the peace and security domain. A deadly fight for military advantage has been the hallmark of the tragic civil war in Syria, in spite of frequent admonitions to the effect that there is no military solution to the conflict. Neglect has supplanted active diplomacy in the search for a two-state solution in the Israel–Palestine conflict. Iraq, Libya, and Yemen face momentous threats to their sovereignty and territorial integrity. A defiant Taliban is a persistent source of instability in Afghanistan.

The absence of progress on the de-nuclearization of the Korean peninsula is a stark reminder of the threat posed by the proliferation of weapons of mass destruction. At the same time, the failure of the 2015 Review Conference of the Nuclear Non-Proliferation Treaty exposed the continuing reluctance of the nuclear weapon states to fulfill their commitments. The persistent deadlock regarding the establishment of a zone free of nuclear weapons and other weapons of mass destruction in the Middle East further highlights the limitations of the Treaty and its regime. The crisis in Ukraine reignited a level of animosity between Russia and the West reminiscent of the Cold War. In Africa, notwithstanding visible progress at sustaining peace in the Western part of the continent, terrorism has spread across a large arc of instability along the Sahel, while promising efforts at stabilization in the Great Lakes region, in South Sudan, and in the Central African Republic cannot be considered irreversible.

As Hugh White elaborates in *The China Choice* (2012), there are many ways in which the potential rivalry between the US and China could escalate dangerously, particularly along the maritime Asian fault lines. De-escalation will require dialogue, diplomacy and compromise, and a political vision capable of creating effective bilateral, regional, and multilateral frameworks to reach the necessary understandings. Such frameworks need to be established with a sense of urgency. It is obvious that the peaceful evolution of the China–US relationship is of paramount significance for the consolidation of a new order of international cooperation.

On the counter-terrorism front, even if a number of initiatives have evoked consensus at the UN, a common sense of purpose based on collectively agreed-upon strategies has yet to emerge in specific situations. As growing attention is given to the protection of civilians in situations of conflict, divergences persist, in particular with regard to the use of force, whether by peacekeepers or others, as legitimate concerns are raised regarding the negative consequences thereof. Mistrust generated by the instability wrought by the NATO intervention in Libya, authorized under a "Responsibility to Protect" mandate, has revived interest in Brazilian proposals on "Responsibility while Protecting." It is ironic to note that the same governments that are most readily inclined to embrace military intervention for the protection of civilians in situations of conflict do not necessarily demonstrate a corresponding humanitarian impulse when it comes to welcoming civilians at their borders who are fleeing conflict.

Subjacent to these problems is the major strategic challenge that Bruce Jones describes as "de-conflicting great power tensions" (Jones 2016: 4–5). Tensions involving the three top military powers might be compounded by several imaginable situations that need not be enumerated. If the UN evolves into a more capable machinery, built on a wider political coalition committed to multipolarity, there may be a chance that the top military powers will be able to develop confidence in such a tool. It is difficult to see how this can happen, however, without the long overdue Security Council reform.

Cooperative multipolarity is achievable

Zbigniew Brzezinski observed in a 2016 presentation in the United Arab Emirates that—in military terms—the current situation may be without historical precedent, with none of the world's three top military powers (the US, Russia, and China) in a position to assume a hegemonic role. In this respect Simon Reich and Richard Ned Lebow correctly point out that "ultimately, hegemony is difficult to reconcile with democracy" (2014: 183). It is undeniable that, in the emerging multipolar configuration of power, divergent agendas and worldviews will continue to collide and could well lead to open hostility and destructive competition. But it is also true that cooperative and increasingly inclusive forms of interaction are happening every day on important, unifying issues, through multilateral arrangements which—although described as "American led" by some—in reality reflect an evolutionary path paved with the engaged participation of many nations large and small.

Cooperative multipolarity is therefore achievable and can be seen as the next, more democratic and just stage in the evolutionary path of the international system that originated at Westphalia. Important achievements, brought about through the active leadership of the victors of World War II, provide a firm foundation for our future efforts. These include the ruling out of the use of military force, except in situations of self-defense or in accordance with specific multilateral authorization; respect for the universality of human rights; and compliance with a vast body of international law establishing rights and obligations on a wide range of topics, from trade, finance and social justice to health, education, and culture.

Of the three "pillars" that compose the triad of the UN's field of activity—namely, development, human rights, peace and security—it is possible to affirm that a process of modernization and adaptation to new contemporary realities has been advancing with respect to the first two. Such is the meaning of the universally applicable 2030 Agenda for Sustainable Development adopted in 2015; such is the sense of the Universal Periodic Review of the Human Rights Council created 10 years ago.

By contrast, in the peace and security realm, there is considerable room for improvement. But the situation is not hopeless. The militarism of the first years of the twenty-first century has come to illustrate the limitations of the use of force to confront the new challenges posed by violent extremism conducive to terrorism, opening opportunities for cooperation on prevention. An effective combination of multilateral and bilateral diplomacy has produced constructive outcomes in dealing with thorny issues, such as the Iranian nuclear project.

This, of course, is insufficient. Multipolarity will not lead to a more stable, cooperative world in and of itself. Governance mechanisms must become more inclusive and democratic. The most powerful will have to relinquish the inclination to view themselves as "exceptional" in favor of a universal proclivity capable of celebrating our common, and diverse, humanity. The rising democratic powers can exercise their growing diplomatic influence by helping to build bridges across ideological divides and reducing the many gaps in communication and understanding that separate countries from different cultural traditions or at different stages of economic and social development, including on issues such as gender equality and access to justice.

Nations of all sizes will need to derive benefits from the sovereign equality of states that lies at the core of our system, through improved and more inclusive multilateral frameworks for decision-taking and cooperation. Civil society groups must be afforded appropriate channels for their voices to be heard, both domestically and internationally. The new UN Secretary General will be called upon to exercise strong leadership, as cooperative multipolarity will not be able to thrive in the absence of robust multilateralism.

A convergence between a multipolar distribution of geopolitical influence and functional multilateral institutions—one that draws strength from confronting collective, unifying challenges absent from previous transitions—can lead to a new international, sustainable, cooperative multipolarity. With enlightened political leadership, diplomatic resourcefulness and social mobilization, the citizens of our interconnected societies, who expect stability and opportunity to realize their potential and pursue happiness, will be supportive and ready.

Postscript: October, 2018

As these thoughts originally were formulated in 2016, it seems appropriate to include a postscript in order to take new developments into account. I would start by saying that the unilateralist impulse, which has come to manifest itself once again, is not anything essentially new. We witnessed it in 2003 with respect to Iraq. As Acharya points out, a neo-conservative disregard for multilateralism at that time may have hastened the end of the unipolar moment rather than enhancing the status of the predominant military and economic power in world affairs (Acharya 2014). In today's more multipolar environment, a renewed disregard for multilateralism could have even more problematic effects.

Moreover, it is worth remembering, as Tourinho (2015) has argued, that the current world order with its multilateral institutions cannot be described properly as led or owned by a single country or region; it has become our collective property. In this sense, it is to be expected that the major players of international society, including governmental and non-governmental actors, will join forces to uphold the tenets of the established order and the international rules-based system. Climate change, the fight against terrorism, and other unifying factors will play a part in exposing the limitations of unilateral approaches to common challenges.

Another set of considerations pertains to the limited power of nationalism to conquer hearts and minds internationally. Defending the national interest remains a priority for every government. But international leadership is difficult to sustain if it is lacking in content of universal resonance. Regardless of audience members' religious affiliations, the words of Pope Francis at the 70th UN General Assembly were greeted with a long, unparalleled standing ovation. His emphasis on the importance of enhancing international cooperation to alleviate poverty and protect the environment inspired and reassured his listeners. This example illustrates the fact that, in our current international landscape, traditional categories of East and West, North and South, may not fully capture the affinities that can arise across and above divisions based on geography, ideology, or level of development.

Multipolarity presupposes a competitive market for international political influence. Diplomatic clout, the capacity to lead and persuade, is not a direct consequence of economic and military power, as the previous reference to the Vatican demonstrates. The rise of the kind of populism that is eschews solidarity, takes a tolerant view of prejudice, and ready to compromise universal values in favor of narrowly defined national interests represents a challenge of considerable scope. The recent electoral successes of this sort of populism merely increase the responsibility of those who see merit in the institutional framework enshrined in our multilateral institutions to work together to preserve it, making adaptations where necessary to the new geopolitical realities of multipolarity, and to join forces across ideologies, religions, and continents to construct a more rational, humane, cooperative international society.

As a concluding thought, may I underline my strong support for the notion put forth by Secretary-General Guterres that a "surge in diplomacy" is urgent and necessary today. I am convinced that a revitalized commitment to dialogue and diplomacy, regionally and globally, is an essential step in the effort to move forward toward a new post-hegemonic multilayered multilateralism.

Notes

1. This text, which I present in my individual capacity, represents an attempt at responding through the language of diplomacy to the very real predicament that the international community finds itself in today. It seeks to outline both the shortcomings in our response to a new historic opportunity for multilateralism as well as the areas of relative success from which to derive encouragement.
2. Substantial portions of this chapter were published previously under the title "Is the World Ready for Cooperative Multipolarity?" in *CEBRI* (Centro Brasileiro de Relações Internacionais), 17(2): October 2018, pp. 8–19. Reprinted by permission.

References

Acharya, A. 2014. *The End of American World Order*. Cambridge, UK: Polity Press

Deutsch, K. & D. Singer, 1964. "Multipolar Power Systems and International Stability." *World Politics* 16(3): 390–406

Gilpin, R. 1981. *War and Change in World Politics*. Cambridge, UK: Cambridge University Press

Ikenberry, J. (ed.), 2014. *Power, Order, and Change in World Politics*. Cambridge, UK: Cambridge University Press

Jones, B. 2016. "The UN at 70—Celebration, or Commemoration? Or: The case for re-tooling the UN's conflict management capacity." Challenge Paper for the UN High-Level Thematic Debate on Peace and Security

Kissinger, H. 2014. *World Order*. New York: Penguin Press

Kissinger, H. 2015. "A Path Out of the Middle East Collapse." *Wall Street Journal*, October 16. Available at www.wsj.com/articles/a-path-out-of-the-middle-east-collapse-1445037513

Reich, S. & R. Lebow, 2014. *Good-bye Hegemony! Power and influence in the global system*. Princeton, NJ: Princeton University Press

Tourinho, M. 2015. *Beyond Expansion: Political contestation in the global international society (1815–1960)*. Geneva, Switzerland: Graduate Institute of International and Development Studies

United Nations, 2015a. *Draft Decision CP21*. Adoption of the Paris Agreement. Paris, December 11. Available at https://unfcc,int/sites/default/files/resource/docs/2015/cop21/eng/10a01.pdf

United Nations, 2015b. "Plan of Action to Prevent Violent Extremism." Report of the Secretary General to the 70th UN General Assembly. Available at https://undocs.org/pdf?symbol=en/A/70/674

Waltz, K. 1964. "The Stability of a Bipolar World." *Daedalus* 93(3): 881–909

INDEX

Page numbers in **bold** denote tables, those in *italics* denote figures.

19th Chinese Communist Party Congress 74, 77

ACFTA *see* ASEAN–China Free Trade Agreement
activism 43, 114–15
Africa 31, 69, 74–7, 103, 108, 120, 212; countries of 69, 75, 183; interregional relations with Europe 75, 77; regionalism in 75
African Union 6, 69–70, 75
AFTA *see* ASEAN Free Trade Area
agenda 9, 13, 79, 122, 131, 136–7, 158, 191, 194, 196–7, 203–4, 209, 211, 214; cultural 122; destabilizing 209; divergent 213; economic 136; international 203; multilateralist 79; national 171; political integration 136; subordinate interregional 71
agreements 12, 56, 60, 84, 95, 106, 116, 157, 180, 183, 196, 206–7, 211; cooperative 60; free trade 179, 182; international 6, 183; interregional 10, 101; legal 11; multilateral 76; regional 12; Westphalian 49
agriculture 172, 210
AIIB *see* Asian Infrastructure Investment Bank
ALBA *see* Bolivarian Alliance for the People of Our Americas
American Declaration of the Rights and Duties of Man 114–15
American Institute of International Law 112
American Republics 111–12
"anchoring practices" 50–2, 54, 61–3
Andean Community (formerly the Andean Pact) 109, 117, 119
Andean Pact 116–17
Annan, Kofi 57, 70, 81, 83, 85, 87
anti-terrorism capacities 72, 148
APEC *see* Asia–Pacific Economic Cooperation
approaches 22, 39, 52, 61, 68, 71–2, 77, 86, 144–5, 154, 159, 194, 209; archaic 129; bilateral 135, 159; constructivist 39; dual-track 159; historical 9, 121; institutional 55, 109; legalistic 55; pan-American 113; regional trade 116; sub-regional 110; unilateral 188, 215
Arab nations 74
Aranha, Oswaldo 113
ARF *see* ASEAN Regional Forum
Argentina 108, 113, 117, 123, 178; leadership role of 117; and the Mercado Común del Sur or MERCOSUR 6, 10, 22, 69–71, 74, 78–9, 100, 108–9, 116–19, 123, 182; rapprochement with Brazil 117
Armenia 73, 131

ASEAN *see* Association of Southeast Asian Nations
ASEF *see* Asia–Europe Foundation
ASEM *see* Asia–Europe Meeting
Asia 24–5, 31, 69, 71, 74, 76, 78–9, 150, 156, 158, 188–9, 191, 193, 195–7, 199; countries of 101, 191, 195, 197–8; and Europe 189–90, 192–3, 195–6, 198–9; and European countries 189, 192–5; and European partner countries 194–5, 197; and European regional entities 12, 190; financial crises 191, 198; growth during the 1980s and early 1990s 190–1; interregional relations 81
Asia Africa Growth Corridor 175
Asia–Europe Business Forum 191, 193
Asia–Europe Economic Forum 191
Asia–Europe Foundation 193–6, 199
Asia–Europe Meeting 12–13, 69, 81, 84, 188–99, 196–7; connectivity 195–8; cooperation 192; countries 193; government sector 193; Infoboard 191, 193; institutions 194; interregionalism 189, 199; leaders 192–3, 195–7; member countries 199; multidimensional cooperation 198; multilateralism 193, 198; Myanmar's membership in 191; partner countries 191; partners 189, 191–8; Pathfinder Group on Connectivity 196–7; process 189–93, 199; summit 81, 84, 191, 196–7; Trade Facilitation Action Plan, adopted 191; Ulaanbaatar Summit 195, 198
Asia–Pacific Economic Cooperation 69
Asian and European 24, 95, 196; businesses and individuals 195; experts 197; governments 195; leaders 197; participants 194
Asian Infrastructure Investment Bank 144
Asian regionalism 24–5
Asian regionalization 25
Asian societies 24
Asian state institutions 25
Asian states 24–5
Asia–Pacific Economic Cooperation 58, 69, 71
Association of Southeast Asian Nations 6, 8, 10–12, 14, 48, 57–63, 69–71, 80, 82–3, 100, 154–60, 183, 189–92, 194–6, 198–9; adapting to norms and rules of the 155, 161; China-ASEAN Summit (1997) 154; China-ASEAN Summit (2018) 155, 157, 197; China Free Trade Agreement 156; China Strategic Partnership Vision 155; code of conduct 159–61; communities 58–60, 62–3; countries 11, 154–60, 183, 185–6; deepening of the integration process 71; for disaster relief and security issues 72; Free Trade Area 58; interactions with China's regional multilateral diplomacy 155, 161; model of multilateralism 154; Regional Forums 58, 155, 157–8; regionalism 57–8; relationship with China 155–8
associations 6–7, 9–10, 13, 68, 83, 102, 105, 134; civil society 83; democratic 134; nationalist 68; regional 6–7, 9–10, 13, 102, 105
Australia 59, 78, 180, 183
authoritarian 3, 6, 21, 41, 105–6; evolution 74; governments 130; hegemons 138; leaders 135; modernization 21; powers 135; regimes 10, 39, 73, 102, 135–6; regionalism 134; rule 135–6
autocracies 6, 10, 73, 132, 135–8
autonomy 18–19, 27, 57, 115, 118; regional 122; relative 41; strategic 9
Axial Age 7, 18, 20, 40

Bangkok 58, 69, 190, 193
Bangladesh 11, 166–7, 171–2
Bava, Ummu Salma 11, 85, 173
behavior 51, 60, 75, 129, 145, 161–2, 206; of China 159; hegemonic 203; human 138; political 23, 42, 171; state 145
Beijing 75, 84, 144, 146, 154, 157–9, 168–9, 171, 175, 192; and cooperation with the Muslim states 11; participates actively in multilateral diplomacy 144; relationship with ASEAN 158; and the standoff with New Delhi 171; thirst for economic benefits from energy and raw materials 75
Belarus 74, 131–2, 135–6, 150
Belt and Road Initiative 9, 11, 69, 74–7, 103, 105, 143, 146, 175, 197–8
Benelux countries 26
Bhutan 167–8, 170–1
bilateral approaches 135, 159
Bilateral Investment Treaty with China 78, 82; agenda 78; negotiations 81
bilateral negotiations 179, 183

Index **219**

bilateral relations with individual member states 9, 105, 133, 146–7, 171–3
bilateral trade 110, 156, 182
bilateral trade deficits 180
bipolar confrontation 69, 76
bipolarity 205–6; *see also* unipolarity
BIT *see* Bilateral Investment Treaty with China
blocs 23, 72, 98, 117; cultural 36; diverse trade 123, 157; military 98; political 48; regional 23, 82, 98–9, 101, 117, 134, 184
Bobbio, Norberto 68, 86
Bolivarian Alliance for the People of Our Americas 74, 110, 118–19
borders 147, 166, 168–71, 173, 213; hardening of 105; national 48–50; shared 149; territorial 28; transcending 173
boundaries 11, 130, 147, 167, 169; defined territorial 19; national 149; political 173; porous 22
Bourdieu, Pierre 41, 68, 86
Brazil 13, 69, 80, 110–11, 119, 122–3, 204, 210; economic and political difficulties 118; Foreign Minister Araújo Castro 113, 202; government of 83; rapprochement with Argentina 117; thumbs nose at international agreements and norms 6; transforms the distribution of power and influence in the global economy 100
Bretton Woods Agreement (1944) 5, 76, 81, 113
Bretton Woods institutions 111, 114, 206
Brexit 8, 26, 57, 62, 73, 105, 204
BRI *see* Belt and Road Initiative
BRICS (Brazil, Russia, India, China, South Africa) group 13, 72, 122, 204, 206, 210
Britain 26, 97–8; control of its empire 5; and the intellectual impulses stemming from political economists of 4; membership in the European Economic Community 26, 99; protects its imperial markets 12
British politics 26
Brookings Institution 211
Brussels 75, 191–2, 196–7
Buenos Aires 108, 117, 178
bureaucracies 136–7
Bush, George W. 71, 205
"Buy American, Hire American" 179

Calvo, Carlos 112
Cambodia 82, 156
Canada 78–9, 82, 116, 180–1, 183, 210
Cancun Ministerial Conference (2013) 210
capital 23, 99, 131–2
capitalism 21–2, 96, 104
Castro, Araújo 113, 202
Castro, Fidel 115
CELAC *see* Community of Latin American and Caribbean States
CENTO *see* Central Treaty Organization
Central America 23, 69, 109, 116, 122
Central American Integration System 119
Central and Southeast Asia 145, 147, 149, 151, 153, 155, 157, 159, 161
Central Asia 10–11, 74, 147–51, 153–4, 158, 160–2; and a prospective Union 150; SCO states 151; and Southeast Asia 144, 146
Central Treaty Organization 23, 168–9
CETA *see* Comprehensive Economic and Trade Agreement
CFAU *see* China Foreign Affairs University
challenges 13, 42, 61–2, 67, 81, 95, 97, 101, 105, 120, 149, 166, 170, 188, 196–9; contemporary 212; cultural 81; domestic 84; existential 95; global 104, 197, 203; new 202, 204, 210, 214; political 24; unifying 214; unresolved international 212
Chile 119, 180, 183
China 8–11, 18–19, 67–9, 71–8, 80–4, 100–5, 143–4, 146–7, 149–62, 168–71, 175, 179–81, 183–5, 203–4, 212–13; accession to TAC 155; and the Association of Southeast Asian Nations 11, 155–6, 160; attitudes toward multilateralism and regionalism 144; and the BRI program 153; bypasses the security dilemma resulting from territorial disputes over the South China Sea 161; and Central and Southeast Asia 145, 147, 149, 151, 153, 155, 157, 159, 161; decision to prioritize individual relations with single EU countries 76; driving role in forming multilateral relations through the SCO 147; efforts to promote international norms 151–2; emerges as the major strategic competitor of the United States 102; endeavors

China *continued*
to promote economic cooperation 152; engagement with the Central Asian Countries 147, 150, 153, 158; forging a strategic partnership with the Association of Southeast Asian Nations 155, 176; goal of achieving "win/win" economic benefits for all countries 11, 156; interregional policies in Asia 74–6; joins Treaty of Amity and Cooperation in Southeast Asia 155; multilateralism 143–4; opened by imperialist Western powers 28; partnership with the European Union 69; relationship with the United States 208; trade war with the United States 179, 185
China-ASEAN Senior Officials' Meeting 160
China–ASEAN Summit (1997) 154
China–ASEAN Summit (2018) 155, 157, 197
The China Choice 212
China-EU Summit 81
China Foreign Affairs University 84
Chinese 77, 85, 104, 143–4, 146, 154; chief negotiators 156; diplomacy 11, 144, 158, 162; economy 185; government 151; interregionalism in Africa 75; investments 75, 153, 175; networking initiatives 147; norms for managing international relations 154; philosophical worldview and cultural identity 146; politics 146; and Russian leaders 151
Chinese Communist Party 83
Christianity 6, 27–30, 43
CIS *see* Commonwealth of Independent States
civil rights 192–3
civil society associations 83
civilizations 1, 6–8, 18–20, 30, 36, 38, 42–4; Axial Age 18–19; East Asian 29; and Eastern religions 29; global 18; human 2; international 30; non-European 20; styles of civilization 42–5; Western 29, 99
climate change 7, 13, 183, 192, 197, 209, 211, 215
coalitions 46, 137, 203–4; culturally based 44; wider political 213
COC *see* code of conduct
code of conduct 159–61
coexistence 31, 61, 117; conflictual 67; peaceful 29

Cold War 2, 5, 53–6, 67, 71, 76, 96, 98–9, 101, 103–4, 115–16, 169, 172, 202, 205–6; mentality 158; and multilateralism 53; period 117, 144, 168
Collective Security Treaty Organization 131, 150
Commonwealth of Independent States 131, 135–6, 150
Community of Andean States and MERCOSUR 10
Community of Latin American and Caribbean States 72, 110, 118–19
Comprehensive and Progressive Trans-Pacific Partnership 157, 180, 182
Comprehensive Economic and Trade Agreement 78, 183
conferences 84, 112, 150, 192, 210; Cancun Ministerial Conference (2013) 210; First Hague Conference (1899) 111, 113; Lima Conference (1938) 113; pan-American 113, 115; Versailles Conference (1919) 76
conflicts 3, 8, 10–11, 26, 45, 70–1, 86, 104, 114, 167, 169–70, 172–3, 179, 181, 188; armed 4; dysfunctional 40; intrastate 172
constitutional monarchy 167, 170
"constrained diversity" 7, 17–19, 21–3, 25, 27, 29–31, 79, 96; coalesces around states that are more similar in form than in substance 31; conditions of 30–1; world of 22, 25; in world politics 31
cooperation 9, 46, 52–3, 60–1, 104–5, 148, 150–1, 153, 155, 166–8, 171–5, 189, 194–5, 197, 207–9; building 99; cross-border 174; cultural 74; developing 153; enhanced 57, 73; environmental 72; external 3, 76; global 6, 13; harmonious 17; institutionalized 54, 70, 87, 172; intra-Asian 191; multidimensional 71, 190; mutual 149; political 3, 41; regionalist 104; sovereignty-hugging 120; strengthening Asia–Europe 172, 197; sustaining multidimentional 189; voluntary 38
cooperative multipolarity 202–5, 207, 209, 211, 213–15
coordination 57, 61, 202; international 210; regional 58
Council of Europe 73–4
Council of the European Union 8, 55–7, 59, 78, 106, 151, 203
counter-terrorism 192, 212

countries 4–6, 11–12, 44–6, 82–4, 105–6, 135–8, 146–50, 152–3, 156–7, 159, 167–73, 178–80, 182–6, 190–3, 195–9; democratizing 136; developed 97, 210; emerging 118; independent 9–10; landlocked 168, 170; less-developed 186; neighboring 66, 146; participating 85, 157, 179, 183–4; post-colonial 85; post-Soviet 131, 133, 136
Court of Justice 8, 55
Cowhey, Peter 54
CPC *see* Communist Party of China
CPTPP *see* Comprehensive and Progressive Trans-Pacific Partnership
CSTO *see* Collective Security Treaty Organization
CU *see* Customs Union
cultural 39–40, 42, 68; developments 18, 172; diversity 3, 66, 150–1, 198; nationalism 2; pluralism 3; regionalism 2; segmentation 45; transformations 45
cultural backgrounds 42, 48, 157, 170
cultural dialogue 70, 74, 79, 83
cultural identity 8, 41, 43, 71, 146, 173; diverse 14; exclusive 13; shared 2; unique 143
cultural politics 1, 3
culture, political 7, 22, 40–2, 44–6, 86, 102
cultures 1–2, 7, 29, 40, 42–5, 50, 63, 67, 86–7, 110, 148, 172, 174, 189, 213; background 77, 84; collective 41; common civic 3; distinctive cooperative 198; dominant 2; ecumenical 45; general 42; of Latin Christendom 27, 29–30; modern 43; national 80; non-European 85; political 7, 22, 40–2, 44–6, 86, 102; traditional 98
Customs Union 10, 23, 26, 116, 131–3, 182

Dario, Ruben 112
DDA *see* Doha Development Agenda
de Aguilar Patriota, Antonio 13
de Gaulle, Charles 26
Declaration on the Conduct of the Parties in the South China Sea 159–61
declarations 59, 62, 160, 208; Comprehensive Economic and Trade Agreement 78, 183; Declaration on the Conduct of the Parties in the South China Sea 159–61
decolonization 31, 98, 114, 166–7
deficits 24, 180; country's trade 179; democratic 134; US trade 180

democracy 1, 4, 7, 10, 43, 73, 102, 132, 134–7, 152, 171, 206, 213; domestic 87; electoral 1; illiberal 106; parliamentary 170; political 6, 20; social 84
democratic associations 134
democratic framework 41, 171
democratization 6, 10, 14, 168, 171, 192
Deutsch, Karl 30, 171, 205
developing countries 13, 115, 122, 146, 172, 186, 206, 210
dialogue 2, 14, 38, 79, 95, 97, 106, 145, 149–50, 155, 192–3, 195, 198, 212, 215; cultural 70, 74, 79, 83; interfaith 192; intercultural modernization 39; interregional multipurpose 84; interregional/transregional 66; multilateral security 158; partners 58, 150, 154
diplomacy 11, 75, 143–4, 208, 211–12, 215; effective 13, 210–11; new 143; of Xi Jinping 75–6, 78, 143, 146
disagreements among states 31, 57, 84, 100
Dispute Settlement Procedure 179, 184
disputes 61, 112–13, 159; maritime 159; settling border 161; territorial 161, 184
diversity 30, 32, 68, 100, 109–10, 151, 154, 173; cultural 3, 66, 150–1, 198; regional 23, 66, 174; *see also* "constrained diversity"
DOC *see* Declaration on the Conduct of the Parties in the South China Sea
Doha Development Agenda 178–9, 184
Doha Development Round 117, 188
domestic politics 6, 49, 81, 185
Dominican Republic 115
Dominion of Pakistan *see* Pakistan
DSP *see* Dispute Settlement Procedure
Dubey, M. 174
Dugin, Alexander 68

EAEU *see* Eurasian Economic Union
East Asia 12, 24–5, 44, 81–2, 120, 156, 159, 178–9, 181, 183, 185–8, 190–1, 196; and China 87; civilizations 29; multilateralizing regionalism in 178–87
East Asia Summit 2018 157, 159
East Asian Co-Prosperity Sphere (1935–45) 9
ECJ *see* European Court of Justice
ECLA *see* Economic Commission for Latin America and the Caribbean
Economic Commission for Latin America and the Caribbean 115–16

economic powers 202, 215
ECSC *see* European Coal and Steel Community
EEC *see* European Economic Community
EFTA free trade area 26
Eisenstadt, Shmuel 7, 18–20, 38–40, 96
Elias, Norbert 42
The End of the American World Order 205
Eurasia 103, 130, 132, 134–8
Eurasian 10, 133, 135–8; bureaucracy 137; countries 131–2, 134, 137, 139; efforts to emulate the EU experience. 131; integration 131; organizations focusing on economic issues 131, 133, 135; post-Soviet regionalism 129–39; societies 139
Eurasian Economic Commission 132, 137
Eurasian Economic Community 131
Eurasian Economic Union 6, 9–10, 74, 103, 105, 131–4, 136–7, 150
Europe 11, 13, 19, 23–6, 44–5, 54–6, 72–6, 80–1, 83–4, 108, 120–2, 189–90, 192–3, 195–6, 198–9; and the 12th Summit theme "Europe & Asia: Global partners for the global challenge" 192, 197; and American policy discourses on Eurasian regionalism 130; and the balancing role played in trans-Atlantic and pan-European relations 75; and Christianity 6, 19, 27–30, 43; and colonialism 110, 120, 188; experimentation with multilateralism 25; highly developed 208; imperialist powers 25; interventionist 111; and the Monroe Doctrine 110; and partner countries 194; and the path to integration 25; regionalism 25
European 2–9, 18–21, 23–6, 54–63, 67–8, 73–6, 78–80, 84–7, 98–9, 106, 110, 116–17, 119–23, 188–95, 197–8; economic interests 198; empires 98–9; geopolitical landscape 207; governments 195; history 26, 86; integration 25, 54, 87; intervention 110; law 26; leaders 26, 197; legalistic tradition 55; models 2, 21, 36, 122–3; multilateralism 51, 55–6, 61, 63; multilateralists 55; nation-states 26; neighborhood policy 74, 133; partners 194, 197–8; politics 80; powers 4–5, 110; regional entities 12, 190
European Atomic Energy Community 55
European Coal and Steel Community 25, 55

European Commission 8, 55–6, 191; called the "Guardian of the Treaties" 56; and the "New Asia Strategy" 156, 191
European Common Market 6
European Council 55–6
European countries 76, 189–90, 192–5; and Asia 189, 192–5; interests in the region shaped by the dynamism of the economies in East and Southeast Asia 190; relationship with China 75; upgrading trade relations 191
European Court of Justice 26, 78
European Defense Community 25
European Economic Community 25–6, 55, 99
European Enlightenment 18
European External Action Service 197
European Organization for Economic Cooperation 76
European Parliament 26, 55, 82, 106, 183; elections 67; and populist nationalist parties 106
European Union 3, 6, 8, 26, 45, 55–60, 62, 84, 119, 132, 174, 180–1, 189; and Association of Southeast Asian Nations 48; institutions 75; Islamic intercultural dialogue 84; Japan Economic Partnership Agreement 81; and the "Joint Communication on Connecting Europe and Asia - Building blocks for an EU strategy" 197; post-Maastricht 116; "refashioned, ostensibly portable" 108
evolution 10, 20, 22, 57, 59, 66, 71, 74, 101, 147, 149, 168, 171, 203; ambiguous 66; controversial 78; historical 137, 209; peaceful 212

fascism 17, 19
fascist thinking 68
financial crash 96, 98, 101, 103
Financial Stability Board 101
First Hague Conference (1899) 111, 113
Fitriani, Evi 12, 85
forces 3, 7, 20, 23, 28, 30, 37, 56, 62, 96, 180, 182, 204, 206–8, 213–15; destructive hegemonic 204; encouraging populist nationalist 101; military 112, 205, 213; political 105; transcendental 31
foreign markets 4, 6, 10, 12, 24–7, 97, 100, 102, 116, 119, 136, 138, 178–80, 182, 184–5; *see also* markets

foreign policy 23, 25–6, 75, 77, 105, 123, 133, 137, 143–4, 146, 154, 160, 175; agendas 134; community 154; initiatives 137, 143; priorities 146; strategies 77
forums 101, 119, 150, 192–5; ASEM 193; first ASEM Social Partners' 192; human rights 194; international 172; multi-actor 193–4, 199; multilateral 118, 159, 190–1, 199; popular 192; unproductive 193
framework 70–1, 95–6, 101, 179, 212; concrete cooperative 195; distinctive civilizational 18; global power 67; trade negotiation 180
France 5, 12, 26, 55–6, 68, 98–9, 207
free movement of people 86, 131–2, 188
free trade 4, 10, 12, 71, 82, 98, 101, 152; agreements 179, 182; areas 10, 23, 26, 69, 71, 109, 116–17, 156; initiatives 157; liberalism 86
Free Trade Agreement 73, 105, 116, 152, 156, 179–80, 183–6; ASEAN–China Free Trade Agreement 156; bilateral negotiations 82, 183–4; networks 183, 185; North American Free Trade Agreement 22, 73, 101, 105, 118–19, 180
Free Trade Area of the Americas 10, 69, 71, 109–10, 116–17
freedom 37, 55, 85, 87
French Revolution 21
FTA *see* Free Trade Agreement
FTAA *see* Free Trade Area of the Americas
Fukuyama, Francis 17, 36, 54, 67, 100
fundamentalism 1, 7, 19, 38, 40–5, 188
fundamentalist religious movements 20

G-7 (Group of Seven) 202
G-20 (Group of Twenty) 101, 202–3
GATT *see* General Agreement on Tariffs and Trade
GEM *see* Global Europe Multilateralism
General Agreement on Tariffs and Trades 52, 61, 144, 185
geopolitical 73, 101, 143, 205; commentary 205; order 207; realities 211, 215; scene 207; shift 202; tension 208; unit of South East Asia 166
geopolitics 68, 211
Germany 26, 45, 55–6, 68, 97–9, 208; Christian Democratic Party 25; and the European New Order 23; military

and nuclear industry 25; preferences for larger and deeper integration 26; and the "principle of taming power" 25, 27; and the Versailles Treaty 207
Gilpin, Robert 53, 95, 205
global 5–6, 8–10, 12–14, 21–5, 27–31, 36–40, 53–4, 66–72, 74–7, 79–81, 95–106, 115–24, 132–5, 186–92, 194–9; free trade 12; institutions 67, 100; multiculturalism 45; multilateralism 5, 10, 12–13, 36–7, 45, 70, 75, 189; politics 22, 31, 119, 135, 168; processes 120, 123
Global Europe Multilateralism 72
global order 13, 53, 69; balanced 189; current liberal 199; multilateral 12; traditional 67
Global South 109, 118, 121
Global Value Chain 186–7
globalism 27, 53, 95, 97, 144
globalization 23–4, 54, 72, 76, 96, 101, 103–4, 116, 166, 170, 173, 189
Good-bye Hegemony 203, 205
goods 5, 23, 30, 99, 123, 131, 156, 181, 183; *see also* public goods
governance 48–50, 70, 81, 83, 85, 87, 100–1, 121, 129, 206; cooperative 84; democratic 68, 167; forest 192; good 7, 38, 41, 44, 46, 49, 51, 53, 55, 57, 59, 61, 63; international 189; mechanisms 203–4, 210, 214; multilateral 57, 80; multilayered 79; regional 54, 112; rule-based 56

Hagerty, Devin 171
hegemon 8–9, 12, 52–4, 56, 61–2, 95, 97, 99, 102–3, 132, 205; global 103; regional 55, 98; single 62
hegemonic 8, 52, 71, 207; behavior 203; defection 54; entrenchment 203; influence 208; multilateralism 9, 48, 52–4, 61–3, 66; regionalism 110; stability theorists 53; wars 185, 205–6
hegemony 41–2, 52–3, 62, 76, 98–9, 118, 121, 174, 213; global 99; international 77; political 40; unipolar 209
hemispheric regionalism 9, 110, 112, 117, 121
Himalayan kingdom 167
history 2, 9, 17–19, 29, 31, 48, 52, 55, 109–11, 120–2, 124, 166, 173–4, 205, 208; colonial 110; economic 24; global 111; human 209; recent 170; regional 121; universal 21

Holocaust 31
"hubs" 146–7, 161, 183, 195
Hull, Cordell 81
human rights 6, 31, 77–8, 82–3, 85, 114, 121, 135, 192, 194, 212–14
Human Rights Council 212, 214
Huntington, Samuel 6–8, 17, 21, 36, 40, 67, 87

ICC *see* International Criminal Court
identities 1–2, 11, 31, 42, 44, 70, 74, 117, 146, 155, 162, 166–8, 171, 173; collective 17–20, 27; common 154–5, 172; defensive 198; gender 212; metaphysical group 45; new 154; pre-national 154; privileged 166; religious 1; shared 67
identity politics 118, 120; language-based 167; and religious and political fundamentalism 1
ideology 29, 31, 135, 215
IFIs *see* international financial institutions
Ikenberry, John 67, 99, 205–6
ILO *see* International Labor Organization
IMF *see* International Monetary Fund
implementation 30, 62, 76, 136, 160–1; COC 160; consistent 83; DOC 160; gap 131
import-substitution industrialization 115–16
India 1, 11, 18–19, 58–9, 69, 80–2, 96, 100–1, 153, 155–6, 166–76, 181, 183, 204, 210; and the Asia Africa Growth Corridor 175; colonial-era 169; economy 173; independence 166; independent 169; and Pakistan 11, 150, 153, 166–73, 176; partition of 167–8; post-colonial 168; response to regional cooperation and multilateralism 167
instability 210, 212–13; political 123; resulting from the military intervention against Saddam Hussein 2003 207
Institute of European Studies 108
institutional multilateralism 8, 48, 52, 54–7, 59, 61–2
institutionalism, relational 57
Inter-American Conference, Washington (1889) 112
The Inter-American Human Rights System 115
intercultural dialogue 69, 82, 86
International Criminal Court 115
international financial institutions 114, 116, 122, 210

International Labor Organization 82, 113
International Monetary Fund 5, 52, 81, 114, 144
international observers 75
international order 28, 37, 52–4, 62, 100, 111, 117; liberal 54; new 99; rules-based 102; stable 54
international organizations 81, 121, 131, 151; launching regional 144; legitimacy of 28
international politics 2, 42, 49, 67–8, 101, 188, 192, 195
international relations 1, 3–5, 8, 11, 31, 41, 44, 68, 71–2, 102, 143, 145–6, 149, 153, 207–8; Chinese norms for managing 154; managing 154; Western theories of 143
international society 48–9, 54, 215; cooperative 215; universal 206
international system 36, 48, 52, 101, 104, 188, 213; new 4; unequal 115
International Union of American Republics (later the Pan-American Union) 112
interregional 3, 9, 69, 75, 79, 84; affairs 3; agenda 123; agreements 10, 101; arrangements 8, 70–1, 73; Belt and Road Initiative 9; cooperation 3, 6, 12, 70, 73, 81, 83, 122, 189, 198; dialogues 66, 104–5; negotiations 78; partnerships 68, 72, 78, 80, 101; unilateral 74
interregional negotiations 78
interregional relations 8, 69–72, 74–5, 77, 79–80, 87, 191, 198; multidimensional 81; multilayered 3; post-revisionist 80
interregionalism 1, 3, 12, 66–7, 70–3, 79, 95–6, 121, 123–4, 130, 189–90, 198–9; bridging different continents 66–7; competing 72; hybrid 70; intercultural dialogue 67, 69, 71, 73, 75, 77, 79, 81, 83, 85, 87; multilateral 100, 188; and new multilateralism 79; policies imperil transatlantic 73; sustaining 86
investments 78, 100, 103, 105, 149, 156, 183, 191–2, 197, 209; Chinese 75, 153, 175
Iran 1, 18, 44, 74, 135, 150, 208, 211
Iraq 71, 202, 207, 212, 215
ISI *see* import-substitution industrialization
Islam 30, 43, 74
Italy 1, 7, 23, 26, 55, 68, 76, 83, 175

Japan 19–21, 24–5, 71, 73, 75, 78–9, 81, 98, 150, 156, 180, 183–4, 190, 208,

210; occupation of China 28; political initiatives in regional institution-building 25; political suspicion of the motives of 25; reconstruction of modernity 20; and South Korea 58, 155
Jaspers, Karl 18
Jones, Bruce 48, 54, 211, 213

Kang, Moonsung 12
Kant, Immanuel 4, 6–7, 9, 13, 36–7, 39, 44, 46, 80, 84–7; concepts 84–5; tradition of constitutionalism 86
Kathmandu 170, 172
Katzenstein, Peter J. 7, 25, 66, 70, 79, 96, 174, 189
Kazakhstan 131–2, 138, 150, 153, 178
Kennan, George 76
Keqiang, Premier Li 159
Kindleberger, Charles 53, 95
Kissinger, Henry 207–8
knowledge 31, 42; implicit political 42; mutual cultural 84
Korea 181, 183–4, 190
Kyrgyzstan 131, 149

labor 131–2, 185; costs 186; law 78; migration 138; rights 78, 82; standards 83
LAFTA *see* Latin American Free Trade Association
language 6, 19, 23, 30, 80, 110, 130, 168, 171; classical 19; common 30, 79; Latin 30; sacred 19; trade war 23; vernacular 19
Latin America 9, 69, 71–2, 74–6, 84, 103, 108–24; and comparative focus 108; countries allowed space in which to advance their political and trade concerns 123; divided countries 115; and East Africa 23; efforts to achieve equality between states and peoples 115; forms a "multiplex" architecture "beyond" hegemony (Amitav Acharya) 124; history of regionalism 111, 121; involvement in the League of Nations 113; participation on the international stage 112; relations with the US 113, 122; states of 110, 113–15, 122
Latin-America, regionalism 108–24
"Latin America first" approach 117
Latin American Free Trade Association 116
Latin American regionalisms (2019) **119**
Latin Christendom 27, 29–30

laws 8, 23, 30, 37, 39, 85; decaying canon 27; national 26; of politics 23; sanctity of 28
leaders 5, 104, 111, 115, 135, 151, 157, 172, 191–2, 194, 196, 198; authoritarian 135; election of 104; European 26, 197; international 54, 215; national 106; prominent South American 9, 112; regional 81; world 5, 207
leadership 53–4, 67, 101, 136, 174; active 213; cooperative 80; enlightened 13, 210; global 53; national 137; shared interregional 77; strong 214; undemocratic 68; *see also* political leadership
League of Nations 5, 36, 113, 122
Lebow, Richard Ned 203, 205, 213
Lerner, Daniel 21
Li Keqiang (Chinese Premier) 157, 159–60
liberal international order 53, 98
liberalism 43
Libman, Alexander 10, 133
Libya 74, 212–13
Lima Conference (1938) 113
Lisbon Treaty 78, 82

Maldives 5, 167, 170–1
Malmström, Cecilia 77, 82
markets 4, 6, 10, 12, 24–7, 97, 100, 102, 116, 119, 136, 138, 178–80, 182, 184–5
Marshall Plan 55, 76
mechanisms 49, 136, 193, 212; auxiliary security 157; collective decision-making 136; enforcement 196; governance 203–4, 210, 214; institutional 59, 148; legal 55; multilateral 198; regional security 157–8; special security 148
media 193, 209
meetings 59, 84, 95, 148, 155, 158, 160, 191–3, 196; ASEM Senior Officials' Meeting on Trade and Investment (2017) 191; decision-making 60; ineffective 193; of world leaders 5
member countries 8, 10, 12, 56–8, 60, 63, 73–4, 76, 78, 85, 105, 134, 136–7, 148, 150–1; ASEAN 183; Asia–Europe Meeting 199; CPTPP 180; European 195; RTA 186
members 25–6, 43, 50–1, 55–9, 113, 118, 123, 146, 149–53, 161, 169, 178, 183, 193, 211–12; founding 108, 114;

members *continued*
  interacting with one another 148; legitimate 38; national 27; newest 191; permanent 5, 203, 206, 211; potential 74; religious affiliations 215
MERCOSUR (Southern Common Market) 6, 10, 22, 69–71, 74, 78–9, 100, 108–9, 116–19, 123, 182
Mexico 79, 113, 116, 119, 122, 178, 180–1, 183
Meyer, John 29
Meyer, Thomas 1–2, 4, 6–8, 10, 12, 14, 36, 38, 40, 42, 44, 46, 84
migration 83, 103, 146, 192, 210
military 99, 103, 131, 158, 208; blocs 98; powers 210, 213; rivalry 67, 103
Misri, Vikram 175
modernism 43
modernities 19
modernity 1–2, 7, 14, 17–32, 38, 43–6, 67, 95–6, 99, 129, 137, 206; civilization of 18–20; cosmopolitan 21; diverse 80; early 19; fake 129–30, 138; general model of 7
modernization 1, 3, 7, 21, 38–41, 44, 46, 68, 95–8, 129, 138; cultural 22; delayed in some community-oriented political cultures 22; illiberal 21; logic of 39–40; military 171; process of 7, 39, 43, 214; theory of 21; variants of 38
Mogherini, Federica 77
Moldova 74
Mongolia 150, 186, 195–6
Monroe Doctrine 110, 113
movements 1, 27, 86; anti-globalization 62; fundamentalist religious 20; indigenous fundamentalist 19; ISIS-led jihadist 28; neo-populist 1; political protest 20; populist 119; post-modern protest 20; religious 20, 27; social 18, 83
multi-actor forums 193–4, 199
multiculturalism 31, 45, 97
multidimensional 3, 25, 80, 190–1, 199; cooperation ranging from political dialogue and economic collaboration to social-cultural interactions 189; multipolarity 203; regional integration 72
multilateral approaches 48, 159; taken by the US after World War II 76; to transnational governance at the global and the regional levels 48
multilateral arrangements 51–3, 55, 61, 83, 213

multilateral cooperation 7, 13, 46, 50, 66, 69, 79, 81, 83, 87, 95, 104–6; financial 81; regional 8–9; wider 103
multilateral diplomacy 144, 146–8, 153, 155, 159–62
multilateral forums 118, 159, 190–1, 199
multilateral institutions 8, 50–1, 53–5, 102, 104, 113, 121, 154, 193, 215; current 204; disparaged 101; functional 214; global 13; new 76
multilateral order 113, 118, 124, 174; rules-based 190; stable 37
multilateral organizations 6, 150, 190
multilateral processes 57, 109, 122, 198
multilateral regional initiatives 150
multilateral trade 156, 178, 182
multilateral trade negotiations 106, 178, **179**
multilateral trading systems 178, 180–1, 184, 191
multilateralism 5–14, 37, 41, 45–6, 48–54, 61–3, 72–3, 79–81, 83–5, 113–14, 143–4, 154, 188–90, 198–9, 204–5; common features and different anchoring practices *51*; cultural foundations for consistent 7, 46; damage at the global level 105; economic 158, 161; flexible 154; and good governance 49, 51, 53, 55, 57, 59, 61, 63; institutional 8, 48, 52, 54–7, 59, 61–2; international 36, 40; new 13–14, 66, 79–80, 83; partial 189, 198–9; regional 6, 11, 14, 36, 55; relational 8, 48, 57–8, 60–2, 86; rules-based 62; self-initiated 150; successful 203; sustainable 37, 41, 79
multilateralizing regionalism 178–87
multiple modernities 2–3, 6–7, 17–18, 20–1, 30, 36–40, 44, 67, 84, 96, 98, 100, 104, 106, 173; approach pioneered by Israeli sociologist Shmuel Eisenstadt 7; and multilateralism 15, 37, 39, 41, 43, 45; paradigm 129; principle 77; and republicanism 38; theme of 19; theory 77; and variants of modernity 17, 24; world of 9, 37, 96, 104, 106
multipolar confrontation 69
multipolar environment 100
multipolar international reality 203
"Multipolar Systems and International Stability" 205
multipolarity 73, 203–8, 213–15
Münch, Richard 40
Murakami, Yasusuke 27, 29

Muslims 58, 167
Myanmar 82, 156, 183, 191, 196

NAFTA *see* North American Free Trade Agreement
NAM *see* Non-aligned Movement
national interests 12, 54, 56–7, 145, 158, 199, 215
National People's Congress 155
nationalism 8, 12, 67, 71, 81, 87, 166, 215; civic 31; ethnic 31; extreme 83, 86; populist 8–9, 67, 97, 103–5; and regionalism 167, 169, 171, 173, 175
nationalist associations 68
negotiations 55, 78, 82, 115–16, 122, 156–7, 159–60, 179–80, 182–4, 186, 210; bilateral 179, 183; bloc-to-bloc 72; diplomatic 82; interregional 78; multilateral trade 106, 178, **179**; peaceful 27; suspended 180; values-based 82
neo-nationalist approaches ("social welfare nationalism") 68
Nepal 167–8, 170–2
"New Asia Strategy" 156, 191
"new multilateralism" 13–14, 66, 79–80, 83
"new regionalism" 2, 9, 70, 95, 99, 108–9, 118
Non-aligned Movement 168–9
North American Free Trade Agreement 22, 73, 101, 105, 118–19, 180
NPC *see* National People's Congress
nuclear weapons 115, 173, 202, 206, 208, 212
Nyerere, Julius 87

OAS *see* Organization of American States
observers 53, 62, 78, 129–30, 189, 194
Onfray, Michel 68
OPANAL *see* Tlatelolco Treaty
Organization for Security and Cooperation in Europe 73–4, 135
Organization of American States (replaced the Pan American Union) 23, 115–16, 119
organizations 10, 58–60, 111, 113, 115–16, 119, 123, 131–2, 136–7, 150–3, 155, 172, 175, 196–7, 211; advanced 10; economic 134; intergovernmental 8, 56, 123; new 117, 119, 191; non-governmental 25, 148, 209; partner 72; political 96; regional 5
OSCE *see* Organization for Security and Cooperation in Europe

PA *see* Pacific Alliance
Pacific Alliance 110, 118, 120, 123
Pacific region 78, 108, 156, 158
Pakistan 11, 120, 150, 153, 166–73, 176; China nexus 171; conflict relationship with India 11, 150, 153, 166–73, 176
Pan-American Union 112, 115
Paris Agreement (2015) (COP 21) 209, 211
Paris Treaty (1952) 55
parliamentary democracy 170
parties 4, 149, 159–60, 179, 183, 190, 206; anti-EU nationalist 73; far-right 67; nationalist 106; political 99; populist 83
partners 69–72, 77, 80, 82, 103, 155, 168, 186, 189, 191, 193, 198–9; consultative 154; continental 75; cooperative 146; global 192, 197; non-state 193; regional 72, 156
Pax Americana 52, 205
peace 4, 37, 57, 59, 80, 86–7, 151, 155, 159, 168, 212, 214; durable 6, 37, 205; perpetual 4, 9, 36, 45–6, 84, 86; preserving 207; regional 158; sustaining 211–12
Peace of Westphalia 1648 4, 213
political 20, 72, 96, 168, 170; authority 30–2, 37, 96, 104; behavior 23, 42, 171; blocs 48; boundaries 173; classes 40, 43; climate 104, 172; democracy 6, 20; dialogue 72, 83, 189, 192, 199; fundamentalism 1, 40, 188; identities 20, 166, 168–9; institutions 19–20, 41, 58, 136, 168; parties 99; regionalism 1, 3, 36; systems 44, 46, 136, 157, 194
political culture 7, 22, 40–2, 44–6, 86, 102; changes in 44; of civilizations 7, 46; community-oriented 22; democratic 45; dominant 40, 45
political leadership 25, 53–4, 56, 67, 101, 136–7, 174, 211; common 30; enlightened 214; national 137; young 194
politics 1–3, 23, 26, 29–30, 41, 46, 73, 84, 148, 155, 166, 174, 211; British 26; Chinese 146; comparative 67; cultural 1, 3; domestic 6, 49, 81, 185; European 80; global 22, 31, 119, 135, 168; international 2, 42, 49, 67–8, 101, 188, 192, 195; jihadist 28; laws of 23; national 22, 174; regional 17, 24, 190; religious 27–8; secular 28
post-Soviet Eurasia 130, 133

Pound, Ezra 68
"power politics" 4–6, 13, 41, 76, 79, 199; assertive 66; big 189; competitive 67; global 10, 66; hard 69; philosophy of 180
powers 4–5, 8–9, 12–13, 26–8, 52–4, 56–8, 61–2, 97–101, 104–5, 131–2, 134, 138, 170, 190, 205–6; democratic 214; economic 202, 215; emerging 144, 174, 202; European 4–5, 110; geo-economic 75; global 75; hegemonic 8, 52–3, 55, 97; military 213; normative 72, 77, 80; political 3, 179; regional 98–9, 122, 208
practices 31, 51, 60–1, 130; alternative 42; diplomatic 146; institutional 31, 38; legalistic 56; political 29–30, 42; trade 179, 184–5
production networks, regional 186
projects 14, 22, 97, 99, 104, 106, 109, 124, 132, 145, 147, 149, 194; ambitious hemispheric trade 116; anti-hegemonic 120; national identity 174; pan-American 123; political 97; regional 102, 117, 132
protectionism 152, 182, 194
protectionist 83, 97–8, 102, 105; anti-multilateralism 1; measures 178, 180; trade policy 81
Prussia 207
public goods 76, 97, 99, 102, 106, 174
Putin, Vladamir 10, 73

Qin, Yaqing 5, 8, 66, 68, 71, 79

Rahman, S.H. 174, 176
RCEP *see* Regional Comprehensive Economic Partnership
reactionary associations 68
regional alliances 23
Regional Anti-Terrorist Structure/Regional Counter-Terrorist Structure 148
regional associations 6–7, 9–10, 13, 102, 105
regional autonomy 122
regional blocs 23, 82, 98–9, 101, 117, 134, 184
Regional Comprehensive Economic Partnership 82, 157, 183–4, 186
regional cooperation 1, 3, 6, 10, 55, 58, 66, 70–1, 73, 87, 97, 99, 103–5, 166–7, 171–4; competing varieties of 95; limiting 73; organizations 74; projects 66; schemes of 172

Regional Counter-Terrorist Structure 148
regional hegemon 55, 98
regional identities 79, 97, 99, 171–2; common 109; fostering of 70; robust 169
regional institutions 25, 189
regional integration 60, 72, 97, 108, 117, 132–3, 135, 172–4
Regional Integration Processes (master's degree program) 108
regional models 67–8
regional multilateral bodies 170
regional multilateralism 6, 11, 14, 36, 55
regional orders 22–4, 26, 112, 118, 173–4
regional organizations 9, 22, 59, 70, 83, 129–38, 172; advanced 132; multilateral 154; non-democratic 136; powerless 136; role of 79–80; undemocratic 135, 138
regional platform 166, 172, 176
regional powers 98–9, 122, 208
regional production networks 186
regional schemes 10, 57
regional security 148
regional trade agreements 12, 182–6; Asian 185; bilateral 186; East Asia 186; since the Trump administration took office **182**; US trading partners in 182
regionalism 3, 5–7, 9–13, 22–5, 95–101, 103–6, 108–12, 114, 118, 120–4, 130, 132, 134–5, 143–4, 173–5; authoritarian 10, 74, 130, 134–5, 137–8; closed 9, 98, 109; comparative 122, 130; contentious 120; deep/institutionalized 74; development of 8–9, 97, 130; effective 120; emergent 97; hierarchical 3; history of 109, 111; illiberal 105–6; Latin-American 108–24; multilateral 73, 185; and nationalism 167, 169, 171, 173, 175; open 9, 95, 97, 100, 103–4, 106, 116; political 1, 3, 36; post-hegemonic 118; post-Soviet 135; processes of 109, 131, 138; and regionalization 22, 27
regionalist 12, 72, 104, 117; blocs 103; initiatives 100, 104–5; projects 95–7, 99–100, 102, 105; reforms 81
regionalization 22–3, 25, 27; political 3; processes 23–4, 26, 30; and regionalism 22
regions 22–4, 30, 40–2, 44–6, 69–70, 103–5, 108–10, 119–20, 130, 148–51, 154, 156–9, 166–76, 185–6, 189–94;

crucial 101; divided 58; extended 175; fast-transforming 173; geo-cultural 36, 44; irreconcilable 67, 87; neighboring 144
Reich, Simon 203, 205
relational multilateralism 8, 48, 57–8, 60–2, 86
"relational regionalism" 10
relations 49, 57, 60, 73, 76, 121–2, 143–7, 150–1, 153–5, 166, 170–1, 175, 189, 192–3, 196; bloc-to-bloc 69; complex 58, 60; conflict-laden 170, 198; cooperative 57, 60; delicate 192; developing 153; dialectical 29; establishing official 154; expanding multilateral trading 77; external 77, 82, 148; financial 192; informal 132, 154; market 24; multidimensional 69; mutual 59; pan-European 75; parliamentary 192; people-to-people 86; social 40; strategic 155
relationships 61, 75, 87, 109, 111, 120, 144–6, 150, 152–3, 155–7, 160, 173; amicable 158; intensive 154; inter-regional 69, 74; intercontinental 67; long-distance 29; maintaining positive 58, 60; personal 62; political 24; reciprocal 40; regional 70; social 8, 149
religions 11, 18, 27–9, 43, 146, 167–8, 171, 215
republicanism 4, 7, 37–9, 84–7
republics 4–7, 37, 154; democratic 167; ex-Soviet 131; federation of (Kantian concept) 13, 37–8
research agenda 42, 72, 79, 130, 135, 138; multidisciplinary 70; new multilateralist 67
resources 39, 97, 147, 195, 199; economic 134, 156; insufficient 199; mobilizing 54
revolution 4, 28, 111, 115; incipient military 28; industrial 188; technological 18
Ricardo, David 4, 12, 86
"Rio process" (between the EU and Latin America) 69
risks 62, 86, 97, 134, 157; of division and political domination 75; persisting security 204; undermining and destroying the nation 85
rivalry 97, 103, 105, 168, 210; bipolar superpower 96; ideological 99; major-power 143; military 67, 103; potential 212

Rodó, José Enrique 112
Roosevelt, Franklin D. 5
RTAs see regional trade agreements
Ruggie, John 49, 52, 76, 79, 100, 173
rule of law 7, 55, 78, 82–3, 97, 151
rules 4, 8, 14, 55–62, 95, 98, 101, 106, 129, 146–7, 152, 155, 185–6, 204, 206–7; colonial 168, 171; constitutive 50; divergent 185; established 56, 97, 208; global 174; hierarchical 74; institutional 61; internal 74; interregional trade 82; majoritarian voting 60; military 167–8; multilateral 74; of origin 186; regional 55
Russia 53–4, 58–9, 72–4, 99–100, 105, 129–38, 147–9, 151, 153, 156, 181, 203–4, 206–7, 210, 212–13; and Belarus regional organizations 131; diplomacy 133; dominated 129; emulates the EU 133; epistemic community of 133; and EU tensions during the Ukranian crisis 133; and Eurasian regionalism 129–39; and the older traditions of rule that dominates 129; persuaded to prefer a bilateral approach to multilateralism 135; portrayed as an example of "fake modernity" 129; propaganda presents the EU as an unsuccessful case ripped apart by contradictions among its member countries 133; resurges and wields considerable military might 208; sanctions against democratizing countries in Eurasia 136
Russian Federation see Russia

SAARC see South Asian Association for Regional Cooperation
SACU see South African Customs Union
SADC see Southern African Development Community
Sales Marques, José Luís de 67, 80
Salvini, Matteo 76, 106
Scharpf, Fritz 68
Schmitt, Carl 68, 80
scholars 4–6, 18, 51, 68–70, 78, 80, 85, 114, 117–18, 123, 134, 154, 188–9, 193–4, 205; ASEM 197; constructivist 118; eminent Chinese 84; legal 112, 114; prominent 72
SCO see Shanghai Cooperation Organization
SEATO see Southeast Asia Treaty Organization

security 71, 74, 109, 111–12, 148–50, 155–8, 172, 185, 194–5, 211, 214; affairs 55, 158; alliances 99; blocs 169; common 26; dilemmas 67, 161, 169, 173; energy 174; global 194; human 48, 194; international 144; political 59; sustainable food 192
security issues 72, 157–8, 161, 195; controversial 158; non-traditional 153; regional 150
security multilateralism 157–8, 161; regional 157; successful 161
Shanghai Cooperation Organization 6, 10, 74, 144, 147–53, 158, 161; agenda 148; institutionalization 147; member states 149–53, 161; process 147, 151, 153; summit in Bishkek 2013 153
"Shanghai Spirit" 150–3, 161
SICA see Central American Integration System
Singapore 58–9, 157, 160, 180, 183
Singer, David 205
Single European Act (1986) 26, 56–7
Sinocentric world order 27–8
Smith, Adam 4, 12, 86, 114
SNA see Social Network Analysis
Snowden, Edward 212
social democracy 84
Social Network Analysis 10, 145–6
social networks 83, 146, 148, 150, 152–3, 160, 162; extended 150; regional 147; relational 155
"social welfare nationalism" 68
societies 2, 21, 40–4, 86, 109, 209; civil 4, 9, 19, 44, 82, 192, 203, 209–10; contemporary 45; human 95–6, 106, 209; international commercial 97; and political elites 45; transnational 49
"socio-cultural milieus" 66, 173
Song, Weiqing 11
South African Customs Union 182
South America 9, 20, 82, 117–19
South Americans 10, 111, 117
South Asia 11, 23, 44, 103, 166–76; countries of 168, 170, 172, 174–5; states of 11, 166, 170, 173
South Asian Association for Regional Cooperation 11, 166–7, 172–6
South China Sea 11, 158–61; dispute over 158; issues concerning 159–60; and signing of the declaration of consensus 160
Southeast Asia 10–11, 23–4, 44, 58–9, 71, 108, 143–7, 149, 151, 153–5, 157–9, 161–2, 190–1, 198; and ASEAN 161; and Central Asia 144, 146; sharing features with China 160
Southeast Asia Treaty Organization 23, 99, 168–9
Southern African Development Community 22, 74, 182
Southern Common Market (MERCOSUR) 6, 10, 22, 69–71, 74, 78–9, 100, 108–9, 116–19, 123, 182
sovereign states 28, 159, 205
sovereignty 8, 11, 14, 49, 56–7, 134, 136, 152, 155, 158, 166–7, 173, 175, 207, 212; claiming 96; exclusive 6; issues 166; national 6, 13, 56, 62, 103; political 168; pooled 174; principles 85; responsible 54; territorial 106
Soviet Union 53–4, 99–100, 130–1, 138, 147, 149, 168, 206–7
stability 44–5, 58, 151, 158–9, 204–5, 207, 214; economic 155; regime 149, 152–3, 161; social 26
"Stability of the Bipolar World" 205
Stalinism 129
state sovereignty 13, 57, 105, 153
styles 41, 44–5, 50–1; cultural 44; decision-making 51, 59; political 77
Summit of the Americas 116
summits 59, 84, 118, 192, 195–6, 198; Asia–Europe Meeting, Ulaanbaatar (2018) 69; Summit of the Americas (1994) 116
superpowers 54, 77, 144, 168–9
supranational 56, 68, 134; bodies 136; bureaucracy 132, 137; institutions 54, 117; integration 62; interests 57
sustainability 53, 197–8, 211
sustainable development 13, 77, 82, 192, 197, 203, 205, 211, 214

TAC see Treaty of Amity and Cooperation in Southeast Asia
Tajikistan 131, 149
tariffs 5, 81, 144, 181, 185
Telò, Mario 8–9, 70, 79–80, 84, 111, 118, 124, 134, 138–9, 195–6
tensions 8, 29, 59, 84, 100, 102, 112, 117–18, 120, 158, 160, 190, 194, 204, 213; bilateral 169; enduring 117; heightened 73, 133; increased military 68, 210; political 3
territorial disputes 161, 184

terrorism 7, 11, 13, 48, 173, 208–9, 212, 214–15; combatting 208; international 148; transnational 149
TFEU *see* Treaty on the Functioning of the EU
"Third Chinese Revolution" 76
threats 28, 48, 73, 87, 95, 102, 110, 149, 155, 185, 199, 202, 207, 209, 212; external security 173; new 208–9; traditional security 173
Tlatelolco Treaty 115–16
Tokugawa (Japan) 19
TPP *see* Trans-Pacific Partnership
trade 4–5, 7–9, 11–12, 68, 74, 76–9, 81–4, 97, 99–100, 149, 180–1, 183–5, 190–2, 195, 197–9; barriers 178–9; bilateral 110, 156, 182; conflicts 179, 181, 185; cooperation 149; dialogues 79; disputes 185; global rules-based 81, 152, 188, 191; increasing 78; international 97; liberalization 116, 152, 156–7, 161; open 196; regional 116, 178, 180
trade agreements 12, 14, 66, 69–70, 73, 77, 82, 179; multilateral free 152, 156; regional 12, 182, 186; trilateral 184
Trade Expansion Act (1962) 185
trade negotiations 82, 179; bilateral 179–80; multilateral 178–9
trade policies 77–8, 179–80, 184–5; common 131; multilateral 6; preferential 156; unilateral free 97; of the United States 25
trade practices 179, 184–5
trade preferences 186
trade protectionism 73, 152, 182, 194
trade relations 2, 12, 152, 188
trade wars 67, 73, 102, 104, 188; aggressive 81; defusing 8; practiced 23
traditions 2, 7, 11, 30, 39, 42–3, 109, 129; civil 152; cultural 6–7, 42, 45, 58, 77, 152, 214; historical 50; political 168; regional 1; religious 18, 20
Trans-Atlantic Trade and Investment Partnership 12, 69, 73, 101, 180, 184
Trans-Pacific Partnership 12, 69, 73, 101, 110, 119, 157, 180, 184
transnational 3, 44, 48–9, 83, 86; anti-globalist movement 104; infrastructure projects 196; interdependence 2; multiple networks 4, 86; norms and rules 162; threats 49, 54
transnational governance 48–51, 56–7, 61–2; legitimacy of 49; purpose of 49

treaties 26, 77, 82, 151, 155, 212; Bilateral Investment Treaty with China 78, 82; multilateral 55–6, 144; Treaty of Amity and Cooperation in Southeast Asia 155, 161; Treaty of Asunción 10; Treaty of Lisbon 77; Treaty of Maastricht 26; Treaty of Rome 26, 55; Treaty of Versailles 207; Treaty on the Functioning of the European Union 77
Treaty of Amity and Cooperation in Southeast Asia 155, 161
Treaty of Asunción 10
Treaty of Lisbon 77
Treaty of Maastricht 26
Treaty of Rome 26, 55
Treaty of Versailles 207
Treaty on the Functioning of the European Union 77
Trudeau, Justin 105
Trump, Donald 25, 54, 61, 73, 78, 80–1, 100–2, 105, 144, 179–80
Trump administration 8–9, 72, 101–2, 104, 178–85
TTIP *see* Transatlantic Trade and Investment Partnership
Turkey 1, 7, 23, 150, 181

UDHR *see* Universal Declaration of Human Rights
Ukraine 73–4, 131, 212
Ukrainian crisis 133
UN 5, 57, 111, 122, 144, 203, 209; Charter 23, 70, 148, 202, 204, 206–7, 211; Environment Program 210; General Assembly 5, 115, 203–4, 210, 215; Human Rights Council 212; International Organization for Migration 210; Security Council 5, 13, 59, 172, 203, 206–7, 211; systems 113, 210
UNASUR *see* Union of South American Nations
Union of India *see* India
Union of South American Nations 110
Union of Soviet Socialist Republics *see* Soviet Union
Union State of Russia and Belarus 131
unipolarity 205–6
United Nations *see* UN
United States of America 5–6, 8–9, 12, 14, 24, 53–6, 58–9, 71–2, 74, 96–105, 110–11, 113–18, 120, 178–81, 183–5; and the "America First" policy 9, 100, 102, 105, 179–80; anti-Communist grand strategy 23; balance of payments

United States of America *continued*
deficits 24, 180; commitment of its power to the construction of the postwar global order 53–4, 61, 102; consumption-driven growth model 24; domestic polity 54; and Europe 24, 40; foreign policy 13; fundamentalist religious movements 20; globalist belief and hegemonic multilateralism 54; hegemony 52, 67, 99; intervention in the Dominican Republic (1965) 115; material capabilities 53; MERCOSUR (Southern Common Market) 6, 10, 22, 69–71, 74, 78–9, 100, 108–9, 116–19, 123, 182; multilateralism 52; postwar planners 52; promotion of regionalism in the 110; protects Western Europe after World War II in security affairs 55; regional alliances 23; regional governance in the 112; regionalism 121, 124; resentment at free-riding by some former allies 100; system of hegemonic multilateralism 9; Trade Representative 178–9; trends in global regionalism 109; unilateralism of 144, 191; and Western efforts to promote democracy 152; Western Europe and the Marshall Plan 55

Universal Declaration of Human Rights 114–15

USTR *see* United States Trade Representative

values 2, 20, 31, 43, 54, 70, 77, 82, 102, 129, 146, 151–2, 180, 198; alternative 42, 74; basic 43; cultural 11, 154; democratic 134; fundamental 82; liberal 175; political 170; shared 30, 70, 147; strategic 191; universal 215

Venezuela 118, 123, 135, 181
Versailles Conference (1919) 76
Vietnam 24, 78, 82, 160, 180–1, 183
Viner, Jacob 17
votes 5, 56–7
voting 8, 56, 59

Waltz, Kenneth 205
Wang, Jianwei 10–11, 159
War and Change in World Politics 205
wars 41, 68, 86, 96, 98, 168–70, 188, 205–6, 210; liberal 71; regional 96; World War I 4–5, 10, 36, 98, 138; World War II 2, 5, 8–9, 12, 45, 48, 52, 55, 76, 81, 98–9, 113, 115, 167, 169
"Washington Consensus" 71

weapons 105, 202, 210, 212; *see also* nuclear weapons
Weber, Max 18, 29, 40
welfare 104, 172–5
West Pakistan 167; *see also* Pakistan
Western: analysis of Chinese diplomacy 162; centrism and fragmented relativism 80; civilizations 29, 99; governments 151–2; liberal order 99; model of modernization 1, 3, 21, 143; modernity 1–2, 37, 188; multilateralism 144; neo-liberal culture 71; powers 28, 98, 206; societies 97
Western Europe 19–21, 46, 55, 169, 172–3, 175, 188, 191
Westphalian system 4, 6, 13, 28, 205
White, Hugh 212
Wong, Kan Seng 59
workshops 197–8
World Bank 5, 52, 61, 81, 144, 191, 210
world economy 96, 100–2, 106, 188, 208
world leaders 5, 207
world order 27, 53, 67, 95–7, 100–1, 106, 205–6, 208; American 202, 205–6; contemporary 206; cooperative 13–14, 196, 198; current 13, 206, 215; Eurocentric 97; law-based international 204; liberal 97–9, 103, 106; multilateral 97; new 96, 101; new multipolar 209; peaceable 37; post-hegemonic 53; religious 28; Sinocentric 27–8; stable multilateral 36
world politics 17, 22, 24, 27–8, 31–2, 48, 62, 173, 205–6; contemporary 17, 23, 28; organized 205; shaped 29; transforming 24
world religions 7, 18, 20
World Trade Organization 5–6, 8, 12, 61, 71–2, 83, 117, 144, 178–9, 181–4, 188, 191, 210; dispute cases with the US as a respondent during the Trump administration (as of March 2019) **181**; Dispute Settlement Procedures 179, 184; Doha Round 188; members 156, 178
World War I 4–5, 10, 36, 98, 138
World War II 2, 5, 8–9, 12, 45, 48, 52, 55, 76, 81, 98–9, 113, 115, 167, 169
WTO *see* World Trade Organization

Xi Jinping 75–6, 78, 143, 146

Yan Xuetong 68
Yeo, L. 189–90, 193, 198
youth 195–6